Screening
Asian Americans

Rutgers Depth of Field Series

Charles Affron, Mirella Jona Affron, Robert Lyons, Series Editors

Edited and with an introduction by
Peter X Feng

Screening
Asian
Americans

Rutgers
University
Press
New Brunswick,
New Jersey, and
London

Library of Congress Cataloging-in-Publication Data

Screening Asian Americans / edited and with an introduction by Peter X Feng.
    p. cm. — (Rutgers depth of field series)
    Includes bibliographical references and index.
    ISBN 0-8135-3024-5 (cloth : alk. paper) — ISBN 0-8135-3025-3 (pbk. : alk. paper)
    1. Asian Americans in motion pictures.   2. Asian Americans in the motion picture
industry.   I. Feng, Peter X, 1966–   II. Series.

PN1995.9.A77 S79 2002
791.43'6520395073—dc21   2001031785

British Cataloging-in-Publication data for this book is available from the British Library

Manufactured in the United States of America

For Mom and Dad

Contents

Contents

Acknowledgments

My greatest debt is of course to the contributors and to the filmmakers who inspired their passionate work. (I want to thank Sabine Haenni and Jennifer Guarino-Trier in particular for agreeing to give their essays their first publication here.) We are all part of a larger community of teachers and scholars of Asian American cinema, and in assembling this collection I was influenced by pedagogical conversations with Nerissa S. Balce, L. S. Kim, Sandra Liu, Aaron Park, Valerie Soe, Elena Tajima-Creef, and Oliver Wang.

Many people offered sage advice and assistance in tracking down authors and copyright holders, including John Bache, Rick Bonus, Gary Colmenar, David James, Don Kirihara, Marsha Orgeron, Deepika Petraglia-Bahri, Francesca Canade Sautman, Alan Sekula, Vivian Sobchack, and Trinh T. Minh-ha. Thanks to Richard Fung, Dorinda Hartmann at the Wisconsin Center for Film and Theater Research Photo Archive, Yun-ah Hong, Chris Kennedy at Vtape, and Helen Lee for providing the images.

I appreciate the guidance of series editors Charles Affron, Mirella Jona Affron, and Robert Lyons. At Rutgers University Press, Leslie Mitchner and Theresa Liu wielded both the carrot and the stick. Thanks to the capable staff at the Press, to David denBoer and Bookcomp, and to the staff of the English department at the University of Delaware for administrative support.

A partial list of my mentors must include Rick Altman, Marina Heung, Sumiko Higashi, Gina Marchetti, Kent Ono, Alvina Quintana, and not least Lauren Rabinovitz. My colleagues and students at the University of Delaware are a continual inspiration.

For sustenance and sanity during the nitty-gritty of editing: thanks to Bill Evans, John Holt, and Sheila Jordan.

Screening
Asian Americans

Peter X Feng

Introduction

It is a salient feature of the Asian American experience to be perceived as eternally foreign. Historian Ronald Takaki notes that

> "Color" in America operated within an economic context. Asian immigrants came here to meet demands for labor—plantation workers, railroad crews, miners, factory operatives, cannery workers, and farm laborers. Employers developed a dual-wage system to pay Asian laborers less than white workers and pitted the groups against each other in order to depress wages for both . . . [leading] white laborers to demand restriction of Asian workers already here in a segregated labor market of low-wage jobs and the exclusion of future Asian immigrants. Thus the class interests of white capital as well as white labor needed Asians as "strangers."[1]

Nineteenth-century Asian laborers were known as "sojourners," a label that expressed the desire that they return "home" when their services were no longer needed. Darrell Y. Hamamoto has referred to this phenomenon as "the simultaneous necessity and undesirability of Asian immigrant labor."[2] This contradictory formulation is expressed in the competing constructions of Asian Americans as "model minorities" (praising their contributions to the economy) and as the "Yellow Peril" (sounding the alarm over unfair economic competition). We could say, then, that the very contradictions in representations of Asian Americans as perpetual foreigners express a crisis in the definition of what it means to be American.[3] The continual conflation of Asian foreigners and immigrants with Asian American residents and citizens has inspired a number of neologisms: David Palumbo-Liu deploys the term "Asian/American," while Hyun-Yi Kang expresses this concept as "Asian (American)."[4] These formulations suggest that we cannot understand what it means to be American without understanding what it means to be Asian American.

    The study of Asian American cinematic representation is crucial in a culture that conceives race in black-and-white terms. The model minority thesis, for example, elevates Asian Americans to "honorary white" status, attributing economic successes and failures to cultural factors and thus denying the existence of structural inequities that systematically disenfranchise people of color. Since the model minority thesis serves to triangulate race relations, Asian Americans become the target for resentment from both white "haves" and non-white "have-nots," as revealed by the destruction of Korean American stores in the L.A. riots.[5] More recently, Asian Americans have found themselves ventriloquized as opponents of affirmative action. As Dana Takagi points out in her study of racial preferences in college admissions, "Asian Americans were the necessary racial subjects in the construction of a political and moral discourse attacking racial preferences in the late 1980s. . . . In fact, the same Asian Americans who felt they were the victims of discrimination almost without exception favored affirmative action and racial preferences."[6] Takagi makes two important points: Asian Americans are "central rather than peripheral to debates about race and equity in the United States," but nonetheless racial politics "are determined and shaped by black experiences, on the one hand, and white experiences, on the other."[7] Asian Americans are alternately claimed as black and white, so the study of Asian American representation is ultimately a study of the construction of blackness and whiteness in racial discourse.

Asians have played significant on-screen roles since the birth of cinema. At the turn of the twentieth century, the novel medium of cinema was given a significant boost by the Spanish-American War. In 1899, Edison's Kinetograph Department employed New Jersey as the backdrop for James White's reenacted battles between U.S. soldiers and Filipino insurgents; African American actors portrayed the Filipino guerrillas.[8] These early movies participated in creating popular support for U.S. imperialism, representing Asians as racial inferiors who would benefit from U.S. rule. In the decades to follow, cinematic depictions of Asians shifted in response to U.S. foreign policy concerns. The devious and brutal Chinese warlords in *The Bitter Tea of General Yen* (1933) gave way to the noble suffering of Chinese peasants in *The Good Earth* (1937), reflecting shifts in U.S. economic interests in the region. The most popular Chinese character of this period, however, was not isolated in China but indeed reached beyond Asia toward domination of the West: Sax Rohmer's Fu Manchu first appeared in print in 1911, on British movie screens in 1923, and on U.S. screens in 1929. In the 1930s, Paramount, MGM, and Republic all released Fu Manchu films. American movies suggested that Asians were either passive peasants or villainous despots.

In contrast to China, the Russo-Japanese War had established Japan as a military force to be reckoned with, but in the cinematic imagination such force was attributed not to strength of will but rather to treachery, duplicity, and deviousness.[9] On the whole, Hollywood was disinterested in everyday Japanese life, devoting its depictions to soldiers and diplomats. (A notable exception were films produced by Hollywood actor Sessue Hayakawa in the late 1910s and early 1920s.) When the United States entered the Second World War, depictions of Japanese as sadistic warriors reached a new low: films like *The Purple Heart* (1944) demonized the Japanese as a ruthless, inhuman society bent on world domination.[10]

Before and after the war, Asia served as a backdrop for a number of movies centering on white characters, as in adventure movies like *Soldier of Fortune* (1955) and the Bob Hope–Bing Crosby "Road" series. These backdrops were often interchangeable: since the aim of such films was to dramatize the white adventurers, stories that turned on Asian issues were passed over for those in which the subjectivity of white characters could be explored. For example, Hollywood produced a number of films dramatizing conflicts between the British Army and tribes in the Khyber Pass while completely ignoring Nationalist uprisings in India. Not surprisingly, Asian subjectivities were given the most attention in the context of romance plots, frequently involving mixed-race characters in an updating of the "tragic mulatto" stereotype.[11] In the mid-1950s, *Love Is a Many-Splendored Thing* (1955) and *Bhowani Junction* (1956) featured A-List actors Jennifer Jones and Ava Gardner, respectively. Many of these films made a profound impression on Asian American filmmakers, judging from contemporary critics and their attempts to read these liminal, East-West hybrid characters as "instigator[s] of . . . processes of self-affirmation."[12] Ironic readings aside, narratives of interracial romance almost always served as cautionary tales, even as they trafficked in the exotic allure of such couplings. And while these melodramas did put Asian women center stage, typically Asian women functioned as "Lotus Blossoms," "passive figures who exist[ed] to serve [white] men." Their evil, active counterparts were the "Dragon Ladies," exemplified by Fu Manchu's predatory daughter.[13]

While Hollywood often traveled to Asia, only rarely did Hollywood films depict Asians who had ventured to America. There were of course a number of domestics, like Tai (Emma Young), Ginger Rogers's maid in *Shall We Dance* (1937), and Sam (Peter Chong), Fred Astaire's valet in *Easter Parade* (1948). (These roles were frequently played by Asian American actors, while leading roles were almost exclusively played by white actors in "yellowface.") Charlie Chan, the popular Chinese American detective from Hawaii in a series of films produced by Fox in the 1930s and Monogram in the 1940s, was in a sense merely a privileged servant, as Charlie Chan films rarely explored Chan's subjectivity but instead focused on the lives of the white characters whom he investigated. Chan's tag-along adult children provided the only glimmer of Asian American subjectivity in the movies, but the films' condescending attitude toward the younger Chans and their use of American slang revealed the limits of Hollywood's willingness to imagine the second generation as full-fledged Americans.

There had been isolated films made by Asian American filmmakers before the 1960s, as with the aforementioned Sessue Hayakawa. Like many of the earliest books published by Asian American writers, many of these early films dealt with Asian subject matter. The conception of Asian American cinema as being centrally concerned with recovering Asian American history and articulating Asian American experiences emerged with the Asian American movement of the late 1960s and 1970s. This wave of filmmaking drew heavily on a documentary ethos: even narrative films were palpably animated by a need to represent Asian American lives with authority and authenticity. The earliest Asian American films have thus been interpreted as actively contesting dominant cinematic representations. Whether documenting issues ignored by the mainstream news media or challenging and interrogating cinematic stereotypes about Asians and Asian Americans, Asian American film is viewed as essentially oppositional. As Rolando Tolentino notes in an essay in this volume, conceptualizing Asian American cinematic practice in a narrowly reactive, oppositional framework ultimately privileges dominant representational strategies: it implies that Asian American filmmakers take their cues from mainstream cinema.

The organization of this collection in a sense reinforces that framework: essays relating the history of Asian American media production and offering readings of specific movies follow a section sketching out the contours of dominant cinematic representations of Asians and Asian Americans. Certainly our interest in marginal filmmakers arises from the presupposition that they will offer a perspective not otherwise articulated by mainstream cinema. However, no marginal movie can be reduced to merely countering racist representations, and indeed as a strategy, critiquing racism is not possible within a strict binaristic framework. The critical project may begin by enumerating racist and stereotypical representations, but it does not end there. For example, Dorothy B. Jones's 1955 study identifies four recurring themes in portrayals of India in the years before World War II: religious mysticism, interracial love affairs, jungle adventures, and isolated uprisings against the British (as in *The Lives of a Bengal Lancer, The Charge of the Light Brigade*, and *Gunga Din*, all from the 1930s).[14]

Jones undertook her research as part of a larger study of international communications, specifically to understand the international ramifications of U.S. movies, and as such her categories are suggestive but lacking in nuance. These categories tend to divide movies into two columns: negative stereotypes and positive characterizations. Such a reduction is apparent when Jones draws the following statistics from Production Code Administration reports dating from 1947 to 1954: in this period, eight films offered sympathetic portrayals of China, two were unsympathetic, eleven films mixed sympathetic and unsympathetic elements, and five films offered indifferent portrayals.[15] It is this logic that leads Jones to conclude that "the philosophy and the way of life of the Far East were given an extremely favorable portrayal" in D. W. Griffith's *Bro-*

ken Blossoms (1919).[16] Jones is unable to distinguish between what Julia Lesage has identified as the film's ostensible message that "Asian Buddhist peacefulness is superior to Anglo-Saxon ignorance, brutality, and strife" and the way that Griffith "hides the social reality of racism."[17]

In the introduction to another volume in this series, Valerie Smith identifies a number of problems with the elaboration of negative images.[18] Chief among them is the virtual impossibility of identifying a *positive* image. It is not simply a matter of proffering the moral inverse of a negative image: the inverse of Fu Manchu (evil mastermind bent on world domination) is Charlie Chan (deferential public servant), but Charlie Chan is hardly a positive image.[19] Instead, Charlie Chan embodies what Frank Chin and Jeffery Paul Chan have termed "racist love," the image of an ethnic minority who unquestioningly accepts his marginal status even as he serves the social order.[20] In a similar analysis, Sut Jhally and Justin Lewis argue that the depiction of a prosperous, upper-middle-class African American family on "The Cosby Show" (1984–92) "implies the failure of a majority of black people who, by these standards, have not achieved similar professional or material success."[21] The Huxtables, surely a "positive image," serve to normalize the middle class and stigmatize the working class.

This collection argues against conceiving of Asian American cinematic production as merely oppositional, while at the same time acknowledging that much Asian American cinema is dialectically engaged with the problematics of dominant cinematic representations. In place of a reductive account that casts marginal filmmakers as activists attacking a monolithic Hollywood, I advance two simple propositions: first, there is no such thing as a positive or negative representation, rather, there are representations that are mobilized positively or negatively depending on discursive context; second, representations created by non-Asian American filmmakers are not necessarily racist, nor are representations created by Asian American filmmakers necessarily progressive. This collection articulates a dynamic relationship between mainstream and marginal cinemas, wherein it is not the images themselves that are contested so much as their discursive deployment. Both mainstream and marginal representations of Asian Americans articulate the terms whereby the borders of the American body politic are policed.[22]

We return to the contention with which we began: the perception of Asian Americans as perpetual foreigners in the United States indicates a crisis in the definition of Americanness. Representations of Asian Americans therefore reveal the contradictions in attempting to define the U.S. body politic. All of the essays in this collection articulate the terms by which Asian Americans are either accepted as citizens or defined as foreigners—this is true of the essays in Part One that focus on dominant representational practices no less than it is of the essays in Parts Two and Three on Asian American cinematic production. These essays explore the ways that Asian Americans are screened: "screening Asian Americans" thus describes a process of evaluation, employing the metaphor of a filter that separates desirable from undesirable elements.[23] Of course, the title of this collection also evokes the process of projecting cinematic images, but to screen also means *to conceal from view*. By combining these different senses into one word, this volume means to suggest that these three processes are mutually implicated. It is not the job of the critic to determine whether a given representation is positive or accurate, but instead to evaluate the discursive context that a representation speaks to.

For example, much of Binita Mehta's essay responds to bell hooks and Anuradha Dingwaney's charge that *Mississippi Masala* conveys stereotypes about race relations between African Americans and Indian Americans in the Deep South. Mehta acknowledges the validity of many of hooks and Dingwaney's claims while situating the film in a specific historic context: Mehta asks us to resist "the temptation to read this family as representative of all Indian immigrants."[24] Ella Shohat and Robert Stam note that "It is not enough to say that art is constructed. We have to ask: Constructed for whom? And in conjunctions with which ideologies and discourses?"[25] Shohat and Stam's "for whom" evokes both filmmaker and audience, situating the artwork (text) in multiple contexts. The critic's job is twofold: to reconstruct the discursive context in which the filmmaker constructed a text, and to discuss the reception of that text in multiple discursive contexts that may or may not align with the filmmaker's. It is therefore entirely possible for Mehta to agree with hooks and Dingwaney that *Mississippi Masala* traffics in racial stereotypes even as she draws different conclusions about the functions of the movie. *Mississippi Masala* can thus be seen as simultaneously purveying and critiquing stereotypes, as promoting its Asian American and African American characters as representative and also as unique, as *screening* Asian Americans in all senses of the word.

This volume serves to constitute Asian American cinematic representation as a coherent object of inquiry, which means that its essays do not merely discuss the processes of screening, but themselves serve to screen Asian American cinema. An anthology succeeds to the extent that it offers a persuasive canon: this is no less true of a collection of critical writings than it is of an anthology of literature. But constructing a canon of Asian American cinema is a problematic endeavor, since (unlike Hollywood) Asian American media production is dispersed and access to films and videos is severely restricted due to limited distribution of titles. Many Asian American film/videomakers and spectators produce and consume movies without awareness of Asian American cinema as an artistic tradition. For example, many of the works shown in the major Asian American film and video festivals (including the annual festivals run by the National Asian American Telecommunications Association in San Francisco, Visual Communications in Los Angeles, and Asian CineVision in New York, as well as competing festivals in Chicago, and irregular festivals in Seattle, Washington, D.C., and elsewhere) were produced by college students enrolled in production courses around the country. These movies, while frequently vibrant and animated by a palpable sense of discovery, are often repetitive in content and formally unsophisticated: they do not build on the thematic and formal discoveries of preceding film/videomakers. (The same observation could be made of much Asian American film criticism: every essay on Asian American cinema is forced to define its parameters, to constitute the field of inquiry afresh.)

This anthology seeks to address this problem by offering a framework that Asian American media criticism can build upon; furthermore, by promoting the study of key cinematic texts, this collection hopes to disseminate information about Asian American media and thereby boost the distribution of Asian American movies. But this process of canonization is not undertaken lightly, for one of the valuable aspects of Asian American media production is *precisely its dispersion*, its independence from the exploitative structures of commercial cinema. So if this volume constitutes Asian American cinema, it is important to note that it does so at a discursive level, by postulating connections among diverse movies, film/videomakers, and institutions—connections that may not be borne out at a structural (economic) level.

A comprehensive history of dispersed cinematic production is impossible; in its place, this anthology offers a number of partial and competing accounts that construct contrasting constellations of Asian American film/videomaking: taken together the essays in Part Two call attention to the multiple explanatory frameworks that can be imposed on Asian American cinema. Helen Lee makes this clear in her subtitle: her account is a "personal genealogy" of films and videos made by Korean American women. Lee does not claim that these movies do not exist in multiple traditions: clearly these film/videomakers have been influenced by a number of cinematic precursors, including the Hollywood studio system, independent film production, avant-garde cinema, and the national cinemas of Korea, Japan, and other Asian countries. Some of these women were born in Korea, some in North America; some were adopted by white families while others were steeped in the culture of the Korean diaspora. To group these movies together because they were all made by Korean American women is to propose one corpus against which individual movies can be judged. The success of Lee's account is attributable not to an objectively defined identity of filmmakers as Korean American women; rather, Lee's genealogy persuades due to the subjective factor of her judgment. By juxtaposing this account with other subjective accounts of the historical development of Asian American cinema, this volume calls attention to the contingency of its claims to constitute Asian American cinema as a field of inquiry.

In an effort to place Asian American film and video production in historical context, the first part of this anthology is devoted to discussions of the role that Asian bodies play in the American imaginary. Asian American media production is dialectically entwined with the legacy of racist depictions of Asian Americans by the dominant culture. But as the preceding discussion should make clear, the reader should resist the temptation to think of Part One as inaccurate, inauthentic representations authored by non-Asians. Rather, the essays in Part One convey what Asian Americans signify in the American imaginary and *what is at stake* in the representation of Asian bodies on American movie screens. Sabine Haenni, Eugene Franklin Wong, and Laura Hyun-Yi Kang each discuss the discursive process by which Asians are incorporated into the American body politic, the screening process by which Asian bodies are evaluated.

Sabine Haenni examines representations of Chinese bodies in early films, arguing that fantasies of Chinese bodily transformation are cinematic manifestations of white spectatorial fascination with U.S. Chinatowns. Haenni's compelling discussion of the consumption of Chinatown in the first decade of the twentieth century suggests some of the contradictions attending America's fascination with Asians in the United States, a fluidity and complexity that later cinematic representations strove to contain. In examining the intersection between movies and the tourism industry, Haenni reminds us that movies are part of a larger system of signification, and that these systems are ultimately predicated on the consumption of difference. The culture of consumption enjoys *sampling* exotic flavors while denying the subtle transformations that attend their ingestion. This denial manifests itself in efforts to regulate consumption, to protect purportedly vulnerable consumers (such as women and children) from harmful contact. Even as Chinatown's exotic appeal reveals spectatorial subjectivities to be fluid rather than fixed, these representations nonetheless serve to stabilize a white, middle-class national identity. The manifest artifice of cinematic Chinatown, what Haenni calls an aesthetic of fakeness, renders Chinatown stimulating but inconsequential, thereby revealing the anxiety about the consequences of the Chinese presence in the United States.

The excerpt from Eugene Franklin Wong's seminal study, *On Visual Media Racism*, focuses on film series (such as Fu Manchu and Charlie Chan) and serials (such as *Patria*). The 1920s and 1930s established Hollywood's Asian tropes, and traces of these films can be felt in virtually all popular cinematic representations of Asian Americans to this day. In the introduction to his study, Wong notes that the U.S. motion picture industry's institutionalized racism manifests itself in role segregation (wherein white actors can portray non-whites, but non-whites can never portray whites), in role stratification (wherein the larger the role, the greater the likelihood that a white actor will be cast), and in the relatively limited (that is to say, stereotypical) dimensions of Asian characters.[26] Wong notes that stereotyping is not an intrinsically pejorative activity: "Accepting stereotypes as a fact of filmic life, the presence of a particular stereotype is not evidence of racism as such. It is the persistence and durability of stereotypes over time which will determine to what degree there has been progress."[27] Wong's account thus allows us to situate Hollywood representations of Asians both in the context of their production and as they persist: indeed, in reading Wong's account more than two decades after it was written, the continuity of visual media racism from the 1970s to the present is even more striking than its persistence from the 1920s to the 1970s.

In "The Other Question: Stereotype, Discrimination and the Discourse of Colonialism," Homi Bhabha famously observed, "The stereotype is not a simplification because it is a false representation of a given reality. It is a simplification because it is an arrested, fixated form of representation that, in denying the play of difference, . . . constitutes a problem for the *representation* of the subject in signification of psychic and social relations."[28] It is ironically the fixity of stereotypes, the fact that they have maintained a remarkable constancy, that lends them their aura of truth. In cinematic terms, Wong notes that in the absence of counterbalancing representations (which he labels "counter-stereotypes or autostereotypes" and notes are unlikely to emerge given the Asian American community's inability to compete on equal footing with the motion picture industry), "Repetitiveness of stereotypes can literally maintain unfavorable images across generations, whereby the consistency and authority of the stereotypes are assumed to be 'almost like biological fact.' . . . the new generation can in turn, having been conditioned, expect or at the very least accept continuation of racist stereotyping in its own motion picture experience."[29]

In an influential formulation, Renee Tajima has noted that Hollywood cinema has represented the Asian female as either a blushing Lotus Blossom or a domineering Dragon Lady. While this dichotomy is in a sense the feminine equivalent of the Charlie Chan–Fu Manchu schema, these female archetypes function within an economy of exchange in which Western superiority to the "Orient" is affirmed through the possession of female bodies. Whereas the cross-racial desire that Haenni discussed can potentially upset white, middle-class hegemony, Laura Hyun-Yi Kang notes that the desire of white women for Asian men is represented as fundamentally distinct from the desire of white men for Asian women; the latter is ultimately indicative of the cultural superiority of the West over the East: "colonial, patriarchal desire is justified and encouraged by an imaginary construction of [the Asian woman's desire] as complementary with it."[30] Kang argues that the Asian women in *Thousand Pieces of Gold, Come See the Paradise,* and *The Year of the Dragon* are mere vehicles for the narrative transformation of white male characters. As Jessica Hagedorn has observed, Asian women on screen are invariably passive (or dead—the Dragon Lady exception proving the rule).[31]

The sexual dimension of the image of Asians and Asian Americans in the American imaginary cannot be overemphasized. Sexual and racial stereotyping are mutually implicated and embedded in discourses of Asian cultural inferiority. Deborah Gee's documentary video, *Slaying the Dragon*, links cinematic representations such as those discussed by Wong and Kang with the iconography of television news, noting that the pairing of older, white, male anchors with younger, Asian, female partners is indicative of U.S. racial formations of Asians as model minorities.[32] David Henry Hwang's *M. Butterfly* suggested that the Lotus Blossom fantasy disseminated by Puccini's *Madama Butterfly* was so compelling that a Western man seduced by the image of a submissive Asian female could allow himself to be deceived by his male lover. Hwang's play further suggested that American and French foreign policies were similarly deluded by the belief that Vietnam and the rest of Asia desired to submit to Western imperialism. Videomaker Richard Fung's study of gay pornography, "Looking for My Penis," shows that Hwang's dramatic speculation is grounded in contemporary practices: sex-race stereotyping has been translated into the homosexual hierarchy of tops and bottoms:[33] "Asian and anus are conflated" (121).[34] Since gay pornography "is never organized around the desire to be fucked, but around the desire to ejaculate,"[35] Asian sexuality is continually subordinated. The conclusion, supported by Haenni, Wong, and Kang, is that the dominant media industry denies subjectivity to Asians and Asian Americans, inviting them to participate in the American body politic at the expense of their agency and individuality.

By contrast, agency is the theme of Stephen Gong's essay on Asian American media arts centers, which offers the first of three different accounts that situate Asian American media production in contrasting aesthetic and material histories. Gong's essay articulates a paradox: how can there be multiple centers? Each organization has its own structure, determined by the exigencies of its local context. The diversity of organizations helps to promote varied forms of media production, even as these groups attempt to coordinate their efforts. In the fall of 2000, twenty years after the Berkeley summit that resulted in the founding of the National Asian American Telecommunications Association (NAATA), the organization hosted a national summit of filmmakers, scholars, media advocacy groups, and arts foundations with the aim of formalizing a national network for the promotion of Asian American media.

The paradox of multiple centers for marginal media production is also the subject of Rolando Tolentino's efforts to reconstruct a history of Filipino/a American media. Writing in response to *Moving the Image: Independent Asian Pacific American Media Arts* (where Gong's essay first appeared) in *Amerasia Journal* (also published by UCLA's Asian American Studies Center, thus offering a friendly if pointed amendment), Tolentino argues against subsuming Filipino/a American media under the umbrella of Asian Pacific American production. The term "Asian Pacific American" can work to obscure the differences among the diverse ethnic and national-origin groups that comprise it, and further cast all "Asian Pacific American" media productions in opposition to monolithic Hollywood. Drawing on Stuart Hall's discussion of black British filmmaking, Tolentino calls for Asian Pacific American media to move beyond refutation of Hollywood racism into a second phase that critiques the construction of ethnic identities and thereby the very politics of representation. Along the way, Tolentino uncovers a group of vibrant films worthy of sustained critical attention.

In "Re/membering Spectators: Meditations on Japanese American Cinema," Kent A. Ono argues that the act of presenting alternative histories (the act of remembering) on film actually brings a Japanese American audience into being.[36] In a similar vein, Helen Lee proposes that the process of filmmaking is a search for a sense of place, which means that cinema becomes home for displaced filmmakers. Lee, a Canadian woman who studied film in the United States, is profoundly aware of the possibilities and inadequacies inherent in terms like "Asian American" and "Korean Canadian." She proposes a diasporic framework, describing herself as *kyop'o* (overseas Korean) and positing a *kyop'o* women's aesthetic practice. Just as Lee's own identities are multiple and situational ("In an American context, we are Korean. In a Korean context, we are women"), so does Korean American women's cinema become Asian American in the context of a feminist film festival, or Korean in the context of an Asian American film festival. By bridging the positions of filmmaker and spectator in this essay, Lee reminds us of the personal stakes in any attempt to construct a history of Asian American media production.

The essays in Part Three situate Asian American films in a variety of sociocultural and aesthetic contexts, including the documentary tradition, avant-garde film and video, the Toronto art scene, Asian American literature, and diasporic audiences. In a sense, then, this section does not argue for a coherent discursive context for Asian American film and video production, but rather articulates numerous discourses as they intersect with Asian American cinema. The section begins with Bill Nichols's discussion of the landmark documentary, *Who Killed Vincent Chin?* The murder of Vincent Chin and the ensuing trial of Ronald Ebens and Michael Nitz raised the fundamental question of whether Asians could become full-fledged American citizens, thereby reinvigorating Asian American activism and Asian American Studies. The Vincent Chin case helped constitute modern Asian American identity, as Yen Le Espiritu argues.[37] Christine Choy and Renee Tajima's film makes clear the inaccuracy of the common misconception that Ebens and Nitz mistook Chinese American Vincent Chin for Japanese even as it thoroughly explores the context of anti-Japanese resentment in Detroit.[38] In doing so, the film poses Chin's murder not as a mystery to be solved (Nichols points out that the film refuses to provide a linear, realist depiction of the murder), but as a paradox about the nature of agency (the film quotes Ebens's use of the passive voice: "It's not something you plan on happening, but it happens"). Did an economic recession kill Chin? Did he die because he deployed macho codes denied to Asian Americans (the fight began as a disagreement between Chin and Ebens in a strip club)? Choy and Tajima's film concerns itself with the very problem of minority representation: does Ebens stand in for white racism? Does Chin stand in for Japanese economic competition? Who speaks for Chin? Nichols argues that the film's formal strategy "sustains that cry for justice which the judicial system has yet to hear"[39] through an experiential form of knowledge that balances abstractions (such as "race" and "class") with the conviction that agency can be assigned: Ronald Ebens and Michael Nitz killed Vincent Chin.

While Nichols attempts to describe a historical method in cinema, Marita Sturken muses on the nature of memory. Sturken situates three videos about the legacy of the World War II internment of Japanese Americans (Janice Tanaka's *Memories from the Department of Amnesia* and *Who's Going to Pay for These Donuts, Anyway?* and Rea Tajiri's *History and Memory*) in the context of experimental video's tradition of countering hegemonic national myth-making with a politics of memory. Tajiri's modestly monumental video does not reconcile personal memory with documented history, instead interrogating hierarchies of documentation that privilege some events as objective, verifiable historical truths while dismissing others as subjective, unreliable memories. Tanaka's videos relentlessly document the present in an attempt to understand the past, such that the past can justify the present. Like *Who Killed Vincent Chin?* these three videos confront a trauma visited upon Asian American bodies and attempt to understand the nature of the conflicting testimonial accounts; the goal is not to discover what actually happened, but to understand the process by which what happened is alternately remembered and forgotten, memorialized and obscured. Like Nichols, Sturken situates these movies not in the context of Asian American culture but in the context of cinema aesthetics.

The next two essays examine the impact of immigrants on established communities of American-born minorities. Of course, the Vincent Chin case and the internment, even as they are manifestations of interracial tensions, also produced interethnic transformations—these events helped to (re)constitute Asian Americans as a political entity. The formation of Asian American political identity can be seen as a claim upon resources: *Chan Is Missing* and *Mississippi Masala* both depict the ways that tenuously established minority communities guard their small slice of the American Pie from later arrivals. My essay suggests that the absent figure of Chan poses a crisis for Chinese American identity, a crisis that calls for the formation of an Asian American identity that can incorporate both immigrants and U.S.-born Asian Americans. This overarching Asian American identity always has the potential to obscure diversities among Asian Americans, but it can also describe a process whereby that diversity is realized, as in Helen Lee's ironic statement, "I became an Asian American before I became Korean American" (in this volume). Binita Mehta's discussion of *Mississippi Masala* is significant for the emphasis she places on the multilayered preconceptions that determine how Ugandan Indian immigrants interact with African Americans in the Deep South. The platitude "United we stand, divided we fall," voiced by one character to imply unity of non-whites in the United States, signals a complicated series of appropriations that draw on the rhetoric of the civil rights movement as well as Revolutionary America. Taken together, these two essays describe the investment that marginal subjects have in maintaining the very class- and race-based hierarchies that disenfranchise them.

Linda Peckham's essay on Trinh T. Minh-ha's *Surname Viet Given Name Nam* functions as a pivot for the four essays that precede it. The state's use of violence against its own citizens to redefine its national identity, the complex structures of remembering and forgetting that such trauma produces, the intersection of multiple discourses in the Asian American body, and the central role that gender plays in mediating all of these processes: Trinh's film brings all of these themes together. Calling the conventions of translation and the documentary interview into question, *Surname Viet Given Name Nam* denies that unmediated communication is ever possible. By problematizing spectatorial identification with the speaking figures on screen, Trinh's film refuses to permit the construction of a unified Vietnamese American women's subjectivity. Peckham's essay reproduces the gaps and silences of Trinh's film: Peckham does not explain the film so much as she meditates on what the film refuses to explain.

Binita Mehta asks us to account for the diversity of experiences within the Indian diaspora; Helen Lee hints at a complex interrelation between Korean American and Korean Canadian identity; and Trinh T. Minh-ha's *Surname Viet Given Name Nam* presents a multiplicity of Vietnamese women, North, South, and overseas. The essays in Part Three have been gradually expanding the definition of Asian American cinema to include spaces throughout North America, Africa, and Asia itself. Of course, all Asian American cinema is in a sense an articulation of how we got from there to here, but these essays all remind us that the very concept of "here" is a construction used to legitimate a hegemonic American identity (which, after all, is not truly native). Locality and rootedness are the themes that Thomas Waugh takes up in his discussion of the videomaker Richard Fung, a gay Canadian born in Trinidad to Chinese parents. Waugh suggests that Fung's videos evoke a complex space, both rooted and dislocated, out of settings that are resolutely specific (a particular spa in Toronto) and manifestly abstract (stylized studio sets).[40] Local spaces intersect with "ethnoscape" and "homoscape," defined as "the transnational scene of sexual spaces, commodities, communications and identity performance." As a videomaker and activist, Fung seems to think locally while acting globally.

A similar tension between the distinctiveness of historical events and locations and a mythic sense of time is also apparent in Yunah Hong's *memory/all echo*, a video adapted from and inspired by artist and writer Theresa Hak Kyung Cha, whom Helen Lee has called the godmother of Korean diasporic women artists. Cinematic adaptations are conceived as isolating the essence of a literary text, which is then translated into cinematic terms. But Cha's *Dictee* is hybrid text, combining semi-autobiographical prose, historical texts, poetry, and visual elements including photography and calligraphy (among others) into a work that calls into question the very ability of language to represent. In Cha's work, language *renders*, it tears apart as it attempts to depict. Jennifer Guarino-Trier's sensitive reading of *memory/all echo* brings out the traces of Cha's text within Hong's video, articulating a process whereby Cha speaks through Hong and Hong speaks through Cha. This continual cycling brings the past into the present as an echo, a manifestation that "refers" to the past but "exists" in the present. In this manner, both Hong's and Guarino-Trier's texts honor the ongoing process that Cha famously captures in her phrase, "Our destination is fixed on the perpetual motion of search."[41]

In our increasingly global culture, new identity formations that situate Asian Americans as citizens of the world are increasingly reflected in Asian American aesthetic production. Aihwa Ong has described a strategy of "flexible accumulation" that disperses the members of family firms around the globe to enable "twenty-four hour responses to a highly uncertain, competitive global capitalism." These transnational business strategies produce new forms of subjectivity as different members of the family maintain multiple residences and search for "local affective and business bonds" that will provide them with a sense of belonging. Family structures undergo an uneven evolutionary process wherein values shift as competing notions of the family's cultural identity assert themselves.[42]

The Wedding Banquet and *Fire* are both products of the transnational cinema marketplace: Ang Lee's film was funded by both the Taiwanese film industry and a New York production company, while Deepa Mehta's film was funded by a combination of Canadian and Indian investors. While *The Wedding Banquet* is set in New York, the New Delhi family depicted in *Fire* is surely not Asian American. However, both films "screen Asian Americans" in a transnational age by articulating the effect of competing nationalist discourses on the Asian diaspora. For example, North American and Indian critics interpreted *Fire*'s representation of lesbian sexuality as indicative of Western cultural influence; New York *Newsday* described the film as a "florid, erotic cross-cultural romance" despite the fact that the two lovers were both Hindu.[43] In the essays that conclude this collection, Mark Chiang and Gayatri Gopinath examine the challenge that homosexuality poses to national identity. Chiang identifies a contradiction in Taiwanese identity arising from the Nationalist Party's imposition of a monolithic Chinese identity upon the ethnically diverse

Taiwanese population. Attempting to explain how a Taiwanese American's homosexuality becomes subsumed by the imperative to procreate, Chiang argues that *The Wedding Banquet* attempts to reconstruct Taiwanese patriarchy in a transnational space. In the absence of a stable homeland, cinema becomes a space where the contradictions of transnational capital are putatively resolved; the movie theater becomes a place of refuge for transnational Asians.

Gayatri Gopinath's discussion of *Fire* proposes two competing interpretations of the film, one grounded in Western conceptions of queer identity, the other attentive to sexuality in an Indian diasporic context. Gopinath argues that *Fire* depicts lesbian desire as an expression of the rejection of "contemporary Hindu nationalist ideologies that rely on women's sexual purity and sanctity to ensure group solidarity." Written in early 1998, Gopinath's essay displays remarkable prescience: in December of that year, the Hindu fundamentalist group Shiv Sena closed down a number of Indian theaters that were screening the film. *Fire*'s distributor, Shringar Films, suspended all screenings, and the Ministry of Information and Broadcasting sent the film back to the Censorship Board for review. On 14 December, Shiv Sena announced that it would withdraw its opposition to *Fire* if the characters named Sita and Radha were given the Muslim names "Sabhana and Saira."[44] Shiv Sena's actions would seem to confirm this collection's thesis: cinematic representation of Asians in their bodily materiality reveals the ideologies that police national identities.

The essays in the final section of this collection have traced an ironic trajectory. Two assaults on Asian American bodies, the Vincent Chin murder and the internment of Japanese Americans, express the persistence of the belief that Asian Americans do not belong "here." As it happens, these two tragedies served as a wake-up call for Asian Americans, who became impelled to redress past wrongs and address present inequities: in both cases, Asian Americans turned to the U.S. judicial system for remedy. Part Three concluded with two films that are not concerned with being here in North America at all: *The Wedding Banquet* depicts the transformation of Taiwanese nationalism in the diaspora, while *Fire* dramatizes the price women pay in contemporary formulations of Hindu nationalism in India. In between, we have examined the complexity of the Asian diaspora (from India to Uganda to the United States, from China to Trinidad to Canada) and the legacy of wars in Korea and Vietnam. These essays suggest that Asian American identity was always transnational in character, that migration from Asia was determined to a great extent by political and economic interests of other nations. In the words of JeeYeun Lee, "I am here because you were there: my location is a direct reflection of nations and peoples shifting and conflicting."[45] The question is not why Asian Americans have come to these shores, but why the United States has reached beyond its borders. The essays in Part Three have shifted our attention away from the United States and onto the world stage.

This shift in emphasis reflects the transformations that globalization is wreaking on the United States and its minority populations.
Asian Americans, defined in terms of their labor in the nineteenth century, find that they continue to function as signifiers of the flow of capital across the globe in the twenty-first century. In the academy, the
discipline of Asian American Studies has traditionally been narrowly
focused on the experiences of Asian Americans in the United States, distinguishing itself from East Asian Studies. However, in an era when Asian
immigrants to the United States outnumber Asian Americans born in this
country, Asian American Studies has necessarily adopted a diasporic
framework to understand the flow of Asian bodies in and out of the United
States. What will racial difference come to mean in a global economy? Will
labels like "Asian American," implying ethnicity and nationality, retain
their relevance? I anticipate that cinematic representations of diasporic
Asians will not immediately adapt to changing economic circumstances.
Instead, I predict that the long-established Asian archetypes of model
minority and Yellow Peril, Lotus Blossom and Dragon Lady, will persist.
These images continue because they divert attention toward putatively
Asian cultural values and away from economic structures that brought
Asians into contact with the West.

NOTES

1. Ronald Takaki, *Strangers from a Different Shore: A History of Asian Americans*
(New York: Penguin, 1989), 13.

2. Darrell Y. Hamamoto, *Monitored Peril: Asian Americans and the Politics of TV
Representation* (Minneapolis: University of Minnesota Press, 1994), 1.

3. For a discussion of the meanings of citizenship for Asian American Studies, see Lisa
Lowe, *Immigrant Acts: On Asian American Cultural Politics* (Durham, N.C.: Duke University Press, 1996).

4. See David Palumbo-Liu, *Asian/American: Historical Crossings of a Racial Frontier*
(Stanford, Calif.: Stanford University Press, 1999). Since writing "The Desiring of Asian
Female Bodies," reprinted in this volume, Kang has adopted the "Asian/American" formu-
lation. See "Si(gh)ting Asian/American Women as Transnational Labor," *Positions: East
Asia Cultures Critique* 5:2 (Fall 1997): 403–37.

5. Dai-Sil Kim-Gibson's *Sa-I-Gu* documents the riots from the perspective of Korean
American women in Los Angeles. Michael Cho's *Another America*, which documents relationships between African American communities and Korean American merchants, argues
that the "Black-Korean" problem is a media construction.

The third section of Palumbo-Liu's *Asian/American* offers an extended discussion of
the model minority thesis and relates this racial triangulation to the L.A. riots.

6. Dana Y. Takagi, *The Retreat from Race: Asian-American Admissions and Racial
Politics*, rev. ed. (New Brunswick, N.J.: Rutgers University Press, 1998), x.

7. Ibid., ix–x, 11.

8. Charles Musser, *Before the Nickelodeon: Edwin S. Porter and the Edison Manu-
facturing Company* (Berkeley: University of California Press, 1991), 146.

9. Richard A. Oehling, "Hollywood and the Image of the Oriental, 1910–1950, Part II,"
Film and History 8:3 (September 1978).

10. For accounts of cinematic representation during the Pacific War, see Michael

Renov, "Warring Images: Stereotype and American Representations of the Japanese, 1941–1991," in *The Japan/America Film Wars: WWII Propaganda and Its Cultural Contexts* (Chur, Switzerland: Harwood Academic, 1994), 95–118.

11. See Donald Bogle's *Toms, Coons, Mulattoes, Mammies, and Bucks* (New York: Continuum, 1989), excerpted in *Representing Blackness: Issues in Film and Video*, ed. Valerie Smith (New Brunswick, N.J.: Rutgers University Press, 1997). For an analysis of multiracial Asian romance narratives, see Gina Marchetti, *Romance and the "Yellow Peril": Race, Sex and Discursive Strategies in Hollywood Fiction* (Berkeley: University of California Press, 1994).

12. Allan DeSouza, "Return to *Bhowani Junction*," *Amerasia Journal* 23:2 (1997): 134. For other ambivalent readings of Hollywood romances, see also Jessica Hagedorn, "Asian Women in Film: No Joy, No Luck," *Ms.* 4:4 (1994): 74–79; and Peter X Feng, "Recuperating Suzie Wong: A Fan's Nancy Kwan-dary," in *Countervisions: Asian American Film Criticism*, ed. Darrell Hamamoto and Sandra Liu (Philadelphia, Pa.: Temple University Press, 2000), 40–56.

13. Deborah Gee's documentary video *Slaying the Dragon* surveys representations of Asian women on film and television. Renee Tajima, "Lotus Blossoms Don't Bleed," in *Making Waves: An Anthology of Writings By and About Asian American Women*, ed. Asian Women United of California (Boston, Mass.: Beacon, 1989), 308–18.

14. Dorothy B. Jones, *The Portrayal of China and India on the American Screen, 1896–1955: The Evolution of Chinese and Indian Themes, Locales, and Characters as Portrayed on the American Screen* (Cambridge, Mass.: Center for International Studies, Massachusetts Institute of Technology, 1955), 52–59.

15. Ibid., 23.

16. Ibid., 15.

17. Julia Lesage, "Artful Racism, Artful Rape: Griffith's *Broken Blossoms*," in *Home Is Where the Heart Is: Studies in Melodrama and the Women's Film*, ed. Christine Gledhill (London: BFI, 1987), 236, 247.

18. "Introduction," in *Representing Blackness: Issues in Film and Video*, ed. Valerie Smith (New Brunswick, N.J.: Rutgers University Press, 1997), 3–4.

19. Gary Okihiro argues that the model minority thesis is an articulation of Asians as a mental threat, connected to the Yellow Peril concept of the bodily threat of Asian masses, and that the two concepts "form a closed loop that ameliorates and reinforces both. Thus, the model minority blunts the threat of the yellow peril, but the former, if taken too far, becomes the yellow peril. I also note that the two stereotypes are engendered categories. . . . The 'masculine' yellow peril is imbued with 'womanly' threats, and the 'feminine' model minority, with 'manly' perils. In fact, the dual natures of both ideas . . . destabilize the borders that delineate power and disempowerment. The perils of the body (the yellow peril) and mind (the model minority) are rooted within a cultural politics of assimilation and exclusion, but they also arise out of economic and political contestation." Gary Okihiro, *Margins and Mainstreams: Asians in American History and Culture* (Seattle: University of Washington Press, 1994), xiii–xiv.

20. Frank Chin and Jeffery Paul Chan, "Racist Love," in *Seeing Through Shuck*, ed. Richard Kostelanetz (New York: Ballantine, 1972), 65–79.

21. Sut Jhally and Justin Lewis, *Enlightened Racism: The Cosby Show, Audiences, and the Myth of the American Dream* (Boulder, Colo.: Westview, 1992), 137–38.

22. This analysis takes its cue from three works that articulate Asian Americans vis-à-vis the body politic: Dana Takagi, Lisa Lowe, and David Palumbo-Liu, all cited previously.

23. I am indebted to Martin Brückner for pointing out this implication of *Screening Asian Americans*.

24. Binita Mehta, "Emigrants Twice Displaced: Race, Color, and Identity in Mira Nair's *Mississippi Masala*," in *Between the Lines: South Asians and Postcoloniality*, ed. Deepika Bahri and Mary Vasudeva (Philadelphia, Pa.: Temple University Press, 1996), 191. Reprinted in this volume.

25. Ella Shohat and Robert Stam, *Unthinking Eurocentrism: Multiculturalism and the Media* (London: Routledge, 1994), 180.

26. Eugene Franklin Wong, *On Visual Media Racism: Asians in the American Motion Pictures* (New York: Arno, 1978), 11–15.

27. Ibid., 20.

28. Homi K. Bhabha, *The Location of Culture* (London: Routledge, 1994), 75.

29. Walter Lippmann, *Public Opinion* (New York: Macmillan, 1950), 93, quoted in Wong, *On Visual Media Racism*, 17–18.

30. L. Hyun-Yi Kang, "The Desiring of Asian Female Bodies: Interracial Romance and Cinematic Subjection," *Visual Anthropology Review* 9:1 (Spring 1993): 8. Reprinted in this volume.

31. Jessica Hagedorn, "Asian Women in Film: No Joy, No Luck," *Ms.* 4:4 (January/February 1994): 74–79.

32. See Michael Omi and Howard Winant, *Racial Formation in the United States: From the 1960s to the 1990s*, 2nd ed. (New York: Routledge, 1994).

33. It is by no means clear that homosexuality borrows heterosexual hierarchies. Orientalism's assignation of deviant sexuality to the East suggests that homosexual fantasy has always been central to Western discourses. See Tom Hastings, "Said's *Orientalism* and the Discourse of (Hetero)sexuality," *Canadian Review of American Studies* 23:1 (Fall 1992): 127–47.

34. Richard Fung, "Looking for My Penis: The Eroticized Asian in Gay Video Porn," in *How Do I Look?: Queer Film and Video*, ed. Bad Object-Choices (Seattle, Wash.: Bay Press, 1991), 153.

35. Richard Dyer, "Coming to Terms," *Jump Cut* 30 (March 1985): 28, quoted in Fung, "Looking for My Penis."

36. Kent A. Ono, "Re/membering Spectators: Meditations on Japanese American Cinema," *Countervisions*, 129–49.

37. In a chapter on the formative role that racially motivated violence has played in constituting Asian Americans as a political entity, Espiritu notes that "though the case did not turn out to the satisfaction of Asian Americans, it did leave an important organizational legacy." See *Asian American Panethnicity: Bridging Institutions and Identities* (Philadelphia, Pa.: Temple University Press, 1992), 143.

38. In a paper presented on 27 May 2000 at the conference of the Association for Asian American Studies (held in Scottsdale, Arizona), Tomio Geron deconstructed these contradictions in representations of the Vincent Chin case ("Vincent Chin and Asian American Politics in the 'Ambiguous' 1980s").

39. Bill Nichols, *Blurred Boundaries: Questions of Meaning in Contemporary Culture* (Bloomington: Indiana University Press, 1994), 137.

40. I discuss Fung's strategies for photographing China, a space thoroughly narrativized by his father's family, by historians and critics, and by popular culture, in "Decentering the Middle Kingdom," *Jump Cut* 42 (1998): 122–34.

41. Theresa Hak Kyung Cha, *Dictee* (New York: Tanam, 1982), 81.

42. Aihwa Ong, "On the Edge of Empires: Flexible Citizenship Among Chinese in Diaspora," *Positions: East Asia Cultures Critique* 1:3 (1993): 759, 761.

43. John Anderson, "Slow-burning Issues Fuel *Fire*," *Newsday* (22 August 1997): II B 8.

44. "Thackeray's Terms for Screening of 'Fire,' " *The Hindu* (14 December 1998): n.a. The name "Sita" had already been changed to "Nita" when the film was dubbed into Hindi, at the instigation of the Censorship Board. The names "Sabhana" and "Saira" refer to two of Deepa Mehta's most vocal supporters (including her lead actress, Member of Parliament Shabana Azmi).

45. JeeYeun Lee, "Toward a Queer Korean American Diasporic History," in *Q & A: Queer in Asian America*, ed. David L. Eng and Alice Y. Hom (Philadelphia, Pa.: Temple University Press, 1998), 186.

Asian American Bodies

Sabine Haenni

Filming "Chinatown":[1] Fake Visions, Bodily Transformations

An 1898 Thomas Edison film, entitled *Dancing Chinamen—Marionettes*, consists of one scene—a stage set on which we see two marionettes on strings next to each other, facing us. For the duration of the brief film the marionettes are pulled up by the strings above ground, then quickly let down until they sit on the ground doing splits, pulled up, let down, pulled up, let down, and so on. This movement within the static shot creates an image of a strangely multijointed body, a body that is definitely "foreign"—coded as "Chinese." Such a mobile body, whose limbs seem to be able to perform physically impossible feats, reveals a strange fascination with precisely this kind of "strange" body and, at the same time, a considerable aggression. After all, the marionettes are on strings, moved by an invisible hand.

Such aggression is much more visible in *Chinese Rubbernecks* (American Mutoscope and Biograph, 1903), in which one Chinese laundry man grabs the head of another Chinese man and pulls it until the neck extends across the entire screen before it springs back, a feat made possible by the use of a dummy head and a dummy neck. Revealing white fantasies about the emerging Chinese presence in the United States, these films suggest not only the physical aggression directed toward the Chinese body, but also a fascination with the Chinese body that gets coded as strangely extendable and mutable. The use of props—marionettes and dummy body parts—in both *Dancing Chinamen—Marionettes* and *Chinese Rubbernecks* ground the representation of the Chinese in fantasies of magical, bodily transformations beyond the physically possible.[2]

More implicitly than explicitly, these two films reveal fantasies not only about Chinese bodies but also about the white spectators' own transformations in the wake of the emergence of U.S. Chinatowns. In the 1890s, as part of the larger development of the intraurban tourist industry, New

21

Figure 1. George Fitch, "'Seeing New York' Through a Megaphone," *Ladies Home Journal* 24 (January 1907): 17.

York City's Chinatown became the object of a considerable slumming craze.[3] American magazines began to feature essays on Chinatowns, describing menus in Chinese restaurants, the offerings in Chinese curio shops, and the enclaves' inhabitants.[4] By 1909, so-called rubberneck automobiles, accompanied by a "megaphone man," who provided a commentary on the urban landscape, would take the curious spectator on a tour through Chinatown, which included visits to a joss house, a theater, and a restaurant.[5] The emergence of rubbernecking as a new form of entertainment—the term was coined in the United States in the 1890s—suggests that the title of *Chinese Rubbernecks* was hardly coincidental.[6] The film displaces rubbernecking onto a racialized body, but its literalization also associates this new form of leisure with bodily transformations. Of course, white rubbernecking tourists would hardly be transformed in such a physical, literal way. With its ascending rows of seats, the rubberneck automobile looked like a moving theater, which suggests that rubbernecking revolved around *fantasies* of self-transformation, rather than physical mutations.

The difference between the rubberneck automobile and the movies lay, among other things, in the price. Chinatown trips cost one to two dollars and would have attracted an (upper) middle-class audience, many of whom must have been tourists visiting New York City.[7] Movies, on the other hand, made Chinatown available for consumption to the masses. Actuality films, such as *Chinese Procession, No. 12* (Edison, 1898), *Parade of Chinese* (Edison, 1898), and *San Francisco Chinese Funeral* (Edison, 1903), captured apparently unstaged scenes in open, urban space, often privileging moments of celebration; more apparently staged films, such as *Scene in Chinese Restaurant* (American Mutoscope and Biograph, 1903), *Chinese Shaving Scene* (Edison, 1902), and *Scene in Chinatown* (American Mutoscope and Biograph, 1903), showed scenes from everyday life; other films, such as *The Heathen Chinese and the Sunday School Teachers* (American Mutoscope and Biograph, 1904) and *Rube in an Opium Joint* (American Mutoscope and Biograph, 1905), exploited popular fantasies about Chinatown; and some films, particularly *Lifting the Lid* (American Mutoscope and Biograph, 1905) and *The Deceived Slumming Party* (American Mutoscope and Biograph, 1908), closely modeled themselves after actual slumming tours. Once they became available for consumption of both working-class and middle-class Americans, Chinatown tours and Chinatown films, I argue in this essay, provided white viewers and slummers with fantasies of magical (self-) transformations.

Such fantasies, as well as the pleasures of Chinatown tourism in general, have received little attention in recent work on American Chinatowns' emergence into national consciousness, which has usually stressed how popular depictions of Chinatown served to reinforce racial distinctions and maintain the status quo. James Moy, for instance, has located early U.S. representations of the Chinese in the context of a commodified, dehumanized spectacle, in which they were exhibited as an "objectified or dead Other," a strategy meant to establish Americans' imperial superiority.[8] And Sumiko Higashi has suggested that slum films "objectified and commodified the urban 'Other' " in order to reinforce "social hierarchies."[9] In the logic of these accounts, Chinatown tourism and early Chinatown films helped stabilize the middle-class, imperial nation.

While I do not disagree with the claim that such representations ultimately maintained racial hierarchies, the focus on stability does not quite explain the fascination with mobility, mutability, and bodily transformations in *Dancing Chinamen—Marionettes* and *Chinese Rubbernecks*. In this essay, I want to address how the production and consumption of Chinatown may simultaneously assert a white hegemony even as it grants its viewers and tourists access to new, rather than old, mobile, rather than static, subjectivities. My objective here is to further explore the cultural logic of commodification by not presuming commodification's static quality but by accounting for its fascination with mutability, mobility, and bodily transformations. In doing so, I partially follow Gaylyn Studlar, who has recently argued that orientalism in U.S. film provided white women with new "transformative identities," as well as Esther Romeyn, who comes to a very similar conclusion in her study of the anti-Chinese hysteria surrounding the murder of Elsie Sigel—a young, white woman whose dead body was found in the apartment of a Chinese man in 1909.[10] I do not presume, however, that Chinatown appealed almost exclusively to women (although its pleasures were certainly gendered), and I do not presume that the "transformative identities" Chinatown offered were congruent with those of the New Woman.[11] Instead, I argue that the commodification of Chinatown and the filming of Chinatown imagined new kinds of vision, and new ways of engaging the racialized metropolis.

I want to bring into view three structures of representation and experience—a surface aesthetic, multisensorial perceptions, and an aesthetic of fakeness—that became available to viewers around the turn of the twentieth century. Along the way, I wish to show how early Chinatown films appropriated a form of urban spectatorship already familiar from sightseeing tours and the popular iconography developed in mass-circulation magazines, while they also struggled to establish the specificity of their own medium. The new kinds of experience and spectatorship made available in magazines, on tours, and on film constituted a complex negotiation of the contradictory presence of the Chinese in the United States, who had been banned by the Exclusion Act of 1882, but who were already present in the country. For David Palumbo-Liu, it is precisely this presence despite the exclusion that makes the Chinese in the United States the harbinger and sign of the modernity of the United States, a nation defined by its new focus on "the management of a newly defined interiority."[12] The emergence of Chinatown in New York City seemed to require some sort of bodily and psychic response and transformation on the part of white Americans. Tours to Chinatown and Chinatown films, I want to suggest, helped manage this new interiority by giving white Americans a new sense of self and a new sensorial experience. On Chinatown tours and in Chinatown films, white viewers and tourists could experience not a stable, hierarchical regime, but a regime predicated on fluidity and bodily transformations, as well as a fundamentally modern subjectivity not grounded in concepts of identification or stable identity. Rather than altering social and racial hierarchies in everyday life, such new ways of experiencing themselves and the city, I would suggest, ultimately allowed white Americans to negotiate—and be in control of—a racialized, urban modernity.

A few years later, such a cultural exchange with the Chinese and Chinatown was theorized by cultural critics across the Atlantic, particularly by Karl Kraus and Siegfried Kracauer. Writing in response to the murder of Elsie Sigel, Kraus, a Viennese satirist, suggested that the outrage generated by the murder revealed white male Western society's fear of a Chinese "superman," who commands past, present, and future, and who can take all guises and perform all roles.[13] Writing a decade after Kraus, Kracauer used a passing reference to the Chinese as a way of thinking about how urban filmic spectatorship allowed its viewers to entertain fantasies of radical transformations: "It [the human spirit] squats as a fake Chinaman in a fake opium den, transforms itself into a trained dog that performs ludicrously clever tricks to please a film diva, gathers up into a storm amid towering mountain peaks, and turns into both a circus artist and a lion at the same time. How could it resist these metamorphoses?"[14] In Kracauer's scenario, modern urbanity in general and the cinema in particular foster a fantasy of a series of transformations that leave the spectator's body behind and that are "global" in that they are not limited by geography, nation, gender, or even species.

Kracauer's reference to a "fake opium den" was hardly coincidental. As this essay will show, Chinatown was indeed associated with such polymorphousness and magical transformations. My point is, however, that while such representations may have originated in a latent fear of "Chinese" polymorphousness (as Kraus as well as *Chinese Rubbernecks* and *Dancing Chinamen—Marionettes* suggest), films dealing more directly with Chinatown rarely bestowed any polymorphousness or magical qualities onto the Chinese. Instead, many such representations allowed the white spectators to imagine a complex white social formation—a new body politic—that could include European ethnic, class, and gender differences; these representations also allowed them to imagine themselves as polymorphously mobile, as capable of taking on any shape, thereby reworking a latent fear into an amazing possibility and into a particularly urban vision of identity. These films attempted to invent subjects that could pleasurably experience the newly racialized metropolis by simultaneously consolidating a new kind of "white" hegemony, and by assigning the Chinese to a limited and constrained space.[15]

Sensational Surface Aesthetics

The Deceived Slumming Party, an American Mutoscope and Biograph film from 1908, on which D. W. Griffith collaborated, is likely the most outrageous early film about Chinatown. The film opens with a location shot on New York City's 42nd Street, a street scene showing how a sightseeing automobile loads passengers. As the publicity material advertises, "Old Esra Perkins and his wife, Matilda, are induced by the glib-tongued bally-hoo to investigate the mysteries of that famous section of our great Metropolis— the Bowery. They are joined by Mr. Reginald Oliver Churchill Wittington, an English gentleman, who was willing to blow his last farthing in order to see the thing to the very limit."[16] The tourists' desire to see things "to the very limit" first takes them to a Chinatown opium joint, where they seem to witness the suicide of one of the young, white girls apparently addicted to opium; next they are taken to a Chinese restaurant, where Matilda, frightened by a rat, accidentally falls into the machine used for making sausages; and finally they visit a Bowery saloon, where they seem to witness a murder. Each time barely escaping with their lives (or so they think), the tourists experience Chinatown at its most sensational.

The film's sensational impulse, its longing not only to exhibit and display Chinatown but its insistence on the unimaginable horrors hidden within Chinatown, emphasizes the exotic difference of the Chinese, their inability to assimilate.[17] Such a view was supported by a larger iconographic geography that emphasized the hidden nature of Chinatown. As one journalist wrote, "There it lies, unfathomed and unknown, in the very ear of the city where all things come to be known—where a pin dropped on the other side of the world is heard an instant afterward—contemptuous, blandly mysterious, serene, foul-smelling, Oriental, and implacable behind that indefinable barrier which has kept the West and the East apart since the centuries began."[18] In this account, Chinatown is the one impenetrable spot in an otherwise utterly transparent city, even a transparent globe. Anthropomorphizing the city, the writer suggests that, as a "blandly mysterious" spot "in the very ear" of New York City, Chinatown disables New York City's body, or at least its sensorium.[19] Chinatown's segregation from the rest of the city, its enclosure within well-determined boundaries—behind a "barrier"—may be reassuring, but it also makes it frightening. Confronted with "a slamming of doors, a shooting of bolts, and snapping of locks," visitors are effectively locked out of Chinatown.[20] In such American fantasies, Chinatown relentlessly produces boundaries; more accurately, it is relentlessly segregated from American public life. Its most typical aspect is its impenetrability, its separation of the public and private realms.[21]

By 1908, the year *The Deceived Slumming Party* was filmed, such an iconography was hardly new. Indeed, in the early 1900s Chinatown often appeared to be experienced according to a sensationalist paradigm familiar since at least the 1850s. Dividing the city into rich and poor, us and them, mid-nineteenth-century, urban, sensational iconography had been committed to evoking a divided, melodramatically polarized city. George Foster, for instance, writing in 1850, invited the reader to "penetrate the thick veil of night and lay bare the fearful mysteries of darkness in the metropolis—the festivities of prostitution, the orgies of pauperism . . . the under-ground story."[22] The most famous example of such a melodramatic urban vision may have been Jacob Riis's *How the Other Half Lives*, published as late as 1890, but which, as Sally Stein has shown, heavily relied on an earlier iconography.[23] Chinatown easily seemed to be assimilated into this well-established, sensational paradigm, which melodramatically spatialized and separated the city into "us" and "them." As Chinatown emerged as a disturbing presence in the "body" of New York, the very familiarity of this segregationist, representational strategy was one way in which white New Yorkers negotiated the emerging presence of the Chinese in the city.

In New York City at least, the hidden nature of Chinatown was accentuated by built space: the narrow streets and the break with the grid system helped characterize Chinatown as labyrinthian. The sharp angle of Doyers Street was named "Bloody Angle," because it was a place where rival tong members supposedly waylaid each other; arcades were closed by the police because they offered criminals easy escapes, as did underground passageways.[24] As generous a commentator as Louis Beck suggested that criminals can "get under cover in the labyrinths of Chinatown."[25] In this scenario, which associated New York City's Chinatown literally with the "underground" and with a maze, the divergence from the urban grid system could easily be coded as foreign: "Doyers street is no good for traffic; it is too narrow; it resembles one of those mean byways in what the A.E.F. [American Expeditionary Force] used to call the foreign sections of French cities. It is little more than two hundred feet in length, and it curves and twists so much that to get from one end of it to the other one could almost follow the directions for reaching the house of Kassim Baba."[26] Doyers Street here becomes a symbol not of knowable foreignness (Frenchness), but of the foreign within the foreign (the foreign in France). If the grid system was indeed associated with the "American" (and with "American democracy"), as Philip Fisher has argued, then Chinatown's "crookedness" denoted the un-American.[27]

And yet, *The Deceived Slumming Party* appears less interested in depicting the sensationalistically conceived horrors of Chinatown than it is in exposing the fakeness of such sensational horrors and in emphasizing that it all is just a "show." The slummers may think that they narrowly escape with their lives on each occasion but we, the spectators, know that these horrifying scenes are staged to con and entertain the slummers. Before the party enters each establishment, we get a glimpse of how it "really" is. In the opium joint, for instance, people are playing cards until someone announces the arrival of tourists. The card players immediately get ready, lying down on beds in couples, faking an opium stupor. When the tourists enter, one white girl melodramatically clings to a lady's skirt, pleading, ultimately pretending to plunge a dagger into her heart. Finally, when the police arrive, the slummers readily pay what appears to be a substantial sum so as not to get arrested. At the end of the scene the money is divided among everybody present—including the police and the tour guide, who all participate in the fake show. As the ad says, "[e]very evening the stage, as it were, is set for this great comedy, and the characters are all made-up and ready for their parts when the 'easy-marks' arrive."[28] In this mutation of the mid-nineteenth-century sensational paradigm, the focus is less on the danger and unknowability of Chinatown than on its excessive well-knownness—its transformation from an obscure slum into a tourist attraction.

The emphasis on fakery shifts the focus of attention within a sensational paradigm, from a fascination with the hidden dangers behind the walls of Chinatown, to a fascination with the "show" itself. Many magazine writers showed little interest in what might be found in the depths of Chinatown, but were captivated by Chinatown's glitzy, gaudy surfaces. Chinatown's decorated buildings appeared to be one of the best shows in town:

> Banners of various designs; paper lanterns of every imaginable shape, size and color; effigies of all manner of repulsive beasts and reptiles, and signs of indescribable design conveying suggestions which are intelligible only to the Chinaman, cover the fronts of the three and four-story buildings, which are themselves painted in red, green, and yellow, and profusely ornamented with gilt and tinsel. Everything is glitter and show. Gaudiness prevails on every hand. Each building rivals its neighbor in its efforts at display and attractiveness.[29]

If in Chinatown "[e]verything is glitter and show," if Chinatown's effort is primarily directed toward "display," then *The Deceived Slumming Party's* exposure of the "show" that Chinatown has become begins to look like a logical sequel to this 1898 text. Magazine accounts, however, can help explain some of the dynamics generated by such a surface aesthetic. The above account, for instance, makes us aware of the writer's apparently confused feelings—his oscillation between revulsion and attraction. Such a mode of display, another writer added, to the degree that it is "of every imaginable" manner, is "bewildering to the average New-Yorker, who has not studied the queer sides of the city."[30] For these commentators, excessive decoration suggests that "Chineseness" itself signifies the ability to read what Americans cannot; conversely, Chinese surface decorations, to the degree that they remain "indescribable," have the capacity to explode the American linguistic system. Ultimately, such accounts of Chinatown's surface aesthetic point to the fear that "Chineseness" may be beyond the bounds of an intelligible identity or a coherent self, especially when excessive decorations seem to mark mere profusion and lack of order. In such a context, Chinatown and the Chinese are marked as "queer," an epithet often used to describe the neighborhood and meant to evoke the indescribability of the neighborhood's identity, its incapacity—or unwillingness—to conform to commonly available concepts of identity itself.[31]

And yet, even as Chinatown's gaudy surfaces raised questions of intelligibility and self-coherence, even as it challenged American journalists' ability to describe it without descending into confusion, the neighborhood's impulse to decorate also resulted in an aestheticization of difference that ultimately promoted the quarter's attractiveness. Louis Beck's description of the decorations comes after an account of the visitor's confusion upon first entering Chinatown. Struck by the "constant moving about," "the incessant jargon with which his ears are assailed, and the tireless bustle," the visitor is finally "attracted to the universal decoration and fantastic painting of the buildings."[32] After a moment of bodily and aural assault, the decorations of Chinatown, as confusing as they may be, appear to stabilize the slummer's gaze, providing a focus in the midst of confusion; at the very least, the decorations are purely visual and stable, rather than mobile, smelly, or loud. Ornamental profusion, even though it is associated with fears of illegibility, is therefore very different from, for instance, fears of contamination. Not understandable as a strategy of containment—in which neither Beck nor the other observers seem to be interested—the journalists' focus on ornamental profusion can produce pleasure and appreciation. Apparently less confusing than the more ephemeral (and maybe more immediate) sensations of smell and hearing, ornamental profusion can be appreciated as "attractive."

The representational strategy of what I have called a sensational surface aesthetic—and more particularly the emergence of signs and other ornaments on the façades of Chinatown—may have quickly located Chinatown within the larger field of emerging mass culture. As one disillusioned writer noticed, the focus on decorated façades was typical of the Bowery, New York City's working-class entertainment district, in general: "And here again is that pretentious exterior—the gay paint, the big signs, all the promise of good things within. . . . Inside it is a sad swindle. . . . It is all fraud, all fake."[33] Interestingly, the cultural illegibility of Chinatown's façades only serves to make it look more like other entertainment establishments. Presumably, it would therefore have been intelligible to slummers according to a newly emerging entertainment paradigm, although such a paradigm of show and fakery was certainly only one way in which an emerging mass culture was being perceived. What I have meant to suggest in this section is that by the turn of the twentieth century an iconography revolving around the consumption of a "surface aesthetic" uneasily coexisted with an older sensational paradigm that associated Chinatown with hidden horrors. One might suppose that the pleasures Chinatown held for white slummers must have been found in the particular mixture of sensational fascination and touristy fakery. The surface aesthetic may have been particularly compelling because it remained connected to a sensational logic promising thrills, even as it was quite clearly and reassuringly an "aesthetic" that one could appreciate. In many ways, however, such paradigms made it difficult to think about Chinese "identity." The decorational aesthetic itself posed questions of legibility, and the very idea of fakeness presumed that whatever is behind the façade is unlikely to be what is advertised on the front. To the degree that Chinatown was conceptualized in U.S. magazines according to the terms of a sensational surface aesthetic, the neighborhood had a profoundly contradictory, incoherent, if not illegible identity. Such incoherence suggests the modernity of even early Chinese/American "identity," but it also must have made the U.S.-Chinese encounter in Chinatown fundamentally problematic, even as the sensational surface aesthetic was presumably part of what made Chinatown an attractive tourist destination.

Multisensorial Transformations

In 1909, William Brown Meloney imagined how a slumming party experienced Chinatown: "The guide is talking; but see, few of his followers are listening to him. They are bewildered, uncertain. They feel they are on the threshold of a mystery. The women are clinging timidly to their escorts or holding one another's hands. The men are trying to look unconcerned as if it were an old story to them." After a visit to a fake opium den, however, "[t]he eyes of the slummers, as they step into the street, are brilliant, dancing, excited, eager. The women have lost their timidity. . . . They talk loudly; they laugh without occasion. . . . They no longer turn their eyes away from the impudent glances of the slant-eyed yellow men staring at them from the shop doors and the dark openings of the noisome tenements. They give back stare for stare."[34] Like Kraus's essay, Meloney's considerably more racist article was written shortly after the murder of Elsie Sigel; he is clearly concerned about the contaminating effect Chinatown supposedly has on white women. Meloney's essay—and the outraged response to the Elsie Sigel murder in general—may therefore be a particularly eloquent articulation of a male anxiety suggesting, as Gaylyn Studlar and Esther Romeyn have argued in different contexts, that U.S. orientalism allowed white women to escape bourgeois normativity and create new roles for themselves.[35]

While this is certainly the case, and while Meloney's essay apparently intends to warn white women of the dangers of such transgressions, his article, when read against the grain, also begins to suggest a larger anxiety. In Chinatown, Meloney suggests, all the slummers' eyes—male and female—become "brilliant, dancing, excited, eager." And while Meloney is clearly anxious about the women, and amazingly unconcerned about the men, he nonetheless implies that in Chinatown everybody may get high and act out of character even without drugs, simply because of the air one breathes and because of what one encounters. Momentarily bracketing the gendering of such anxiety, I want to take the trope of "being high" seriously and suggest that part of what Chinatown offered was indeed an intensified sensorial experience, and, by extension, a new concept of subjectivity grounded in sensorial perception.

Meloney's anxiety about slumming tours, to say the least, seemed exaggerated, even though it can be explained as a reaction to the Sigel murder. A photo of (mostly female) tourists that accompanies his article, although suggesting the bodily contortions and the undeniable mobilization of the female gaze that rubbernecking involved (both of which, of

Figure 2. William Brown Meloney, "Slumming in New York's Chinatown," *Munsey's Magazine* 41 (September 1909): 826.

course, may have been deemed improper behavior for middle-class women), hardly conveys a sense of a lack of respectability or impending miscegenation.[36] The automobile tours seemed respectable enough, especially if we consider that other automobile tours offered by the "Seeing New York" company included visits to Central Park, Grant's Tomb, and Fifth Avenue.[37] The context of such official New York City sights and monuments must have bestowed an aura of legitimacy on the Chinatown trip, even if, as an evening trip departing at 8:30, it still promised to uncover the dark, seamy underworld of the splendid new cosmopolis that the daytime tours advertised. Explanations by the tour guide and a strict temporal regime dictated the tourists' access to Chinatown in a way that prevented in-depth encounters.

At the theater, for instance, there was a special box reserved for "Americans," and by all accounts, slumming parties often stayed only 10 to 15 minutes before they were shepherded on to the next attraction. Sometimes, theater companies apparently disrupted their regular play, and put on a special, brief show for the tourists, because the Chinese play was deemed too obscene.[38] The entire tour seems to have been comprised of a series of brief "scenes" at best gesturing toward an always absent whole. This institutionalization of ephemerality constructs Chinatown in a way quite similar to the surface aesthetic, as an aggregated, non-coherent surface beyond which the slummers never penetrate. These impressions certainly did not provide coherent narratives, but may have been not unlike early films, which, as Lea Jacobs and Ben Brewster have argued, were understood not as a collection of shots but as a collection of "scenes."[39] The institutionalization of the tour, while certainly promising potential danger, must have made it rather safe.[40]

Despite the tour's apparent safety, Meloney's anxious fantasy, which troped the slummers' experience in terms of addiction, was hardly coincidental. Magazine essays very often—and quite obsessively—focused on Chinatown's "opium dens" and the attraction they represented for white Americans.[41] While some commentators sensationalistically announced the "startling facts with regard to the evil in the United States," others feared the possibility of reverse assimilation. "The people of America are quick imitators of the fashions and follies of others, and are as abject slaves to habit as any other class of people on earth," one writer wrote, as if fearing that Americans might become "Chinese."[42] The fascination with opium dens itself was quickly commercialized. Some places in Chinatown appeared to have staged fake opium dens for tourists, which may have been visited during slumming tours; people not inclined to go slumming could still visit the opium den displayed at Huber's museum.[43] The emphasis on opium dens in the American press made "addiction" a crucial metaphor that could govern the ways in which white Americans' relationship to Chinatown was figured: "An American who once falls under the spell of *chop sui* may forget all about things Chinese for weeks, and suddenly a strange craving that almost defies will power arises and, as though under a magnetic influence, he finds that his feet are carrying him to Mott Street."[44] While this account betrays a less anxious, transitory temporality of addiction, it nonetheless confirms that to the degree that all of Chinatown was a sensuous experience, Chinatown was perceived as potentially addictive.

The trope of addiction inevitably pointed to social consequences and radical transformations. "The opium eater," one commentator reported, sacrifices "[t]ime, wealth, energy, self-control, self-respect, honesty, truthfulness, and everything that is honorable in a man."[45] More specifically, fictional opium "dreams"—a literary genre in itself—frequently revolved around social mobility; this perception was apparently so common that Dr. Kane felt the need to attack the "complete absurdity" that the smoker almost inevitably "imagines himself as immensely wealthy or possessed of magnificent fame."[46] According to these accounts, opium smoking had the same kinds of effects that Hollywood would later be accused of producing through such institutions as the star system. It may therefore be no surprise that opium smoking was associated with leisure tout court, with "a state that approaches as closely as an American can ever come to the *dolce far niente* of the Italian."[47] In both more anxious and more optimistic versions of the discourse, opium addiction always seemed to result in a transformed self implying a change in social relations; at best, it may induce a different state of mind that mimics the one of a more desirable (but similarly "foreign") ethnicity. What concerns me here is that Chinatown, to the degree that it was figured through the trope of addiction, was assumed to have a transformative effect. Chinatown, that is, was assumed to have the power to change a person, to reconfigure American subjectivity.[48]

As the construction of the Chinatown experience via the rubbernecking tours indicates, spectator-participants on slumming tours hardly experienced Chinatown in terms of addiction. Nonetheless, these commentators' obsessive focus on Chinatown's sensuality and transformative potential provides a clue, for much of Chinatown's attraction must have been connected to its capacity to engage all the senses. The restaurant, the joss house, the theater, and the opium joint may appear to privilege particular senses—the restaurant the sense of taste, the theater, sight and hearing, and so on. But in fact each of these institutions was understood as providing a sensorial overload, a sensorial confusion and turmoil. Such overstimulation may have been most apparent at the theater, where visitors were not only fascinated by what they saw onstage, but also by the dense "tobacco smoke" that made the visitors wonder "that one really can live breathing something besides the common or garden variety of air"; by the orchestra's "shrieking and clashing descriptive music," by the "Crash! bang! shriek!"; and by the gorgeous costumes that were a "delight to the eye."[49] Commentators on restaurants noted the "Chinese lanterns" as much as they did the "seductive dish[es]."[50]

It is not surprising, then, that in *The Deceived Slumming Party*, one of the slummers, upon entering the restaurant, immediately proceeds to examine the various decorations; a "Chinese" restaurant was supposed to provide visual stimulus and to satisfy the taste buds. In fact, Chinatown itself was often characterized by its sensorial excess, particularly by its odor and sound: "This pronounced odor will be apparent to the visitor even before he comes in sight of Chinatown, and will prove a sure guide to that locality. . . . It is all a riddle to the uninitiated observer, suggestive of what must have been the experience when the confusion of tongues occurred at the tower of Babel."[51] Of course, such comments reveal white racism, but presumably, the neighborhood's alleged sensorial overstimulation was one of its main attractions, one major reason why tourists would be curious to visit the neighborhood. In Chinatown, so it seems, slummers could have a multisensorial experience; they would become aware of their senses in a way they never had before. To recall the promotion material of *The Deceived Slumming Party*, they would experience their senses "to the very limit."

If Chinatown promised a multisensorial experience, it immediately raised the question of one particular sense: touch. While many male commentators were irritated by what one may see, hear, and smell in Chinatown, they were scandalized by what women might touch. The Chinatown tour did not include visits to stores, but the stores, maybe especially the curio stores, invited tourists to "own" and take home a piece of Chinatown; they may also have invited a subsequent return, without a guide. Fearing exactly this, Meloney reported (or fantasized) how a young white girl on a slumming tour looked at a shop window, "pointing unashamed at an article of feminine finery."[52] Although he refrains from mentioning actual touching, the connection that he makes between touching a commodity and sexual intimacy is telling. In this somewhat suppressed fantasy—the girl never enters the store—the trip to the Chinatown store inevitably seems to lead to fantasies of miscegenation. In a particular twist on Marx's commodity fetishism, where the commodity becomes a "social hieroglyphic" obscuring social relations, the Chinatown commodity seems to figure social relations all too clearly, expressing the fear of an altered racial (and hence social) hierarchy.[53] In this anxiety-ridden account of capitalistic, commodified culture, the selling of a neighborhood by necessity involves touching, and, by implication, the touching of another person; even as the customer may touch only the commodity, such a commodity is always attached to a vendor. And yet, such miscegenation as a by-product of a capitalistic economy cannot be visualized. Meloney's essay features a picture of two white, working-class men who interestedly examine the commodities on display, rather than a photograph of a woman in a store. Even this essay displaces the fear generated by the fact that white women touch the "Chinese" commodity onto a different social group, inadvertently documenting how Chinatown must have attracted men as well.[54]

Unlike journalistic accounts of Chinatown, which, as I have argued in the previous section, frequently rendered Chinese subjectivity as contradictory and confusing, slumming tours to Chinatown allowed white slummers to experience their own bodies as contradictory, complex, and multisensorial. On Chinatown tours, one might suspect, tourists may have feared the strangeness of "Chinese" bodies and identities, but could ultimately undergo a multisensorial experience that had the capacity to produce a new kind of subjectivity for them. Miriam Hansen has argued that film and other modern entertainments aimed at "producing a new sensory culture"; that they "produced and globalized a new sensorium; . . . constituted, or tried to constitute, new subjectivities and subjects" by engaging the "contradictions of modernity at the level of the senses."[55] We might read the Chinatown experience according to the paradigms provided by Susan Buck-Morss, who, in a rereading of Walter Benjamin, has suggested that in response to the "shocks" of modern industrial life (epitomized by the factory but also by the new urbanity of streetcars, elevated trains, and automobiles), which injure "every one of the human senses," institutions, such as the department store, sought to

Figure 3. William Brown Meloney, "Slumming in New York's Chinatown," *Munsey's Magazine* 41 (September 1909): 819.

provide a remedial sensorial experience but ultimately had "the effect of anaesthetizing the organism, not through numbing, but through flooding the senses."[56]

In this account of modern anesthetics, modern entertainment, like opium, is understood by its promoters as a cure that supposedly revives the senses, when, in effect, it only furthers the numbness.[57] It is certainly difficult—if not impossible—to know how individual slummers would have reacted to the Chinatown experience, even more so since individual experience must have been influenced by the specific collective dynamics of the slumming group. And yet, the kind of sensory stimulation that Chinatown provided, it would seem, would be unlikely to provoke an overstimulation resulting in numbness, although it may have in particular instances. It is important to remember that even though an automobile carried the passengers to Chinatown, because of Chinatown's narrow streets, slummers often had to proceed on foot; Chinatown itself was likely to be understood as a non-technologized enclave in an increasingly technologized city. Unlike other attractions, such as the movies, which one would visit repeatedly, Chinatown was more likely to be a destination that one visited once, a destination outside one's everyday routine. Chinatown, that is, was unlikely to be a frequent experience; more likely, it retained a sense of the irregular in both the slummer's life and the city's urban fabric. To be sure, the newness of such an experience might result in shock, and yet this possibility would be minimized by the careful institutionalization of the tour and the guidance of the megaphone man.

It may be best to understand the Chinatown tour as providing a range of sensorial confusions that are not quite experienced as shocking to the degree that they are channeled according to the paradigms of tourism, but which also do not amount to some carefully orchestrated totality. It would appear that sometimes sensory overstimulation may occur, such as at the theater when a variety of senses are simultaneously engaged in a confined space. At other moments, however, overstimulation may be lessened because one sense would be foregrounded, such as at the restaurant when slummers would actually eat. And sometimes, sensory stimulation must have been temporalized, for instance, on the automobile, when quickly passing scenes may have resulted more in a sense of sensory fragmentation, a sense of an always absent whole, rather than in a sense of condensed overstimulation. Even visitors to the theater may have experienced a sort of sensory fragmentation, a sense that their senses—for instance, what they heard and what they saw—did not add up to some coherent whole. The sensory experience of Chinatown, that is, was various, rather than unified to produce some total effect; a sense of sensory fragmentation may be followed by a sense of sensory condensation and overstimulation. A Chinatown tour, that is, may have provided a range of sensory confusions that varied in intensity and effect. Chinatown's extraordinariness, its insistence on confusion, and its ability to vary the sensorial experience during the course of the tour, it would seem, might have been frightening to some, and yet for many it must have been pleasurable, not least because it offered the opportunity of giving in to one's sensorial confusions, of simply experiencing the "uncivilized and uncivilizable trace" inherent in the senses.[58] At its most extreme, such a tour through one's sensorium may have resulted not just in the loss of an experiential coherence and the loss of a coherent subjectivity, but in the opportunity to inhabit a purely sensorial subjectivity not predicated on a sense of coherent "identity."

Fake Visions

As a primarily visual and, even in the silent period, aural medium, the cinema cannot quite reproduce the kind of multisensorial, bodily experience that slumming tours to Chinatown promised, even though, as *Lifting the Lid* and *The Deceived Slumming Party* show, early Chinatown films also modeled themselves after the tours. Many of the early Chinatown films, including *Chinese Rubbernecks,* appear to focus on more easily representable bodily transformations. *The Deceived Slumming Party,* for instance, emphasizes the possibility of bodily attacks and bodily mutilations. The tourists often get involved against their will: in the opium joint a desperate woman clings to another woman's skirt right before she commits suicide and slummers witness the thrill of a police raid; in the restaurant, when a tourist collides with a waiter, food is spilled over him; in the restaurant's kitchen, a woman falls into a huge kitchen machine; and at the bar the tourists become involved in a fistfight.

Such bodily assaults appear to put these films into what Linda Williams has termed "body genres"—films that, as Steven Shaviro has put it in a different context, insist on "the visceral immediacy of cinematic experience," so that "perception becomes a kind of physical affliction."[59] Both Shaviro and Williams, of course, have much later cinema in mind, and for Williams, at least, such bodily reactions remain both limited to specific genres and contingent on "the perception that the body of the spectator is caught up in an almost involuntary mimicry of the emotion or sensation of the body on the screen."[60] Early cinema's "aesthetic of astonishment," not least because generic conventions and formulas are not yet clearly established, works according to a somewhat different logic; as Tom Gunning has argued, in early film "some sense of wonder or surprise" (what Shaviro might call "affliction") is often combined with "an undisguised awareness of (and delight in) film's illusionistic capabilities."[61] Paying attention to both the representation of bodily afflictions and transformations on screen, and the potential disjunction between the characters' and the viewers' bodily experience, I want to look more closely at *The Heathen Chinese and the Sunday School Teachers* and *The Deceived Slumming Party.* Thematizing white tourists' bodily involvement with Chinatown, these films represent the Chinatown experience as above all a bodily experience that requires an appropriate mode of bodily engagement. Responding to the anxiety that the commodification of Chinatown may alter social relations, *The Deceived Slumming Party,* in particular, also attempts to reimagine this anxiety as a mode of pleasure.

The representation of Chinatown on film, I want to suggest, does not so much bodily "afflict" the viewer, as it transforms Chinatown into a fantastic place of wonder and possibility where bodily transformations appear easily possible. This focus on Chinatown as a magical—and magically staged—place has an effect quite similar to the multisensorial transformations made possible on slumming tours: it provides white viewers with a pleasurable, yet thrilling, experience of modern urbanity, with the possibility of imagining themselves as having modern, complex, and fluid identities that are not grounded in concepts of stability or sameness.

The Heathen Chinese and the Sunday School Teachers comments on the anxieties and possibilities surrounding the commodification of Chinatown, on the new economic and psychic regime that such a commodification entails. The film consists of four scenes: in the opening scene, female Sunday school teachers distribute promotional material in a Chinese laundry; in the next scene, we see the Chinese men (all played by white actors) attending Sunday school; in the third scene, the Sunday school teachers visit an opium joint located right across from the laundry; in the final scene, and after the police have raided the opium den, we see various Chinese characters (including those from the laundry) behind bars, when the Sunday school teachers come in and bring them what appears to be food, chopsticks, towels, and even flowers. In an odd, quasi-happy ending, the prisoners are freed and the ladies are chased away by the police officer. The film, withholding moral judgment, may typify the "irreverent and risque films of the earlier period,"[62] and yet the ending, which visually separates the Chinese from the teachers, at least symbolically prevents miscegenation, even as it frees the Chinese. The fictional film may pretend to be realistic, but its social geography is fantastic, not least because most Chinese laundries serving white customers were not located in Chinatown and were hardly across the street from opium joints.[63] The Sunday school teachers' transformation, however, seems to depend on the opium den's geographic, imaginary, and psychic proximity to the laundry. The exchange occurring in the place of business (the laundry, a business dealing with issues of intimacy) inevitably leads to personal contact, to touching, to altered social relations, and to a different white self-understanding.

The Chinese store in this film not only generates fantasies of miscegenation, it also becomes the locus of intimate self-transformations. Before we see the Sunday school teachers enter the laundry, we see another customer, who picks up her laundry, inspects the Chinese man's queue, and, in a telling gesture of intimate touching, puts her foot on a stool in order to retrieve her money from her shoe. This emblematic scene suggests that what happens in a Chinese business is always more than a business transaction; the woman not only makes a sensuous if not sexual object of herself, but also seems to thoroughly enjoy herself.[64] Likewise, by simply entering the laundry, the Sunday school teachers inevitably seem to discover their other senses and other racial imaginaries. In the opium joint, their bodies relax and loosen up as they lie on a bed; at the end, when they bring food to the jail, they also seem to have discovered a different sense of taste. In this film, which suggests that acquiring a consumerist identity may mean leaving social identities behind, the Chinese store becomes the place of origin for changed social relations and a new sense of self grounded in a different experience of one's senses.

If *The Heathen Chinese and the Sunday School Teachers* helps uncover a potential anxiety about the effects of Chinese business and the commodification of Chinatown in the United States, *The Deceived Slumming Party*, filmed four years later, has overcome all anxiety about this new economic and psychic regime. Delighting in exposing how Chinatown is being staged for the pleasure of the white slummers (male and female) and for the financial benefit of those who stage it (Chinese men and white working-class men and women), the film simply implies that the commercialization and spectacularization of Chinatown result in a capitalist democracy in which the staging of racial difference can be used to redistribute wealth. After all, everybody profits from the staging of Chinatown, and ultimately no one gets hurt either physically or financially (the slummers simply appear to be able to afford the bribes). By emphasizing Chinatown's fakeness, it would appear, the film has left behind all the anxieties surrounding the commodification of Chinatown.

The tourists in the film, of course, experience all the anxiety Chinatown can generate because they do not know that Chinatown is fake, and therefore do not know how to properly engage it. Such an insistence on the characters' lack of experience and lack of knowledge places the film, along with other Chinatown films, such as *Lifting the Lid* and *Rube in an Opium Joint,* in the "rube" genre, which includes films showing characters in a variety of new environments (for instance, *Rube and Mandy at Coney Island* [Edison, 1903], *Rube in the Subway* [American Mutoscope and Biograph, 1905], and *Rubes in the Theater* [Edison, 1901]). The last scene of *Lifting the Lid,* the other film modeled after a Chinatown slumming tour, shows a couple entering a *café concert.* Rube immediately climbs up on the stage in order to participate in the show, and is promptly disciplined by the megaphone man. For Rube, the slumming tour apparently promised physical participation, the ability to get onstage. His problem is that he does not understand the complicated rules for participating and viewing: after all, the tour allows slummers to participate in the opium den and in the restaurant, whereas at the theater and other places of entertainment, they have to remain spectators. If rube films such as *Uncle Josh at the Moving Picture Show* (Edwin S. Porter, 1902) thematized appropriate ways of watching and engaging a film, not least by insisting that spectators know how to distinguish between reality and filmic illusion, then films such as *Lifting the Lid* and *The Deceived Slumming Party* thematized appropriate ways of engaging the racialized city, which required not just an appropriate way of watching, but an appropriate sense of when to watch and when to participate, as well as the ability to differentiate between the "authentic" and the "fake" parts of the city.[65]

Unlike the slummers in the film, the spectators of *The Deceived Slumming Party,* having much more knowledge than the tourists, are presumed to know how to engage the racialized city and can therefore experience and enjoy it very differently. Granted a peek behind the scenes, the viewers of the film are discouraged from identifying with the tourists in the film, even those viewers who may not know New York City or who may be tourists themselves. Feeling knowledgeable about the city, feeling superior to the tourists in the film, they know that the scene of seeing New York itself has become a spectacle to be watched and enjoyed. This lack of identification with the tourists entering Chinatown aligns the spectator with the other white characters in the film who are indispensable for the profitable staging of Chinatown, such as the megaphone man whose "expert" voice constantly delivers the "right" explanations and who participates in the fake staging, the woman who poses in the opium den, playing the "victim," and the policemen who participate in the fake raid.

The staging of Chinatown crucially depends on the mediation of these white, lower-class characters, male and female. The film uncovers a classed and racial hierarchy, that is, in which white gender differences are apparently overcome, and which allows white, lower-class characters to join the ranks of entrepreneurs, while the Chinese are dependent on white initiative even as they profit financially as well.[66] This may suggest that the film must have appealed to white, lower-class spectators. At the same time, middle-class spectators, both New Yorkers and tourists, share knowledge and a cognitive position with the white, lower-class characters in the film, and can encounter Chinatown as connoisseurs who can easily negotiate the complexities of the Chinatown economy and Chinatown illusions. Ultimately, the staging of the fake Chinatown in *The Deceived Slumming Party* enabled the emergence of a heterogeneous white population that was complexly stratified in terms of class, gender, and (European) ethnicity, while at the same time such a racial economy suspended conflicts among the white characters in the film, thus consolidating their dominance.[67]

Beyond positioning the white viewer as an urban connoisseur and beyond enabling a heterogeneous white alliance, *The Deceived Slumming Party*'s insistence on fakeness made it possible to provide spectatorial thrills hardly available on actual slumming tours. The assumption that Chinatown is an elaborately staged, virtual reality allows the film to incorporate incredible horrors, while also turning horror into pleasure and allowing spectators to enjoy the experience. The most telling moment is the scene in the Chinese restaurant's kitchen, when a female slummer falls into a sausage machine. We already see the woman being transformed into sausage links, when someone simply cranks the machine backward until she reappears whole at the other end of the machine. Sausage machine routines had been produced quite frequently onstage as well as in earlier films—maybe because they demonstrated the magical capabilities of the cinema—but in the context of Chinatown, the machine, now coded as Chinese, also acquires another significance, if only because sausage machine routines usually did not turn people into sausages.[68]

The outrageousness of the woman's transformation into sausage is perhaps the moment when a viewer may most easily have a visceral reaction to the film, and yet, such a bodily reaction is immediately tempered by the reversibility of experience, which promises that no bodily state is necessarily permanent, and which transforms the most frightening event into a pleasurable thrill. The scene, a self-conscious reflection on the cinematic experience and cinematic possibilities, points to the intervention of the cinematic apparatus by implying an analogy between the sausage machine and a movie camera, which were cranked in similar ways. In a time when relatively new technologies, such as projectors and movie cameras, were attractions in themselves, and starred in films such as *The Story the Biograph Told* (American Mutoscope and Biograph, 1903), spectators may have been likely to make this connection.[69] It is the movie camera, then, rather than the Chinese machine, that performs the "trick" and transforms the woman into a sausage and back into a woman again. According to this logic, it is the cinema that enables bodily, spectatorial transformations that transcend the physical limits of the body, but ultimately also guarantees a safe restoration of bodily coherence. The insistence on fakeness, while it may seem a concession to the cinema's lack in realism, allowed the cinema to both capitalize on and differentiate itself from other leisure practices, such as the slumming tour, while also taking the promise of bodily transformations to another level.

While the insistence on Chinatown's and the cinema's fakeness may have enabled more excessive bodily thrills, it also circumvented the spectators' "education"—their ability to know how to engage Chinatown and to distinguish between the "authentic" and the "fake." *The Deceived Slumming Party* ultimately implies that the city itself is fake—at least the racialized parts of the city where one might go slumming. The city in the film, the spectator is made to understand, becomes a kind of virtual reality where everything is possible, where the body can be transformed and transcended in the exchange with a racialized minority. Of course, we can only speculate what this may have meant for the spectator who may (or may not) visit Chinatown after seeing the film. One might understand the film as an attempt to prevent spectators from visiting Chinatown, and as a way of luring them into the movie theaters instead. In case spectators saw the film and also visited Chinatown, it is difficult to know to what degree they would maintain a distinction between Chinatown as seen on film and Chinatown as it existed in New York. To be sure, since the film foregrounded fakeness, spectators may easily have made such distinctions. And yet, the film also deliberately blurred the boundaries between fiction and reality, not least by opening with a location shot on 42nd Street. We might assume, then, that to the degree that such films also shaped the way in which spectators would experience, perceive, and engage Chinatown, *The Deceived Slumming Party* may have made it easier for spectators to imagine themselves as experts in Chinatown, even as, paradoxically, the film's persistent focus on the fakeness of Chinatown ultimately denied the existence of a Chinese culture in New York. At best, the particular encoding of Chinatown as "fake"—an encoding magnified by the surface aesthetic propagated in other media—may ultimately have left actual encounters particularly unscripted. At worst, it may have made white slummers' engagement with the actual Chinatown much more difficult.

While presumably a film that mediates between two cultures, and indeed a film that allows white spectators to enjoy the newly racialized metropolis, *The Deceived Slumming Party* may ultimately have defamiliarized the actual Chinatown.

Coda

In this essay, I have elaborated some paradigms that emerged in the context of the commodification of Chinatown—the sensational surface aesthetics, the possibility of multisensorial transformations, and the insistence on fakeness. While hardly accounting for all Chinatown representations, these paradigms provided ways in which Chinatown could be experienced. In these contexts, Chinatown, the Chinese body, and Chinese identity emerged as particularly complex and contradictory, if not incoherent. I have suggested that both slumming tours and early Chinatown films transformed this racial imaginary in such a way that it allowed white spectators to acquire, or try out, a new kind of subjectivity grounded in sensorial experiences, and in a new kind of transformable and transcendable body. By insisting on Chinatown's fakeness, early Chinatown films, in particular, could imagine a new kind of spectatorship in both collective and individual terms. Collectively, such a spectatorship imagined a heterogeneous, widely stratified "white" identity that was modern precisely because it did not assume homogeneity; individually, such spectatorship allowed viewers to indulge in the fantasies of having modern, transformable bodies, bodies that may not necessarily be grounded in any simple concept of "identity," and bodies that could negotiate the new metropolis precisely because of their mutability. Ultimately, these paradigms—the sensational surface aesthetic, the sensorial transformations, the possibilities connected to fake visions—allow us to rethink the complexities of the processes of commodification. Much more than resulting in the objectification of people, commodification here has the capacity to reimagine social relations, to generate new alliances, new modes of experience, and new kinds of subjectivities.[70]

It is, of course, difficult to know what the commodification of Chinatown—and the new modes of experiences that accompanied it—may have meant to particular people. For white, middle-class men and women, it may have been a temporary experience, a kind of virtual reality in which they could experience a variety of transformations that remained absent from their everyday lives. The commodification of Chinatown may have provided new ways of experiencing themselves and the world in the realm of leisure, while in everyday life racial and social hierarchies remained fixed. The anxieties surrounding the commodification of Chinatown, of course, particularly as they emerged in the context of the Elsie Sigel murder, had everything to do with the fear that because Chinatown was, after all, not just a virtual reality but an actually existing neighborhood, such new ways of understanding individual and collective identity carried over into everyday life. Despite fears that Chinatown may have permanently transformed some middle-class visitors, it may have been white working-class men and women above all whose self-understanding was lastingly altered. Meloney's essay, although suppressing questions of class, is clearly anxious about working-class, white women permanently living with Chinese men, and some fiction of the period suggests that for some working-class women, such arrangements, particularly marriage to a Chinese merchant, may have meant social mobility.[71] And we have already seen how for some white men, the staging of Chinatown provided the opportunity to enter a "business." By the same token, Chinatown may have been more than a temporary distraction to African Americans, if only because (some) Chinatown restaurants apparently did not segregate, so that spending leisure time in Chinatown may have responded to some real need for social change and held some real social significance.[72] Because Chinatown was more than a virtual reality or a space of amusement, because Chinatown did, after all, exist, the change in individual and collective identity it made possible may at times have carried over into everyday life, especially as far as disenfranchised populations were concerned.

The structures of experience made available in the context of the commercialization of Chinatown, while telling us a great deal about how white visitors could, at least temporarily, experience a new sense of self and a new sense of the world, ultimately has little to say about how the Chinese inhabitants of New York experienced such a regime of psychic and bodily transformations. Presumably, to the degree that it affected its inhabitants' everyday lives, the commodification of Chinatown made it the locus of Chinese American modernity rather than a traditional authenticity. Some of the Chinese would have participated in the production and circulation of Chinatown, as extras in the staging of the slumming tours or as owners of Chinese restaurants and shops. These participants, one would imagine, must have been very self-conscious about the deliberate staging of Chinatown. Even the Chinese who did not directly participate in the production of Chinatown must have experienced the commodification of Chinatown as spectators. There is no evidence that there were nickelodeons in Chinatown, but at least four nickelodeons were located on the part of the Bowery bordering on Chinatown, so that movies would have been easily available.[73] Because it revolved around the naivete of white tourists, *The Deceived Slumming Party* would probably have been considered less offensive—and more entertaining—than many other films.

But, then, the Chinese inhabitants of the neighborhood did not have to go to the movies to wonder about white tourists' leisure practices. A photograph of New York City's Chinatown shows a number of Chinese

Figure 4. William Brown Meloney, "Slumming in New York's Chinatown," *Munsey's Magazine* 41 (September 1909): 820.

rubbernecking, lined up along the sidewalk, curiously watching a "slumming party entering the quarter," as the original caption tells us. Although it may be perverse that even this moment was captured by the photographer of *Munsey's Magazine*, it suggests that the tourists themselves may have been transformed into a form of entertainment for the inhabitants of the quarter, that the commodification of Chinatown also allowed for the emergence of a Chinese gaze and a new kind of Chinese American spectatorship that, at least in this photograph, seems to be collective (even as it appears to include a white woman) and grounded in a sense of (however underdefined) curiosity. Likewise, for the many Chinese who worked in laundries throughout the city and visited Chinatown only on Sundays, the neighborhood would also become a site of leisure.

While Chinatown offered at least some possibilities of spectatorial and performative participation, and may have fostered the emergence of a Chinese American gaze, in the films themselves the roles of the Chinese seemed more severely limited. It is ultimately important to notice that in *The Deceived Slumming Party* (and other films) even the "Chinamen" are fake, that all the Chinese characters in the film are played by white actors in yellowface.[74] Such yellowface is not only an example of early film's racism (its unwillingness to let white and Asian actors share the same stage), but proves crucial to at least *The Deceived Slumming Party*, since the effect of the film depends on all being fake. In order to film

Chinatown, and for inviting fantasies of transformation, in other words, no Chinese are necessary. Instead, this regime, by appropriating "Chineseness" ultimately offers white actors and spectators one more possible racial transformation, a transformation of which early film was very conscious. *The Mission of Mr. Foo* (Edison, 1914), for instance, opens with a shot dividing the screen into three sections: in the middle of the scene we see a statue that slowly transforms into the white actor (Carlton King) playing Mr. Foo; to his left we see the actor made up as a Mr. Foo in an "American" outfit; to his right, we see the same actor as Mr. Foo in a "Chinese" outfit. The white actor's mastery of identities testifies to both his liberty and presumed superiority, while at the same time the film clearly bars the Chinese from participating in such plays of transformation. This essay, in a way, has attempted to place "role segregation"[75] into a larger cultural context, in which the ability and freedom to perform roles and to inhabit mutable bodies become a sign of adaptability to the modern, racialized metropolis.

While the structures of experience elaborated here point toward (but certainly do not explain) how the commodification of Chinatown may have become a site for Chinese American modernity, they do suggest how Chinatown contributed to the modernity of the white, urban as well as the filmic experience. Most simply, this essay has shown how the orientalist tropes, for which the cinema—and movie theaters—would become famous in the 1910s and the 1920s, were at least partially grounded in a particular moment of U.S. racial history. More important, films such as *The Deceived Slumming Party* at least suggest, on the one hand, that Chinese racial tropes could be used to consolidate (although not homogenize) a heterogeneous white public, an issue that had become urgent by 1908 when the cinema attempted to court a middle-class audience without alienating the working classes.[76] On the other hand, these films, as marginal as they may seem, also point toward a film aesthetic that was not grounded in questions of identification or even identity, but that was fueled by a desire to experience alterity and subjective polymorphousness. Taking it as their task to mediate a racial alterity present within the United States, even as they remained committed to maintain social and racial hierarchies outside the cinema, films such as *The Deceived Slumming Party* helped the cinema become an institution making racialized, urban modernity available for pleasurable consumption.

NOTES

For readings, comments, and insights that have helped shape this essay, I wish to thank Leigh Anne Duck, Peter Feng, Oliver Gaycken, Tom Gunning, Ivan Kreilkamp, and Jacqueline Stewart.

1. The scare quotes indicate the phantasmatic nature of this Chinatown. I have refrained from putting "Chinatown" in scare quotes in the body of the essay, in part for the

sake of legibility, in part because this essay very much tries to elaborate how the fantasies surrounding Chinatown were elaborated in dialogue with the actual Chinatown in turn-of-the-century New York.

2. Katie Trumpener has orally commented on the "multi-jointed body" in the context of a symposium on early colonial films. For a report, see Sabine Haenni, "Colonial Imaging: Early Films from the Netherlands Film Museum," *Screen* 39.3 (Autumn 1998): 303. Such a fascination with a mutable body also emerges in other films. For instance, *The Yellow Peril* (American Mutoscope and Biograph, 1908), mostly a slapstick comedy, centers around a Chinese servant who wreaks havoc in an American household. Slapstick comedy, of course, has been credited with thematizing and negotiating the fate of the body in modernity. On the body in slapstick and other comedy, see Miriam Hansen, "Of Mice and Ducks: Benjamin and Adorno on Disney," *South Atlantic Quarterly* 92 (Winter 1993): 27–61, and Tom Gunning, "Crazy Machines in the Garden of Forking Paths: Mischief Gags and the Origins of American Film Comedy," in *Classical Hollywood Comedy*, ed. Kristina Brunovska Karnick and Henry Jenkins (New York: Routledge, 1995), 87–105; on race and slapstick comedy, see Eileen Bowser, "Racial/Racist Jokes in American Silent Slapstick Comedy," *Griffithiana* 53 (May 1995): 35–43, and Charles Musser, "Ethnicity, Role-playing, and American Film Comedy: From *Chinese Laundry Scene* to *Whoopee* (1894–1930)," in *Unspeakable Images: Ethnicity and the American Cinema*, ed. Lester D. Friedman (Urbana: University of Illinois Press, 1991), 39–81. Sometimes anxieties about the Chinese body were located in the biracial body. See, for instance, D. S. Denison's play *Patsy O'Wang* (1895), which revolves around an Irish/Chinese character's radical transformations as he oscillates between being Irish and being Chinese; the play is reprinted in *The Chinese Other, 1850–1925: An Anthology of Plays*, ed. Dave Williams (Lanham, Md.: The University Press of America, 1997), 125–48; on the play, see also Robert G. Lee, *Orientals: Asian Americans in Popular Culture* (Philadelphia, Pa.: Temple University Press, 1999), 78–81.

3. For the emergence of New York City as a site of tourism, see Neil Harris, "Urban Tourism and the Commercial City," in *Inventing Times Square: Commerce and Culture at the Crossroads of the World*, ed. William R. Taylor (Baltimore, Md.: Johns Hopkins University Press, 1991), 66–82.

4. See, for instance, William Brown Meloney, "Slumming in New York's Chinatown," *Munsey's* 41 (September 1909): 818–30; D. E. Kessler, "An Evening in Chinatown," *Overland* 49 (May 1907): 445–49; George H. Fitch, "A Night in Chinatown," *Cosmopolitan* 2 (September 1886–February 1887): 349–58; Julian Jerrold, "A Chinese Dinner in New York," *Illustrated American* 22 (4 September 1897): 312–13; Allen S. Williams, "Chinese Restaurants in New York," *Leslie's Illustrated Weekly* 82 (9 January 1896): 26–28.

5. Karl Baedeker, *The United States with an Excursion into Mexico*, 3rd ed. (Leipzig: Baedeker; New York: Charles Scribner's Sons, 1904), 17; Karl Baedeker, *The United States with Excursions to Mexico, Cuba, Porto Rico and Alaska*, 4th ed. (Leipzig: Baedeker; New York: Scribner's, 1909), 19.

6. *Oxford English Dictionary*, 2nd ed., s.v. "rubberneck." The word seems to have emerged in working-class circles; in an essay about the work of department store salesgirls, the *American Journal of Sociology* understood "rubbernecking" as part of the "language of the shop." Although it was often applied to middle-class tourists, lower-class workers could apparently think of themselves as "rubbernecks" as well; in George Ade's Chicago novel, *Artie* (1896), Artie, a boy working in a business office, applies the term to himself. "Rubbernecking" appeared to encompass all classes of whites. See Anne Marion MacLean, "Two Weeks in Department Stores," *American Journal of Sociology* 4 (May 1899): 726; and George Ade, *Artie and Pink Marsh* (Chicago: University of Chicago Press, 1963), 19.

7. For a fictional account of a rubberneck tour, see O. Henry, "Sisters of the Golden Circle," in *The Four Million* (1906; New York: Doubleday, Page, 1920), 197–207. The rubberneck automobile may well have modeled itself after the cinema, attempting to provide similarly "moving" thrills; at the same time, as I discuss later, films imitated—and fiction-

alized—the kind of tour the automobile made possible, which points to a rather complex interaction between sightseeing practices and early cinema.

8. James S. Moy, *Marginal Sights: Staging the Chinese in America* (Iowa City: University of Iowa Press, 1993), 14.

9. Sumiko Higashi, *Cecil B. DeMille and American Culture: The Silent Era* (Berkeley: University of California Press, 1994), 62, 61.

10. Gaylyn Studlar, "'Out-Salomeing Salome': Dance, the New Woman, and Fan Magazine Orientalism," in *Visions of the East: Orientalism in Film,* ed. Matthew Bernstein and Gaylyn Studlar (New Brunswick, N.J.: Rutgers University Press, 1997), 106; Esther Frédérique Romeyn, "My Other / My Self: Impersonation, Masquerade, and the Theater of Identity in Turn-of-the-Century New York City" (Ph.D. diss., University of Minnesota, 1998), 70–110. For an argument about how "a scenography of the Orient" enabled artists to "redefine the image of the body," see also Peter Wollen, "Fashion/Orientalism/the Body," *New Formations* 1 (Spring 1987): 5–33. Twenty-two-year-old Elsie Sigel, the granddaughter of a well-known Civil War general, had volunteered in Chinatown; her mother taught at a Chinese Sunday school. Sigel was apparently murdered by a former Chinese lover in an act of jealousy. On Sigel, see also Bonner, *Alas! What Brought Thee Hither?,* 120–22.

11. For this argument, see Studlar, "'Out-Salomeing Salome,'" 106. I need to add here that Studlar mostly discusses orientalism (rather than Chinatown) in fan magazines of the 1920s, when orientalism in film may have been much more stabilized, ritualized, and formalized.

12. David Palumbo-Liu, *Asian / American: Historical Crossings of a Racial Frontier* (Stanford, Calif.: Stanford University Press, 1999), 18.

13. "He [the Chinese man] is old-fashioned because he is not done with the treasures of thoughts that have been piled up in the course of millennia. He has a great future and survives the evils that have been caused by medicine and technology in other worlds. He has no nerves, no fear of germs, nothing can happen to him even when he is dead. He is a juggler who plays skillfully with life and love when the athlete has to give it all he has. He works like a dozen white men and enjoys like a hundred of them. He keeps pleasure and morality separate and thus keeps them both from becoming irritating." Karl Kraus, "Die Chinesische Mauer," *Die Chinesische Mauer* (1910), vol. 12 of *Werke* (Munich: Albert Langen Georg Müller Verlag, 1964), 286–87. My translation. Kraus here satirically evokes and lists common stereotypes; on these, see Palumbo-Liu, *Asian / American,* 36.

14. Siegfried Kracauer, "Boredom" (1924), in *The Mass Ornament: Weimar Essays,* trans. Thomas Y. Levin (Cambridge, Mass.: Harvard University Press, 1995), 332.

15. That "Chineseness" would ultimately be theorized in Austria and Germany suggests how quickly it became a global commodity. Although it is beyond the scope of this essay to explore how filmic representation detaches a specific spectatorial economy from its immediate U.S. urban context, I should note that "Chinese transformations" also became a topic in other film industries. Georges Méliès, for instance—not coincidentally the French filmmaker most closely associated with the trick film—explored such polymorphousness in *Tchin-Chao, the Chinese Conjurer* (1904) and *The Dream of an Opium Fiend* (1908). Such films would have to be read in the context of French orientalism, even though they were also shown in the United States and may well have been assimilated into the cultural logic that I elaborate here.

16. Kemp R. Niver, *Biograph Bulletins, 1896–1908,* ed. Bebe Bergsten (Los Angeles, Calif.: Locare Research Group, 1971), 372. A board visible in the first shot also promises a visit to the morgue, although the film does not include such. On similar excursions in fin-de-siècle Paris (including visits to the morgue), see Vanessa R. Schwartz, "Cinematic Spectatorship before the Apparatus: The Public Taste for Reality in Fin-de-Siècle Paris," in *Cinema and the Invention of Modern Life,* ed. Leo Charney and Vanessa R. Schwartz (Berkeley: University of California Press, 1995), 297–319.

17. Like other films of the same genre, such as *Lifting the Lid,* the film does not restrict itself to Chinatown. The last scene in the saloon clearly displays an immigrant (presumably Irish), working-class environment. The film's main focus remains quite clearly on Chinatown,

but the ways in which other working-class neighborhoods were thought to hover on the edges of Chinatown give at least a sense of how connected Chinatown issues were thought to be to larger urban issues, and how the lines of racialized exclusion, at least in this period, remained rather unstable, even if, as I argue later, *The Deceived Slumming Party* creates an alliance between working-class (and potentially immigrant) whites and the spectators of the film.

18. Meloney, "Slumming in New York's Chinatown," 819. Meloney writes shortly after the murder of Elsie Sigel.

19. Such anthropomorphization of the city was not uncommon in the period. See, for instance, Ernest Poole's "A City's Dream of a City" (*Everybody's Magazine* 23 [July 1910]: 1–13), where anthropomorphizing the city enables the writer to think about ways of "curing" the city of its problems.

20. Meloney, "Slumming in New York's Chinatown," 826.

21. The perception that Chinatown was very much a world apart was aided by the sense that it maintained a separate legislation and government, and was therefore not under American jurisdiction. See, for instance, Louis J. Beck, *New York's Chinatown* (New York: Bohemia, 1898), 13–22. George Fitch, writing on San Francisco's Chinatown, virulently articulated the anxiety generated by Chinatown's apparent foreignness: "After more than thirty years of residence in San Francisco, the Mongolian is little better known to the authorities than he was when the gold rush first brought him to the coast. He is entirely beyond the control of our laws now, as he has always been. He metes out unsparing vengeance upon delinquents of his own race, precisely as though he were in his native province of Quoang Tung. He has secret tribunals and a code of law which are inscrutable mysteries to Americans, as they are to all other foreigners." "A Night in Chinatown," 357.

22. George G. Foster, *New York by Gas-Light and Other Urban Sketches*, ed. Stuart M. Blumin (Berkeley: University of California Press, 1990), 69.

23. Sally Stein, "Making Connections with the Camera: Photography and Social Mobility in the Career of Jacob Riis," *Afterimage* 10, no. 10 (May 1983): 9–16. Stein traces Riis's concept of "the other half" to an 1884 cover of *The Daily Graphic*. By the turn of the century a countericonography surrounding European (rather than Asian) immigrants had emerged, which was less invested in a melodramatically polarizing, urban vision. See, for instance, John Corbin, "How the Other Half Laughs," *Harper's New Monthly Magazine* 98 (December 1898): 30–48. Of course, the melodramatic, urban vision would not entirely disappear; in *The Mission of Mr. Foo* (Edison, 1914), for instance, Mr. Foo, the villain, owns a secret underground apartment from where he plots a rebellion in the homeland.

24. Herbert Asbury, *The Gangs of New York: An Informal History of the Underworld* (Garden City: Garden City Publishing, 1928), 308–9.

25. Beck, *New York's Chinatown*, 127–28.

26. Asbury, *The Gangs of New York*, 300. Kassim Baba is Ali Baba's brother in "Ali Baba and the Forty Thieves." The reference to this tale from *Arabian Nights* is telling; for one thing, "Ali Baba," a story of dubious origin not part of the original *Arabian Nights*, establishes a connection to European orientalism; more important, the spatial imaginary of the story is fascinating. Asbury's reference does not only seem to point to the famous "open sesame" but to the thieves' desperate attempts and near-inability to locate Kassim Baba's house. For an overview of the publication history of *Arabian Nights*, see Husain Haddawy's introduction to *The Arabian Nights* (New York: Norton, 1990), ix–xxix.

27. Philip Fisher, "Democratic Social Space: Whitman, Melville, and the Promise of American Transparency," in *The New American Studies: Essays from Representations*, ed. Philip Fisher (Berkeley: University of California Press, 1991), 70–111.

28. Niver, *Biograph Bulletins*, 372.

29. Beck, *New York's Chinatown*, 25.

30. Anon., "Our Chinese Colony," *Harper's Weekly* 34 (22 November 1890): 910.

31. For uses of "queer," see, for instance, Beck, *New York's Chinatown*, 3, 4, and passim.

32. Beck, *New York's Chinatown*, 25.

33. David Graham Phillips, "The Bowery at Night," *Harper's Weekly* 35 (19 September 1891): 710.

34. Meloney, "Slumming in New York's Chinatown," 820, 823.

35. Studlar, "'Out-Salomeing Salome,' " 99–129; Romeyn, "My Other / My Self," 70–106. On the Elsie Sigel murder, see note 10 above.

36. Lauren Rabinovitz has suggested that at the turn of the twentieth century, middle-class women were still severely restricted in their ability to become urban *flâneuses*, and has argued that the Chicago World's Columbian Exposition of 1892, as well as the movies more generally, made possible a female gaze not quite allowed in urban space. The development of the intra-urban tourist industry, and the commodification of neighborhoods such as Chinatowns, is another way in which the city itself was made available to the female gaze. See Rabinovitz, *For the Love of Pleasure: Women, Movies, and Culture in Turn-of-the-Century Chicago* (New Brunswick, N.J.: Rutgers University Press, 1998).

37. Baedeker, *The United States with Excursions to Mexico, Cuba, Porto Rico and Alaska,* 4th ed., 19.

38. See, for instance, Bonner, *Alas! What Brought Thee Hither?,* 91–92.

39. Ben Brewster and Lea Jacobs, *Theatre to Cinema* (New York: Oxford University Press, 1997), 4. Brewster and Jacobs trace an early film aesthetic to a pictorial tradition in the theater, particularly that of the *tableau.* For an account of the general importance, beyond theater and film, of the concept of the "scene" in turn-of-the-century urban culture, see also my "Visual and Theatrical Culture, Tenement Fiction, and the Immigrant Subject in Abraham Cahan's *Yekl,*" *American Literature* 71 (September 1999): 503–8. Numerous films, of course, had the word "scene" in their title, including *Scene in Chinatown* and *Scene in a Chinese Restaurant.*

40. Not a single scene in Charles Hoyt's successful play, *A Trip to Chinatown* (1891), is set in Chinatown. Knowing that they would never get permission to go to a masquerade ball, Tony and Flirt, two girls in the play, ask Tony's uncle, Ben Gay, to let them go on a trip to Chinatown. Although he first hesitates, he lets them go, in part so that he can go to the masquerade ball himself. Apparently, a trip to Chinatown is thought to be much safer than the promiscuousness a masquerade ball implied. The play is reprinted in Douglas L. Hunt, ed., *Five Plays by Charles H. Hoyt,* vol. 9 of *America's Lost Plays* (Princeton, N.J.: Princeton University Press, 1941), 105–48.

41. D. W. Griffith's 1919 film, *Broken Blossoms,* also features an opium den in London's Limehouse district—a "scarlet house of sin" peopled by "Chinese, Malays, Lascars," as the intertitles tell us. The scene, which focuses prominently on the many white women in the den, and which also features a black man, might be understood as an amazing conflation of a U.S. racial and a British imperial narrative.

42. Anon., "The Opium Curse: Startling Facts with Regard to the Evil in the United States," *The Illustrated American* 4 (29 November 1890): 545–55; Beck, *New York's Chinatown,* 139.

43. Meloney claims that fake opium dens were visited on slumming tours; see "Slumming in New York's Chinatown," 821–22; for a photo of Irish hanger-on Chuck Connors' fake opium den, see Asbury, *The Gangs of New York,* between pp. 328 and 329; on the practice of slummers visiting actual dens, see Beck, *New York's Chinatown,* 163; on Huber's opium den, see Odell, *Annals of the New York Stage* (New York: Columbia University Press, 1927–49), 13:729. In terms of Americans' fascination with opium smoking, it is telling that Beck's book on Chinatown devotes four chapters to the subject, while he deals with all other topics in a single chapter.

44. Williams, "Chinese Restaurants in New York," 28.

45. Beck, *New York's Chinatown,* 143. Unlike slummers, opium addicts were often (but not always) figured as male.

46. H. H. Kane, "American Opium Smokers," *Harper's Weekly* 25 (8 October 1881): 683. For an example of "A Hop Fiend's Dream" that emphasized wealth, see Beck, *New York's Chinatown,* 165–66.

47. Kane, "American Opium Smokers," 682; for another evocation of the *"dolce far niente,"* see Beck, *New York's Chinatown,* 151.

48. Curtis Marez has linked Freud's psychoanalytic theory to his reflections on cocaine and argued that "Freud translates an imperial map into a psychic map that relocates 'South America' within the shifting boundaries of a polymorphously perverse and 'primitive' unconscious." See Marez, "The *Coquero* in Freud: Psychoanalysis, Race, and International Economics of Distinction," *Cultural Critique* 26 (Winter 1993–94): 66.

49. Edward W. Townsend, "The Foreign Stage in New York IV: The Chinese Theatre," *Bookman* 12 (September 1900): 41–42. Will Irwin, "The Drama in Chinatown," *Everybody's Magazine* 20 (June 1909): 861.

50. Jerrold, "A Chinese Dinner in New York," 312; Williams, "Chinese Restaurants in New York," 28.

51. Beck, *New York's Chinatown,* 24, 26.

52. Meloney, "Slumming in New York's Chinatown," 823. In *Broken Blossoms,* the "Yellow Man" and Lucy first exchange gazes through the man's shop window. Although his gaze seems to express sexual desire, hers focuses on the dolls in the window and is apparently motivated by a longing for beauty and childhood play.

53. Karl Marx, *Capital,* vol. 1, intro. Ernest Mandel, trans. Ben Fowkes (Harmondsworth: Penguin, 1990), 167.

54. The pearl-button jacket identifies the man on the right as Chuck Connors. Chuck was the most celebrated hanger-on in Chinatown, who guided white tourists through the neighborhood. Chuck himself was the object of many journalistic sketches. See, for instance, William Norr's "The Romance of 'Chuck' Connors," in *Stories of Chinatown* (New York: William Norr, 1892), 5–13. On Chuck, see also Alvin F. Harlow, *Old Bowery Days: The Chronicles of a Famous Street* (New York: Appleton, 1931), 428–35, and Asbury, *The Gangs of New York,* 316–20.

55. Miriam Bratu Hansen, "The Mass Production of the Senses: Classical Cinema as Vernacular Modernism," *Modernism/Modernity* 6 (1999): 70–71.

56. Susan Buck-Morss, "Aesthetics and Anaesthetics: Walter Benjamin's Artwork Essay Reconsidered," *October* 62 (Fall 1992): 17, 22. For a historical contextualization of the economy of shocks generated by the new urban traffic systems (such as the streetcar, the elevated train, the automobile), see Ben Singer, "Modernity, Hyperstimulus, and the Rise of Popular Sensationalism," in *Cinema and the Invention of Modern Life,* ed. Leo Charney and Vanessa R. Schwartz, 72–99.

57. See Buck-Morss, "Aesthetics and Anaesthetics," 18–22, for an account of opium.

58. Ibid., 6.

59. Linda Williams, "Film Bodies: Gender, Genre, and Excess," in *Film Genre Reader II,* ed. Barry Keith Grant (Austin: University of Texas Press, 1995), 140–58; Steven Shaviro, *The Cinematic Body* (Minneapolis: University of Minnesota Press, 1993), 36, 52.

60. Williams, "Film Bodies," 143.

61. Tom Gunning, "An Aesthetic of Astonishment: Early Film and the (In)Credulous Spectator," in *Viewing Positions: Ways of Seeing Film,* ed. Linda Williams (New Brunswick, N.J.: Rutgers University Press, 1995), 125, 129. See also Gunning's earlier essay, "The Cinema of Attractions: Early Film, Its Spectator and the Avant-Garde" (1986), which emphasizes early cinema's confrontational aesthetic. The essay is reprinted in *Early Cinema: Space, Frame, Narrative,* ed. Thomas Elsaesser (London: BFI, 1990), 56–62. By 1908, the year in which *The Deceived Slumming Party* was filmed, the cinema was often less confrontational, including many more narrative elements than it had in its earliest phase. On the development of early film aesthetics, see, for instance, Gunning, *D. W. Griffith and the Origins of American Narrative Film.*

62. Gunning, *D. W. Griffith and the Origins of American Narrative Film,* 157.

63. On Chinese laundries in New York City, see Bonner, *Alas! What Brought Thee Hither?,* 68–70.

64. The scene also recalls Edwin S. Porter's *The Gay Shoe Clerk* (Edison, 1903), a film

where the close-up of a woman's ankle immediately leads to inappropriate behavior on the part of the clerk.

65. On *Uncle Josh at the Moving Picture Show*, see Hansen, *Babel and Babylon*, 25–28.

66. Chuck Connors was probably the most famous of these white, working-class mediators. See note 54 above.

67. Such a racial economy does not simply allow for the emergence of "whiteness" but for the emergence of a complexly stratified and nuanced whiteness. Some "whiteness" studies make similar observations. Joyce Flynn comments on how the adoption of blackface could allow European immigrants to keep (or assume) various "un-American" accents and dialects; and Michael Rogin notes how blackface in films such as *The Jazz Singer* (Alan Crosland, 1927) "helped create New World ethnic identities—Irish American and Jewish American—that were culturally pluralist within the melting pot." See Flynn, "Melting Plots: Patterns of Racial and Ethnic Amalgamation in American Drama before Eugene O'Neill," *American Quarterly* 38 (1986): 426. Rogin, *Blackface, White Noise: Jewish Immigrants in the Hollywood Melting Pot* (Berkeley: University of California Press, 1996), 57.

68. On the sausage machine gag, see Gunning, "Crazy Machines in the Garden of Forking Paths," 98. The standard gag, of course, was to feed animals into one end of the machine, and have cuts of meat and links of sausage come out at the other. In *The Dog Factory* (Edison, 1904) sausages are fed into one end and puppies emerge at the other.

69. Of course, *The Story the Biograph Told*, which shows how a movie camera can be used to publicly expose a private love affair, suggests a very different function of the cinema. My point here is that it also reveals that cameras were quite visible in public life.

70. For a compelling way of thinking about how "capital/commodity has heterogeneity and incommensurability inscribed in its core," see Dipesh Chakrabarty, "The Time of History and the Times of Gods," in *The Politics of Culture in the Shadow of Capital,* ed. Lisa Lowe and David Lloyd (Durham, N.C.: Duke University Press, 1997), 35–60, 57.

71. For an example of such fiction, see Norr, "A Chinatown Tragedy," in *Stories of Chinatown*, 54–72. Although the story presumes the depravity of Chinatown, it also explains why poor, white women may find it attractive. This particular point also begins to suggest some of the differences between the commodification of Chinatown and the commodification of Harlem, which emerged into national consciousness somewhat later. Because Chinatown's population was mostly male, it generated anxieties about miscegenation in a way quite different from other enclaves. Harlem certainly shared with Chinatown a sensationalistically sensuous image. In 1930, James Weldon Johnson wrote: "Within the past ten years Harlem has acquired a world-wide reputation. . . . It is farthest known as being exotic, colourful, and sensuous; a place of laughing, singing, and dancing; . . . New Yorkers and people visiting New York from the world over go to the night-clubs of Harlem and dance to such jazz music as can be heard nowhere else; and they get an exhilaration impossible to duplicate." (*Black Manhattan* [New York: Alfred A. Knopf, 1930], 160.) The passage begins to suggest a different concept of non-white physicality, one that is much more grounded in the sensuous materiality of the body. (On the body in blackface minstrelsy, see Eric Lott, *Love & Theft: Blackface Minstrelsy and the American Working Class* [New York: Oxford University Press, 1993], 111–35.) It is beyond the scope of this essay to explore this issue fully, although it would appear that Chinese physicality is much more grounded in the magical, the not-quite-comprehensible. In a story first published in the 1890s, George Ade seems to elucidate the magical quality of the Chinese body: "on Sunday the Chinaman bubbles up out of his basement and discusses the silver question with other Chinamen who have bubbled up out of their basements" (George Ade, "Clark Street Chinamen," in *Chicago Stories* [Chicago: Henry Regnery, 1963], 163). The "bubbling" capacity of the Chinese seems to have a more tenuous connection to the body's materiality than the scene Johnson writes about. This is not to say, of course, that physical stereotypes, such as the coolie, did not persist on the stage and elsewhere. (On the coolie, see Lee, *Orientals*, 51–82.) It nonetheless seems important that despite their focus on the Chinese body, neither *Dancing Chinamen—Marionettes* nor *Chinese Rubbernecks* is grounded in physical bodies. This lack of materiality, it would seem,

makes possible such magical transformations as depicted in the sausage machine scene in *The Deceived Slumming Party.*

72. In 1902, a *Tribune* journalist reported that in Chinese restaurants "Negroes are in disproportionately large numbers." Quoted in Bonner, *Alas! What Brought Thee Hither?,* 105. According to Bonner, some chop suey places catered exclusively to African Americans, because white patrons would avoid restaurants with black patrons. Jacqueline Stewart has located an early African American film, *A Reckless Rover* (Ebony Film Corporation, 1918), in which the part of a Chinese laundry owner appears to be played by a black actor. See Stewart, "Migrating to the Movies: The Emergence of Black Urban Film Culture, 1893–1920" (Ph.D. diss., University of Chicago, 1999), 237, note 24.

73. Ben Singer, "Manhattan Nickelodeons: New Data on Audiences and Exhibitors," *Cinema Journal* 34 (Spring 1995): 10. When the Chinese theater closed in 1910 because of its involvement in tong wars, it briefly became a cinema, which apparently failed; the building then became the property of the Rescue Society. See Asbury, *The Gangs of New York,* 309.

74. That the state of film technology and the absence of close-ups often makes it difficult to "see" the race of an actor adds yet another level of complexity to these films, particularly on the level of audience reception. For a discussion of this issue in relation to African Americans, see Stewart, "Migrating to the Movies," 179–96.

75. On role segregation, see Eugene Franklin Wong, *On Visual Media Racism: Asians in the American Motion Pictures* (New York: Arno, 1978), 11–15.

76. The mayor of New York closed down all the nickelodeons on Christmas Eve of 1908, which in part triggered the attempt to appeal to a better class of patrons. See, for instance, Gunning, *D. W. Griffith and the Origins of American Narrative,* 151–54. On the related attempt to produce quality films, see William Uricchio and Roberta E. Pearson, *Reframing Culture: The Case of the Vitagraph Quality Films* (Princeton, N.J.: Princeton University Press, 1993).

Eugene Franklin Wong

The Early Years: Asians in the American Films Prior to World War II

Introduction

The American film industry's early feature-length productions and serials depicting Asians, Asian Americans, and various Asian themes reflected American society's general ignorance (with rare exceptions) of the people and thematic materials depicted. The element of ignorance was pivotal and non-problematical within the time period because the level of ignorance was reciprocal between the industry and society. Arguably, if not having accurate knowledge of a given content area or social condition or phenomenon is a charitable definition of ignorance, then the definition is neutral in its connotation. The definition is neither condemnatory nor salutary of the state of being ignorant but rather simply acknowledges its existence.

In historical retrospect, if there is justification to scrutinize critically the film industry's products, and by inference American society's acceptance, even demand, of the products, it is predicated upon the conviction that the degree of ignorance of Asians, Asian Americans, and Asian themes was *avoidable*. Compounded over time, there was, and to a large extent still is, a seemingly conscious unwillingness (an even deliberate intellectual parsimoniousness) to learn about, and hopefully to know, the human and thematic area depicted. It is that realization that warrants a critical judgment of the industry and the society from which it was spawned. The true witness of judgment is the irreparable longitudinal damage effected by such social callousness and professional carelessness. Cutting unchecked across generations of viewers, the full imaginal ignorance persists unabated, uncorrected, and ultimately reaffirmed by more recent reincarnations of the original social-perceptual sins.

Reproduced by permission of Ayer Company Publishers from *On Visual Media Racism* (New York: Arno Press, 1978), pp. 88–119.

Whenever empirical validity is precluded as the base from which literary and cinematic license is taken; whenever character imbalance is modeled upon a debased conception of human nature; and whenever the social responsibility of an industry's or a society's policies and practices are evaluated within the same ideology with which they were initiated, there can only be a resultant cry of outrage from those whose humanity and imagery have been sacrificed in the name of entertainment.

—Eugene F. Wong (6 February 2001)

Against the background of the Paris Peace Conference and the tension between the United States and Japan, the appearance of the film serial *Patria* was as ill-timed as it was ill-conceived. The United States, particularly in light of its own expansionist drive, had for at least three Administrations followed a complex, and oftentimes contradictory, relationship with Japan. Largely because America's fundamental perception of Japan was that of a militarily powerful nation not averse to speaking the Western "language of shot and shell,"[1] *Patria* came as an unwelcome and potentially incendiary article bearing upon relations between Japan and the United States. Perhaps not surprisingly, William Randolph Hearst, whose anti-Asiatic views were well-known to Americans, was responsible for the financing and production of the film. By 1917, the year in which the United States entered the First World War, Hearst had become intensely anti-Japanese—no doubt conditioned by the fact that Japan had become an Asian *power* and one whose emigrants had been the center of racial difficulties between the United States and Japan—and highly critical of the United States' foreign policy. Hearst believed that the Japanese would attack the United States behind her back once the decision had been made for the United States to enter the War. That Japan might become an ally of the United States apparently escaped Hearst altogether. That Japan became an ally of the United States seemed not to affect his fundamental distrust of the Japanese.

For the most part, Hearst's Yellow Peril alarmism, as manifested cinematically, was on the surface a product of his own dissatisfaction with "sundry items related to American defense efforts over the previous few years,"[2] earlier films which concentrated upon the race issue and the supposed aggressiveness of the so-called Yellow Menace,[3] and a disreputable and highly propagandistic translation of an otherwise obscure book printed in Japan. The book's incorrect American title was *The War Between Japan and America*. The New York *American* ran an article purporting to delineate the contents of the book. Under the heading "Japan's Plans to Invade and Conquer the United States," the American people were informed of Japan's plot to invade and overrun the United States, with the assistance of Mexico, after which the Panama Canal would be destroyed. Equally incorrect and misleading was the report that the book had sold nearly one million copies in Japan, presumably an indication of the Japanese people's, not the military's, support of the impending war with America. The Japanese representatives in America reacted quickly to the story. In an effort to discover the alleged source of the anti-Japanese upsurge, the Japanese consul-general in the United States, after having communicated extensively with his home government, was able to locate a book written in Japan which was anti-American only insofar as the author was disturbed and embittered over the treatment of Japanese nationals in the United States. The consul-general, in fact,

> learned that the original book had been written by a Japanese newspaperman to exploit the measures against Japanese in California. It was a flimsy effort that sold only a few thousand copies, had no official support and was ignored by the intelligent public. Its true title was *The Dream Story of the War Between Japan and the United States*. In it there was no mention whatsoever of the Panama Canal. The 'translation' for the Hearst press was no translation at all but included many inventions calculated to inspire fear. It was, in short, a fake.[4]

Regardless of the obvious falsehoods surrounding the *Dream Story* at the hands of the Hearst press, the serial *Patria* was, to all intents and purposes, the motion picture equivalent of the literary distortion, complete with its undeniable anti-Japanese, and anti-Mexican, biases.

Patria was originally begun in 1917; it was intended to become a fifteen-chapter serial, at a cost of approximately $90,000, starring Warner Oland[5] as the sinister Japanese baron and Irene Castle as the white starlet. Filmed over an extended period of time, and released in 1919, the serial was a sensation in the United States, "playing to packed houses but gravely offending Japanese Ambassador Hanihara."[6] The President, himself directly involved with the Japanese over a number of emotional and potentially explosive issues, not the least of which were Japanese emigration, the United States' anti-Asiatic immigration policy, and the racial equality clause controversy, took particular note of the film. In fact, *Patria* "incurred the deep displeasure"[7] of President Wilson. In an unprecedented action, the President asked Hearst to recall the film from distribution in order that *certain alterations* might be made. In a letter to Hearst, Wilson stated:

> May I not say to you that the character of the story disturbed me very much. It is extremely unfair to the Japanese and I fear that it is calculated to stir up a great deal of hostility which will be . . . extremely hurtful. I take the liberty, therefore, of asking whether the Company will not be willing to withdraw it.[8]

Hearst complied with the president's wishes, and the appropriate alterations were made in the film, "with the result that the film appeared primarily anti-Mexican."[9]

The President's action had essentially accomplished the task of postponing a substantially anti-Japanese position in the American films, whether serial or feature. However, the anti-Asiatic, that is, anti-Sinitic, efforts of the industry were beginning to crystallize throughout the 1920s into the 1930s, with the Chinese, and the Japanese to a lesser degree, serving as the representatives of all Asiatics. In the evolution of perhaps the most famous and infamous of all Asian serial characters, Fu Manchu, at least two earlier cinematic characters were subsumed in rapid sequence before the final product was presented to the American public. The ominous Long Sin appeared in the serial *The Exploits of Elaine*, with Pearl White in the leading role (1916). As the prototype of the Chinese villain, that is, the monstrous Mandarin, Long Sin's only conspicuously Asian characteristic, excluding his peculiar name, was a drooping mustache, later to be known as the Fu Manchu mustache.[10] Apparently, Long Sin only whetted the industry's desire to create a Chinese character of the most demonic proportions, playing upon the American fascination with the Yellow Peril as well as the structure of serials in general. In the second serial starring Pearl White, *The Perils of Pauline* (1919), Long Sin had been replaced by a more sinister Chinese character, Wu Fang. As one observer remarked:

> Beside Wu, the inscrutable, Long Sin, astute though he was, was a mere pigmy—his slave, his advance agent, as it were, a tentacle sent out to discover the most promising outlet for the nefarious talents of his master.[11]

Given the profitability of the anti-Chinese serials, Wu Fang was so popular that he became Miss White's personal Fu Manchu and a more exciting contemporary of Ali Singh. Thus, largely based upon the Chinese characters Long Sin and Wu Fang, with Ali Singh as a less durable entity,[12] by the "mid '20's the Master Oriental Criminal was solidly established in the [American] cinema."[13] However, it was not until the advent of the talkies (1926) and the full-fledged arrival of Sax Rohmer's Dr. Fu Manchu that the epitome of Chinese treachery and cunning was to satisfy the apparent white racist craving for an Asian enemy whose avowed purpose would be the total subjugation of the white race, exposing in the process the exotic and mysterious world of the East.

Dr. Fu Manchu was not an American invention. He was an English export to the United States, although his creator was of Irish descent. Sax Rohmer was born Arthur Henry Ward in Birmingham, England, in 1883, of Irish parents. During his late teens, Ward dropped his given middle name and replaced it with Sarsfield, perhaps for romantic reasons and as a gesture to a legendary character in England's past. Having tried his hand at a number of professions, among which were finance, art, journalism, musical composition, and the theater, Ward finally turned to writing. The Fu Manchu character was unquestionably Rohmer's[14] most successful literary accomplishment as well as being the most fascinating manifestation of Rohmer's personality. The first of the thirteen Dr. Fu Manchu novels was begun in the latter part of 1911.[15] Rohmer had always possessed a vivid imagination. He was especially eccentric and given to the occult, in fact believing as a devoted Egyptologist that in an earlier life he had originated somewhere along the Nile. Rohmer's attraction for the exotic, coupled with a magazine editor's commission for a story on Limehouse, that is, London's Chinatown, proved to be the initial introduction to Mr. King, perhaps the real Dr. Fu Manchu.

At some unspecified date in Limehouse, Rohmer made the acquaintance of a Mr. Fong Wah. Rohmer would often go to Limehouse, braving the fog and possible danger from the more unruly members of the Chinese community, for the sole purpose of talking, actually listening mostly, to the old Chinese man. There is no indication that Rohmer associated with any other Chinese inside or outside of Chinatown. Mr. Wah told Sax tales of old China, while Rohmer's adult imagination, changed little from boyhood, embellished Wah's every word. To Rohmer, Chinatown represented, as it did to most white Englishmen and Irishmen in London, a living mystery filled with the enchantments, dangers, and wonders of the ancient East. And like many whites, Sax was preoccupied with the more seamy aspects of Chinatown, both real and imagined. Murder, intrigue, narcotics, and assorted villainy all came to a head in Rohmer's perception of a man, presumably a Chinese, known only as Mr. King. Who Mr. King was, or if he truly existed outside Sax's own imagination, is perhaps the greatest mystery surrounding the origin of Dr. Fu Manchu.[16] What is known is that Mr. King was to Rohmer the most evil, mysterious, frightening, and unwholesome character—perhaps Rohmer's boyhood nightmare—ever to walk the London streets. Ironically, Rohmer had never seen Mr. King. Sax openly admitted that, in creating the image of Dr. Fu Manchu, the visualization of Fu himself was a particular dilemma. With his limited contact with real Chinese and his generous imaginal conception of Chinatown, Rohmer, the man who created the single outstanding personification of anti-Sinicism, confessed his ignorance of the Chinese people, stating: "I MADE MY NAME ON FU MANCHU BECAUSE I KNOW NOTHING ABOUT the Chinese," after which he slyly commented, "I know something about Chinatown. But that is a different matter."[17] Rohmer's perception of Chinatown was that of a faceless, exotic and mysterious evil, buttressed by traditional English prejudices and the recent embers of the Boxer Rebellion in China.[18] The otherwise problematical visage of Dr. Fu Manchu, however, revealed itself to Rohmer on one traumatic and terrifying night in London's Limehouse. Someone, possibly Fong Wah, had informed Sax that he might witness Chinatown's most notorious inhabitant if he were to secret himself late at night in the doorway of a particular house in Chinatown. Rohmer followed the information and was later to recall:

"Minutes passed and I continued standing there in the grip of such excitement as I had never felt before. For a mere instant while the light flooded out from the opened door, I had seen the face of the man in the fur cap, and in that instant my imaginary monster came to life. His face—well, I needn't describe it."

"Was it 'Mr. King'? I don't know, and it doesn't matter. 'King' was only a nickname or a part of his real name, anyway. Whether or not it was the same man whom I saw ceased to interest me. I knew that I had seen Dr. Fu Manchu. His face was the living embodiment of Satan."[19]

Thus, Dr. Fu Manchu was fully conceived in the mind of Sax Rohmer, and given to the world at a time when China, rather than fitting the image of the Yellow Peril, was turning to the West, especially to the United States, for friendship and democratic guidance.[20]

The English motion picture industry, specifically the Stoll Picture Corporation, released *The Mystery of Dr. Fu Manchu* in 1923, followed by two fifteen-chapter serials under the title *The Further Mysteries of Dr. Fu Manchu* in 1924. Paramount Studios was the first of the American industry to seize upon Dr. Fu Manchu. In 1929, *The Mysterious Dr. Fu Manchu* starred Warner Oland as the Dr. *The Return of Dr. Fu Manchu* and *Daughter of the Dragon*[21] were released in 1930 and 1931, respectively, by the same studio. In 1932, Metro-Goldwyn-Mayer starred Boris Karloff as Dr. Fu Manchu in *The Mask of Fu Manchu*.[22] And Republic Studios, in 1939, went into the production of *The Drums of Fu Manchu*, in serial, starring Henry Brandon as Dr. Fu Manchu. Released in 1940, the serial was condensed into a seventy-minute feature in 1942. NBC began a series of Dr. Fu Manchu thrillers, in 1950, starring Sir Cedric Hardwicke as Nayland Smith, Fu's nemesis, but difficulties and dissatisfaction with the sponsors permanently halted completion of the series. Finally, Rohmer reportedly sold the television, radio, and film rights to Dr. Fu Manchu to Republic Pictures for the sum of $4 million in 1955. In the same year, Hollywood Television Productions, Inc., a subsidiary of Republic Pictures, started a serial of no less than seventy-eight one-half hour episodes under the general title of *The Adventures of Fu Manchu*. Given the institutionally racist nature of the American motion picture industry, controversies involving Dr. Fu Manchu, including some English imports of the cheap variety, continue to smolder.[23]

Throughout the first four decades of the twentieth century, the Asian serials (many of which were thematically anchored in Hollywood's creation of Asian racism, the goal of which was "the destruction of the white race")[24] constituted a significant aspect of the American motion picture industry's stock in trade. Nonetheless, the fact remained that although the industry was conspicuous in its efforts to encourage the belief that whites were being victimized by the Chinese, the white "star system"[25] and the general profitability of the serials excluded the Asian artists from both stardom and profit, while accounting for a simultaneous increase in cinematic and social anti-Sinicism. Because all major Asian characters "were played by white men in yellowface,"[26] the industry had a free hand in racially portraying Asian characters. Notably, augmenting Fu Manchu who had become a substantive factor in America's perception of the Chinese, Victory Studios' *Shadow of Chinatown* serial (1936), which was delivered in fifteen episodes, used the figure of an insane Eurasian chemist, Victor Poten (portrayed by Bela Lugosi), not only to propagandize on the undesirability of interracial marriages between whites and Chinese, but also more importantly to emphasize the enfeebled and socially unacceptable character traits allegedly inherent to the offspring of such unions. Although Poten's own devilry was superlative, he nevertheless remained a subtly pathetic creature whose personal dilemma was rejection by whites and Chinese alike, and whose personal and social degeneracy lurked in his hatred for "both the Chinese and the white races."[27] Residing somewhere between Dr. Fu Manchu and Poten was Universal Studios' most expensive, and possibly most popular, serial: *Flash Gordon*. Begun in 1936, and originally completed in thirteen episodes, the *Flash Gordon* films introduced the American people to a futuristic Yellow Peril, Emperor Ming, the Merciless, who was portrayed by the white actor Charles Middleton. One observer of the films remarked on the depth of the anti-Asiatic tradition of the industry:

> Such is the villain in *Flash Gordon*—a trident bearded, slanty eyed, shiny doomed, pointy nailed, arching eyebrowed, exotically garbed Oriental named Ming, who personifies unadulterated evil. A heavy [a villain] like Ming is not contrived in a comic strip writer's imagination during a coffee break, but rather is the product of perhaps the richest and longest tradition of all of Hollywood's ethnic [racial] stereotypes, one which has spawned many grotesque offspring and conceived innumerable variations of deformity.[28]

At the same time, against the film industry's concentration upon Asian villainy, the arrival of an otherwise sympathetically portrayed Asian character, necessarily played by a white actor, was the product of historical happenstance, not social deliberation.

In 1919, the same year in which *Patria* appeared, with its anti-Japanese intent, author Earl Derr Biggers while in Hawaii read about a Chinese detective, Chang Apana, on the Honolulu police department.[29] The idea of a Chinese detective, of whom there were presumably few, fascinated Mr. Biggers. By no means a writer of import, Biggers' character creation, Charlie Chan, might have achieved much of his success not only from his assumed uniqueness, both in terms of personality and profession, but also from the anti-Asiatic catharsis administered by the United States' passage of the 1924 Alien Land Law–Immigration Act.[30] Less than a year after the passage of the legislation, Biggers' first Charlie Chan novel, *The House Without a Key*, was published. The novel was a relative success, as were others published by Biggers in the late 1920s. However, the motion picture producers, conditioned and guided by traditional anti-Asiatic imagery and sentiment in the industry and in America as a whole, "were cautious in springing an Oriental 'good guy' on audiences in large doses and, thus, introduced Charlie [Chan] only casually."[31] In fact, in the first Charlie Chan film, *The House Without a Key* (1926), which was titled after the novel, Charlie Chan was not the "polite, mild mannered, gracious" Chinese detective with "an endless capacity for calling forth the wisdom of the past in application to the present situation,"[32] but rather a supporting character of little actual importance to the film. Largely because of the producers' caution in developing a more noticeable role for the detective, George Kuwa, a Japanese actor, played the minor character of Charlie Chan. In 1927, *Behind That Curtain*, the following Chan film, was released with E. L. Park (possibly a non-white) in the role of Chan. However, Chan was of such minor significance in the film that Park's name appeared last on the billing. Another Japanese actor, a favorite of Douglas Fairbanks and one best known for his villainous-looking face, Kamiyama Sojin portrayed Chan in the 1928 production of *The Chinese Parrot*. Charlie Chan thus remained a character of only casual interest.

Not until the 1931 release of *Charlie Chan Carries On* did the otherwise sympathetically portrayed Chan[33] become popular. Warner Oland, who had filled the roles of Wu Fang and Dr. Fu Manchu earlier, starred as the Chinese detective. Although Oland's personality had much to do with the success of Chan,[34] it is likely that the final immigration measures taken by the United States Government, and the subsequent social relief accompanying the end to the Asian immigration problem,[35] gradually provided a psychological incentive and social climate given to the acceptance of an image of a non-villainous Asian. Chan's un–aggressive persona, rendered affectedly quaint by an "abundance of apho-risms"[36] oftentimes prefaced by "Confucius say,"[37] was as remotely threatening to white Americans as the continuing fear of an Asian immi-gration deluge was at last superfluous. Although anti-Asiatic motion pic-tures persisted mostly because anti-Asianism per se had become standard institutionalized practice—with Asians represented as a racial threat only through the "crude efforts of the Hollywood writers"[38]—Chan became symbolic of the harmless and comical[39] cultural and racial characteristics of a people barred from American shores because of their race.

Oland starred in a total of sixteen Chan films. Upon his death, in 1938, Sidney Toler assumed the role of Chan for eleven productions. Roland Winters continued the series after Toler's death, in 1947, playing Chan in over twenty pictures. The character of Charlie Chan, much like that of Dr. Fu Manchu, has not diminished in popularity over the years.

The films have been continually brought to the American viewing public on television:

> The Chan movies themselves, staples on television for years, in the early 1970s suddenly found themselves the center of a new cult, part of the general craze for nostalgia of the thirties and forties. As a result, they were repackaged, their television licensing fees skyrocketed, and, placed on the 16-mm market, they commanded hefty rental rates commensurate with fees for major classics.[40]

Newer Chan-related materials, despite repeated protest by Asian actors and charges of racism,[41] have found their way into the American market and the American home.

Not all of Chan's sympathetically portrayed contemporaries fared so well, however. Chan's Japanese counterpart, Mr. Moto, appeared in 1937 at the Twentieth Century-Fox Studios. Having found a successful "formula with its oriental detective series *Charlie Chan*,"[42] the industry attempted to duplicate the success. Also a detective,[43] albeit one with a propensity to "lisping, bowing, and foot-shuffling,"[44] Mr. Moto was based upon the late John Marquand's character. Despite his "impeccable English,"[45] in marked contrast to Charlie Chan's pidgin English, Mr. Moto remained essentially an inscrutable personage, as described by Marquand:

> He was a small rather chunky Japanese, in well fitting European clothes, . . . I remember exactly the way the light struck Mr. Moto's face, bringing out the eager, watchful lines around his narrow eyes, and making his blunt nose cast a sideward shadow on his coffee colored skin. I remember that he was smiling, with the curious reflex action of his race that makes the lips turn up at unconventional moments into a parody of merriment.[46]

With Peter Lorre in the starring role, Mr. Moto was capable of physical violence, unlike Chan, and would sometimes "engage in some extremely lively fight scenes which often brought the films to a much more rousing conclusion than the predictable confrontations of the Chans."[47] Unfortunately, the Mr. Moto character fell victim of international tensions between the United States and Japan. The increasing aggression in Asia of Japan's militarists, particularly when England's interests in south Asia were being threatened, was largely responsible for a new wave of anti-Japanese sentiment in the United States.

> The movie industry [decided] to abandon the Mr. Moto series of detective stories because anti-Japanese feeling [was] running so high in America that audiences [could] no longer take pleasure in the courage and astuteness of a member of that nation.[48]

Dutifully, the American motion picture industry put Mr. Moto into "his wartime internment camp,"[49] as would the Government of the United States 110,000 Americans of Japanese descent.

Mr. Moto was not released from his internment for over sixteen years. In 1957, Twentieth Century-Fox Studios finished shooting *Stopover Tokyo* which was filmed entirely in Japan. Hailed as "the latest and finest of the 'Mr. Moto' stories,"[50] the motion picture itself made no reference to the Japanese detective. In fact, the screenplay not only "dropped the name Moto"[51] from the lead role, filled by Robert Wagner as agent Mark Fennon, but also "completely eliminated"[52] Mr. Moto from the story. To all intents and purposes, Mr. Moto had been thoroughly emasculated by the Studios' efforts. In 1965, more peculiarly, with the increasing emphasis upon the surrealistic thrillers, many of which had anti-Asiatic overtones, Warner Brothers Studios released *The Return of Mr. Moto*, which starred another non-Asiatic, Henry Silva,[53] in the role of Mr. Moto "to cash in on the *James Bond* super agent cycle."[54] Thus, finally assisted by a dismal performance by Silva, Mr. Moto appeared to have found release from both the internment camp and the motion picture screen.

The last of the sympathetically portrayed Asian characters was Mr. Wong, Detective.[55] Two Asian detectives might have proved sufficient by any American standard. However, Monogram Pictures, in 1938, hoped "to duplicate the success of the Oriental detective craze."[56] The rights to Hugh Wiley's short-story character, Mr. Wong, Detective, were bought by the Studio. Several white actors, in accordance with the Studios' practice, were tested for the part of Mr. Wong. After some deliberation Boris Karloff (an actual Eurasian actor of East Indian and English descent, and a former portrayer of Dr. Fu Manchu) secured the part. Although only three Mr. Wong, Detective, films were made, the short-lived series was important in one respect. Karloff, after having made the first two films, left the series; and Keye Luke, a real Chinese actor, was able to try the role in the third film, *Phantom of Chinatown*. While *Phantom* was a particularly interesting film, the white film exhibitors, who were only interested in Karloff, "lost interest in the series, and it was dropped."[57] Primarily as the result of the exhibitors' bias, the only series that might have starred an actual Asian was terminated.

The collective impression of Asians created by the American motion picture industry prior to the Second World War was one of cultural condescension and open racism. Yet a definitive irony lay in the fact that the industry while profiting from its racist view of Asians was simultaneously offending a growing nationalism[58] among Asians. Moreover, the United States' anti-Asiatic policies, formally culminating in 1924, served to insult and humiliate all Asian governments and peoples. Considering the nature of Japanese-American relations, coupled with the rising expectations of an especially high-strung, modern Japanese nationalism, it was not surprising that Japan should determine to offset the United States. In like fashion, the American film industry, which throughout the years had remained more heavily anti-Sinitic than anti-Japanese, would act as one of the most vicious weapons in America's struggle against Japan's aggression.

The United States' passage of the Immigration Act in 1924 severely wounded Japanese pride both nationally and racially. The insult and trauma to the Japanese nation were so overpowering that "the train of events that culminated at Pearl Harbor may be said to have been set in motion in 1924."[59] In Japan, protest against the Act was unanimous. In addition, it "created a tremendous antagonism in Japan and inspired the growth of militaristic and anti-foreign elements who were given the excuse to wage war against the United States."[60] After what was for Japan a long contest with the white nations, most outstandingly the United States, on the issues of national and racial equality, the 1924 Immigration Act was a stunning defeat, the disgrace and humiliation of which was unprecedented. Perhaps reluctantly, the Japanese had begun to realize that regardless of Japan's industrial achievements and military successes, and despite her attempts to impress the white nations with her non-Asiatic capabilities, the ultimate barrier to equality was race. Thus it was remarked:

> Previously the quest for equality had been seen largely in terms of the ac-quisition of Western economic, political, legal and cultural institutions; the barrier of Western racism had been either ignored or thought inappli-cable to the Japanese case. The removal of most other barriers to accept-ability, however, raised a depressing spectre, the growing awareness that the dream of equality might in the end be frustrated by an ingrained un-willingness among Europeans and Americans to accept those of other races as equals under any circumstances. For many, the elimination of racial prejudice as a barrier to international acceptability eventually be-came the single final achievement necessary before Japan could take her rightful place among the advanced nations of the world. To them, with-out this ultimate acceptance, all Japan's achievements to date would be worth little.[61]

At the same time, however, Japan's final realization that in the eyes of the whites the Japanese were not superior to the other Asian nationalities, but merely a variant form of the Yellow Peril, drove the Japanese more closely to the other extreme of stationing themselves as the assumed head of the Asian races.[62]

Japanese nationalism, and its inherent "call for 'a militarily pow-erful Japan,' "[63] was intensified by the United States' behavior in 1924. Racial rejection of Japan by the United States enlivened the concept of a united Asia ready to reverse the gains made by the whites in Asia. How-ever, the Pan-Asiatic ideal, perhaps Japan's regional expression of Japan-ese nationalism, was based upon contradictory goals. On the one hand, Japan's ideal Pan-Asianism would cast out the white powers from Asia, thereby destroying "the Western imperialistic structure in the Orient."[64] On the other hand, Japan would replace the white powers in Asia, thus in essence making "serfs"[65] of the supposedly liberated peoples. For the

Eugene Franklin Wong

Japanese, peculiarly, the diametrically opposed purposes "were insepara-
bly fused together and internalized in the national ideology."[66] Resentment against the United States continued to mount in Japan.[67] In 1926,
Vice-Admiral Reijiro Kawashima argued that a war between the United
States and Japan had been decreed by Heaven, and Teisuke Akiyama, the
editor of the *Niroku* and a man influential in politics, said that a war
against the United States would be a moral tonic for the Japanese people.[68]
In fact, the Japanese press had become highly anti-foreign, reacting wildly
to Japan's rejection on racial grounds, with the United States and the other
Anglo-Saxon nations as primary targets:

> More probably the anti-alienism of Japan is now displayed in hopes of
> bringing to Japan the headship of an Asiatic federation against white ag-
> gression. "The whites," says *Kokumin*, "are robbers. They have long been
> brutally and cruelly unjust." The influence of Japan, the *Nichi Nichi*
> thinks, will, in the future, control the fate of Asia. The time will come,
> *Yamato* said in 1925, when Japan will wage herculean struggle against the
> Anglo-Saxon races on the plains of China, and the *Mainichi* warned the
> world what fate befell those nations who purposely and unnecessarily in-
> sulted Dai Nippon.[69]

Japan's martial spirit had been excited by the United States' anti-Asiatic
racism. Indeed, all Asians felt the sting of America's racism. With the flame
of a Greater East Asia Co-Prosperity Sphere kindled, the Japanese seethed
under the sometimes placid surface of resignation. In 1930, eleven years
after the release of *Patria* had so gravely offended him, and six years after
the passage of the Immigration Act of 1924, ex-Ambassador Hanihara
Masanao reflected, in the most ominous tones, upon Japan's humiliation:

> "the resentment is felt now as it was then, nor will it ever die out so long
> as the wound inflicted remains unhealed."[70]

A year after the ex-Ambassador's words were spoken, the Empire of Japan
fatefully invaded Chinese territory. Although most Americans paid little
attention to Japanese aggression against China in 1931, despite Chinese
efforts to seek the assistance of the United States, the course had been set.
America and the American motion picture industry would on 7 December 1941, acknowledge Japan's unhealed wound, but not America's white
racism, in the cry: "The Japs have just bombed Pearl Harbor!"[71]

NOTES

1. Kyoshi K. Kawakami, *Asia at the Door: A Study of the Japanese Question in Con-
tinental United States, Hawaii and Canada* (New York: Fleming H. Revell, 1914), 27.

2. Kalton C. Lahue, *Continued Next Week: A History of the Moving Picture Serial*
(Norman: University of Oklahoma Press, 1964), 48.

3. *The Yellow Menace* serial dealt heavily with the race issue, depicting the yellow
race as especially treacherous and aggressive. A "Mongolian" by the name of "Ali Singh"

plotted to overthrow the white race from within the United States. Singh, whose name suggested an East Indian origin, possibly Sikh, despite the fact that the character was Mongolian, was one of the first (1916) fifth-column scares in American films. While the conquest of the white race by the yellow race was an American projection onto the yellow race of what appeared to be the white race's conquest of yellow Asia, Singh's ultimate defeat by the United States' Secret Service was viewed as, in Kalton C. Lahue's succinct terms, "the supremacy of right and white," *Continued Next Week*, 40. *The Yellow Menace* serial, in addition to depicting Asians as a fifth-column threat, also filmically critiqued the assumed apathy and neutrality of the United States prior to that country's entrance into the War. Likewise, there was a particular irony in the fact that the German forces in World War I were referred to as "Huns." Once again, the West had projected its cultural racism onto the Asians. That the Germans, then considered to be the worst and most aggressive of the whites of Europe, were likened to the Huns reveals that Asians served as the reference point of evil, especially international and military evil. Although it has not yet been determined to what extent the Huns were Asian, it is generally accepted that there was "a Mongolian strain in the Huns." So, too, it has been established that "many Huns were halfbreeds," that is, Eurasians. See, for example, J. Otto Maenchen-Helfen, *The World of the Huns, Studies in Their History and Culture* (Berkeley and Los Angeles: University of California Press, 1973), 363–64.

    4. W. A. Swanberg, *Citizen Hearst, A Biography of William Randolph Hearst* (New York: Charles Scribner's Sons, 1961), 296–97.

    5. Warner Oland was not only one of the first white actors to use racist cosmetics in portraying Asians in the films, but he was also later to portray two of the best-known and ambivalently designed Asian characters, Charlie Chan and Fu Manchu, about whom more will be said shortly.

    6. Swanberg, *Citizen Hearst*, 297.

    7. Raymond William Stedman, *The Serials: Suspense and Drama by Installment* (Norman: University of Oklahoma Press, 1971), 41.

    8. Swanberg, *Citizen Hearst*, 297.

    9. Stedman, *The Serials*, 41. It should be noted that *Patria* became far more controversial than *The Yellow Menace* not because it was more racist, but because it was manifest in its identification of the Japanese as the Asian peril to the United States. As was mentioned earlier, the President felt a special obligation to recall the film in order that its more blatant anti-Japanese features be edited out. The resulting anti-Mexican emphasis marked an important subtheme in the film. In defending the Japanese, Kawakami remarked: "The spectre of [a] Japanese invasion in Mexico was conjured up, it seems, as a scheme of boosting a real estate enterprise by those American interests holding immense tracts of land in Lower California" (*Asia at the Door*, 37). Hearst's mother owned, that is, held, ranch, oil, timber, mining, and chicle property in Mexico. Indeed, the Hearst holdings were conservatively estimated at $4 million, and they were under the political protection of Porfirio Diaz. With Diaz's exile in 1911, however, the Mexican revolutionaries determined to drive out the Yankee "imperialists" and to ferret out those Mexicans who had supported them under Diaz's tough regime. The pending threat to the Hearst family's financial and territorial holdings no doubt colored William Randolph Hearst's increasing anti-Mexican sentiment, as incorporated into *Patria*. So, too, Hearst's Babicora ranch, located in Chihuahua, was repeatedly attacked and finally overrun by Pancho Villa's men. It was reported that Pancho Villa personally appropriated upwards of 60,000 of Hearst's cattle.

    10. Sax Rohmer's first Fu Manchu publication, *The Insidious Dr. Fu-Manchu*, appeared in 1913. It is very likely that the Americans knew of the Fu Manchu character as early as that date, and that Long Sin and Wu Fang were incipient Fu Manchus. Wu Fang was alternately played by Frank Lackteen and Warner Oland, both of whom were white men in Asian character parts.

    11. Stedman, *The Serials*, 39.

    12. William Randolph Hearst was also responsible for the financing of *The Yellow Menace* film in which Ali Singh appeared.

13. Bradford M. Day, *Sax Rohmer: A Bibliography* (New York and Denver: Science-Fiction and Fantasy Publications, 1963), 33–34.

14. From Arthur Sarsfield Ward, Rohmer went through another name change. Being of a very nervous character with habits to match, Rohmer is reported to have taken a long trip to Europe (the Continent). When he left, he was Arthur Sarsfield Ward. Upon his return, he was Sax Rohmer. The given name "Sax" was derived from the ancient Saxon word for "blade." "Rohmer" as a surname was likewise derived from the ancient Saxon, meaning "roamer." The exotic-sounding name did not inhibit Sax's literary career. On the contrary, Rohmer himself was under the impression that it assisted his literary career.

15. The last Dr. Fu Manchu novel was completed in 1959, the year of its author's death. Sax had also written other novels as well as numerous magazine articles, some on Dr. Fu.

16. Rohmer actually mentions a Mr. King in one of his earlier novels dealing with the Chinese, although not with Dr. Fu Manchu. In *The Yellow Claw* (New York: McBride, Nast, 1915), 242, Dr. Cumberly, one of the characters, says: "He is a certain shadowy being, known as Mr. King." "Mr. King being the chief, or president, of a sort of opium syndicate, and, furthermore, it points to his being a Chinaman."

17. Cay Van Ash and Elizabeth Sax Rohmer, *Master of Villainy: A Biography of Sax Rohmer* (London: Tom Stacey, 1972), 72. Rohmer's propensity for the occult, it is worthy to note, was epitomized in an episode he and his wife, Elizabeth, had with a ouija board. While fooling with the ouija board one night, Sax asked the board, "How can I best make a living?" As it was a time before the Fu Manchu creation, Sax and Elizabeth were astonished when "the pointer moved rapidly over the chart and, not once, but repeatedly,spelt out: C-H-I-N-A-M-A-N" (63).

18. The Boxer Rebellion (1900) made an impact both upon Rohmer and the film industry. The Boxers were intensely anti-foreign, anti-Christian, and particularly anti-white. On more than one occasion whites in China were killed by the enraged Chinese. Rather peculiarly, the one redeeming aspect of Dr. Fu Manchu, that is, an understanding of why he hated whites, was a product of the Boxer Rebellion. In the film *The Return of Dr. Fu Manchu* (Paramount, 1930) with Warner Oland as the Dr., an explanation is given for Fu's evil. At Dr. Fu's assumed demise, two white characters expressed a kind of remorse:
Inspector Smith: "Before Fu Manchu went insane, he was a magnificent scientist working for mankind. And not only that, during the Boxer Rising, he was the best friend the white man had in China." [In reaction to a Boxer attack near Fu's house, English and other white soldiers were forced to open fire] "the white troops were obliged to fire, and Fu Manchu's wife and little son, whom he adored, were killed before his eyes."
Newspaper Man: "Is that why he went insane?"
Inspector Smith: "Yes. And in the mistaken belief that his white friends had intentionally fired on his house, he swore to his gods that he'd wipe them out to the third generation, and that he'd use the child, Lea Eltham, in his vengeance."
The inspector went on to state that the Dr. had earlier hunted down Russian, German, and French men who were also responsible for the deaths of Fu's wife and son. Likewise, Fu's symbol, a blood-stained dragon, represented his wife's blood. Day, *Sax Rohmer*, 33–34, says that film treated Fu too kindly, that is, "Fu Manchu became a poor, misguided oriental who sought revenge on the English for killing his wife during the Boxer Rebellion." Apparently, Day missed the overall intent of the film.

19. Cay Van Ash and Elizabeth Sax Rohmer, *Master of Villainy*, 77. Rohmer's description of Dr. Fu Manchu's physical being was as contradictory and ambivalent as was the Dr.'s character. Physically speaking, Dr. Fu Manchu was quite non-Chinese. He was "a tall, cat-like individual possessing a Shakespearean-yet-Satanic countenance, close-shaven skull, and magnetic feline eyes." See Jack Mathis, *Valley of the Cliffhangers* (Northbrook, Ill.: Jack Mathis Advertising, 1975), 137. In considering the importance attributed to the difference between the occidental and the oriental eyes, perhaps the most peculiar dissonance lies in the fact that Dr. Fu Manchu was supposed to have had powerful *green eyes*. In Sax Rohmer [Arthur Sarsfield Ward], *The Island of Fu Manchu* (New York: Doubleday, Doran, 1941), for

example, Kerrigan, a white character opposing Fu's evil, says: "I recognised the fact that this power emanated entirely from his [Dr. Fu's] eyes" "and I knew that his power resided in a tremendous intellect, for it shone out like a beacon from those *strange green eyes*, feverishly brilliant in cavernous shadows" (37, italics added). It is also instructive to note that at a time when the superiority of the white race was still a foregone conclusion, the white characters should recognize Fu's superior intellect, that is, "Dr. Fu Manchu, embodiment of the finest intellect in the modern world" (3). Likewise: "There was no man whom I feared as I feared the brilliant Chinese doctor" (4).

20. Raymond Durgnat, "The 'Yellow Peril' Rides Again," *Film Society Review* Volume 5, Number 2, October, 1969, 38, states that "Fu Manchu was created in the era of Sun Yat-Sen and so represents the West's fear of China as the sleeping giant whom she'd have done better not to awaken." Dr. Sun Yat-Sen was friendly toward the United States and was in Denver, Colorado, when the 1911 Chinese revolution erupted. Sun had approached the United States for financial support on several occasions, without success. In frustration, he turned to the Russians, and later to the Soviets.

21. Anna May Wong portrayed Dr. Fu Manchu's daughter, Fah Lo Suee, who was supposedly Eurasian. Rohmer may have had erotic feelings toward Eurasian females, particularly in light of his own personally progressive attitude toward sex and marriage. In *The Yellow Claw*, 155, he sensually wrote: "She had the pallidly dusky skin of a Eurasian, but, by virtue of nature or artifice, her cheeks wore a peach-like bloom. Her features were flawless in their chiseling, save for the slightly distended nostrils, and her black eyes [not green] were magnificent. She was divinely petite, slender and girlish; but there was that in the lines of her figure, so seductively defined by her clinging Chinese dress, in the poise of her small head, with the bluish rose nestling amid the black hair—above all in the smile of her full red lips—which discounted the youth of her body, which whispered 'Mine is a soul old in strange sins.' " Rohmer did have at least one extramarital relationship with a white woman. And during his Limehouse escapades his wife, Elizabeth, feared that he might have had a Chinese (Fong Wah's daughter), possibly a Eurasian, relationship. There is, however, no solid evidence to support the possibility.

22. Durgnat, "The 'Yellow Peril' Rides Again," 36, says this film depicted Dr. Fu as "preaching genocide and race-rape" of the whites, screaming: "Kill all the white men and take their women!"

23. The increased social and political awareness among Asian Americans of the issue of anti-Asiatic white racism, certainly as it applies to the mass media as a whole, has oftentimes accounted for outspoken criticism of individuals and institutions. However, little attention or coverage has been given specifically to Asian protest against anti-Asiatic racism in the United States. One of the few incidents that did in fact receive coverage by the media concerned the showing of a Fu Manchu film on television in 1972.

"Members of several Asian-American groups Friday protested the showing of the film 'The Brides of Fu Manchu' by television station KTLA [channel 5].

"The film was denounced by the groups as being 'racist and distorted.' They demanded a public apology by the station as well as equal time to present a more accurate portrayal of Asians.

"Among those represented at a press conference were spokesmen for the Los Angeles Joint Chinese Students Association, the Japanese American Citizens League and the Chinese Community Council of Greater Los Angeles.

"Richard Fong, president of the USC Chinese Students Association, said the film 'perpetuates a false stereotype and racial image of Asians in America.'

" . . .the manager of the station said his station did not intend to schedule the movie again." See *Los Angeles Times*, 13 May 1972, MPAS Collection.

24. Ken Weiss and Ed Goodgold, *To Be Continued . . .* (New York: Crown, 1972), vii.

25. Thomas W. Bohn and Richard L. Stromgren, *Light and Shadows* (Port Washington, N.Y.: Alfred, 1975), 192–93.

26. Richard Griffith and Arthur Mayer, *The Movies* (New York: Simon and Schuster, 1970), 108. The institutional exclusion of real Asian performers from primary roles vis-à-vis the use of racist cosmetics had become established practice as early as the late 1910s.

27. Weiss and Goodgold, *To Be Continued . . .*, 86.

28. Robert Barshay, "Ethnic Stereotypes in Flash Gordon," *Journal of Popular Film*, Volume 3, No. 1, Winter 1974, 24–26. Barshay also notes other important elements in the *Gordon* serial. The projected white racist sexual phobia was an inherent part of Ming's master plan for universal domination: "the evil Ming is perversely attracted to the fetching Dale [the white female heroine], and much of the action revolves around the emperor's diabolical insistence on marrying her and ridding himself of a potential suitor, Flash. (The theme is peculiar because at the time the serial was made, the United States had miscegenation laws prohibiting the marriage between Asians and whites.)

"What could be more psychologically excruciating and suspenseful to an American audience than the personification of evil of obviously alien [Asian] extraction lusting after the pure blue-eyed, blond-haired American virgin of genteel breeding? The mythical attraction of a vile, corrupt and sinister Oriental's pursuit of a self-contained unit of almost prenatal innocence, then, manipulated and exploited the commonly embraced stereotypes in the American imagination for commercial success" (20).

29. Frank Chin, "Interview: Roland Winters, the Last Charlie Chan of the Movies," *Amerasia Journal*, Volume 2, Fall 1973, 16.

30. The primary intention of the 1924 land and immigration legislation was to deny admittance to the United States of any and all aliens (Asians specifically) who were by law "ineligible for citizenship." See Connie Young Yu, "The Chinese in American Courts," *Bulletin of Concerned Asian Scholars*, No. 4, Fall 1972, 28. Since Asians were prohibited by law from becoming American citizens, the legislation in effect served as the final step in excluding Asians from American shores. Added to the tension between the United States and Japan, especially over the Japanese emigration to the United States and Japan's demand for equal treatment of her nationals in the United States, the 1924 legislation was destined to have a devastating impact upon American-Japanese relations, as will be seen presently.

31. William K. Everson, *The Detective in Film* (Secaucus, N.J.: Citadel, 1972), 73.

32. Dorothy B. Jones, *The Portrayal of China and India on the American Screen, 1896–1955: The Evolution of Chinese and Indian Themes, Locales, and Characters as Portrayed on the American Screen* (Cambridge, Mass.: Center for International Studies, M.I.T., October 1955), 32–33. It should be noted that the Charlie Chan features and serials numbered an impressive forty-seven. Likewise, the Charlie Chan character has been a traditional favorite among Americans and non-Americans alike. The popularity of Chan as a detective is reportedly second only to Sherlock Holmes.

33. A sympathetic portrayal should not be construed as necessarily non-racist. Although Chan was not a villain, the portrayal of Chan is racist if only on the basis of racist cosmetology, and the fact that the institutional exclusion of the Chinese accounts for Chan's "never having been portrayed by a Chinese actor." See Chris Steinbrunner and Otto Penzler (eds.-in-chief), Marvin Lachman and Charles Shibuk (senior eds.), *Encyclopedia of Mystery and Detection* (New York: McGraw-Hill, 1976), 72.

34. Everson, *The Detective in Film*, 73.

35. Maisie Conrat and Richard Conrat, *Executive Order 9066, The Internment of 110,000 Japanese Americans* (California Historical Society, 1972), 21. The Conrats say, for example, that the 1924 Exclusion Law put an end to the "burst of active anti-Japanese agitation in the United States," although anti-Asiatic imagery persisted.

36. James Robert Parrish, ed., *The Great Movie Series* (New York: A. S. Barnes, 1971), 90.

37. Jones, *The Portrayal of China and India*, 34.

38. Harold Isaacs, *American Views of China and India: Images of Asia* (New York: Capricorn, 1962), 117.

39. Everson, *The Detective in Film*, 79, notes that the second-generation Chans, sons and daughters, were generally engaged in "sleuthing misadventures." The Chan films were the only vehicles, however, through which Asian actors did not have to speak pidgin English. Keye Luke played Chan's No. 1 son, Layne Tom Jr. and Victor Sen Yung appeared as

No. 2, Benson Fong as No. 3, Edwin Luke as No. 4, Frances Chan as daughter Frances, and Marianne Quon as Iris Chan.

40. Everson, *The Detective in Film*, 80.

41. The most recent Asian and Pacific American protest against the continued presentation of Charlie Chan took place on 3 August 1977. Asian and Pacific actors and actresses went to Los Angeles' Chinatown to protest the filming of a Charlie Chan commercial for Dodge Aspen automobiles, with Chinatown as a mere background. The Chan character was portrayed by white actor Ross Martin. The Association of Asian/Pacific American Artists argues that the character is stereotypical, affected, and negative, as well as being a continuation of the use of racist cosmetology. The persistence of racist cosmetics is not restricted to Chan. For example, the Japanese American actor Mako was reportedly turned down for an Asian role in *Rashomon*. In reading for the role, Mako was told by David Susskind: "You gave a great reading. But as a real Japanese you'd be too conspicuous. All of the other actors are white made up to look Japanese." Mako did not get the role. See Irvin Paik, "The East West Players: The First Ten Are The Hardest," *Neworld*, Winter 1975, 31.

42. Parrish, *The Great Movie Series*, 259.

43. In the film *Charlie Chan in Honolulu* (1938), Chan, played by Toler, actually made professional reference to Mr. Moto: "Am expecting visit from distinguished colleague, Mr. Moto, shortly—must be prepared for same." See film and final script, 3. It is curious that as part of Chan's pidgin English and affected Asian humility, as conceived by whites, he was never allowed to speak in the first-person singular.

44. Stephen Birmingham, *The Late John Marquand: A Biography* (New York and Philadelphia: J. B. Lippincott, 1972), 78.

45. Steinbrunner and Penzler, *Encyclopedia of Mystery and Detection*, 291.

46. John P. Marquand, *Thank You, Mr. Moto* (New York: Grosset and Dunlop, 1936), 31 and 105.

47. Everson, *The Detective in Film*, 80.

48. Jacobus ten Broek, Edward N. Barnhart, and Floyd W. Matson, *Prejudice, War and the Constitution* (Berkeley and Los Angeles: University of California Press, 1954), 32.

49. Everson, *The Detective in Film*, 79.

50. From Harry Brand, Director of Publicity, 20th Century-Fox Studios, Beverly Hills, "Vital Statistics on 'Stopover Tokyo,' " 1.

51. *Reporter*, 28 October 1957, MPAS Collection. In the original story, Mr. Moto was definitely the character who was later eliminated by the Studios. Marquand himself identified Moto when he wrote: "Yes, it's the same name, . . .'Moto. Yes, I've got it now. Your nephew gave me your name in San Francisco.' " See John P. Marquand, *Stopover Tokyo* (Boston, Mass.: Little, Brown, 1956), 71.

52. John Scott, "'Stopover Tokyo' Tale of Intrigue in Orient," *L.A. Times*, 8 November 1957, MPAS Collection.

53. *The Green Sheet*, The Film Board of National Organizations, New York, December 1965.

54. Parrish, *The Great Movie Series*, 259. The racist character of the Bond films is emphasized by Bond's lines: "I don't think I've ever heard of a great Negro criminal before," said Bond. "Chinamen, of course, the men behind the opium trade. There've been some big-time Japs, mostly pearls and drugs." See Vincent Canby, "In 'Live and Let Die,' the Bad Guys are Black," *The New York Times Film Reviews*, 1973–74, 80.

55. Mr. Wong, Detective, should not be confused with a villainous character, called Mr. Wong, in a film starring Bela Lugosi. They were two entirely different characters.

56. Richard Bojarski and Kenneth Beale, *The Films of Boris Karloff* (Secaucus, N.J.: Citadel, 1974), 132.

57. Everson, *The Detective in Film*, 82.

58. Jones, *The Portrayal of China and India*, 37, remarks that by the 1930s, when China had begun to take her place among the family of nations, "the Chinese government began to express itself with respect to the manner in which China and Chinese customs and people

were being portrayed in American motion pictures." Paul K. Whang, in his "Boycotting American Movies," *The World Tomorrow*, August 1930, stated: "whenever a Chinese is portrayed on the screen he is depicted as a dope fiend, gambler, murderer or something equally bad. Being far away from China, the public has nothing better to do than take these misrepresentations at their face value." "Thus to exaggerate the evils of Chinatown on the screen will not only arouse the ire of the Chinese people, but will reflect no good upon the reputation of the American government" (339). From a more nationalistic perspective, Whang lamented the use of Japanese actors in Chinese character parts, who he said misrepresented the Chinese "for the benefit of their own country" (339). In general, however, Whang took issue with Harold Lloyd's *Welcome Danger*, in which Chinese were portrayed as opium-smugglers, kidnappers, and gamblers. Additionally, a young Chinese boy in Singapore decried: "We don't eat rats and mice. We like candy, cake and ice cream, just like other kids. You think all Chinese boys run laundries and are washermen. Say! We want to be policemen, firemen, doctors, lawyers and soldiers, too. When my daddy takes me to America, I am going to say 'Hello' to Jack Dempsey, Mayor Jimmy Walker, Lindy, Charlie Chaplin and President Hoover." See "Byrd Again in NewsReel," Chinese Boy in Singapore Talks in English for Film at Embassy, *New York Times Film Reviews* (1913–1931), 15 April 1930, 638–39.

59. Kimitada Miwa, "Japanese Images of War with the United States," in *Mutual Images: Essays in American-Japanese Relations*, ed. Akira Iriye (Cambridge, Mass.: Harvard University Press, 1975), 115.

60. Albert M. Robbins, "Exclusion as a Factor in the Relations of Japan and the United States, 1913–1924" (Unpublished M.A. thesis, University of Southern California, January 1954), 172.

61. Lee Arne Makela, "Japanese Attitudes Towards the United States Immigration Act of 1924" (Unpublished Ph.D. diss., Stanford University, 1973), 3. It should also be noted that 1 July 1924, the day the Act was passed in the United States, was celebrated as National Humiliation Day in Japan.

62. Japan's own prejudice against the other races and nationalities of the East literally undercut the idea of Pan-Asianism. Hence: "The Japanese demanded equal status with the advanced Western imperialist countries; but they ignored the unequal treatment they accorded their Asian neighbors," Iriye, *Mutual Images*, 8.

63. Matsumoto Sannosuke, "The Significance of Nationalism in Modern Japanese Thought: Some Theoretical Problems," *The Journal of Asian Studies*, Volume 31, No. 1, November 1971, 53.

64. Joyce C. Lebra, ed., *Japan's Greater East Asia Co-Prosperity Sphere in World War II* (London: Oxford University Press, 1975), 4.

65. Edwin O. Reischauer, *Japan: The Story of a Nation* (New York: Knopf, 1970), 204.

66. Sannosuke, "The Significance of Nationalism," 55.

67. In the third week of June 1924, Shochiku, one of Japan's leading motion picture production companies, began a general boycott against American products and refused to screen American films. The boycott was a failure, however, largely through the efforts of Makino Shozo, a film director, who said Shochiku was exploiting the situation in order to promote the sales of Japanese films.

68. Harry Emerson Wildes, *Social Currents in Japan, with Special Reference to the Press* (Chicago: University of Chicago Press, 1927), 88.

69. Ibid., 93.

70. Makela, "Japanese Attitudes Towards the United States Immigration Act of 1924," 268–69.

71. *Wake Island* (1942), Brian Donlevy as Major Geoffrey Caton speaking.

Laura Hyun-Yi Kang

The Desiring of Asian Female Bodies: Interracial Romance and Cinematic Subjection

Western anthropology has yet to significantly move beyond the earlier premise of studying and evaluating difference over there. In their introduction to *Anthropology as Cultural Critique*, George Marcus and Michael Fischer posit:

> In using portraits of other cultural patterns to reflect self-critically on *our* own ways, anthropology disrupts common sense and makes us reexamine *our* taken-for-granted assumptions. (1986:1)

Who is figured in the unquestioned, first-person plural "we" in firm possession of its own ways and assumptions? This is not a rhetorical question but one that is motivated by my own uneasy ambivalence around inclusion/alienation each time I come upon such assertions of collectivity. This essay hopes to provoke a rethinking of the assumptions around who can speak about what and for whom and in which cultural, disciplinary contexts.

Due to the political pressures of various racial-ethnic communities *back here*, within the nation-state borders of the United States, and the growing body of their critical and cultural productions, anthropology and the practice of ethnographic discourse has had to rethink its assumptions about the distance separating here and there and the cultural differences manifested in these presumably distinguishable locales. This has unsettled any fixed, reliable conceptualizations of both the familiar and the exotic. James Clifford expresses this challenge in the introduction to his *The Predicament of Culture*:

> This century has seen a dramatic expansion of mobility, including tourism, migrant labor, immigration, urban sprawl. . . . In cities on six

continents, foreign populations have come to stay—mixing in but often in partial, specific fashions. *The exotic is uncannily close.* (1989:13)

I am interested in that uncanniness, that inexplicable "somethingness" of the (abrupt) realization of the (sudden) closeness of the unfamiliar-distant. An exploration of such disorientation could be illuminating, not only for a reconceptualization of ethnographic practices but more important for how difference continues to support power inequalities even after—and often accentuated by—the acknowledgment of its proximity.

One approach is to be attentive not only to what these (formerly) foreign, exotic populations have to say but to the way in which they represent not only themselves but precisely these historical shifts and the broader sociopolitical stage. Two essays that appeared in the fall 1991 issue of *Visual Anthropology Review* articulate a growing awareness about the need to read ethnographic narratives of culture and difference alongside and against a vibrant field of postcolonial, multicultural discourse that is emanating from within the geopolitical borders of the West. Bill Nichols begins his essay, entitled "The Ethnographer's Tale," by positing: "Ethnographic film is in trouble." He attributes this predicament to its own mistakes and shortcomings but also to "the ground-breaking, convention-altering forms of self-representation by those who have traditionally been objects (and blindspots) of anthropological study: women/natives/others." The essay goes on to call for an "ethnotopia" that would encompass both ethnographic discourse and these diasporic articulations. I believe that a critical consideration of one discursive terrain with and against the other could be instructive for both and possibly complicate assumptions about their distinct if not adversarial goals and methods. However, I would add that such a broadened "ethnotopia" must be mindful about the differential access to funding and resources, to circuits of distribution/viewership, and to institutional legitimation that ethnographic and diasporic film/videomakers must contend with.

Later in the same volume, in an essay entitled "Speaking For, Speaking About, Speaking With, or Speaking Alongside: An Anthropological and Documentary Dilemma," Jay Ruby also acknowledges that the previously assumed "right and ability of outsiders to represent accurately minorities has been repeatedly questioned" by critical scholarship and by cultural productions transmitting from those previously (mis)represented groups. He begins this particular section on "Films by *The Other*" by announcing what is fairly evident: "African Americans, Asian Americans, Native Americans, Hispanics, the poor and the homeless, gay people as well as women, have been seeking to represent themselves for some time." Immediately, I am struck by the sheer diversity and vast numbers of persons included on this list and then further troubled by his unqualified reference to them as "minority filmmakers" in the following discussion. While Ruby points out that there are "other 'new' filmmakers (who) are more interested in the construction of an alternative practice that remains deliberately outside the establishment," his discussion focuses greatly upon compromised, self-serving filmmakers, who have (possibly) become tainted by the dominant worldview in the process of their acquiring the dominant methods of image making (1991:60). He spells out the dilemma: "Learning mainstream means of expression fits the liberal/social reformist notion that society can accommodate everyone's voice within existing structures."

This is no news to those of us who are invested in the production of counterhegemonic representations. Ruby's discussion of the risks of a depoliticized celebration of difference—even if it would be enunciated from previously marginalized sites—that would easily be co-opted by the still dominant institutions of representation could present an illuminating balance to Nichols's consideration of an "ethnotopia" in a critical rethinking about the boundaries of ethnographic versus "subject-generated" representations of difference. I say "could" because his sobering cynicism about the unquestioned "authenticity" of self-representation gives short shrift to the politically subversive, counterhegemonic, and often visionary accomplishments and possibilities of those self-willed acts of representation by feminists, people of color, lesbians and gays, the poor. A glaring way in which he reduces and silences these voices is his problematic categorization of mainstream, Hollywood-generated distortions of African Americans—he cites "the so-called blaxploitation films like *Super Fly* or the television series, 'I, Spy' "—as a "variety of 'minority' imagemaking" along with those invested in "the creation of a cinematic form that allows minorities to express uniquely their cultural identity." While his warning of how "diversity is mainstreamed" is well taken, it falls short because he does not adequately distinguish the externally imposed distortions from the self-willed articulations and therefore prematurely condemns all attempts at self-representation to a destiny of co-optation —all of this while he positions himself throughout his essay as an able assessor of cultural authenticity and its representation.

Nichols's affirmative call for the consideration of multicultural, diasporic articulations and Ruby's critical assessment of the "taken-for-granted" authenticity and authority of such cultural productions mark encouraging movements in ethnographic discourse. While both essays attempt to push the limits of ethnographic representation, neither author adequately interrogates the taken-for-granted arrangements of who gets to observe—even if it be a Chinese American film rather than a Chinese American person—evaluate, and pass judgment on whom. Here, I want to suggest yet another terrain of cultural production that could be revealing about how difference is represented and also complicate the binary of ethnographic films and "films by the Other." I am thinking of U.S. popular culture/mainstream media/advertisements. Maybe the "we" would know more about its shared ways and assumptions through a studying not of *them*, over *there* or even back here, but through a critical, vigilant attention to the manner in which their growing presence here provokes doubts, anxieties, and reconfigurations of who "we" are and should be.

The following critical exploration of a certain figuring of difference through the Asian female body does not fall neatly into ethnographic discourse or self-representation—even though I hope that it can be illuminating for both discursive terrains. I look at three recent representations of the Asian woman in U.S. cinema: *Thousand Pieces of Gold, Come See the Paradise*, and *The Year of the Dragon*. I am primarily interested in deciphering the stories they tell about racial, gendered difference as it is inscribed on an Asian female body and ultimately apprehended by white masculinity. Much of this essay will read as exegetical—but, with a difference—as I attempt both to explicate my own admittedly situated and selective viewing of the three films *and* to look at the white, masculine gaze that they serve to uphold. Therefore, I will begin by presenting my own critical retelling of each filmic narrative. My analysis focuses on their constructing a familiar and reassuring version of national and masculine identity in an increasingly fluid and heterogeneous era of (1) growing racial diversity through continuing immigration from Asia and Latin America, of (2) the threats to masculinity posed by the demands of feminism within the United States, and of (3) the declining status of U.S. hegemony—which has been cast as invariably WASP and masculine—in the global scene in terms of both economics and geopolitics. All of these tensions are reduced to the manageable realm of interracial, heterosexual romance between white male and Asian/American female. Racial conflict and sexual domination are reconstructed as complementary difference. The familiar plot of the romance that introduces barriers—here multiplied and exacerbated by racism, class differences, languages—yet ends ultimately in the lovers' (re)union casts these multiple plots and actors into the economy of white male desire, thus displacing the other scenes of racist, sexist domination, exclusion, exploitation, and harassment in these films.

The American cinematic representation of the Asian female bears traces of a long and complex genealogy of orientalist discourse in the patriarchal Western psyche. Here, I want to refer to two works on European orientalism(s) that could be illuminating to my subsequent analysis of the three films. In an edifying essay on the orientalism of European paintings entitled, "The Salon's Seraglio," Rana Kabanni writes that the oriental woman was constituted in the imaginary of the West as aesthetically pleasing, sexually willing, and speechless. Yet as the dark and primitive Other, who lacked subjectivity and existed beyond the terms of Victorian morality, her body was available without emotional or economic demands. Kabanni goes on to discuss how the desiring of oriental female bodies in these paintings was accompanied by establishing a rigid and conflictual difference between these female subjects and their oriental male counterparts.

If the women of the Orient were exotic and enticing, the men were "almost always portrayed as predatory figures . . . as ugly or loathsome." In contrast to the gender hierarchy of male/female in the West, the gender non-equivalence of the East was reversed, positioning the oriental female as aesthetically superior to the oriental male. The sense of complementarity in the Western conception of sexual difference is then impossible between the oriental male and the oriental female, and the neat dyad of man/woman is uncoupled for *these others*:

> This leaves the (Oriental) woman *free for the abduction of the viewer's gaze* since she is not attached within the painting, being mismatched with a male who is her obvious inferior. Thus, *she must desire to be saved* from her fate in some way. By such projection, the European fantasized about the Eastern woman's emotional dependency on him. (1986:79, emphasis mine)

If the Eastern woman desired to be liberated into the arms of the Western male, these paintings represented the Eastern male as both impeding that union *and* facilitating her availability:

> The villainy of Oriental men is aggravated by the fact that they are portrayed as *traders in female bodies*. They are *the cruel captors who had women in their avaricious grasp*, who use them as chattels, as trading-goods, with little reverence for them as human beings. This idea was highly important in distinguishing between *the barbarity of the Eastern male and the civilized behavior of the Western male*. One tied women up and sold them at slave auctions; the other revered them and placed them on pedestals. The European (and the Englishman in particular) cherished *the notion of his added gentlemanliness among savages. It was one way of convincing himself that he was born to rule over them.* As Mark Girouard has suggested, the sources of imperialism and the sources of the Victorian code of the gentleman were so intertwined that they were often indistinguishable from each other; and affected the way the Empire was run. (1986:79, emphasis mine)

Such visual representation of the Orient and its inhabitants was mirrored in the contemporary narrative representations as well. In her critical examination of the heterogeneous orientalisms of eighteenth- and nineteenth-century French and British literatures, Lisa Lowe observes a similar stereotyping of the Orient in terms of an excessive male tyranny and female licentiousness. The travel narratives too were filled with images of oriental men who enslaved women and oriental women who were highly sexualized. Lowe sees the focus on oriental misogyny by Jean Dumont, one French writer of such travel narratives, as "a displacement of European misogyny which disguises its European character by figuring women's subjugation in an oriental context" (Lowe 1992:44). The contradictory pressures of the oriental male's measures of confinement and the sexual abandonment of the oriental female are cast as an internal and preexisting conflict, thus setting the stage for the colonial struggle between the oriental male and the occidental male over both territory and female sexuality.[1]

My pointing to Kabanni's essay on orientalist paintings and Lowe's book on orientalist literatures is meant to reveal how the desiring of oriental female bodies and the construction of the Asian woman in Western art and literature have been effected through multilayered ideological processes. Not only is the racially and sexually other body (re)presented as exotic object to be desired, but that colonial, patriarchal desire is justified and encouraged by an imaginary construction of *her desire* as complementary with it. However, a seeming contradiction is glossed over in this match—how oriental men are simultaneously "cruel captors who hold women in their avaricious grasp" and "traders in female bodies." The first sets them up as in opposition to Western male desire while the second indicts them as actively complicit in the objectification and exchange of oriental female bodies. This unexamined contradiction serves to posit the Western male's moral superiority and to justify his inevitable victory through his virility. The struggle over indigenous female bodies is then metonymical of the struggle for geopolitical territory that is the goal of imperialist domination. Lisa Lowe points to "an established association of the oriental with the feminine erotic."[2] This colonizing, masculinist gaze constructs both territory and 'native woman' as erotically enticing and passively available. Casting territorial struggle in terms of an exotic/erotic encounter with the Eastern female conceals and justifies the realities of forced penetration, territorial dispossession, and colonial domination.

These arbitrarily constructed and contradictory thematics—disseminated in another era and in reference to another geopolitical context—are echoed in several recent cinematic representations of the Asian/Asian American woman[3] in the United States Cinema as signifying practice that operates within a vastly different set of economic, historical, and psychological considerations than do the orientalist paintings that Kabanni describes or the orientalist literatures that Lowe analyzes. I mean in no way to equate the two instances of representation. Neither do I intend to argue for a historical continuity from one ideological construction to the latter.[4] While there are numerous differences, there are ideological and representational strands that are present in both that refute the developmental narrative of a singular history that has departed from a racist colonial past to a more enlightened postcolonial multiculturalism. Positing these two instances alongside and against each other is my attempt then at a Foucaultian genealogical critique of the category of the Asian woman in the shifting discourses of the West.[5]

Here, I must clarify that the Asian woman as I will be discussing *her* in this essay is a representation that is distinguished—but not separated— from Asian women as historical subjects and their heterogeneous experiences. Furthermore, "Asian (American) women" is itself an unstable identity category that runs the risk of displacing or disguising national, ethnic, cultural, and geographical specificities. My aim here is not to indict such representations as simply negative or inaccurate to an-other realness that could be confidently articulated otherwise—I do not profess to know/tell what she is thinking about *him* let alone herself. Rather, I venture a critical examination of how *he* has been thinking about her, of how such ideological constructions of racially and sexually other bodies and identities are revealing of the racially and sexually familiar masculine self of Western discourse. By interrogating it on its own terms, I seek to reveal the cracks, fissures, and contradictions of the seeming coherence, certainty, and stability of white male identity as it is articulated against the Asian female body.

There have been some critical discussions of the media stereotypes of the Asian/American woman by Asian American women. There is the video documentary *Slaying the Dragon* and an essay in *Making Waves: An Anthology of Writings By and About Asian American Women* by Japanese American filmmaker Renee E. Tajima entitled, "Lotus Blossoms Don't Bleed: Images of Asian Women." In the essay, she identifies two dominant stereotypes of the Asian woman that have remained more or less constant in the sixty-year history of her representation in U.S. cinema:

> There are two basic types: the Lotus Blossom baby (a.k.a. China Doll, Geisha Girl, shy Polynesian beauty), and the Dragon Lady (Fu Manchu's various female relations, prostitutes, devious madams). There is little in between, although experts may differ as to whether Suzie Wong belongs to the race-blind "hooker with a heart of gold" category or deserves one all her own.[6]

These two seemingly contradictory stereotypes were mobilized to posit the Asian woman's passive welcoming of the American male on the one hand and to reinforce the sexual perversity and moral depravity of Asians in general. Asian men, in turn, were painted as tyrannical and lecherous, cruel in their treatment of their women while lusting after the Euro-American woman. Such characterizations of the Asian male as an enemy rival—albeit inferior in both physique and ethics—to the white male's visions of sexual and territorial conquest, together with the Lotus Blossom/Dragon Lady nexus, justified and affirmed U.S. motives of imperialism in Asia. These cinematic distortions have been naturalized by the representations of Asians as largely interchangeable—a cinematic articulation of the age-old "All Orientals Look Alike." The genericization of Asian identities has been reinforced by the commonality of 'non-language' that these Asian female characters embody. Tajima defines this 'non-language' as "uninterpretable chattering, pidgin English, giggling, or silence." The Asian woman, thus caught in the filmic gaze of Hollywood image making, possesses no means of asserting her specificity.

Given this cinematic inheritance of (mis)representation, the Asian female protagonists of the three films—*The Year of the Dragon, Come See the Paradise,* and A *Thousand Pieces of Gold*—are noteworthy on several points. First, I set them apart from other, earlier representations because of the placement of the Asian woman not in Asia but within the nation-state borders of the United States.[7] The three films, seen together, provide a certain historical mapping of the Asian American experience. *Thousand Pieces of Gold* is set in the period of early Chinese immigration to the United States in the nineteenth century. *Come See the Paradise* tackles the internment of Japanese Americans during World War II. *The Year of the Dragon* is set in an established, even affluent Chinatown in the 1980s. More significantly, the protagonists *appear* to depart from the old stereotype of Asian women as passive and silent or evil and scheming. They are a new prototype of the Asian female—spirited, proud, resourceful. Tracy Tzu in *The Year of the Dragon* is a career-oriented, articulate television news reporter. She is certainly modeled after Connie Chung, that most visible Asian/American woman in recent public consciousness. Lily in *Come See the Paradise* is a young nisei working woman who defies her parents to elope with the white protagonist. She is also the narrator of the film. Lastly, Lalu Nathoy, or Polly Bemis, is a gutsy pioneer woman. She fights off lascivious white males, defies her indenture servitude to Hong King, chooses to have a non-marital sexual relation with another Chinese man, and establishes her own laundry business. While their bodies and faces may evoke the exotic and unfamiliar, the personal narratives of these women invoke the familiar elements of socioeconomic mobility, forbidden love, entrepreneurial know-how, and heterosexual romance.

Given the historical, geographical, and ethnic diversity of the films, it is significant that all three narratives revolve centrally around an interracial sexual relationship between a white male and an Asian female. I examine how these films portray the Asian woman through the interaction of her sexuality with her ethnic identity and white masculinity, ultimately reaffirming the primacy of the white male over both the Asian woman and the Asian males of her community. The Asian female character in each of these films comes into comprehensibility precisely through her romantic/sexual liaison with a white male protagonist. As his chosen object of desire—all three males, Charlie Bemis, Jack McGurn, and Stanley White are presented as self-assured, confident men who could have choice in such matters—the Asian woman is rescued from the perpetual facelessness and otherness that mark the other Asian bodies in the films, male and female. She becomes a subject in both senses of the word: she is granted (relative) subjectivity through her (understandable) desire for the white male hero but this is crucially contingent upon whether and how she is subjected to *his* desire.

Thousand Pieces of Gold in its prior manifestation was a historical novel written by Ruthanne Lum McCunn. It is based on the life of Lalu Nathoy (later anglicized to Polly Bemis),[8] a Chinese immigrant woman in the nineteenth century. The filmic interpretation was produced by Kenji Yamamoto, a Japanese American man, and directed by Nancy Kelly, a Euro-American feminist filmmaker. It was produced through the American Playhouse and is periodically aired on PBS as the token Asian American cultural text, thus marking it as a product of the new mainstreamed multiculturalism. Its categorization by many as an authentic and representative artifact of the Asian American experience is noteworthy in illustrating that works considered as "self-generated representation" are not necessarily liberatory, counterhegemonic, or even politically unproblematic. I say more about this at a later point in the essay.

Rather than give an account of the film myself, I *defer* instead to its own alluring advertisement. Such frozen instances of self-promotion are significant because they refer directly to the political economy of film production, distribution, and possible viewership;[9] they demonstrate the terms of social appeal and financial viability of the film. On the back of the video release of the film, there is this short description of the film:

> DENNIS DUN ("The Last Emperor," "Big Trouble in Little China") stars with ROSALIND CHAO ("White Ghost") in this *incredible—and true —* story of a young Chinese woman *torn from her homeland* and forced to survive in the frontier land of America.
>
> An *innocent woman* in an Idaho mining town's *thriving bordello*, Lalu (Rosalind Chao) rebels and pays a terrible price for her fight against racism and sexism. Wagered as a piece of property, Lalu is finally handed over to her new owner Charlie (CHRIS COOPER "Guilty by Suspicion," "City of Hope") who *opens the door to a whole new life* for Lalu—*and himself.* (emphasis mine)

Dennis Dun, who plays Polly's Chinese male love interest, Jim, gets top billing in the first paragraph, but his name and character completely drop out in the second paragraph that sets up the drama of the film's narrative. While it may sound titillating to some, there is no "thriving bordello" in the film. There is a small saloon and Polly is the main and only attraction. That the film will be about the relationship between Polly and Charlie is firmly established and promised by the photographic image on the front of the video cover: the towering image of a naked Charlie (Chris Cooper) is holding an implicitly naked Polly (Rosalind Chao).[10] He is upright and she is prone, their eyes fixed on each other in a passionate embrace. Between their faces is text that reads, "A TESTAMENT TO THE STRENGTH OF THE HUMAN SPIRIT"—racial and sexual differences apparent on the bodies of this white male and Asian female are collapsed into a unifying humanness. It is important to note that this embrace never appears in the film.[11] The only implicitly nude sex scenes in the film take place between Polly and Hong King—following a rape—and a more consensual encounter between Lalu and Jim. Beneath this image on the video cover is another still from the film: a diminutive Jim on horseback with a slightly sinister smile leading a sullen-faced Polly who trails behind him, fully clothed in Chinese dress. This layered image establishes the sexual potency of the white male and highlights the romantic embrace he offers the Asian female by setting it in unequal contrast to the sexual subordination that is her unhappy fate with the Asian male counterpart. The narrative is already thus visualized for the prospective viewer.

How can a story be both "incredible" and "true"? Certainly many of the reviewers for *Thousand Pieces of Gold* assumed both its historical accuracy and by extension its representativeness of the Chinese/American experience. Here, I think that it becomes crucial to my analysis of the cinematic fixation upon the Asian/American female body to point out the distortions that would keep an arbitrary and controlled representation from being collapsed with a 'real' Asian/American woman. While Ruthanne Lum McCunn laboriously researched the material for the book, it is a constructed account of the real-life story of Lalu Nathoy, containing several fictional aspects. Even though it claims a certain biographical and historical authenticity, the cinematic interpretation differs significantly from the already fabricated text. While the novel spans the entire life of Lalu Nathoy until her death in 1933, Yamamoto and Kelley's chosen end to Polly Bemis's "film life" focuses on various male struggles—relinquishments and victories among Jim, Charlie, Hong King, and the white male miners—over her body and ends with her reconciliation with Charlie.

Significantly, in addition to elaborating on the romance of Charlie and Polly, the film greatly emphasizes the misogyny of Chinese men. What sets up a long chain of her mistreatment at the hands of Chinese men is the early scene in which Polly's father deliberately sells her—and his patriarchal authority—to another Chinese male. The novel is much more ambiguous about whether her removal from her family was a kidnapping or a cold economic exchange. Also, the film is much more explicit in portraying her rape and mistreatment by the lascivious Hong King. Finally, whereas the novel only hints at romantic stirrings between Lalu and Jim, the film depicts them in a full-scale sexual relationship (who said Asian men and women are never portrayed having sex?). Their affair ends when Jim returns to find her living with Charlie. Although the audience knows that this is a purely platonic arrangement at this point, this "discovery" provokes such jealous resentment in Jim that he literally turns around and walks away from Lalu and the movie without saying a word. That a cinematic interpretation of "this incredible—and true—story of a young Chinese woman" departs so remarkably from a linear birth to death novelistic account and focuses almost exclusively on Polly's sexual relationships with men —Chinese and Euro-American[12]—provokes a critical consideration of the limits and possibilities of this narrative genre and how it serves to affirm the dominant economy of desire with its certain fixation upon Asian female sexuality.

While the three male characters are in competition over Polly's sexuality, they are not completely uncooperative with each other. After all, it is Jim who purchases Polly from the kidnappers in Chinatown, San Francisco, and delivers her to Hong King. Even though he is fully aware of Hong King's plans for Polly, he carries out his contract and accepts his payment. Charlie owns the saloon that Hong King leases as a place of business. They have a friendly relationship. One of the clearest instances of this masculine bonding over the body of the Asian woman can be seen in the scene of Lalu's arrival at Warren's Diggens. When Jim and Lalu ride into town, the camera shows a crowd of white men gazing at Lalu, thus emphasizing early on her "to-be-looked-at-ness." The camera's gaze eventually rests on the face of Charlie, who has been watching and assessing Polly from the saloon. He tells Hong King who is seated next to him: "Boy, you're a lucky man." Charlie then gives Jim an affirmative pat on the shoulder for his good delivery. The established intimacy of the three men will be tested by the ensuing competition among them over the sexual-romantic possession of Lalu/Polly.[13] Her body both unites these men and provides the field of their power struggles.

The three male characters are, however, fairly distinguished from each other in their sense of ethics and degree of masculine strength. It is worth noting how the varying claims that Hong King and Jim make to Lalu's sexuality are cast in terms of race-ethnicity and class. When Jim returns for the first time after leaving Polly in town, she must reassure him by telling him that she has "not gone with ghosts," only Hong King. He finds this acceptable enough and proceeds to offer to buy her from Hong King with his life savings. Hong King quotes a price and then "allows" Jim to sleep with Polly. He spies on their sexual encounter, but is careful not to disrupt them. However, he decides to punish Polly later on. Even though he has promised her to Jim, his jealous resentment aroused by his perverse voyeurism motivates him to hold a lottery for the white male miners: the winner can have Polly "show him the pleasures of the East." When Jim returns once again with the money and discovers Polly living with Charlie, he is possessed by such quiet anger that he leaves without a word. If Hong King would will Polly to sleep with white men rather than another Chinese male, who is his socioeconomic subordinate, Jim is willing to accept her rape at the hands of Hong King so long as she remains untouched by white males. Both situations reiterate the long-established, contradictory stereotype that Chinese—and by extension Asian—males are so blindly territorial about their woman that even though they may actively facilitate the circulation of her body, they are unable to bear the thought of her sexual involvement with other men.

In contrast to the utter greed and remorselessness of Hong King and the utter helplessness of Jim in defending Lalu from the white miners, Charlie is able and willing to express his disapproval about her enslavement/mistreatment and assists her on occasion. However, for much of the film, Charlie is clearly ambivalent and often does not intervene on her behalf. On occasion, he willingly participates in the sexual harassment of Polly along with the other miners. One notable scene—from which derives the advertisement still for the film's theatrical run—involves the indistinguishable miners, each taking turns forcing Polly to dance with them. Disgruntled after a loss to Hong King in a card game, Charlie too takes his turn with Polly. It is significant that a snapshot of this coercive situation is taken out of context and deployed as a romantic embrace to attract viewers to go see this film. On the one hand, it is inappropriate and misleading;

on the other, it is reflective of Charlie's moral and sexual ambivalence toward Polly. When Lalu moves out of his house to be a manager at a local boarding house, Charlie and Hong King commiserate over a bottle of whiskey. Lastly, when the Chinese are being driven out of town at the end of the film, Charlie helps Hong King to escape without harm.

Even though she has been thus constructed as the field of struggle and the sexual prize for these three men, the film ends with Polly having to make a difficult decision between staying in an obviously anti-Asian town with Charlie or joining the Chinese men who are being driven out. Initially, she refuses the offers of Charlie and chooses to leave and eventually make her way back to China. When Li Dick, the old and wise herbalist, advises her to drink from the "River of Forgetfulness" and begin a new life in the United States, she abruptly turns her horse around and heads back toward Charlie. She emerges on horseback from the crowd of faceless Chinese men who are leaving on foot; this scene splendidly visualizes her individualization from racial-ethnic anonymity and her exceptional incorporation amid Chinese exclusion as a climactic moment of personal agency. This return is the end of her journey; yet, another narrative also demands closure.

Charlie's story frames Polly's story as he is *the one* "who opens the door to a whole new life for Lalu—and himself."[14] It is he who must resolve his ambivalence toward Polly: is she the racial Other/sexual Object deserving of mistreatment, or a possible romantic partner worthy of his protection? As much as Polly is the one who decides to stay behind in Warrens, her options are ultimately dictated by how Charlie Bemis will respond to this question. The final shot of the film shows a pastoral landscape with text that informs us that Charlie and Polly settled down to a life along the "River of No Return." While I agree that their isolation from both the Chinese and the white community does not fit neatly into the trajectory of assimilation into the dominant culture,[15] the ending nevertheless situates them in the tradition of rugged individualism and pioneer life that is one of the central American cultural myths. In the end, I read *Thousand Pieces of Gold* as the story of Charlie's redemption from a life of alcohol, prostitutes, and moral ambivalence. Such a simple happy finale is possible only by disregarding the exclusion, discrimination, and harassment suffered by Chinese/Americans in the nineteenth century. The nostalgic return to the wild, pristine frontier represented in the closing shot of a female figure—presumably Polly Bemis—standing on the shores of a glistening Salmon River allows a revisioning of U.S. history that not only incorporates but *relies upon* the dark, female body to redeem the American myth of manifest destiny and its white male actors.

Alan Parker is credited with both directing and writing *Come See the Paradise*.[16] Here, I quote the video cover synopsis of the film:

> *Come See The Paradise* is *a deeply touching love story* set against *the backdrop* of a dramatic and controversial period in American history. It

follows the romance and eventual marriage of Jack McGurn (Dennis Quaid), a *hot-blooded Irish-American*, and *a beautiful Japanese-American*, Lily Kawamura (Tamlyn Tomita), at the outset of World War II. The *clash of cultures*, at once painful for the two lovers, becomes insurmountable after the Japanese bomb Pearl Harbor. Lily and the Kawamuras are relocated to a bleak, outdoor internment camp in California. Jack is drafted into the Army, powerless to help the woman he loves . . . abandoning all hope of ever winning her family's approval. This *gorgeously photographed* film is brought faithfully to the screen by Alan Parker, the director of *Mississippi Burning* and *Midnight Express*. (emphasis mine)

In an interview published upon the theatrical release of the film, Parker openly admitted that he did not choose the historical setting to educate or inform the audience about the internment of Japanese Americans during World War II. Rather, he chose it as an interesting backdrop for a compelling story of star-crossed romance.[17] Not coincidentally, that is what I find most problematic and dangerous about this film: while it focuses greatly on this horrific historical event, and is indeed quite critical of it, the film nevertheless renders it as secondary if not merely spectacular to the romantic fable, using it to propel plot-movement but completely displacing its many significances in the happy ending.

Come See the Paradise is constructed as a retrospective first-person narrative by its nisei female protagonist Lily to her biracial daughter. It opens with a shot of the two walking down an unidentifiable country road singing a song in Japanese. As Polly's story ends with Charlie, the story Lily tells begins not with her own beginning but in "Brooklyn, New York 1936" with Jack McGurn, a well-read labor activist for the Film Projectionists' Union. In fact, much of Lily's narration is told from Jack's perspective. When he is implicated in the firebombing of a theater, Jack is forced to leave town and heads toward California. This westward movement marks the beginning of his renewal and redemption in the film.

The film then shifts to "Little Tokyo, Los Angeles" to a social function replete with a band, a Japanese American crooner, and people dancing in period costume. We meet the Kawamuras, a large family of eight. The nisei children are represented from the beginning as acculturated. Their contrast to the Japanese Japanese guests further emphasizes just how 'American' they are. The first son Charlie is a baseball fanatic and the second son Harry is a movie actor who is a small celebrity in the community even though, as someone says in the film, he can only play "Chinese houseboys." Somebody else says of the oldest daughter Lily that "she only speaks Japanese at meal times." As one reviewer astutely observed: "Parker is careful to make the Kawamura's as American as possible (Lily's two older brothers are 'hepcats'). It's as if he's afraid anything Old World (sic) would alienate us."[18] The film establishes an assimilationist liberalism that seems to tell the audience that Japanese Americans are really like or dearly aspire to emulate the dominant WASP culture.

This liberalism is undercut by the construction of the father character in ways that dearly echo the contradictory representation of 'oriental' males in my earlier discussion. Unlike a benevolent 'American' father, Mr. Kawamura is portrayed early on as an insensitive tyrant who cares only about his gambling. He has already amassed a large debt and promises Lily to an older widower to assist the family economically. Their exchange indeed takes place in the midst of a card game and the casualness and certainty with which it is enacted serve to reinforce Western impressions of Asian patriarchal tyranny.

The Kawamuras run a Japanese movie house that shows films imported from the homeland. When the alcoholic projectionist, Mr. Ogata, commits suicide, Jack McGurn is hired as the new film projectionist. This is a suggestive reversal of the economic relations and representational authority between a white male and a Japanese male, but such a socioeconomic arrangement was highly unlikely in the racist and segregationist mood of the period. Jack is employed by Mr. Kawamura and he is in no position to actively decipher and re-present the Japanese others; rather than film them as another intercultural traveler would, he can only project films that have been constructed elsewhere and imported to the United States.

Jack soon develops a friendly relationship with Charlie. There is an interesting sexual tinge to their interactions. For example, when Charlie is acquainting Jack with the operation, they have this exchange:

Charlie: "The projectors are very old. So you have to treat them like a woman."

Jack: "With love?"

Charlie: "No, with patience."

However, their masculinities are in no way commensurate. Shortly thereafter, there is a scene with a reversal of the dominant direction of acculturation; rather than an alien other immigrating into a familiar all-American space, a white male enters and adapts to a racial-ethnic community. Jack even learns to sing in Japanese from his work. In the next scene, Jack performs a masquerade dance with Charlie in the theater lobby in which Charlie takes on the role of a shy Japanese maiden to Jack's samurai. Even while the Japanese male may occupy a fraternal relation to the white male in their shared objectification of women, ultimately, if one needs to be feminized to enact sexual difference, it will have to be the Japanese male. Conversely, the white male protagonist never stops being man, even if that fixity may require the demasculinizing of the other man of his new environment. Later, when Jack shows an interest in his sister Lily, Charlie attempts to dissuade him by reminding him: "She's *Japanese*, Jack. We'll find you a nice *American* girl." Again, there is an unequal but consensual cooperation between white man and Asian man in the negotiation of sexual difference and the circulation of woman. But here, it is ironically an acculturated Japanese/American male that espouses a racial-ethnic essentialism that reifies a clear distinction between Japanese and American.

Unswayed by this counteroffer, Jack begins to pursue Lily, and the film then traces the development of their romantic relationship. In one of their initial encounters, Lily gives Jack a history lesson in anti-Japanese legislation and discrimination, again marking out their racial differences. When Mr. Kawamura learns of their affair, Jack is fired and Lily is forbidden to see her white male lover. While Mr. Kawamura is casually willing to offer Lily to a gambling partner, he is possessive and obstructs the way of the white male suitor—demonstrating the contradictory construction of Asian men that I mentioned earlier. When Jack confronts the intransigent Mr. Kawamura, he blurts out in his frustration, "What I can never be . . . not ever . . . is Japanese." Despite his entry and acculturation into a Japanese/American community, this statement asserts a racial-ethnic essence that cannot ultimately be attained. Simultaneously, it is an ironic reversal of the power dynamics of the dominant model of assimilation in which a WASP, English-fluent, bourgeoisie grants acceptance to a transformed racial-ethnic immigrant Other. I do not see this reversal as a critique of the dominant pressures of assimilation but as positing the impossibility of transcending clear and fixed demarcations of race and ethnicity. For if Jack can say he can never be Japanese, the flip side of that essentialist declaration would be that what Mr. Kawamura can never be . . . never . . . is American, which was the foundational logic of Japanese/American internment.

Against the specter of such impossibility, Lily and Jack decide to elope, but, as Lily tells her daughter, due to the anti-miscegenation laws in the state of California at the time, they go to Seattle and begin a new life there. Immediately after the ceremony, the newlyweds happen upon another, almost entirely white wedding celebration. This festive scene replete with a band and numerous guests dancing and frolicking is contrasted to both the loneliness and isolation of their own illegal/forbidden marriage and the earlier opening party in Little Tokyo. Lily proceeds to dance with a series of white male guests, showing her entrance into the dominant white society and the greater tolerance of these partygoers for this Asian female body than the exclusivity of the Japanese/American community, especially the intransigence of Mr. Kawamura. Jack takes a job working at the docks while Lily makes herself into the picture of domesticity. With the birth of their daughter, they comprise the ideal American nuclear family. However, Jack's involvement as a labor activist increasingly interferes with their marital bliss. When Lily voices her opinions to Jack ending with "You can't spit against Heaven," he replies, "Don't give me that Japanese shit."

Lily then decides to return to her natal family with her biracial daughter. Even though in the voice-over narration, Lily states that she does not know what motivated her to leave, it is fairly evident that the motivation is Jack's jarring reminder of her inescapable difference together with the degrading of her ethnicity. Mother and daughter arrive in Los Angeles to find that Mr. Kawamura along with many issei men has been arrested for possible espionage. Just at the moment of her return to her family and the Japanese American family, the social costs of her ethnic difference manifest themselves in a most glaring manner. She resumes her job at the costume shop, but this time she has to take charge as Mr. Matsui too has been taken away.

Shortly thereafter, Jack appears at the shop; he too "returns" to Little Tokyo (not) coincidentally after all the forbidding patriarchs have been forcibly removed. After a passionate reunion in the back room of the shop, Jack tells Lily, "You are braver than anyone that I ever knew. *You have everything that I never had.*" While this statement seems to admit of a lack on his part, I see it more as establishing their complementarity, for the next scene shows a family gathering for Christmas in which Jack appears to fill the absence of Mr. Kawamura. It is a picture of interracial harmony and cross-cultural fluidity. The Kawamuras dance and sing period songs in English. When prodded to sing himself, Jack chooses a sad Japanese ballad.

Come See the Paradise does attempt to cast the Japanese bashing after the bombing of Pearl Harbor as unjust and hysterical. When Franklin Roosevelt signed Executive Order #9066, the U.S. government and military undertook the internment of those of Japanese descent living on the West Coast. The film does point to the human costs of the internment. As the Kawamuras prepare to leave, they must burn their letters and books in Japanese and sell their belongings at low prices. The film also portrays the gradual displacement of the Japanese/American male characters. Mr. Kawamura slowly loses his sanity and dies a lonely death in the camps. Charlie, who answers "no" to two loyalty oath questions, is relocated to Tule Lake and later chooses repatriation to Japan. The only other distinguished Japanese male, Henry the second son, decides to serve the U.S. military and dies in combat.

In the end, the reconstituted family contains the Kawamura women and Jack, who literally replaces the Japanese males. Although all of these characters and plots are significant, especially given the historical context, the film never attends to their political complexities in a meaningful manner. Rather, the film ends with the happy reunification of Jack, Lily, and their daughter. One reconstituted family is celebrated, displacing the ruptures in Japanese American family structure as a result of the internment. Thus, an atrocious episode in U.S. history—full of the ugliness and terror of human suffering, mass imprisonment, and near total disempowerment—is rendered by Alan Parker as dramatic backdrop to a more reassuring narrative of interracial romance and a multicultural picture of the American nuclear family.

The Year of the Dragon begins with a careful disclaimer that the film does not represent any real Asian American persons or situations.[19] Based on Robert Daley's novel, *Year of the Dragon*, the screenplay was written by Michael Cimino and Oliver Stone—two image makers arguably most responsible for the Vietnam War genre—and reflects perhaps the most unabashedly distorted depiction of Asian Americans. The movie opens with a Chinese New Year's Parade, focusing on the Dragon Dance. Shortly thereafter, gang warfare breaks out, disrupting this cultural celebration. During the mayhem, a community patriarch is assassinated by a Chinese youth.

We are first introduced to Tracy Tzu as she is covering the funeral procession of this slain leader, Jackie Wong. She is shown interviewing a white police officer who sits perched on a horse. Even while she is the interrogator, she must speak up to him as he speaks down to her due to their physical positioning to each other. Meanwhile, the camera shifts toward the face of another white male whose assessing gaze focuses knowingly on Tzu. We soon learn that he is Stanley White, a New York city cop who has just been promoted to be the new head of the Chinatown precinct replacing the officer on the horse.

One of White's first actions as a precinct head is to invade a meeting of the Chinese community leaders. When they remind him of the historical collusion of the police department and the Chinatown leadership, White declares in the language of another invasion: "new marshal in town—new marshal means new rules." When the Chinese leaders make an appeal to traditions thousands of years old, he reminds them: "This is America you're living in and it's 200 years old." The next scene shows Stanley White at a police department meeting. He articulates his theory of how the Chinese are poised to take over New York—yet another articulation of the "yellow horde." Their first target is the Italian organized crime syndicate: "The Mafia concept is not even Italian. It's Chinese." This positioning of racial invasion against white ethnicity is especially telling in that we learn that despite his unsubtle surname, White himself is not an Anglo-Saxon Protestant but Polish.

The earlier, unevenly positioned conversation between Tzu and the police officer on horseback is reenacted in a later scene between White and his wife. She sits on the floor of their home attempting to fix a kitchen sink. Stanley sits on a chair addressing her from a higher stance. A seemingly tough and independent woman, she is almost a stereotypical picture of the liberated woman—brash, sassy, physically strong, complete with wrench in hand. Telling him that he's "breaking her balls," she is clearly shown as not the least bit hesitant about challenging his masculinity. They then proceed to have an argument about paternity, alluding to his sexual impotence.

Following this challenge to his masculinity, a later scene finds White in a meeting with Tracy Tzu at a Chinese restaurant. The sarcastic banter signals that theirs will be a classic love-hate relationship. A Chinese American, born and raised in the Bay Area, Tzu demonstrates herself to be well acculturated—"I like Italian food better (than Chinese food)." She also shows a good grasp of her own family history and how it has been affected by racist exclusion laws and economic exploitation. Both her grandfather and great-grandfather worked on the construction of the transcontinental railroad but returned to China because they were discouraged from staying on permanently. Rather than being enlightened, White demonstrates himself to be already well-informed about Chinese American history. He proceeds to give Tzu a revisionist history lesson on Chinese American exclusion and marginalization. He ends with a resolute critique of the erasure of this history: "No one remembers, that's the problem." Tzu responds to this by telling White that he sounds just like her father; his seeming concern for Chinese American history imbues him with the aura of Chinese patriarch in her eyes.

Having established this connection, White presents himself as a social reformer and proposes that Tzu conduct a series of exposés on Chinatown corruption. Assuming the position of "good father," White enlists Tzu's help in overthrowing the "bad fathers" of Chinatown, those Chinese men of the implied Mafia. Earlier in the conversation, he compliments Tzu on her greater sexual desirability compared to "other journalists." His choice for Tzu to do the exposé is certainly related to her feminine appeal; but, as he points out later, the greatest motivating factor is her racial-ethnic identity and the authenticity it guarantees: "If it's some white broad, they would say it's racism. With you, it looks like it's in the up and up." Stanley White is knowledgeable about the codes of authenticity in the multiracial, multicultural era. It is he, not Tzu, who knows the corrupt secrets of the Chinese and wants her only to be his credible voice.

At the end of this conversation, there is a gang attack on the restaurant. While the faceless masses of patrons run amok in terror, White is shown as the only one who would bravely fight back and pursue the attackers. For her part, Tzu has hidden herself in a phone booth. When he finally locates her, she is blabbering and near-hysterical, and it is in this state of terror and disarray that White first kisses her. He is the lone brave hero who rescues and comforts this Chinese woman from the irrational acts of violence and destruction perpetrated by a literally faceless gang of young Chinese men.

Their next meeting has suddenly moved them to her elegantly furnished and almost entirely white penthouse apartment. They continue their love-hate verbal exchange:

> Tzu: The first time I saw you I knew you were cracked and a racist too. Were you in Vietnam?
>
> White: Yeah. Why?
>
> Tzu: I knew it. It ruined you.
>
> White: The first time I saw you I hated your guts. I think that I hated you even before I met you. *I hated you on TV—I hated you in Vietnam.* You know what's destroying this country. It's not booze. It's not drugs. It's TV. It's the media. It's people like you, vampires. I hate the way you make a living by sticking microphones in everyone's faces. I hate the way you lie every night at six o'clock. I hate the way you hide real feelings. I hate

everything you stand for. Most of all, I hate rich kids and I hate this place. So why do I want to fuck you so bad?

Note how his soliloquy moves quickly from racism to an attack on the media and then to a rant on class differences. Like Lily to Jack, Tracy is everything that he is not; her differences are what repel and attract him to her.

It is evident in this conversation that he has already been watching her and has judged her authenticity. His hateful voyeurism is at once revealed and justified since she, as a television news reporter, has already offered herself up to his gaze. That she is a willing performer leads him to suspect her of conscious dissemblance. In her seminal essay on feminist film criticism, "Visual Pleasure and Narrative Cinema,"[20] Laura Mulvey argues for the centrality of sexual difference in both narrative and cinema. Building on the psychoanalytic insight that woman represents lack (of a penis) and therefore poses the threat of castration for the male spectator-subject, she proposes:

> Thus, the woman as icon, displayed for the gaze and enjoyment of men, the active controllers of the look, always threatens to evoke the anxiety it originally signified. The male unconscious has two avenues of escape from this castration anxiety: preoccupation with *the re-enactment of the original trauma (investigating the woman, demystifying her mystery), counterbalanced by the devaluation, punishment or saving of the guilty object;* or else complete disavowal of castration by the substitution of a fetish object or turning the represented figure itself into a fetish so that it becomes reassuring rather than dangerous (hence, overvaluation, the cult of the female star).
>
> This second avenue, fetishistic scopophilia, builds up the physical beauty of the object, transforming it into something satisfying in itself. *The first avenue, voyeurism, on the contrary, has associations with sadism:* Pleasure lies in ascertaining guilt (immediately associated with castration), *asserting control and subjugating the guilty person* through punishment or forgiveness. This sadistic side fits in well with narrative. Sadism demands a story, depends on *making something happen, forcing a change in another person,* a battle of will and strength, victory/defeat, all occurring in a linear time with a beginning and an end. (Mulvey 1975:21–22)

If woman by her sexual difference presents a threat to the male unconscious, Tracy Tzu provokes multiply exacerbated anxieties in Stanley White due to the many other axes of difference that she embodies for him. In his eyes, she is a hostile, foreign country, a lost war, a manipulative social mechanism, and class antagonism. She is so excessive of him and that is "why he wants to fuck her so bad"—to bring her within the terms of his comprehensibility and sexual agency.

However, when he tries to initiate sex, she stops him by claiming that she is tired from having "just spent all afternoon with her boyfriend." He responds to her rejection first with surprise and then indignation. He subjects her to this line of questioning:

White: So, what's his name? Is he rich?

Tzu: You want to know if he's Chinese, right? That's what you want to know. So ask it.

White: Yeah . . . so that's the question.

Tzu: He's white all right. He went to Princeton. His name is Roger and he's a lawyer.

White: Well, I hate lawyers and I wouldn't want to make love to a woman who just got done screwing a lawyer anyway. So does he have a lot of money, this Roger Pumpernickel III?

Tzu: Well, yes and he's not a crackpot racist.

White: Oh yeah. What does he do? Play tennis, golf, go out sailing on a yacht? What's with all these machines here? What are you with AT&T? What do you got everyone in town jumping in and out of bed? . . . I'm gonna go home to a woman who at least acts like a woman. If this Roger's so great, how come he didn't want to marry you. What he didn't want a slant-eyed Roger IV at Princeton?

This barrage reveals how a masculinity along the lines of race and then class is inscribed on the body of this bourgeois Chinese American female body. White is concerned not so much with Tzu but his own identification in relation to the Chinese male, the WASP elite class male, and ultimately the white female.

This anxiety around social identity and sexuality is compensated for by the subsequent purging of Chinatown that White commands. A montage sequence reveals the seamy and illicit depths of Chinatown beneath the surface of orientalist exotica. What is presented are crowds of indistinguishable Chinese in garment sweatshops and restaurant kitchens. In one scene, White literally goes underground to cavernous structures that process some strange meat product amid damp darkness. He proceeds to close down garment sweatshops and restaurants for health violations.

Even when other police officials criticize his ruthless zeal for reform, he remains resolute, arguing, "This is a fucking war. And I'm not going to lose it. Not this one. This is Vietnam all over again. It's all about politics. Nobody wants to win this one. Not all the way. " His efforts are revealed not as selfless social reform but as an act of retribution against another battle waged against another Asian-ethnic group. Not only is he unable to distinguish between Vietnam and Chinatown, New York City, a decade later, but the perceived loss in the Vietnam War is the lens through which he sees Tracy Tzu as well. He tells her: "It's Nam all over again. We lost because *you* were smarter than us." She has become a metonymic figure for the early loss of face of both American masculinity and national identity. Despite this close association and its attendant hostilities that are directed at Tzu, he can express his need for her in the same breath and she lovingly responds. However, he will not be easily rehabilitated by his romantic counterpart. When Tzu tells him that she "loves" him after having sex, White's response is to again assert her alienness: "There's no Chinese word for love." His sadistic desire for Tzu is a harder version of Charlie's and Jack's ambivalence toward Polly and Lily.

To retaliate against White's aggressive reforms, Joey Tai, the new Chinatown leader, orders some young Chinese gang members to rape Tzu. It is the trauma of this experience that finally propels Tzu to tell White the truth about herself—that there is no Roger and that she made the whole thing up. His purging of Chinatown has indirectly effected the purging of Tzu as well. Having solved her mystery and without any anxiety around class positioning thus resolved, the rape of Tzu is the impetus for White to pursue his reform efforts even more zealously. In the end, he coordinates the death of Joey Tai, signifying his superior virility, retribution for the rape of Tzu, and his victory in the war against the corrupt Chinatown leadership. As she has been denuded of her own secret sexuality, Tzu finally decides to conduct the exposé of Chinatown. The last scene of the film returns to yet another scene of a mass gathering in Chinatown. An angry, uncontrollable mob of Chinese attacks White but Tzu saves him. She has chosen to save him this time, from the irrational mob violence of the ethnic community. The reconciled lovers begin to walk away as the credits roll. Romantic reunion brings narrative closure, leaving unanswered the contradictions and questions about the havoc of an ethnic community under siege.

These representations incorporate a seemingly independent, articulate, and some would even argue feminist Asian woman into the familiar boundaries of both the patriarchal and the colonial imaginary. However, the costs of her comprehensibility and social acceptability are hinged on the repudiation of her ethnic community. It is choice between romance, safety, liberation, and voice within the white community and the significantly more backward, more patriarchal, and more oppressive Asian ethnic community. Her sense of individuality and strength already marks her alienation from the ethnic community, which requires her to be passive and submissive to patriarchal rule.

Appearances are deceptive; appearances—to be visible, to be embodied—are sinister precisely by being able to hide, to distract from their often duplicitous, contradictory, fabricated, and ideologically tinged foundations. To varying degrees, all three films *appear* to pose the narrative dilemma, the central conflict as a matter of choice between ethnic loyalty-erasure-oppressive culture and individuation-subjecthood-interracial romance for the Asian woman. Certainly, these female characters are the highlighted objects of the gaze—of the spectator, the camera, and the male protagonist[21]—effected by lingering, isolated close-ups of their faces and nude bodies. Such a reading, even if it may be explicitly critical of that binary, cannot get beyond the pre-given terms of that oppositional logic. Furthermore, it prematurely positions the Asian female as the central protagonist who possesses the agency to both dictate the terms of her own life as well as the cinematic narrative that would purport to be *about* her. Instead, I read the films as *not about her* after all; if you refuse the peaceful dyad of the interracial romance and the closure of that story by the reunion of the lovers, you see that the narrative that frames the Asian woman in all three films is after all *his story*—the transformation of the white male protagonist through Polly, Lily, and Tracy.

While several feminist film theorists have articulated a cogent analysis of the way sexual difference operates within narrative and cinema to dictate the terms of desire and indeed subjectivity, much of these feminist critiques do not account for other differences, like race-ethnicity, nation, and class. My intention in pointing out this lack is not a superficial call for an easy or immediate inclusion of these other lines of social difference. Nor is it meant to suggest that a consideration of race-ethnicity take primacy over the consideration of sexual difference. Rather, I am concerned that the lack of a more heterogeneous analysis limits a full deconstruction of the representation of Asian woman, which is my purpose here. One of the most significant insights that women of color thinker-writers[22] have provided is that of the multiple and mutually implicated nature of our social experiences and critical insights. Several black feminist thinkers have proposed the useful notion of "a system of interlocking race, class and gender oppression"[23] that black women experience simultaneously.

I extend this insight then to my project to deconstruct the above cinematic representations of the Asian woman. In a patriarchal and racist culture, the image of the Asian woman simultaneously signifies sexual difference and racial otherness—not to mention the boundaries of culture, language, and class. She is precisely not what the male protagonist is.[24] Her multiple negativities—an excessive alienness—threatens to unsettle the neat dyad of man and woman.[25] How is this racially other body *to be apprehended* as the familiar woman to the familiar man?

Here, I turn to the critical insights articulated by Teresa de Lauretis in her book, *Alice Doesn't: Feminism, Semiotics, Cinema*. In the chapter entitled "Desire in Narrative, " she borrows the insights of Vladimir Propp's analysis of plot structures to illustrate the recurrence of a male subject who undergoes some passage and transformation in Western discourses.[26] De Lauretis then extends Jurij Lotman's concepts of plot typology and the types of characters that occupy the narrative landscape to conclude:

> In this mythical-textual mechanics, the hero must be male, regardless of the gender of the text-image, because the obstacle, whatever its personification, is morphologically female and indeed, simply, the womb. The implication here is not inconsequential. For if the work of the mythical structuration is to establish distinctions, the primary distinction on which all others depend is not, say life and death, but rather sexual difference. . . . Opposite pairs such as inside/outside, the raw/the cooked, or life/death appear to be merely derivatives of the fundamental opposition between boundary and passage; and if passage may be in either direction,

from inside to outside or vice versa, nonetheless all these terms are predicated on *the single figure of the hero who crosses the boundary and pen-
etrates the other space.* In so doing the hero, the mythical subject, is
constructed as human being and as male; he is the active principle of culture, the establisher of distinction, the creator of differences. (1984:119;
my italics)

Complicating the binary of "the two positions of a sexual difference
thus conceived: male-hero-human, on the side of the subject; and female-
obstacle-boundary-space, on the other" (De Lauretis 1984:119), the Asian
female character also undergoes passage and transformation in the course of
each of the three films. Polly Bemis is brought forcibly to the Idaho town;
but she soon learns to adapt to her new environment, making apple pie and
running a successful laundry service. She eventually manages a boarding
house, tending to its male tenants who had harassed her in the saloon not so
long before. She forces their respect by threatening them with a huge buck
knife, soon earning the honorary status of "not Chinese," even as they are
strategizing about a racist attack on the town's Chinese residents. Lily leaves
the confines of Little Tokyo to start a new life with Jack in Seattle. Her passage from the Japanese enclave to the "real world" is represented when the
newlyweds crash an all-white wedding party and Lily is shown exuberantly
dancing with a series of white men. Tracy Tzu, as an Ivy League educated,
acculturated television news reporter, has already moved out of the dreary,
insidious atmosphere of Chinatown. However, *her story* lacks autonomous
significance; in terms of the romantic plot, her story is significant only insofar as it and she fit into the story of the male protagonist.

Consistent with these paradigms of the working of narrative in
Western discourse, the white male protagonist of each of the films undergoes some type of travel into another space. Each crosses the racial-ethnic
boundaries to enter the Asian enclaves in their separate worlds. This intercultural travel is reminiscent of yet another significant strain of the Western narrative tradition—that of the anthropologist who enters the social
space of the cultural other to observe, decipher, and reveal to those at home
the (exotic) cultural truths of its inhabitants. What is notable is that these
borders exist within the supposedly familiar and reliable borders of the
United States. Although *Thousand Pieces of Gold* is set in a historical era
of severe racial-ethnic segregation, Charlie Bemis easily moves in and out
of the small Chinese settlement at the outskirts of Warrens. He receives
acupuncture from a wise, old Chinese man. He accompanies Lalu to a "Chinese shindig"—a New Year's celebration complete with firecrackers and a
dragon dance; he even speaks a little Chinese. Having been exiled from his
native scene of white-working class New York, Jack McGurn invents a new
identity in the midst of Little Tokyo, Los Angeles, including learning to sing
in Japanese only after a few days. While his biracial daughter, his nisei wife,
and her family are interned in desert camps that imprison them with barbed
wire and armed guards, Jack is able to go in and out. Finally, Stanley White

invades and wreaks havoc on Tracy's posh penthouse apartment as well as New York's Chinatown, crossing boundaries of both class and ethnicity.

I read all three narratives in terms of whether and how each of these white male figures will manage the challenge to their identities that is posed by the racially, and sexually, Other body of the Asian woman. The central question is not how this contact with the feminine exotic/erotic will provoke a rethinking of the masculine familiar. Rather, the question that is negotiated and too simply resolved is this: how does the masculine familiar *apprehend* the differences in these unfamiliar settings while remaining who they are/should be? This metaphoric challenge of maintaining a dominant and unassailable form of white masculinity is especially salient in the challenging historical moment of the late twentieth century and in the United States.

The past few decades have seen the increasing preoccupation with Asian/American bodies within the nation-state borders of the United States. After nearly a century of Asian exclusion, immigration laws were liberalized in 1965, owing to the efforts of the civil rights movement. Since then, 40 percent of all new immigrants to the United States come from Asian countries, resulting in the establishment of distinct Asian-ethnic enclaves as well as increased visibility and socioeconomic mobility for some. This growth has also necessitated new hegemonic strategies of containment and control like the model minority myth. The United States has also been attempting to recuperate from and reconstruct its imperialistic struggle with Asian bodies in the Korean and the Vietnam Wars. Lastly, the decline of U.S. hegemony in the world, experienced most immediately in the unstable domestic economy, has motivated the construction of Japan as the central nemesis. Consequently, there has been a significant rise in anti-Asian sentiments that are increasingly manifested in frequent perpetrations of hate violence on Asian Americans in the United States, challenging many a fantasy of multicultural harmony in diversity.

Meanwhile, the pressures of various feminist and anti-racist new social movements have forced a reluctant acknowledgment of many marginalized narratives, such as that of Asian/American historical presence in the United States. In the guise of a liberal multiculturalism, there have been articulations of a revised history that points to racial-ethnic differences without reflecting upon material realities of past and continuing domination. This has given rise to such cultural productions as *Thousand Pieces of Gold, Come See the Paradise,* and, to a lesser degree, *The Year of the Dragon,* in which narratives of immigration exclusion, sexual exploitation, mass internment, and police harassment are left unanalyzed and depoliticized while simultaneously serving as compelling backdrops to the familiar interracial, heterosexual romantic plot. While they all necessitate individuation and rejection of ethnic community for the Asian woman, these narratives of the white male/Asian female union are not advocating full assimilation; rather, I see them articulating a certain fantasy of manageability about social and cultural differences. In his rescue of her from the silent, alien margins, then, the white American male is redeemed of a racist past through the romantic embrace he grants—and has been granting since the nineteenth century, if we believe the premise of *Thousand Pieces of Gold* —the Asian/American woman. The recurrence of the romantic plot ultimately reveals the films as re-visionings of Asian/American history that reprivilege the white male in the picture. As for the production and dissemination of these films in the past decade, they serve to reassure the centrality of white, male identity and agency in an era of increasing multiplicity and hybridity. Such subtexts of reducing difference into complementarity that upholds power arrangements should alert filmmakers and critics who endeavor "to know difference differently" (Williams 1991:12) to be more vigilantly attentive to how "subjected-generated" and ethnographic representations coexist and must interact with these other politically problematic articulations of identity and difference in the contemporary cultural field.

NOTES

Acknowledgments: I would like to thank the following persons for their helpful and provocative suggestions on this essay: Paul Yi, Angela Davis, Teresia Teiawa, and Donna Haraway.

1. I do not mean to render invisible the role and experience of women but to point to how the colonial struggle, especially in terms of territory, had been cast metaphorically as profoundly masculinist by both colonizing and nationalist forces.

2. Lisa Lowe, Chapter 1, "Discourse and Heterogeneity: Situating Orientalism," in *Critical Terrains* (Ithaca, N.Y.: Cornell University Press, 1992). In her examination of Flaubert's writings, she argues that "Masculine romantic desire is often introduced by an oriental motif. . . . Such associations of orientalism with romanticism are not coincidental, for the two situations of desire—the occidental fascination with the Orient and the male lover's passion for his female beloved—are structurally similar. Both depend on a structure that locates an Other—as woman, as oriental scene—as inaccessible, different, beyond" (2).

3. These two different—although not unrelated—and internally plural identity categories continue to be collapsed as one and the same in the discourses of the West. To note this tension between diversity and homogeneity, I will employ the term "Asian/American woman."

4. Lisa Lowe sets forth a cogent articulation of the heterogeneity of multiple orientalisms.

> My study treats orientalism as one means whereby French and British cultures exercised colonial domination through constituting sites and objects as "oriental." The discussions that follow are inscribed within an unqualified criticism of the persistent hegemonies that permit western domination of non-Europeans and the Third World. Yet, as much as I wish to underscore the insistence of these power relations, my intervention resists totalizing orientalism as a monolithic, developmental discourse that uniformly constructs the Orient as the Other of the Occident. Therefore, I do not construct a master narrative or a singular history of orientalism, whether of influence or of comparison. *Rather, I argue for a conception of orientalism as heterogeneous and contradictory; to this end I observe on the one hand that orientalism consists of an uneven matrix of orientalist situations across different cultural and historical sites, and on the other, that each of these orientalisms is internally complex and unstable.* (1992: 4–5; my italics)

5. Feminist thinker Judith Butler has articulated such a project of critical inquiry as follows: "A genealogical critique refuses to search for the origins of gender, the inner truth

of female desire, a genuine or authentic sexual identity that repression has kept from view, rather, genealogy investigates the political stakes in designating as an origin and cause those identity categories that are in fact the effects of institutions, practices, discourses with multiple and diffuse points of origin." From *Gender Trouble: Feminism and the Subversion of Identity* (New York: Routledge, 1990), x.

6. Renee E. Tajima, "Lotus Blossoms Don't Bleed: Images of Asian Women," in *Making Waves: An Anthology of Writings By and About Asian American Women*, edited by Asian Women United. While Tajima's article articulates many well-researched and insightful readings of filmic representations, one of my critiques of the piece is that it ends by positing self-expression as the answer to these (mis)representations rather than addressing the broader social and historical stage that constructs the Asian woman.

7. There have been several notable films in recent memory that have echoed the earlier exotic/erotic representations of Asian female sexuality. They have ranged from major studio productions like Bernardo Bertolucci's *The Last Emperor* to Dennis O'Rourke's "ethnographic" film, *The Good Woman of Bangkok*, and the narrative films of Asian directors like Im Kwon-Taek and Zhang Yi-Mou. The films of Im and Zhang deserve a separate careful analysis of how their deployments of the denuded and multiply exploited body of the Asian female protagonist as a way of critically commenting on the decay of the larger social body of Korea and China are received in the West, where these films are widely and warmly circulated.

8. I will refer to her subsequently as Polly Bemis since I focus not on her biography but on the two fictionalized texts —one a novel and the other a film. In an early scene from the film, Jim tells her as they anticipate their arrival in the small Idaho town: "They'll call you China Polly or China Mary. You won't have your real name." I choose Polly not in conformity with this racist dehumanization but precisely to emphasize and insist on the character "Polly" as distorted representation. I also keep her married surname Bemis because it fits into my argument that she is only significant in terms of her relationship with Charlie Bemis.

9. Stephen Heath calls this the "narrative image" in his *Questions of Cinema* (Bloomington: Indiana University Press, 1981), 121. "Narrative contains a film's multiple articulations as a single articulation, its image as a single image (the 'narrative image,' which is a film's presence, itself talked about, what it can be sold and bought on, itself represented as—in the production stills displayed outside a cinema, for example)."

10. In a conversation with Asian American actor Ken Narasaki, he informed me that the male body here is Dennis Dun and not Chris Cooper. This embrace is taken from the film, but the face of Cooper was later superimposed onto the body of Dun. This small insight adds a further ironic twist to the multiple displacements and layerings of this 'narrative' image.

11. The print ad that appeared during the theatrical release of the film also was greatly decontextualized and focused on Lalu and Charlie. It shows Lalu dancing with Charlie, and without having seen the film, can easily be viewed as a romantic embrace. However, the still is taken from a scene of sexual harassment and objectification in the film. After Lalu has refused to prostitute herself to the white male patrons of the saloon, as was the intention of Hong King in "buying" her, by resisting one man by putting a knife to his throat, she is put to work "to earn her keep otherwise"—according to Charlie's advice to Hong King. She must cook, clean the saloon, and wait on tables. A series of men force her to dance with them. Charlie cuts in on one of these men and begins to dance with her. Even though she expresses less terror with Charlie, Lalu soon runs out of the room.

12. The only interaction that is not sexually charged is the scene in which an African American man informs her that slavery is no longer legal and that she should be free.

13. One reviewer pointed out this quadripartite narrative as follows: "Nancy Kelley's stirring feminist Western, '*Thousand Pieces of Gold*,' comes with a rare delicacy, like that of a small, four-character off-Broadway play that's been carefully—and handsomely— 'opened' up for the screen. There are other characters here, as well as a lot of action and plenty of panoramic scenery swirling around the four main characters. The film always seems in motion. And yet a certain stillness prevails as the main foursome continually pairs off in twos in scene after scene, each one usually played out in small, restful rooms lighted by a golden gaslight—settings which make most of them seem quiet and contemplative even

when there's a lot of shouting" (in "'Pieces of Gold' Strikes It Rich" by Joe Baltake in *The Sacramento Bee*, 1 August 1991). I am struck by the harmonious and intimate picture painted here; the author does not discern the subtexts of masculine bonding/competition and the politics of race, class, and gender at work here.

14. A feature article on Rosalind Chao in the *San Jose Mercury News* reveals: "Chao realizes how lucky she was that '1000 Pieces of Gold' even was made with Polly/Lalu as the leading role. Director Nancy Kelley, who struggled for years to get the film financed, had to fight distributors who wanted her to rewrite the story so that Lalu/Polly would become the movie's focus." Ron Miller, "Internment on T.V.," Friday, 1 May 1992.

15. Donna Haraway shared this insight with me.

16. The film narrative is strongly reminiscent of *Farewell to Manzanar*, a personal memoir written by nisei Jeanne Wakatsuki Houston. There are too many coincidences in the two stories: the emasculation of a tyrannical Japanese father, a strong older brother, the repeated use of the phrase "Shigata Ga Nai." One scene in which the Kawamura siblings destroy their old Japanese phonograph records as a way of venting their confusion and suppressed rage is reminiscent of Mrs. Wakatsuki smashing all of her nice dishware rather than sell it to a scavenger.

17. In a newspaper interview, Alan Parker is quoted as saying, "'I set out to do an interracial love story. And that just happens to be the most significant thing that happened to that particular ethnic group, the fact that they were interned and had their civil rights taken away from them. So I just couldn't ignore it.' It's not his problem, he says, that no American filmmakers have tackled the subject. 'So I'm suddenly responsible for telling the entire story of the internment of Japanese-Americans—as if it's my fault that no one ever touched it before or had the guts to do it,' he says indignantly" (in "American Lesson, British Eyes: 'Paradise' Director Alan Parker Attacks U.S. Social Problem Through Love Story," by Sara Frankel, in the *San Francisco Examiner*, 23 December 1990). Parker's superficial appropriation of this horrific and painful historical event is evident in the ironic and potentially misleading title, *Come See the Paradise*. The inappropriateness of the title is borne out in Parker's ultimate failure to represent the internment of Japanese Americans in any meaningful complexity. If an ironic commentary about the discrepancy between the American promise of a land of milk and honey, freedom, and opportunity is intended and the actualities of forced removals and systematic incarcerations of its citizens, it is never satisfactorily borne out and displaced by the happy ending of the film.

18. "Love Story Weakens Heartfelt Pulse of Pain in 'Paradise' " by Joe Baltake (see above review of *Thousand Pieces of Gold* by same author), in the *Sacramento Bee*, 1 February 1991.

19. This disclaimer was begrudgingly added following much protest from the Asian American community. A $100 million suit was filed for defamation against the studio.

20. Laura Mulvey, "Visual Pleasure and Narrative Cinema," *Screen* 16, no. 3 (Autumn 1975).

21. "Classically, cinema turns on a series of 'looks' which join, cross through and relay one another. Thus: 1) the camera looks (a metaphor assumed by this cinema) . . . at someone, something: the profilmic; 2) the spectator looks . . . at—or on—the film; 3) each of the characters in the film looks . . . at other characters and things: the intradiegetic." From the chapter on "Film Performance" in Stephen Heath, *Questions of Cinema* (Bloomington: Indiana University Press, 1981), 119.

22. Some names that come to mind are Elaine Kim, Angela Davis, Cherrie Moraga, Gloria Anzaldua, Lisa Lowe, Patricia Hill Collins, Rigoberta Menchu, Judy Yung, Barbara Christian, Paula Gunn Allen, Evelyn Nakano Glenn, June Jordan, Chandra Mohanty, Barbara Smith, bell hooks, and many, many more.

23. Patricia Hill Collins, *Black Feminist Thought* (Cambridge: Unwyn Hyman, 1990), 226. Collins quotes bell hooks and her naming of this as a "politic of domination" that "refers to the ideological ground that they share, which is a belief in domination, and a belief in the notions of superior and inferior, which are components of all of those systems. For me, it's like a house, they share the foundation, but the foundation is the ideological beliefs around which notions of domination are constructed" (hooks 1989: 175).

24. After their passionate reunion, Jack McGurn tells Lily, "You have everything that I don't."

25. Describing how narrative works to construct and maintain sexual difference—

"a mapping of differences, and specifically, *first and foremost*, of sexual difference"—De Lauretis argues that narrative plays an active and generative role in the dissemination of possible subject positions for its audience through the process of identification. She states: "Much as social formations and representations appeal to and position the individual as subject in the process to which we give the name of ideology, the movement of narrative discourse shifts and places the reader, viewer, or listener in certain portions of the plot space. Therefore, to say that narrative is the production of Oedipus is to say that each reader—male or female—is constrained and defined within the two positions of a sexual difference thus conceived: male-hero-human, on the side of the subject; and female-obstacle-boundary-space, on the other." *Alice Doesn't: Feminism, Semiotics, Cinema*, 121.

26. De Lauretis posits: "How ever varied the conditions of presence of the narrative form in fictional genres, rituals, or social discourses, its movement seems to be that of a passage, a transformation predicated on the figure of a hero, a mythical subject" (113). She then proceeds to include the semiotic insights of Jurij Lotman's concept of plot typology and the types of characters that recur in Western narratives. In a lengthy citation by De Lauretis that I think is worthy of full rearticulation here, Lotman writes: "Characters can be divided into those who are mobile, who enjoy freedom with regard to plot space, who can change their place in the structure of the artistic world, and cross the frontier, the basic topological feature of this space, and those who are immobile, who represent, in fact, a function of this space. Looked at topologically, the initial situation is that a certain plot-space is divided by a single boundary into an internal and external sphere, and a single character has the opportunity to cross the boundary. Inasmuch as closed space *can be interpreted* as 'a cave,' 'the grave,' 'a house,' 'a woman' (and correspondingly, be allotted the feature of darkness, warmth and dampness), entry into it *is interpreted* on various levels as 'death,' 'conception,' 'return home' and so on; moreover all these acts are thought of as mutually identical" (118).

BIBLIOGRAPHY

Asian Women United of California, ed. *Making Waves: An Anthology of Writings By and About Asian American Women.* Boston, Mass.: Beacon, 1989.

Butler, Judith. *Gender Trouble: Feminism and the Subversion of Identity.* New York: Routledge, 1990.

Clifford, Jim. *The Predicament of Culture.* Berkeley: University of California Press, 1989.

Collins, Patricia Hill. *Black Feminist Thought: Knowledge, Consciousness, and The Politics of Empowerment.* Cambridge, Mass.: Unwyn Hyman, 1990.

De Lauretis, Teresa. *Alice Doesn't: Feminism, Semiotics, Cinema.* Bloomington: Indiana University Press, 1984.

Heath, Stephen. *Questions of Cinema.* Bloomington: Indiana University Press, 1981.

Kabanni, Rana. "The Salon's Seraglio." In *Europe's Myths of the Orient.* New York: Macmillan, 1986.

Kim, Elaine. "Sex Tourism in Asia: A Reflection of Political and Economic Inequality." *Critical Perspectives of Third World America* 2:1 (1984): 214–32.

Lowe, Lisa. *Critical Terrains.* Ithaca: Cornell University Press, 1992.

McCunn, Ruthanne Lum. *Thousand Pieces of Gold.* Boston, Mass.: Beacon, 1988.

Marcus George E., and Michael M. J. Fischer. *Anthropology as Cultural Critique: An Experimental Moment in the Human Sciences.* Chicago: University of Chicago Press, 1986.

Mulvey, Laura. "Visual Pleasure in Narrative Cinema." *Screen* 16:3 (Autumn 1975): 6–18.

Nichols, Bill. "The Ethnographer's Tale." *Visual Anthropology Review* 7:2 (1991): 31–47.

Ruby, Jay. "Speaking For, Speaking About, Speaking With, Speaking Alongside: An Anthropological Dilemma." *Visual Anthropology Review* 7:2 (1991): 50–67.

Williams, Sarah. "Suspending Anthropology's Inscription: Observing Trinh Minh-ha Observed." *Visual Anthropology Review* 6:3 (1991): 7–14.

Histories of Asian American Cinema

Stephen Gong

A History in Progress: Asian American Media Arts Centers, 1970-1990

Asian American media arts organizations are at a critical juncture: arguably the best organized of any alternative media arts by people of color in the United States, yet too fragmented to constitute an effective national network. Asian American media arts organizations consist of three major centers: Visual Communications (Los Angeles), Asian CineVision (New York), and the National Asian American Telecommunications Association (San Francisco). These are complemented by three smaller organizations: King Street Media (Seattle), Asian American Resource Workshop (Boston), and Asian American Arts and Media (Washington, D.C.). Several other groups also serve Asian American filmmakers and media artists, like Third World Newsreel, Women Make Movies, and the Downtown Community Television Center (all located in New York City).

These centers face chronic funding problems from an economy hostile to artistic and educational endeavors (a legacy of the Reagan years), and an even greater problem of passing over two decades' worth of commitment and idealism on to the next generation of producers, media activists, and administrators. Yet, the presence of the Asian American voice and image on movie screens and through the airwaves has never been more assured. Where we go from here in sustaining a community of cultural organizations committed to "moving the image" of Asian Pacific Americans depends on how we assess the development of our efforts to date. What follows is a description and assessment of Asian American media arts organizations and their development from 1970 to the present.

From *Moving the Image: Independent Asian Pacific American Media Arts,* edited by Russell Leong (Los Angeles: UCLA Asian American Studies Center, 1991), pp. 1–9. Reprinted with permission of the UCLA Asian American Studies Center.

Background—The 1960s

The genesis of any social movement begins with the influences that shape its artists, leadership, and directions. The Asian American media community emerged from the movements for racial and social justice and cultural affirmation of the 1960s. The institutions themselves—as media arts centers—were both unplanned and unprecedented. Mostly, Asian American media arts was developed by relatively small groups of diverse individuals, from suburban southern California to New York's Chinatown, from the campuses of Los Angeles City College to Harvard, who held two beliefs in common. The first was that being Asian American transcended the experience of being solely Chinese, Korean, or Japanese American. The second was a belief in the power of the media to effect social and cultural change, in response to the negative power of Asian stereotypes in the mainstream media. At the time, the tools of media production were becoming affordable and available for community and individual use in a way not possible earlier. Many foresaw the opportunity of replacing negative media stereotypes with more authentic and affirmative images.

What is a "Media Arts Center"?

The term is generally self-descriptive, and applies to several types of non-profit organizations that provide services to support media activity, generally in production, exhibition, distribution, and advocacy. According to the Membership Directory of the National Alliance of Media Arts Centers, there are approximately 125 organizations in the United States that so define themselves. These centers serve constituencies of artists and producers working in film, video, and radio, but they also help present these works to a larger audience. Some media arts centers, like the Community Film Workshop of Chicago, concentrate their efforts on one area of media activity, in this case, in film production training for minority youth. Others, such as the Film Department of the Museum of Modern Art, emphasize exhibition, distribution, and film preservation, working on an international level with film archives and cinematheques in other countries. Whether connected to museum or university or not, media arts centers tend to support an alternative vision of media, or at least one that transcends the commercial Hollywood industry. The media arts, as opposed to the media industry, covers social issue documentaries, experimental film and video art with regional, gender, and multicultural diversity.

The media arts field is organized through mutual consent—on the part of the organizations listed above, and the hundreds of producers, filmmakers, and video artists they represent. The rules of the game, in terms of grant support, are supplied by federal (the Arts and Humanities Endowments) and state (such as the New York State Council on the Arts and the California Arts Council) funding agencies, private foundations (especially the MacArthur Foundation and the Rockefeller Foundation), and the public broadcasting system (through the Corporation for Public Broadcasting).

Asian American media arts centers should be viewed within the larger context of the field of media arts centers. After all, they share a common agenda of social and cultural change. More important, if this agenda is to be realized, they will have to work together to achieve it. But it is these very groups that also compete for limited funds from government agencies and private foundations. This paradox of interdependent competition is worked out in practice, as all intertribal relationships are, through unwritten protocol and obligations.

The Models—Visual Communications and Asian CineVision

> *In the beginning none of us knew what we were doing—*
> *and that made for some difficult challenges. But that's*
> *also what made it so much fun.*[1]
> —Robert Nakamura

In 1970, a small group of Asian Americans in Los Angeles came together to produce a photographic exhibit about the Japanese American internment during World War II. This was the first project by the group, which began calling itself Visual Communications, or VC. The founders of VC, Robert Nakamura, Eddie Wong, Alan Ohashi, and Duane Kubo, had been deeply influenced by the civil rights and anti-war movements that had stimulated student and community activism. In the Japanese American community, community-based organizations such as Gidra and Storefront were established; at UCLA, a number of the key VC members went through the Ethno-Communications Program and made their first films, and were involved in developing the Asian American Studies Center.

Initially producing posters, leaflets, and photographs for Asian American community groups, VC was incorporated as an independent nonprofit organization in 1971. VC members recognized that these modest projects with their uncertain funding were inadequate to realize their larger goal of effective sustained social and cultural change. Nonprofit status allowed VC to seek support from a broader set of funding sources, especially through publicly legislated programs such as the Comprehensive Employment and Training Act (CETA) and Emergency School Aid Act (ESAA). These programs provided key staff and production support early on; later, the Media Arts and Expansion Arts programs of the National Endowment for the Arts (NEA) became mainstays for VC's sustained development as an arts organization.

From 1972 to 1977 VC produced some ten films of increasing sophistication, including *Pieces of a Dream, Wataridori: Birds of Passage,* and *Cruisin' J-Town,* as well as a major photographic publication, *In Movement* (1974), and work in video. "It was not easy," Bob Nakamura recalls, "because the community at that time was really fragmented, with many different viewpoints and conceptions of what the Asian American community was and how people should serve it. The radical left and the conservatives of the community had very different ideas about the role of media. We were criticized by both sides."[2] Since there were no precedents for the films VC was beginning to make, people in the community felt proprietary about the content and treatment. Some criticized these early works based on their accuracy and historiography. Ironically, for some, the VC films were too technically proficient, too slick, and too indebted to Hollywood and network television.

The pressure of being responsive and accountable to the community while at the same time trying to develop the craft of filmmaking continually challenges those in Asian American media. Steve Tatsukawa, the late and greatly missed VC administrative director, once observed,

> We have to fight the tendency of becoming isolated as filmmakers who happen to be Asian Americans. I think we like to see ourselves as Asian Americans who know how to make films. . . . Time and again we have sat down and said no, it's not just going to end in a production company that grinds out films for the sake of the dollar. We have some real stories that have to be told and some histories that have to be analyzed.[3]

VC thus defined and established an oppositional stance to commercial mainstream productions. In doing so, for the time being, they left unanswered the question of art-for-art's-sake, and media artists working in experimental genres that were more revelatory of personal vision than of community history.

As Visual Communications was becoming one important model of a media arts center, in 1976, a complementary organization was established in New York City: Asian CineVision.[4] Founded by Peter Chow, Christine Choy, and Tsui Hark, Asian CineVision was conceived originally as an organization to provide workshops to train the New York Chinatown community in basic video techniques, so that it, in turn, could produce half-hour video programs for the newly developed cable access channel on Manhattan Cable. The intent was to teach the community to produce programs to effect positive change in areas such as housing, redevelopment, and health care. In 1977, ACV-trained producers were creating a half hour of programming per week. By 1982 they were producing a nightly hour-long news program in Chinese. In time, however, ACV stepped away from the workshops, having found doing a daily video production and training facility too hard to maintain, especially since other media arts centers such as Downtown Community Television and Young Filmmakers (now Film/Video Arts) were able to fulfill this need adequately.

Peter Chow, ACV's executive director and guiding spirit, has long been a master of program diversification, and so ACV began to develop programs in exhibition, distribution, and information services. In 1978, ACV, with help from Daryl Chin and Danny Yung, organized its first Asian American Film Festival. The aim was to showcase independently produced films by Asian American filmmakers. The festival seemed to signal a coming of age for the 1960s generation. Because it was more of an experiment than the inauguration of an event, few ACV staff members thought that there would, or could be, a second festival. The film festival is programmed by a committee whose selection process, stormy at times, has over the years helped to shape the definition of what the Asian American media arts are, and who is considered an Asian American media artist. This definition has ranged from the narrow to the non-specific: from the epigrammatic "films by, for and about Asian Americans," and "positive images and truthful portrayals of the Asian American experience," to experimental and personal works by artists like Fu-Ding Cheng, Gregg Araki, and Trinh T. Minh-ha. The evolution to a more inclusive definition of Asian American media work indicates a steady maturation of the field, a growing assurance that once the basic history of exclusion and internment has been told we are free to tell more personal tales and follow other topics and impulses.

The festival was subsequently enlarged to include Asian films along with Asian American works, a move that acknowledged the cultural interconnectedness of Asian and Asian American work. It also enabled ACV to take advantage of Asian films in slack periods when Asian American works were scarce. The Asian American International Film Festival tours to other cities around the country, although some sites occasionally supplement the selection with additional works.

Other key programs offered by ACV have included the Asian American Video Festival, two editions of the *Asian American Media Reference Guide*, and *Bridge* magazine, which up until 1986, when it was replaced by the more modest *CineVue*, presented an important mix of news, essays, film criticism, book reviews, photography, and poetry from an "Asian American perspective." *Bridge*, published as an irregular quarterly, was expensive to produce but it offered a distinctive point of view and gave a coherent voice to the emerging Asian American media community.

For the Asian American media centers that followed in Boston, Seattle, and Washington, D.C., Visual Communications and Asian CineVision have served as models and as sources of encouragement and support. The support has often been mutual. In 1980 VC produced *Hito Hata: Raise the Banner*, breaking ground as the first Asian American feature film. Unfortunately, the organization was faced with a substantial debt that threatened not only the film's completion but the future of the organization itself. Following the inception of the first Friends of Visual Communications support group in Los Angeles, numerous other ad hoc chapters came together in these and other major communities across the nation. It was not only an inspiring show of community support, but a catalyst in stimulating the formation of other groups.

Coast to Coast: The Network Grows

Seattle

In Seattle, interest in the emerging Asian American media was concentrated in the offices of the *International Examiner*, where several staff writers and photographers, including Bill Blauvelt, Ken Mochizuki, and Dean Wong, formed King Street Media.[5] Although incorporated separately as a nonprofit organization, King Street has never emerged from the confines of the *Examiner* and in fact has never had a paid staff. But an informal organizational structure may have been the appropriate approach given the needs of the community and the interests of the members. King Street still manages to mount a film festival in order to broaden exposure for Asian American films, and it also presents area premieres of significant Asian American features, such as *Dim Sum* (1985) and *Living on Tokyo Time* (1987), usually to benefit the *Examiner*. Their most ambitious project to date was the production of *Beacon Hill Boys* in 1985. Co-directed by Blauvelt, Mochizuki, and Dean Hayasaka, this featurette (at forty-eight minutes) was a well received coming-of-age story of Japanese Americans in Seattle. At the time that this was written, the King Street members were at work on another screenplay and were also planning for another film festival.

Boston

The Asian American Resource Workshop was founded in Boston in 1979 by a group that included Mike Liu, Fred Ho, Ramsey Lieu, Irene Wong, and Albert Lau.[6] Boston has many of the same elements found in New York City, albeit on a much smaller scale. It's an old Eastern city, within an urban context of diverse and turbulent ethnic groups, as well as a plethora of colleges and universities. So, Asian American Resource Workshop developed many of the same programs as ACV, including video workshops for the community, and film festivals and premieres. Later on, however, as chronic funding problems set in, the organization modeled itself more on the lines of VC, which worked with AARW to develop a long-range plan. Continual financial struggles and dismal funding prospects from the Massachusetts Council on the Arts and Humanities have kept AARW from developing as expected. Today, according to Helen Liu, the Workshop is in a "survival mode," concentrating on the provision of media services to the community and local colleges. Community workshops on video production are produced through contracts, as income-generating services become vital to the organization's existence. Still AARW is the fourth largest Asian American media arts center in the country, which itself is a sobering fact.

Washington, D.C.

In Washington, D.C., the flame is being kept alive by a small group of true believers, including Theo-dric Feng, Laura Chin, Lori Tsang, and Wendy Lim. For more than ten years this group of volunteers have maintained an Asian American media presence in the nation's capital. Incorporated finally in 1985 as Asian American Arts and Media, Inc. (and known conversationally as Arts and Media), the group's efforts are impressive given the scarcity of resources and inherent limitations to organizational development. Arts and Media presents an annual film festival (a supplementation of ACV's touring festival), and activities and visual arts exhibits in conjunction with the Asian Pacific American Heritage Month. Theo Feng hosted "Gold Mountain," a weekly hour-long radio program covering Asian American political and cultural issues, on WPFW, a Pacifica Foundation station. Some of these activities are not necessarily Arts and Media projects but are undertaken by, inevitably, the same group of people. Because of the lack of Washington, D.C.'s foundations and corporations, the modestly budgeted D.C. Commission on the Arts and Humanities is the only source of public funds.

San Francisco

By 1979 the Asian American media arts field had a national network of organizations. In San Francisco, there was no formal media organization, although filmmakers and producers like Loni Ding, Felicia Lowe, Emiko Omori, Geraldine Kudaka, Christopher Chow, and Curtis Choy had for years worked in and around the commercial and public spheres of television and film. Yet, a growing sense of frustration was developing there as well, especially with regard to equal access to public television (PBS) and radio. In response to more than a decade of criticism, the Corporation for Public Broadcasting, which has been created by Congress to channel public money to the public broadcasting system free of political pressure, responded by convening a national blue ribbon task force which produced a comprehensive report entitled "A Formula for Change." Its recommendations for inclusion of minority-produced programming and increased training opportunities for minorities in public broadcasting stations were initially acknowledged and then generally ignored. For the Asian American media community, the most significant result of these efforts was a growing sophistication in dealing with "the system" and resolve to claim a fair share of public broadcasting. These efforts culminated in a gathering of tribes: the first conference of Asian American filmmakers and producers held in Berkeley in 1980. Organized by an ad hoc committee headed by Loni Ding, an independent television producer and instructor in the Ethnic Studies Department at the University of California at Berkeley, the conference brought together Asian American producers and media activists from across the country. From the VC contingent decked out in Hawaiian shirts to the worldly-wise and slightly cynical group from New York, the Asian American media community was meeting face to face for the first time.

By the time the three-day conference ended, the groundwork had been laid for an organization that would acquire, package, and distribute television and radio programs on Asian American history and concerns. The new organization would also advocate against racist and stereotyped images of Asian Americans and support and encourage greater participation by Asian Americans in public broadcasting. Originally the organization that was to become the National Asian American Telecommunications Association (NAATA) encompassed Pacific Islanders within its mandate to CPB. However, the effort splintered even before it was formally organized. Members of the Pacific Island media community argued for, and formed, a separate organization to provide relevant programming to the public broadcasting system.

NAATA, formally established in late 1980 in San Francisco with James Yee as its founding executive director, was conceived as a national organization with a board made up of representatives from regional chapters. This structure has given way to a board of both local and national representation and a mix of national and local services and programs, including the television series (under the "Silk Screen" banner) and specials, like *The Color of Honor* (1987); sponsorship of original radio dramas such as "Quiet Thunder," "Juke Box," and "The Last Game Show"; "Cross Current" media distribution; and, more recently, workshops and exhibitions in the San Francisco Bay Area. NAATA has also played a highly visible advocate role in both the commercial and public film and broadcasting worlds, assuming a position against stereotyped depictions of Asian Americans in films like Michael Cimino's *Year of the Dragon* (1985).

NAATA's accomplishments, although significant, have always been tempered by the modest support provided by CPB[7] (roughly $135,000 per year throughout the 1980s)—less money than is spent on the production of a single half-hour program on public broadcasting, or of a thirty-second commercial on network television. And yet this amount was supposed to provide for a significant and ongoing Asian American presence on public television and radio.

During the early 1990s NAATA's Yee worked with other independent media arts organizations to increase the amount of money for independent multicultural programming for public television. At the time this was written, it appeared that the amount of funds for program development available specifically for Asian American works would double in the near future. In addition, sources and overall funding for independent production were sought from the Independent Television Service. However, it is difficult to believe that all of these potential changes will, in fact, come to pass. The record to date suggests protracted struggle with the system.

Ten to the Twenty-first: Questions and Choices

What choices will we have to make in the next decade? Some are organization-specific, although of a depressingly common genre: how to survive budgetarily. VC, ACV, and NAATA have all participated in arts stabilization (so-called advancement) grant programs through the NEA and state arts agencies, yet still face ongoing budgetary problems. Worse, administrators find themselves spending more time seeking grants and contributions than they do in managing services to filmmakers and the community.

The question now arises, was it the ultimate goal of the Asian American media arts movement to get grants from Chemical Bank and Anheuser Busch? The Asian American media arts movement from its inception was an alternative movement developed in opposition to mainstream strategies and structures in the film and television industries.

Other challenges are how to continue to serve the ever-changing Asian American community (especially with recent immigrant groups from Southeast Asia, who have little in common with your typical highly assimilated third-generation Asian American). This issue underscores the fact that the Asian American media arts field is fundamentally a political (rather than a cultural or ethnic-based) movement.

A related concern is how to attract and hold on to the next generation of filmmakers, producers, activists, and administrators. Will the next generation be willing to accept lower salaries and career mobility for jobs of increasingly dubious social prestige?

Each of the centers has and continues to struggle with the issue of Pan-Asian representation. Situated in L.A.'s Japanese American community, VC's Executive Director Linda Mabalot (herself a Filipino American) has struggled to diversify VC's board, staff, and collaborators to include Chinese, Koreans, Filipinos, and Pacific Islanders, while at the same time continuing to draw upon the tremendous support offered by the Japanese American community. In these efforts VC can call upon a history of working successfully with a variety of community organizations in workshops and exhibition programs.

In New York, Asian CineVision, originally a Chinatown group, has made concerted outreach efforts to include Indian and Filipino works in the film festival and publications. NAATA, too, has diversified its board and staff and has struggled with the delicate issue of representation of and services to the Pacific Islander community ever since the initial splintering of the group in 1980. (The group originally recognized as representing the Pacific Island community by CPB is no longer functioning and a process is underway to replace it.) The Asian American media arts center field has also diversified from its original dominance by men to greater inclusion of women in key administrative and board governance positions.

Not all of its challenges lie within the inner circle. It has also become increasingly clear that the Asian American media arts centers may play a key role in the current cultural debate over "multiculturalism," whether it is the rhetoric about marginalized classes and ethnic communities or something more potent. As institutions, Asian American media arts centers must play an activist role on all levels of municipal, state, and federal arts funding. The recent attacks on the National Endowment for the Arts and the issue of federal funding for arts activities reflect both a continuation of a fight for freedom of expression and equity in support for the arts that is both decades old and a harbinger of things to come.

NOTES

1. Interview with Robert Nakamura, *In Focus*, Vol. 6, No. 1, Winter 1990, 3.

2. Ibid.

3. Jeanne Joe, "Visual Communications: A New Image on the Screen," *Neworld*, No. 6, 1979, 54.

4. Interview with Peter Chow, May 1990.

5. Interview with Dean Wong, June 1990.

6. Interview with Helen Liu, June 1990.

7. Adequate support is relative. The entire Asian American media arts field is woefully undercapitalized. The three largest centers, VC, ACV, and NAATA, have budgets under $400,000 per year. The Asian American Resource Workshop has a cash budget of less than $50,000 per year, and Arts and Media and King Street have no permanent staff and individual project funding only.

Rolando B. Tolentino

Identity and Difference in "Filipino/a American" Media Arts

The continuing unevenness of conditions and developments among specific groups' media arts is already being concealed by the weight of the category "Asian Pacific American." The "Asian American," and the later term "Asian Pacific American," have been made to encompass the multiplicity of various peoples' experiences, implying the formation and transformation of a mass for two opposing objectives: a homogeneity of other peoples and cultures that becomes the basis of racial stereotyping ("massification") and which, in turn, forms a base experience among various peoples and cultures that becomes the foundation for coalition-building ("critical mass").[1] While the solidarity articulated largely in political bondedness has been useful in the pronouncement of the Asian Pacific American's transformation into a critical mass, the category fails to inscribe the specificity and historicity of included and excluded groups. With the growing body of works in Filipino/a American media arts, a need arises to locate the space of the "Filipino/a."[2] It is along this area that I would like to explore the issues of constituting the category of "Filipino/a" within "Asian Pacific American" media arts, addressing both the dominant representations of "Asians" and "Pacific Islanders," and "Asian Pacific American's" marginalization of the "Filipino/a American" range of experience.[3] The pioneering book *Moving the Image: Independent "Asian Pacific American" Media Arts* (1991), a collection of fifty essays by media and cultural workers, provides the juncture to situate the discourse of "Asian Pacific American" media arts.[4] The experience of Filipino/a Americans marks both commonality and difference with other Asian Pacific Americans. In this essay, however, I emphasize *difference* as a way of rethinking both identity formation (characterized by "heterogeneity,

From *Amerasia Journal* 23:2 (1997): 137–61. Reprinted with permission of the UCLA Asian American Studies Center.

hybridity, multiplicity") and minority discourse ("to describe and define the common denominators that link various minority cultures").[5] I then map out the three waves of media output by Filipino/a Americans, connecting the different representational issues associated with each wave. For readers unfamiliar with Filipino/a American media texts, I present readings of works representing each wave. I focus on the specificity of racial identity as this has been represented by the media artists. I am putting terms I am taking issue with in quotation marks (Derrida's *sous rature*) to call attention to the problematics of inadequacy yet indispensability of the terms to account for the multiplicity of experiences they purport to encompass.

"Asian Pacific American" film and video arts have come a long way from their initial productions in the early 1970s. These earlier productions resulted mainly from the Ethno-Communications Program at UCLA.[6] As an affirmative action program, Ethno-Communications provided for the representation of Asian Americans, African Americans, and Chicanos to study filmmaking in the university. What then resulted were initial works that would eventually progress into the body of productions of each of these groups. From initiation to and empowerment of the tools of film-making, these filmmakers realized shared conditions and aspirations. The radicality of the margins-in-solidarity in the 1960s drew from the national liberation struggles in and of the "Third World." Deriving from the radical politics of "Third Worldism," the legacy of Ethno-Communications persists, most significantly in the continuing growth of film, and consequently video productions among these specific groups. Batch mates Duane Kubo, Steven Tatsukawa, and Eddie Wong would join Robert Nakamura to form Visual Communications, which remains the "oldest and most prolific of Asian American production entities."[7]

 Some twenty-five years later, Asian American media artists continue to mark their works in the category of "Asian" rather than to specify their own differences within the grouping. The category fails to represent the differences in strides made in media arts and the heterogeneous ways of identity formation of the various peoples. Furthermore, Pacific Islanders have been amassed in the swelling category of "Asian Pacific American." The developments in various groups' media arts have been uneven, yet the category remained the same. The prominence of certain groups has eclipsed other groups in the category. Japanese and Chinese Americans remain frontrunners in the field, also having the longest continuing immigration history among Asian Americans. The absence of other national groups—like peoples of Indonesia, Singapore, Papua New Guinea, and Ceylon, for example—in the area of media arts is further obscured by "Asian Pacific," made to stand in for the experiences of these absent groups. The category also conflates specific boundary formations, as in the case of Chinese American filmmaking, made to encompass the diaspora of (at least) the "three Chinas." The category has also failed to reflect either the more recent strides made by Filipino/a, South Asian, and Korean Americans or the lag of Samoan and Laotian Americans in media productions. With just one masters output so far, "Thai American" filmmaking has yet to become a category. Furthermore, "Asian Pacific American's" primary construction as a racial category fails to account for the "internal," intraracial, and interethnic differences and commonalities, such as the related and divergent positions of gays, women, and other local and sectoral groups. Important too are the differences in assimilation and resistance factors in the immigration experiences of the various groups. Issues of contraction and constriction in immigration, income, generational, local, and sectoral differences are some factors that have come to play a role in the constitution of communities or the so-called internal exile experience, and which are not encompassed by the "Asian Pacific American" experience. While the category remains functional to some extent, it has proven to be limiting and limited to other pressing and long-term concerns of specifying cultural formation.

The book *Moving the Image* documents these issues and scopes as linked to the "Asian Pacific American" media arts.[8] It has presented these issues, however, in terms of its oppositionality to white racism and Hollywood dominance. Mainstream media has constructed the dominant image of the "Asian Pacific American," which has perpetuated the racism against these groups and individuals. The task assumed is to represent these images by way of recuperation (to re-present) of dominant representations or to *present* counterimages of Asianness and Pacificness. In the introduction, Russell Leong asks, "whose eyes ultimately are seeing? what do they see, and what do they do with what they have seen?"[9] This directs us to an "image of" studies of "Asian Pacific American" media arts. The privileged markers of oppression are Hollywood and racism—what images are produced, and how? The general assumption of the texts is that all of Hollywood images are racist. Asian Pacific American filmmakers are thereby framed in a reactive stance—what images can counter the mainstream media's production of the "Asian Pacific Americans," and how. The effect is an oppositional space of difference from Hollywood and whiteness. It, however, has produced an undesired side-effect: the oppositional space of difference between the Asian Pacific American artists and critics and Hollywood has also collapsed differences within the Asian Pacific American group.

The discourse is shifted to an exclusive and overencompassing position of the *our*. Thus, the following interrelated issues are reposed:

> What are the implications of the critical academic terms and cultural/political definitions used to view and interpret our media works? Do terms such as postcolonial and postmodern, for instance, apply to "Asian Pacific American" media arts?
>
> In turn, how do we develop our own interpretative critical language, and create our own metaphors for experience?

How can our media arts productions serve as a tool to educate for action?[10]

Linda Mabalot's *Preface* puts it in a similar way: one of the four goals in publishing the book is "to begin to develop new languages, both critical and cinematic, for assessing our work—a new cultural literacy which places cultures of color at the core."[11] There is a dual desire at stake here—one is to be central by a reversal of the hierarchy, the other is to work outside the critical and cinematic languages of the status quo. There is a confusion as to the level at which such terms are to be taken. For to take these literally is to fall short of real power structures at work: can the margins truly assume a privileged position on a sustained basis in the social structure? On the other hand, to take these symbolically is still falling short of the real dynamics of the power structure that has consequently dominated structures of beings and feelings: can one really work outside the language of power? Such a choice—to work *outside* the technologically and culturally inscribed hegemonic media—undermines the possibilities of repowering the language for the margins, if not in its utopian entirety, in its potentially subversive and liberating aspects. While positions of power, as "post-" theories would state, implicate both self/other or involve interchangeable subject positions, the violent history of internal colonialism and racism can also be easily elided in this ("post-") refiguration of power. This move to fix the space of the "enemy" and "victim," after all, seems to be the stance taken in positioning the group within a nationalist Asian Pacific American perspective: to serve as a counterregister/memory of the group's experiences with racism and oppression.

The essays do not distinguish any space between the filmmaker and writer, and indeed, most of the writers are themselves filmmakers. This can be read in its historical setting: that at this moment of "Asian Pacific American" media arts, the mode of reading their media texts has not been foregrounded by critics and scholars, or that there is no distinction between film practice and theory as both can be assumed by the political body of the filmmaker articulating his or her filming strategies, or that the film text opens up its own reading strategies. What then unfolds, for the most part, are the more-than-substantial justifications for the political mode of filmmaking and, consequently, for the political mode of film criticism. This politics, however, remains grounded in the notion of the "Third" Cinema and "Third World" Cinema, and to some extent, in the notion of the historical avant-garde. "Third" Cinema called for a new cinematic language appropriate to the "Third World's" experience of colonialism and imperialism, and the collective struggle against these oppressions. The historical avant-garde espoused notions of anti-art and anti-art establishments, and a re-turn of art to the praxis of everyday life. Being that these promises remain undelivered, the essays have yet to problematize their relationships to oppositional notions of art and cinema which, for the most part, the authors have chosen to align themselves with.

Besides contesting the image, there is a second proposition in the book: to accept the discussions as "the way things are," as inherent and formless to the state-of-affairs of "Asian Pacific American" media arts and this community. Trinh T. Minh-ha refers to "a feeling that has found its form in its formless nature."[12] This "formlessness," however, can be interpreted as a built-in defensive justification of the state of "Asian Pacific American" media arts in particular, and the state of the Asian Pacific American community in general. What this logic succeeds in doing is to historicize the past as its source, create the present as its perennial justification, or even as its perennial state. What it fails to do is to specificitize and historicize contradictions within this formlessness of the present. "The way things are," therefore, becomes the differentiating aesthetics of "Asian Pacific American" media arts. There is an ahistorical ideology to this: lost ground is simply appropriated back, not interrogated. The ideological imperative in this logic is the erasure of the fascist history of racism as experienced by the various groups in the United States. Furthermore, the logic rides with the way the hegemonic culture has pigeonholed Asian Pacific Americans in their Asianness/Pacificness, thereby maintaining the distinguishing space of Americanness for the privileging of its own racial imperatives. "Formlessness" becomes the recourse against the oppressor's fascination with forms, fixation, and fetishism. Consequently, "formlessness" becomes its own form and its own fetishism. This reading subsequently underscores the reactive relationship of the margins to the oppressor: when the center sneezes, the margins catch a cold.[13]

Equally problematic is the margin's discursive placing of the site of subversion and liberation: the mode of transformation as conduit to the space of the oppressor. Trinh, for example, states that "transformation requires a certain freedom to modify, appropriate and reappropriate without being trapped in imitation."[14] The issue of agency is assumed to exist: who can transform the image, the power structure, and so on? Mimicry of power, along these lines, reifies the liberal-plural individual subject as one is assumed to be capacitated with freedom. Furthermore, because of the nature of independent production, the filmmaker remains as the privileged agent and subject of transformation. The obvious problematic in this elitism (similar to "Third" Cinema and the historical avant-garde) is that the promise of alternative filmmaking and spectatorial practices remains largely undelivered.

Another serious ramification of this construction of identity is the failure to see "white" as also another racial category; in the same instance whiteness never assumes itself to be one. The "Asian Pacific American" still heavily draws from the paradigm of binary opposition, the reversal of which merely reconstitutes a similar power structure. In doing so, "whiteness" consequently assumes a non-racial/ethnic position—but nevertheless othered—from which to draw the construction of an "Asian Pacific

Rolando B. Tolentino

American" identity. Stuart Hall forewarns us that "we . . . are ethnically located and our ethnic identities are crucial to our subjective sense of who we are. But this is also a recognition that this is not an ethnicity which is doomed to survive, as Englishness was, only by marginalizing, dispossessing, displacing, forgetting other ethnicities."[15] Chon Noriega further notes that these positions often reduce the margins "to an unenviable position of defiant invisibility or of reforming something that is just plain wrong."[16] He then posits an engagement for a "politics of representation to a second degree" for Latino film criticism. This call can also be useful for Asian Pacific American media texts. Noriega is going beyond the "images of" studies to a discursive construction of representation via identification and difference. This space allows for the interrogation of structural and institutional foundations where these images are constructed in the first place, calling into question the very politics of *representation* itself.

Similarly, black filmmaking practices in Britain, as Hall also mentions, have generated a two-phase movement: "from a struggle over the relations of representations to a politics of representation itself."[17] The initial phase of Asian Pacific American filmmaking and criticism can be likened to correspond to the first phase of black British filmmaking, the struggle to change the "relations of representation," as "predicated on a critique of the degree of fetishisation, objectification and negative figuration which are so much the feature of the representation of the black [in our case, Asian Pacific American] subject."[18] The principal objects of this first phase of critique are: "first, the question of access to the rights of representation by black artists and black cultural workers themselves; secondly the contestation of the marginality, the stereotypical quality and the fetishised nature of the images of blacks by the counter-position of a 'positive' black imagery."[19] Judging by *Moving the Image*, the state of criticism in "Asian Pacific American" media arts falls under this first phase.

The second phase of critique, however, moves from a simple substitution to a displacement of the politics that constructs representation itself—a struggle to "reorganize and reposition the different cultural strategies in relation to one another" or a struggle of "the burden of representation." This struggle of artists and cultural workers deals in two fronts: "how to characterize this shift—if indeed, we agree that such a shift has taken or is taking place—and if the language of binary opposition and substitutions will no longer suffice."[20] Similarly, in terms of a homogeneously conceived "Asian Pacific American" media arts, it is difficult to conceive whether these have moved into the threshold of the second phase, remain within, or overlap with the first phase. The determination of the shift (from relations of representation to politics of representation) can only be conceived through the analysis of a specific group's media arts. In theorizing the concept of difference in identity formation, "a new cultural politics engages rather than suppresses difference and which depends, in part, on the cultural construction of new ethnic identities."[21]

Further specifying difference on two levels is integral in the second phase: first, within the level of theoretical contact between the Eurocentric discourse that has largely framed the issue of representation and an ethnic cultural politics; and second, within the level of the ethnic cultural politics itself that marks an "end of innocence" to an essentially national(ist) subject.[22] Thus, a *new* cultural politics, as Hall suggests, involves an inside view (an introspection) of ethnicity itself: how "we are all . . . ethnically located and [how] our ethnic identities are crucial to our subjective sense of who we are."[23]

By specifying and historicizing the "Filipino/a American" media arts, the "Asian Pacific Americans" and their media arts can undergo an unpacking of excess assumptions and scopes. However, it is within the context of the "Asian Pacific American" media arts and criticisms' own history that such practices become filters to better understand the framing of the "Filipino/a" and its media arts' visibility and invisibility. One begins with the "image of" studies to periodize the two generations of Asian Pacific American filmmakers. The attempt to *fit* the "Asian Pacific American" identity formation into an oppositional stance with the hegemonic culture is grounded to the first of, so far, two periods in the Asian Pacific American filmmaking. I think of this periodization as a form of a "working category" that illuminates race issues related to the group's media arts and its identity formation, at the same time that it calls attention to its tentativeness, inventiveness, and constructedness. In attempting to simply reverse the hierarchy of power, as mentioned earlier, the framework of oppositionality in filmmaking and film criticism has become problematic. The lineage of the 1960s radicalism to the Ethno-Communications Program to Robert Nakamura and his batch mates, and to the Visual Communication marks this first period. Visual Communications becomes the model of an oppositional filmmaking operation, emphasizing collectivity against individuality in film production, community focus and involvement instead of the individual/personal centeredness, and the construction of countermemory and counterhistory instead of Hollywood and racism's erasure of minority history and memory.[24] Collective film production becomes the metaphor for constituting the community ego-ideal. Tasked with retrieving the community's history and emphasizing its uniqueness, the documentary becomes the preferred film type.

The first wave of output of this period utilized, not surprisingly, the avant-garde and documentary techniques dominant in the burgeoning 1960s alternative filmmaking scene. In productions such as Danny Kwan's *Homecoming Game*, Brian Maeda's *Yellow Brotherhood*, and Duane Kubo's *Cruisin' J-Town*, the everyday narratives of young Asian American lives are documented using an absent omniscient narrator, extended takes, quick edits, dutch angle shots, self-reflexive camera presence, and fragmented storytelling. A second wave sprang from the avant-gardist documentary mode, using more straightforward documentary (presence of an omniscient narrator, talking heads, and historical evidences) and narrative (featurized representation, organic structure) film techniques. Filipino/a Americans entered the media arts in this second wave. These later documentaries represented straightforward narration of erased histories.

As the agenda of filmmaking was retrieval of the community's history and emphasis on its uniqueness, the immigrant experience becomes the privileged subject matter marking the beginning of the group's contact with U.S. history. Any discussion, therefore, of a politics of representation in the documentary of the "Filipino/a American" experience is linked to the immigration experience and the changing demography. Filipinos were the first Asian immigrants to the United States; Filipino sailors jumped ship in the galleon trade and established a community in New Orleans in the 1700s. As a mass exodus, however, Filipino/as make up the third wave in Asian migration, after the Chinese and Japanese. This bit of information may further be linked to the larger media arts output by Chinese and Japanese Americans. As incomes tend to increase over generations, more time and money can then be spent for leisure. Indulgence in Western art, such as filmmaking, is considered a form of leisure, alienated from the function of everyday life or of compensated labor. With increasing incomes, tolerance and awareness of art-as-profession increase.

Educational institutions play an important role in "Asian Pacific American" media arts. Although still pressed by the problem of representation in film schools, those who do make it contribute significantly toward enriching the body of productions of their community. Even more significant is the link between film schools and the Filipino/a American media artists. The earliest link dates back to Doroteo Ines as a film student at the University of Southern California (USC). He is credited with the first known "Filipino American" film with the work entitled, *A Filipino/a in America* (1938).[25] As a fictional record of Ines' student life, the film features the issues encountered by a Filipino studying and working in the United States; specifically, the film deals with encounters with racism and romance with an Anglo-Saxon. Another pre–World War II USC film student, Isagani Pastor, eventually worked for Walt Disney Productions. The recent generations of A Filipino in American filmmakers are also mostly trained and/or based in academic institutions. Mar Elepaño studied in USC, where he now teaches animation and graphic arts. Fruto Corre and Desireena Almoradie are graduates of New York University. Marlon Fuentes studied at Temple University. Daniel Tirtawinata is a graduate of the University of California at Los Angeles, where Celine Salazar Parreñas is winding up her program. Rachel Rivera finished at UC Berkeley. Antonio de Castro was affiliated with the San Francisco State University, where Melissa Cruz also did her filmmaking degree. Recent entrant John Manal Castro is a graduate of California State University at Long Beach. As the demand for more professionally trained artists increases, Filipino/a media artists are sharing with the other filmmakers, whether Anglo-Saxon or people of color, the general movement toward formal film education as an avenue not only for training, but also exposure and networking. However, filmmakers without academic training or bases are also working to expand and deepen the range of Filipino/a images and representational issues.

It is noteworthy to emphasize here the three waves of Filipino/a immigration to the United States. This, after all, becomes the initial subject explored in the documentary's retrieval of the Filipino/a's history with the United States, the originary moment attributed by filmmakers that produces the bicultural "Filipino/a American" experience. The first wave of immigration was at the turn of the century with the influx of Filipino/a agricultural workers into Hawaii, Alaska, and California that replaced Chinese and Japanese labor for two reasons. Immigration policies greatly restricted the influx of Chinese and Japanese nationals; Chinese and Japanese workers, then, were instigating the formation of unions, becoming too unruly for management to handle. Filipino immigration, however, was tied to U.S. colonial policy. U.S.-Philippine relations in the 1930s, for example, considered Filipino/as as "wards under American tutelage" without rights of citizens. The passage of the Tydings–McDuffie Act in 1934 effected a promise of Philippine independence, but it immediately gave alien status to Filipino/as. It was only after fighting as allies during World War II that Filipino/as were granted citizenship in the United States. Thus, the second wave began when veterans were allowed to petition for women to become spouses. Before this point, women were generally either not allowed or discouraged to immigrate. However, when Filipina immigration was finally allowed and tolerated, the earlier male immigrants were considered too old for marriage. The third wave started in the 1960s, allowing professionals and technically skilled personnel to immigrate. With diminishing opportunities in the Philippines, the "brain drain" era persists as more professionals opt to work abroad.

The first contemporary Filipino/a American production began with this immigration experience, in 1974 with Leonardo Ignacio's documentary entitled *The Filipino Immigrant*. The film presents the social problems encountered by Filipino immigrants in the United States. The thrust of succeeding documentaries was also tied to this retrieval of the history of male pioneers, placing them in the nexus of U.S. national history. Succeeding works on the initial wave of primarily male immigrants included *Manong* (1978) by Linda Mabalot, *The Fall of the I-Hotel* (1983) by Chinese American Curtis Choy, *A Dollar a Day Ten Cents a Dance* (1984) by Geoffrey Dunn and Mark Schwartz, *In No One's Shadow: Filipinos in America* (1988) by Mabalot and Antonio de Castro, and the most recent *Filipino Americans: Discovering Their Past for Their Future* (1994) produced by the Filipino American Historical Society. Other projects in progress or on hold along this thrust include one on women immigrants and two on specific pioneers—a feature film adaptation of Carlos Bulosan's autobiographical novel *America is in the Heart*, and another documentary based on the oral history of trade unionist Phillip Vera Cruz. Later on, the straightforward narrative mode is also privileged in this period. Daniel Tirtawinata's *Day the Dancers Came* (1993) adopts Bienvenido Santos's short story of the lonely and forgotten aging Filipino elderly. Gene Cajayon's *Debut* (2000)[26] deals with the more recent generation's identity problems, and their differences with later generations and their value systems; Castro's *Diary of A Gangsta Sucka* (1993) is an irreverent account of a young filmmaker's contact with a gang member, and the film encounter that ensues between the filmmaker and the gang with its culture.

Marlon Fuentes' fictional documentary *Bontoc Eulogy* (1996) dramatizes the search for a national ethnic identity as imbricated in the imperialist history of the United States. Using autobiographical documentary techniques, the viewer is subjected to a similar identity-formation and quest as the main character in order to deconstruct the fictionality of hegemonic structures.

The second period of "Asian Pacific American" media arts overlaps with the first. The second period is marked by a divergence from the pounding emphasis on the notion of the political as expressed in the emphasis upon issues of collectivity and foregrounding of the group's macrohistory. What occurs in the second period are shifts back to some notions of the individual, personal, and microhistory that mark a third wave of output in media arts. Films by Japanese Americans Gregg Araki and Roddy Bogawa, part-Filipino Rico Martinez, Filipino/a Americans Noel Shaw and Angel Shaw, and Filipino immigrant Elepaño are some examples of this maneuver. While these works are still marked by their oppositional difference to Hollywood in terms of film style and content, the "Asian" and "Pacific" content value in these films may just become incidental. Or it can be, as in the case of Angel Shaw's *Nailed* (1992), that the individual subjectivity in the media work is coursed through the webs of the hostland and the homeland's social histories. In this second period, media categories (whether animation, narrative, documentary, or experimental mode) tend to cross over boundaries in retelling personal, collective, or more *universal* narratives. In the *Asian American Media Reference Guide*, for example, "experimental" becomes the convenient classification for films that shift between modes, although some media artists prefer the term "mixed genre."[27]

Elepaño's animation, for example, has moved back and forth from representational to abstract films. Images of his Filipino and American experience seemingly get eroded to more general categories of "alienation effect" and "black" humor. Martinez's *Glamazon: A Different Kind of Girl* (1992) is a documentary on a non-Filipino/a and non-Asian American subject, tackling the story of "she-male" Barbara LeMay, a former queen of the burlesque dancers and "ex-carnival freak." Informed by film education, Martinez aspires for a queer cinema "in between *Valley of the*

Dolls, Saturday Night Fever, and Kenneth Anger's *Scorpio Rising.*"[28] Araki's feature films, on the other hand, explore the fringes of decay and taboo of queerness. Preferring "non-traditional" topics, he states, "I found my subcultures to be more repressive, more straightjacketing, more tunnel-vision than the majority culture which they so relentlessly and demonstratively attack."[29] Martinez is equally pronounced: "God! Why do we have to see another film about their grandmother? It seemed to me embarrassing in a way, because I was thinking people are going to think that's the only thing we can do."[30] Elepaño, however, thinks of his works as a phase of grappling with the developments in the media. Currently not doing any animation, he is using the period to rethink his own relationship with identity issues on the one hand, and the technology of computerized animation and interactivity on the other. He, however, warns of the danger of thinking of every film by specific artists as embodying the requirement of specific identity citation.

To think, for example, of "Filipino/a American" films as an embodiment of solely or purely "Filipino/a American" issues is problematic. The expectation that the other remains confined in predetermined terms—in cultural and political constructs of identity politics and marginality—reifies the orientalist position of exoticizing and homogenizing the other, and consequently defines Western subjectivity and selfhood. The idea that the Filipino/a and Asian Pacific Americans can only work within the confines of their experiences is suspect; the modes by which these groups have been historically marginalized and disenfranchised may continue to operate as forms of othering and homogenizing identities. As such, having experienced the postmodern conditions in the belly of the "First World," more recent Filipino/a and Asian Pacific American media artists are incorporating these modes of experienciation with the available new technologies in problematizing their own positions in U.S. culture and cultural politics.

Thus the media artists and their works are getting more and more caught up in the liminal space of historically established expectations—analogous to Trinh's notion of a subject that is at once "transient and constant," or the overarching notion of the hybrid subject—a juncture for considering newer configurations of racial, cultural, and aesthetic (trans) formations.[31] In Noriega's conceptualization, the racialized subject is both a national (American) and nationalist (Filipino/a, Japanese gay, East Asian woman, or Asian, for example).[32] With the notion of liminality in mind, the media artist then foregrounds complementary and contradictory subject positions. Martinez—being part-Filipino/a and part-Mexican American, and gay—is able to move between various racial and sexual cultural constructs. Issues of transnationalism prefigure prominently in "Filipino/a American" media texts. As a Filipino exchange scholar, Corre in *Women of Waray Waray* (1990) reposits the colonial and neocolonial relations as the necessary context for interrogating the construction of

Imelda Marcos's pop culture iconography in the United States, as simply the penultimate exemplar of "Third World" conspicuous consumption. What Corre is attempting in the politicized music video is an imperialist critique implicating Imelda's excess as conjured from the violent legacy and reality of U.S.-Philippine relations. Angel Shaw's two video diaries and Rivera's own *Sin City Diary* (1992) also draw heavily from these relations, returning to the Philippines to weave personal subjectivity with the nation's cultural identity. Lavrente Indico Diaz's *Sarungbanggi ni Alice* (*One Night of Alice*, 1994) documents a Filipina rape victim, seeking solace in the United States only to experience further abuse in her newfound homeland. Parreñas's *Mahal Means Love and Expensive* (1993) deals with a poetic vision of female sexuality and creativity, and issues of race and transnationality. Walter Baitan Hangad's *Blood, Sweat and Lace* (1994) deals with the injustice in the garment subcontracting business, focusing on the alleged abuses committed on immigrant women workers by Jessica McClintock's empire.

This notion of the hybrid subject can be elaborated further by a third term, the "homeland" as the liminal space of identification and difference between the nation of origin or national background on the one hand, and the nation of immigration or the hostland on the other. While national origin refers to the "unchosen" (one does not choose one's national background, one is born into this category as in race and color), the place of immigration is defined by the notion of choice (one chooses or is forced to choose one's place; a Hawaiian, for example, displaced in the islands migrates to the mainland). By "homeland," however, I refer to the location of affinity that the individual consciously chooses to position himself or herself within a group. As a political affiliation, therefore, the homeland is an internal nationally defined experience that considers the differences between how Hollywood, racism, and neocolonialism have been enforced by the hegemonic culture and made sense of by marginal cultures. As such, the "homeland" is related to ongoing demographic changes: "demographic change in the growing mass of Filipinos in the U.S. provides an opportunity to assert an autonomy from the sweep of 'Asian American' even as Filipinos continue to unite with other Asians in coalitions for greater political demands."[33] Next to the Chinese, Filipino/as comprise the second largest Asian group in the United States, half of which is settled in California. Over 170,000 Filipino/as legally enter the country each year. As of 2000, there are some 2 million Filipino/as; and by these indications, Filipino/as may soon comprise the biggest Asian group.[34] For the immigrants, connections between the nation of origin and the hostland persist as instances of familial and national bonds imbued in neocolonial relations. Fifty thousand Filipino/a American nurses, for example, remit over $100 million annually to the Philippines. Annual cash remittance from the United States is estimated to be at $1 billion. Cultural connections have already been concretized in the immigration experience, as each

Filipino/a has at least one family member here. (However, for Filipino/as born in the United States, racial identity formation takes the form of a more conscious effort to retrace both the histories of the Philippines and its imbrication in the U.S. national history. It also takes the form of learning the Filipino language that was denied access by parents believing that such action would quicken the process of assimilation to U.S. society.) Yet the astounding demographic figures do not easily correspond to the Filipino/a American visibility in the political and cultural spheres. One wonders why the Filipino/a American presence has yet to be seen and felt; given its quantity, what accounts for its invisibility?

In attempting to unravel this complex issue, an analysis of race in "Filipino American" media arts presents some of the issue's folds. What I am considering here is how race is differentiated (made specific and historicized) in the documentary, feature, and "experimental" waves of output. Each of these outputs foregrounds particular issues of race and representation. In doing so, I am also attempting to foreground some of the stakes involved, as Filipino/a Americans represent and position themselves in their media arts. The documentary mode provides a trope to make visible an obscured Filipino/a American identity, its Philippine interdeterminations, and consequently its unique position as diasporic peoples of former colonized subjects in the United States.[35] Filipino/a American documentaries mark the originary point of insertion—the manongs' contact and experience in the United States—in national history that eventually paves for the birthing, so to speak, of Filipino/a Americans. (*Manong* is a respectful and endearing term for the male elderly, and the bachelor society in the first wave of immigration.) *In No One's Shadow* is one documentary that deals with the affect of guilt, loss, and nostalgia as differentially experienced by Filipino/a Americans. In differentiating the experience, the documentary also positions the Philippines. It begins with an invocation of fantasies of America:

> Manong: "We heard so much of America, you know . . . America being so beautiful. All you have to do is to pick up that money right over there—either they grow on trees or lie on the streets. See, that's the reason I came over here."

> Woman: "Just to hear America, it tickles us. We also think of coming over here when we graduate."

> Man: "I dream about reaching the U.S., and this is the only way—the navy—to see the U.S."

> Woman: "I came here to do more work in dance, and at that time I had several professors who had been in the U.S. I was interested in doing work in what we call modern dance or contemporary dance. The only place where I can get advanced training, knowledge of modern dance was in the U.S."

Seemingly enunciating a colonized's fantasy of incorporation within the spatial national body of the colonizer, the statements do evoke naivety on the one hand—presenting an immaculate innocence of the literal and epistemic violence inflicted in the Philippine colonial and neocolonial histories. On the other hand, taken as the psyche's working of a fantasy scenario of geophysical movement and social mobility, the statements foreground the defining mark of fantasy, that the act of fantasizing is a substitute for unattainable pleasure. The non-realization of expectations and pleasures becomes predicated on the very nature of fantasy. The filmmakers, then, proceed to catalog the various moments of contacts between the colonized's originary innocence as affected by the adverse conditions in the colonizer's space, consequently producing struggle, survival, and endurance as legitimate bases for insertion within this national space and history. In the filmmakers' discursive construction, the statements are imbued with a sexualized vocabulary of colonial rescue and feminization. The ways in which America is imagined and constructed as imaginable are emanating from the imagination of the other, that of the Philippines—a colonial landscape that does not function for its people, and whose intertwining history with the United States and colonial abjection by the United States are simply not conducive to the imaginary process. Thus the oppressive and repressive realities staked in the colonialization of the Philippines find relief in the act of imagining (re: idealizing) America, culminating in the relief becoming real in the act of coming to the United States. A double rescue takes place: a psychical relief maintained within the colonial space and predicated by the U.S. colonialist imperative of constructing the Philippines "in our image"; and a physical relief through the geopolitical movement of the body. The Philippines is placed in a feminine position, awaiting imperial rescue. Rescue, however, connotes a biblical worthiness based on certain assimilable national characteristics (after all, only the most worthy is deserving of American legitimization: visa, greencard, or citizenship); of which survival and endurance become raw materials to the Protestant work ethics' construction of the liberal-plural individual. Furthermore, this rescue scenario ideologically justifies two issues: the colonization of the Philippines and the absent presence/present absence of the Filipino/a in the United States. The former is used to justify the latter in a cause-effect logic, thereby reappealing to an imperial ethos for recognition as positioned internally (an imperial interiorized voice). The film thus appeals to a colonialist guilt, nostalgia, and loss for the validation of Filipino/a American presence here.[36]

The testimonies via talking heads end, a music track heralding a shift comes in as black-and-white graphic images of Filipino/as flood the screen (with two females, a Filipina holding an infant and a child beside her), the title is posted above these images. The narrator then is introduced in a background shot of a recognizable American structure, the Golden

Gate Bridge, proudly announcing "we are the largest Asian American population in the nation today." The narrator, from a later generation, gives the pedagogical greeting, *"Mabuhay!"* ("Long Live!"), introduces himself, and begins the chronicle of Filipino/a affairs in the United States. *In No One's Shadow* becomes a paradoxical title to the various intertexts called upon to locate and produce the Filipino/a American discourse. It is precisely this connection with the various intertexts (colonial history, present politics, neocolonial relations, culture) that locates a unique history of the Filipino/a Americans. To stretch the documentary's own metaphor, it is the various shadows that hover and subsist in the Filipino/a Americans' own that make distinct its identity formation and critical transformation. The narrator ends with the same shot composition as his introduction sequence began, "the story of Filipinos in America is far from over. Each day is a new step, a new beginning. Filipinos are learning to flex their muscles of social and political influence. We are taking our place in the forefront of American life, standing in no one's shadow." The film posits a nationalist discourse—based on survival amid adversity, endurance amid oppression—only to make it integral for assimilation within the American landscape that claims plurality and multiculturalism as its basis. Interestingly, the narrator's syntax (progression, flexing of muscles, forefronting) claims a remasculinization in its stake in Filipino/a American affairs within American life.

An early film that maps out race relations is *A Filipino In America*. The film deals with the manong experience but on two different levels—from a relatively more privileged position as a student in the United States, and from a narrative feature mode. The feature mode has been similarly used as the straightforward documentaries, drawing on the emotive force of the experience of oppression and endurance to mark its space of identity construction. Another similarity is the way the feature condenses the "Filipino/a" experience in the United States, cataloging issues and events resulting from the contact production and recognition of difference. A recourse through the manong experience condenses issues of racial oppression and resistance in the straightforward documentaries. The feature, however, does not use documentary evidences to make its point; it is a fictional account of the lives of the manongs, and more recently, of the latter generation of young Filipino/a Americans. As such, the feature mode allows for a typology of characters that construct a microcosm of community in narrativizing issues of Filipino/a American identity. Consequently, Filipino/a American features can be read allegorically of the Philippine and U.S. national contexts.

What is interesting in this silent film is the representation of the Filipino's experience with racism. The experience of racism abounds in the film, immediately debunking the American imaginary of Los Angeles skyscrapers, Anglo women, social mobility even within a racial hierarchy, overabundance, and modernity. A fascination with an Anglo woman is initially reciprocated, only to be ignored, and later outright resisted. The transnational connection—the white woman's father's common experience in Manila with the Filipino character "brings immediate friendship"—becomes crucial to the initial and consequent invitations to the woman's house. In other words, the Anglo woman, not the father, becomes the racialized agent body for the eventual othering of the Filipino. In a second incident, the Filipino is forced out of his church seat. The experience in church, a central fixture in the lives of Filipinos, deconstructs the American imaginary, portrayed as being both racist and unchristian. (It is this scene that equally deconstructs the negative representation of the recourse to Filipino public spheres in another straightforward documentary *Dollar A Day*; even "positive" spaces, after all, are not conducive to Filipino identity formation.) The third experience with racism deals with employment after graduation from engineering school; he moves to the job site only to find that the job awaiting him is dishwasher. He is enraged, goes back to his room, and stares at a knife. In this brief contemplation of suicide, he reads an announcement: "the President of the [Philippine] Commonwealth asks students to come home." A salary of $250 a year is also posted. He then decides to return. The final sequence consists of shots of him on a ship exiting the harbor, ending in a close-up of his face superimposed on the Philippine flag.

The Filipino's experience with racism is pervasive in the film, with the educational institution providing the only "neutral" public space, and his room the only private space for negotiating racism and the mythical American imaginary. However, racism is not represented as oppressive enough to cause a return to the native land, as even these experiences remain bearable for the character. What becomes the last straw is the chronic lack of economic opportunities equivalent to his new stature as a college graduate. Academic capital becomes the class characteristic differentiating a student from an agricultural worker—the latter category being the one in which most Filipinos were placed in the same migration period. In the end, he equally realizes the dream of social mobility through education, a value ingrained in the U.S. "benevolent assimilation" of the Philippines which introduced the public school system in the country.[37]

The third wave of output is the "experimental" or "mixed-genre" mode. In this mode, the interrogation of identity moves in the liminality of self and nation, Filipino/a and American, masculinity and femininity, and the like. In other words, now that the documentary has been able to insert Filipino history within U.S. history, the pivot for further specifying identity is through explorations of individual subjectivity. The earlier precursor to this mode is the animation and experimental works, similar to those done by Elepaño; each short film represents the psyche in abstract or "pure" terms of free association. While the feature mode presents an almost equal representation of men and women media artists, the "experimental" mode is largely dominated by women media artists. This flexible mode has been especially instrumental in positioning more women media artists in the forefront, and the different styles and approaches they utilize in narrativizing life stories with political and poetic themes. Parreñas, for example, utilizes the polemical and the poetic in *Mahal Means Love and Expensive. Nailed*, on the other hand, is an autobiographical documentary of a spiritual journey of sorts for the video artist, Angel Shaw. The video chronicles her journey to the Philippines in her quest for identity. Spirituality becomes the primary focus of her search, manifested in her identification with Lucy, one of the thirty-three women who allow themselves to be nailed on the cross every Good Friday as an expression of religious devotion. Lucy is also a medium for the Santo Niño, the child Jesus, and practices faith healing. Divided into four sections, *Nailed* interrogates the religious notions of reverence, ritual, redemption, and salvation.

The film begins with the video artist's epigraph on culture and national identity, "to understand the Philippine struggle was also [her] own struggle." There is a continuous sliding of personal vision, engulfed in myth, lore, dreams, and history, to the problematics of the native land's religiosity and spirituality on the one hand, and of indigenous and Catholic religions on the other. After the epigraph, against the backdrop of images of blue skies and white clouds, her voice-over of a dream of good and bad angels, and the difficulty of deciphering who is what foreshadows the engagement of the mythic with the real, or of the symbolic with the social constructs. Performances by Jessica Hagedorn, Han Ong, and the media artist herself punctuate the search, calling into focus the notion of performativity in identity construction. Thus, her identity is bifurcated yet both Filipina and American sides remain intact. The search that begins with a confusion of identifying "good" and "bad," comes to a halt with the acceptance of both positions imbricating the other.

By the end of the video, Shaw is more able to come to certain terms with her hybrid spiritual self (enmeshed in both animism and Catholicism) as prefiguring her (colonial) national and bicultural identities. The problematic of multiple identities is embedded too in the notion of diaspora— Filipino/a American identity, which Shaw is a part of, is only beginning to emerge as a culturally significant and politically potent national Asian minority. Somehow, its absence defines its presence here. Subjectivity, therefore, is enmeshed in a (dis)jointed cultural desire for historical integration with the U.S. national culture, and a resistance-against-assimilation through the acknowledgment of neocolonial and familial ties with the native land. As Shaw's race becomes an "unchosen" factor, her interrogation of American and Philippine national identities becomes indistinguishable as the split has incorporated one with the other. This means that in every aspect of her being, she is both American and Filipina.

The notion of the "homeland" is significant in positioning her choice of affinity. In her turn to the native land, she privileges this space as the site for exploring her spiritual identity; yet being raised in a U.S. cultural environment, her manner of inquiry (e.g., film ethnography of

Lucy, Christian baptism, and indigenous celebration of christening) primarily interrogates from an internal position in Eurocentric discourse. Lucy is turned into a spectacle for Shaw's identity retrieval, so is the geography of the Philippines as similarly embodied in the extended and recurring shots of a pig being slaughtered for ritual. Shaw's voice and resonance of liminality enclose the video diary. While the "experimental" mode has given the filmmaker a space for articulation, the other woman in her text has yet to speak. This absence of the speaking subject in film, addressed only en masse in straightforward documentaries, is an area that needs further exploration in refiguring "Filipino/a American" formation that does not replicate the binary logic of self/other.

What has been presented thus far are the various issues involved in the categories of "Asian Pacific American" and "Filipino/a American" media arts. It is useful to remind ourselves of Hall's point, of thinking of identity "as a 'production'" that is never complete, always in process, and always constituted within, not outside representation."[38] Without losing sight of the politics of location already gained in the first generation of Asian Pacific American filmmakers and in the civil rights movement, media artists continue to explore the various issues that confront their personal and community's identity.[39] The prospects for "Filipino/a American" media arts and artists are indeed encouraging, discursively alluding and directing to heterogeneous identity formations and the "Filipino/a Americans' " critical transformation. By foregrounding these problematics as a way of refiguring difference in identity formation, the possibilities for bondedness in media arts become more historically concrete and culturally specific. The problematics also allude to crossing-overs of boundaries in figuring identity politics. If as a film critic says of alternative cinemas that "films are only the forms of appearance of the cinemas they [in this case, Filipino/a and Asian Pacific Americans] organize," then alternative film practices can also be refigured for the organization of a politics of social formation and transformation within the group, across groups, and outside the margins, thereby displacing center-margin relationships.[40] This figuration of the collective and specific identity (trans)formation presents some issues of a dialogue in an engagement with notions of individual subjectivity, citizenship, and nationality on the one hand, and of recasting issues of class, gender and sexuality, race and ethnicity on the other hand. In this essay, I hope I have implied some grounds that shift the focus from "what is or ought to be?" to "what is to be done?"[41]

NOTES

Finalization of this essay was made possible through a grant from the office of the vice-chancellor for research and development of the University of the Philippines.

I am especially grateful to the following people for their encouragement and helpful comments: Peter Britos, David Li, David James, Elaine Kim, Kyung Hyun Kim, Lisa Lowe, and Bhaskar Sarkar. This essay is also made possible through interviews with Claire Aguilar, Mar Elepaño, Abraham Ferrer, and Linda Mabalot, and through the assistance of Jerome Academia of Visual Communications and Elsa Eder of the National Asian American Telecommunications Association for facilitating my viewing of Filipino/a film and video productions.

1. Experience in immigration has brought about this contestation for authority to speak for and to define the group, in what terms, and for whom. According to Arif Dirlik in *What is in a Rim? Critical Perspectives on the Pacific Region Idea* (Boulder, Colo.: Westview, 1993), the hegemonic culture's insistence on viewing Asians in their Asianness distinguishes this racial trait from its own Americanness: "in the perception of the hegemonic 'Anglo-Saxon' culture in the United States, Asian Americans were irretrievably Asians. Their trans-Pacific ties served not to further recognition of an Asian presence in the national formation of the United States, but to deny its members' Americanness" (325).

This essay finds affinity in the works of colleagues Peter Britos, "Point of Origin: Recent Hawaiian Filmmakers at the University of Southern California, School of Cinema-Television," and Chia-chi Wu, "Chinese American Independent Filmmaking" (unpublished manuscripts, 1995). Both essays specify and historicize not only the particular groups' experience in the media arts, but also the very concept of difference in reconfiguring race and identity discourse.

2. This is not to say that the "Filipino/a" is in itself devoid of problematics. Categorical questions do arise, as well as the epistemological ones. The issues of nativism and essentialism on the one hand, and assimilation and integration on the other hand, become contending premises that bear impending ideological ramification: is there such a distinct national essence called the Filipino/a as configured in its contact with America? Cultural categories of gender and sexuality, regional and ethnic differences, religious orientation, class origin, and political affiliation further circuit the epistemological imperative to greater complexity. These multiple categories, therefore, already preclude any sweeping subordination of *every* experience under "Filipino/a." As the issue bears weight in my discussion of Filipino/a identity politics, I am thus using "Filipino/a" in a move to call attention to other sexual and gender positionalities that provide modes of critical interrogation to the hegemonic construction of "national" identity as represented in its media arts.

3. David James, in relation to avant-garde film, already mentions in *Allegories of Cinema: American Film in the Sixties* (Princeton, N.J.: Princeton University Press, 1989) the need to determine linkages and dialectics between alternative cinemas and Hollywood on the one hand, and of the "interdeterminations" of various alternative cinemas on the other hand. Although obvious shifts in the Filipino/a image in Hollywood films are manifested— from feminized houseboys and chattering maids to World War II valiant foot soldiers and loyal American (and anti-Japanese) followers, for example—the relationship between Hollywood and Filipino/a American media arts has not been equitable, to say the least. As such, rather than focus on the hybridity of Filipino/a American media arts, for an initial essay on the area such as this, the need to foreground the operations of a *marginal* category (Asian Pacific American) within which this category functions to create a dialectics of solidarity and marginality among its various margins may be more productive in destabilizing center-margin relations within a specific media sphere.

4. Russell Leong, ed., *Moving the Image: Independent Asian Pacific American Media Arts* (Los Angeles, Calif.: UCLA Asian American Studies Center and Visual Communications, 1991).

5. For a discussion of minority discourse, see Abdul R. JanMohamed and David Lloyd, "Introduction: Toward a Theory of Minority Discourse: What is to be Done?" in *The Nature and Context of Minority Discourse* (Berkeley: University of California Press, 1990), 1. For "identity formation," refer to Lisa Lowe, "Heterogeneity, Hybridity, Multiplicity: Marking Asian American Differences," *Diaspora* (Spring 1991), in which she stresses the three terms of her title in an argument on cultural politics, "the ultimate argument being to disrupt the current hegemonic relationship between 'dominant' and 'minority' positions" (28).

6. Refer to Renee Tajima's discussion of the program in "Ethno-Communications: The Film Program That Changed the Color of Independent Filmmaking," in *The Anthology of Asian Pacific American Film and Video* (New York: Third World Newsreel, 1985).

7. Ibid., 42.

8. Although the book claims to be "the first effort to define independent Asian Pacific American media arts and to describe its development from 1970 to 1990," other initial attempts to historicize and synthesize the group's media arts, however, predate the book. Earlier efforts are the *Anthology of Asian American Film & Video Arts* (1985) and the *1987 Asian American International Film Festival: First Decade Celebration* (New York: Asian CineVision, 1987).

9. Russell Leong, "To Open the Future," in *Moving the Image*, xvii.

10. Cindy Wong, "Rituals Revisited," as quoted in Leong, *Moving the Image*, xiv.

11. Linda Mabalot, "Preface," in *Moving the Image*, viii.

12. Trinh T. Minh-ha, "Bold Omissions and Minute Depictions," in *Moving the Image*, 87.

13. Kyung Hyun Kim reminds me of the geopolitical connection in the social sciences' framing of U.S.-Latin American relations, of which the same idea can be paralleled to traditional working of center-margins and Hollywood-alternative cinemas relations.

14. Trinh, "Bold Omissions and Minute Depictions," 88.

15. Stuart Hall, "New Ethnicities," in *Black Film British Cinema* (London: BFI, 1988), 28.

16. Chon Noriega, "El hilo latino: representation, identity and national culture," *Jump Cut* 38.

17. Hall, "New Ethnicities," 27.

18. Ibid.

19. Ibid.

20. Ibid., 24.

21. Ibid., 29. Hall clarifies that the term "ethnicity" acknowledges the place of history, language and culture in the construction of subjectivity and identity, as well as the fact that all discourse is placed, positioned, situated, and all knowledge is contextual."

22. Ibid., 27–28.

23. Ibid., 28. It would be useful to consider culture as an integral categorical force to the dominant political emphasis in identity formation. Antonio Gramsci's reframing of civil society gives culture a privileged function; and as David McLellan states in *Marxism After Marx* (Boston, Mass.: Houghton Mifflin, 1979), "civil society denoted for Gramsci all the organisations and technical means which diffuse the ideological justification of the ruling class in all domains of culture" (188). Thus, culture's function in civil society can be interpreted as allowing the possibility of a counterhegemony, that is, as a means of forging dissent as well as consent, laying bare the contradictions as well as the stability in "the ideological hegemony of the capitalists . . . to represent their own interests as those of society as a whole" (186). As a challenge to ideological hegemony, culture in the public sphere can be read as a potential allied sphere for marginal and subaltern groups. In *Hegemony and Socialist Strategy: Towards a Radical Democratic Politics* (London: Verso, 1985), Ernesto Laclau and Chantal Mouffe further rework the concept of hegemony that validates new social movements, releasing the category from prior Marxist (even in Gramsci's "historical bloc") totalizing and essentializing usages that have historically privileged a unitary class category. This move allows for a "pluralistic" and radical politics and sites of negotiation in the seemingly irreconcilable arenas of the socialist project within the democratic revolution initiated by capitalism. Although remaining largely silent on their specifics of radical democracy and overall conception of socialism, Laclau and Mouffe's allotment of a critical space for new social movements remains significant as a mode of "identify[ing] the discursive conditions for the emergence of a collective action, directed towards struggling against inequalities and changing relations of subordination" (153). Culture, then, returns as a more viable force for empowerment in realizing a pluralistic and radical democracy.

24. Refer to Jeanne Joe's discussion of Visual Communications under Robert Naka-mura's term in "Visual Communications: A New Asian Image on the Screen," *Neworld* No. 6 (1979).

25. This 16mm film is presently being restored in video under the sponsorship of Pamana, a Filipino American cultural organization based in Los Angeles.

26. *The Debut* premiered in May 2000 at the Los Angeles Asian Pacific Film & Video Festival (ed.).

27. Bill J. Gee, *Asian American Media Reference Guide*, 2nd ed. (New York: Asian CineVision, 1990).

28. "Directors' Profile," *16th Asian American International Film Festival Program* (New York: Asian CineVision, 1993).

29. Gregg Araki, "The (Sorry) State of (Independent) Things," in *Moving the Image*, 69.

30. Kim Yutani, "On the Fringe: Young, Hip Filmmaker Explores the Peculiar," from the file *Asians in Film*, compiled by the UCLA Asian American Studies Center.

31. Trinh, "Bold Omissions and Minute Depictions," 85.

32. Noriega, "El hilo latino," 46.

33. E. San Juan Jr., "The Predicament of Filipinos in the United States: Where Are You From? When Are You Going Back?" in *The State of Asian America: Activism and Resistance in the 1990s*, ed. Karin Aguilar-San Juan (Boston, Mass.: Southend, 1994), 206.

34. For further discussion of demographic changes, refer to *The State of Asian Pacific America: A Public Policy Report* (Los Angeles, Calif.: LEAP, 1993); Paul Ong and Tania Azores, *Asian Pacific Americans in Los Angeles, Calif.: A Demographic Profile* (Los Angeles: LEAP, 1993); H. Brett Melendy, "Filipino Immigration—Seeking a Share of the American Dream," in *Asians in America* (Boston, Mass.: T. Wayne, 1977); and Bill Ong Hing, "The Filipinos," in *Making and Remaking Asian America Through Immigration Policy 1850–1990* (Stanford, Calif.: Stanford University Press, 1993).

35. Britos in "Point of Origin" cites the central role of the documentary, in what I will term as "visibility construction" in the libidinal economy of identity politics, as "the desire to set the record straight, to give voice to those marginalized or overlooked by mainstream western preoccupations, to problematize imposed social structures, or to celebrate unique aspects of a cultural heritage" (3).

36. Colonial ties that have constructed a mythical American imaginary became the psychical drive to immigrate to the United States. The immigrant's economic motivation, to seek a better life elsewhere, is also a product of U.S. colonial adventurism. As the imaginary has been proven otherwise by actual immigrants' experience, the economic imperative to survive became the imminent drive to maintain presence here. Unwittingly, the immigrants' continuing presence *here* instead of *there* further fuels the mythical American imaginary in the Philippines. However, the desire to return to the homeland is compounded by guilt, loss, and nostalgia. Guilt results from the notion of forsaking the originary homeland, family, and nation; of initiating the cut that physically and psychically distances the self from these communities. Nostalgia is aggravated by the everyday experience with racism, sustaining and deepening the feeling of isolation and unhappiness *here* versus the imagined originary plenitude experienced *there*. Loss marks the impossibility of a return, the absence of a territorial space in the originary homeland. It also results from "face-saving," as those who return are expected to be economically successful.

It is no wonder that these psychical imperatives become the basis of maintaining transnational business with the older generation of Filipino/a Americans—the substitution is performed through a shipping package, long-distance call, or cash remittance, providing temporal relief from this psychic torment—a business of compressing spatial difference.

37. A more historically situated documentary on the manongs is made by a non-Filipino/a. Done by Curtis Choy, *The Fall of the I-Hotel* details the struggle for survival and dignity among the manongs threatened by eviction in the 1970s, and consequently evicted from their place of residence, the International Hotel on Kearney Street, San Francisco. In the larger context, the I-Hotel became an icon of the struggle against hegemonic planning

and enforcement of urban renewal that marginalizes the already traditionally marginalized peoples incapable of residing elsewhere. The documentary also highlights the ensuing solidarity among Asian Americans and other races around the cause.

38. Quoted in Roddy Bogawa, "An(Other) Reflection on Race?" in *Moving the Image*, 210.

39. One of the creative ways in which "Asian Pacific" American has been utilized is through the form of pragmatic tactical maneuvers within the hegemonic system that purport to be liberal-pluralistic and multicultural. "Asian Pacific American," as a cultural category, has been utilized by practitioners within the group to assert funding (e.g., National Endowment for the Arts and private foundations) and exposure (e.g., Public Broadcast System and museums) of their arts. Such maneuvers have constituted the group as a viable force within the system, placing access to funding and exhibition as integral to the system's enunciation of its liberal-pluralist agenda. (With the recent attack on affirmative action, however, the system once again makes visible its Janus face, now invoking the marginal's access as excess and falling within the logic of unfair competition, and therefore "undemocratic" [*we* of course ask: *for whom?*]. This attack is but one of the nodes of the system's recurring countermaneuvering for self-preservation and self-perpetuation of its liberal/conservative legacy, that is, the backlashing onto bodies of marginal groups as both rationale and scapegoat of its hegemonic yet contradictory agenda.)

40. James, *Allegories of Cinema*, 23.

41. JanMohamed and Lloyd, "Introduction," 16.

Helen Lee

A Peculiar Sensation: A Personal Genealogy of Korean American Women's Cinema

> *Her hair is wrapped smoothly in a possibly comfort-*
> *able bun, higher than seems right but that was the style*
> *then. She is perched on a rock, near flower bushes,*
> *smiling. My mother clutches a small handbag with*
> *gloved hands, her legs neatly arranged. Like my father,*
> *she wears a crisp suit. I don't know what color because*
> *the image is from a black and white photograph, not a*
> *memory. They are about the same age as I am now.*

As adults, I think we are haunted by an image of our parents in their youth, a time we never knew them. For child immigrants, these images of the past also come from another place. Not here. A place far enough away that a telephone call occasions worry first, not joy. My parents left Seoul when I was three years old. A year later, my sister and I joined them in Toronto, Canada. Our young tongues, trained in Korean food and language but unschooled and now unhomed, were soon eager for french fries and making friends in English. I think that age especially, around three and four (just prior to grade school, when private home life becomes formatively public), was critical when I try to recall where photographs end and memory begins. It isn't clear.

It is a kind of curse, I think, to leave your birthplace when you are young enough to lose your mother tongue but old enough not to forget the loss. For my generation, Korean American/Canadian women filmmakers who were born there but raised here, the utter contemporaneity of our experiences means "back there" and "back then" as much as right now. As someone who writes and makes images about such tongue-tying experiences, I would like to try to remember this particular haunting of representation and subjectivity, where language is the spine of memory. Through our images, the faded pictures of our mothers speak with new force, saying something about our lives here. I am certain we all became filmmakers as soon as we stepped off the plane.

For now, let's put away those childish wishes for assimilation and discover a new desire for affinity. This essay represents the desire to look at the work of my peers, other Korean American women filmmakers,[1] and discover the connections among their work and also the films I have made. I wondered if there was anything specific about the efflorescence of media work over the past few years that represented commonalities of location. How did our experiences as *kyop'o* (overseas Korean) women inform our aesthetic practices? How did these works function from the perspective of cultural displacement and feminist intervention, where race and gender identifications were prominent? How did the imbrication of Korean diasporic sensibilities (our *"kyop'o*-ness" or identities as overseas Koreans), and our multivalent positioning and constant negotiations as women and artists of color in this new world, reflect in our work? What kinds of representational strategies were being deployed, and what did this new visual culture signify[2]—simply, what were we saying, and how were we choosing to say it?

First, I am quite struck by the fact that most Korean American filmmakers are, in fact, women. For a generation destined, according to classical immigrant narratives of social and economic progress, to be brilliant doctors and lawyers (and by patriarchal imperative, good wives to boot), this is a startling find. Given the male-centered legacies of cinema history, theories of the cinematic apparatus, and the world of film production itself, it is also extraordinary. Was the desire for self-representation so intense as to supersede all the traditional barriers that usually placed women and people of color as outsiders looking in? Or, in the case of Korean American women filmmakers, did our peripheral status accord a privileged view—a "double vision"?

I imagine a girl standing before a mirror, or a woman holding a camera to her eye. Slowly, she turns to behold her image reflected back at her, like a doubling or twin. Not identical, different but same. She sees herself, as if for the first time.

A kind of "double consciousness"[3] is available to us as minority women in the white-dominant culture of North American society. In an American context, we are Korean. In a Korean context, we are women. These media works embody an ambivalent and contingent status of American/Korean, white/other, here/there, and very often a place in-between. Issues of race and gender are impossible to ignore when their privileges and oppressions affect dimensions of everyday life, not to mention the critical and artistic expressions we try to bring to it. Aptly named a "triple bind"[4] by Trinh T. Minh-ha, alluding to competing allegiances to differ-

ent communities, this unique equation of subjectivity—Korean/woman/
artist—can also prove immensely enabling. Could it be that patriarchal
expectations for the son have, ironically, liberated the daughter? (Sometimes I do wonder if I would have engaged in such an unstable profession as
filmmaking if I'd been expected to be the family breadwinner.) More likely
though, the Korean daughter became a feminist with something to say.

Our issues are different from what I imagine our female contemporaries in Korea, immersed in anti-colonial, nationalistic discourse in
conjunction with feminism in a neo-Confucian context, might take on. In
the 1980s, while Korean students were taking to the streets, the business
of assimilation and dreams of professional prosperity were occupying
Korean American youth. Immigrant success meant moving into ivory
towers, not smashing them. But this is a crude simplification (especially
now, with government gestures toward political reform stymieing former
student movement members of the 1980s, we are faced with a Korean society as economically stratified as ever in the post–Korean War era; as well,
Asian Americans are coming to the economic and political fore as never
before). Ultimately, for individuals and organizations devoted to progressive change, the question of what comprises socially committed, critically
informed work is answered by where we are located. While cut from the
same anti-imperialistic cloth as our Korean colleagues, I think we're more
likely to critique ideals of Western democracy and liberal society as illusions, than to claim them. Too many encounters with racism make it
impossible to be a chest-beating American nationalist (and for a Canadian,
it is downright anachronistic). Still, for mostly middle-class Korean Americans, the seduction of capital usually overrides considerations of class
and sometimes even race. That's why when I speak of "identity," it is less
a personal one (although it may be that, too) than a socially constructed,
politicized identity that needs to be "earned" or declared. Although I have
always been Korean, becoming "Korean American" or "Korean Canadian"
was a longer, self-examining process. Acts of community in the context
of racism and acute marginality are, in this way, themselves political.

These films and videos by Korean American women are highly
conscious, artistically and theoretically mediated works (all produced by
filmmakers with full benefit of college educations or art/film school, usually both). They are not "naive" in any sense, taking part in this highly
politicized arena with strategies of reinvention and resistance. Much of
the groundwork laid by feminist cinema and Asian American media has
informed our filmic practices and we, in turn, extend those histories.[5] For-
tified by debates around political and "third"[6] cinema, the rigidities of
realist filmmaking and pressures to produce only "positive images" of the
community, we roundly reject the banality and victimology associated
with "minority" filmmaking. Mere oppositionality, stereotype-fighting
documentaries, or simplistic "identity" films ("I am Korean American,
and this is a portrait of me") do not constitute this oeuvre. Like some
nationalistic Korean, I am proud of this. A fierce and prodigious discur-

sivity is at work; like a persistence of vision, these plural or multiple forms of consciousness pervade our films. The combined forces of our immigrant family pasts, the lingering effects of Korean male patriarchal traditions, Korea's own colonial national history, they all feed into our contemporary North American perspectives. Sometimes there's time to kick at the can of postmodernity and cultural theory, too. As signposts of new knowledges and new subjectivities, these media works represent complex and personal articulations of race and gender, representation, and the politics and aesthetics of identity formation in film.

> *Born with a veil, and gifted with second-sight.*
> —W. E. B. DuBois

If there is a "godmother" to this recent flowering of work, it is the late Theresa Hak Kyung Cha. Her profound, luminous legacy of critical and poetic writing, performance art, and film and video work has left its traces. Although few of the film/videomakers discussed here would regard Cha's influence as a direct one (I knew only her name when making my first film), the themes and formal concerns of her media work during the 1970s and early 1980s surface again and again in these contemporary films. Cha's semiotic explorations of language, memory, and subjectivity in the context of feminism and Korean colonial history are especially prescient. While the feminist, postcolonial writings and films of Trinh Minh-ha gripped me as a cinema studies undergraduate during the mid-1980s, I didn't yet know of Theresa Hak Kyung Cha before her. Like Trinh, Cha can be at once poetic and interrogative in her unusual forms of address, which are almost oracular. As a body, Cha's work rematerializes the site of Korea-as-Cold-War-victim, and remaps the emotional and cognitive terrain of "Korea" into something tangible for *kyop'o* understanding, a groundswell of critical fictions, diasporic imagination, and genuine political struggle.

Talk about marginal. Until a few years ago, an identity as specific as "Korean American" filmmaker was an impossibility in the American cultural consciousness, even in its alternative quarters. When I made my first film, *Sally's Beauty Spot* (1990), and was living in New York, the prevailing term, politically and organizationally, was "Asian American." For someone from Canada coming to the States, even Asian American sounded great. To encounter organizations such as Asian CineVision in New York, Visual Communications in Los Angeles, and the National Asian American Telecommunications Association in San Francisco was a revelation. This history of Asian American filmmaking, I discovered, was predominantly Chinese American and Japanese American, and consisted primarily of documentaries. These organizations, devoted to supporting the production, promotion, and exhibition of media work by Asian American film/videomakers, also mounted annual film festivals. I decided I was going to make a film to show specifically at ACV's New York festival. The film wouldn't be documentary and wouldn't be earnest, but elliptical, theoretical, feminist, and hopefully, funny and accessible. This Asian American audience would be my primary audience. Besides, how could they turn me down; just how many Asian American filmmakers were out there, anyway?

Enough, I guess. I showed the selection committee a silent cutting copy, which kept falling apart in the projector. They turned down the film. Come back next year, they said, when it's finished. I did.

Sally's Beauty Spot is an image-and-idea-driven film. Rather than focusing on character or story, the deconstructionist tendencies of the film and its hybrid aesthetics were inspired by a personal excitement with theory. Using a despised black mole on a young woman's breast as a metaphor for the threat of cultural difference, the film explores Western notions of Asian femininity and idealized romance. Sally tries rubbing, scrubbing off, and covering up the skin blemish. Made without a script per se, the piece collages together my interest in postcolonial and feminist film theory with pop cultural elements. At the time, I was researching the representation of Asians in the history of American film and television. In the postwar period, a spate of Asian/white romances had emerged from Hollywood, what I call "miscegenation melodramas." Ubiquitous among them, and my clear favorite, was *The World of Suzie Wong*, starring William Holden and Nancy Kwan. Revisionistically speaking, I should spit out this bit of colonial candyfloss I know, but in truth I've loved eating it since childhood. The film was shown regularly on TV, and Kwan's prostitute was one of the few popular images of Asian women around. This kind of obsessive, acculturated form of spectatorship was interesting in itself: Korean girls in Canadian suburbs, glued to California sitcoms and old Hollywood movies on the tube; we were not exactly the intended audience for this once racy bit of entertainment. True, during all those times of looking, rarely did any of these images look back at me. But this one did.

Kwan's Suzie Wong was Dragon Lady and Lotus Blossom rolled in one, but caught in a racist time warp, could you really blame her? She was beautiful, feisty, and deserved reclaiming. Homi Bhabha's seminal retheorization of the stereotype[7] was the trick. Instead of arguing the derogatory or false nature of racial and sexual stereotypes, Bhabha reconceptualized them as "arrested" forms of representation. Stereotypes should be viewed "relationally" according to other representations, he suggests, rather than held up to any picture of reality, thereby releasing them from burdens of truth or moralism. My "Suzie Wong" was a total fiction, pulp romance. As a Korean growing up in North America, it was impossible to be a real essentialist. No one knew where Korea was, so what could they really know about you, if they didn't even know where you came from? In this way, I became an Asian American before I became Korean American. Pillaging troves of Hollywood fare such as these "mixed race" dramas, I found all the Asian characters were

Japanese or Chinese anyway (although I don't want to fight for orientalist crumbs, this problem of the lack of a popular Korean signifier still dogs me to this day). Although Suzie Wong herself is from Hong Kong, the main character in *Sally's Beauty Spot*, while played by my sister, Sally, is not specifically named as Korean, Chinese, or Japanese, to underscore the shared dimensions of Asian American women's experience.

Sally's Beauty Spot tries to give a pulse to these linchpins of racial and sexual identity, in tandem, as inseparable preoccupations. The discourse of race in the United States was, and still is, overpoweringly white versus black. If Asians are admitted into the dialogue, it is almost exclusively in relation to white-dominant culture. Such a status quo-reinforcing focus on the white/other dynamic is not only supremely irritating, but it reflects the workings of power, not our multiracial society. Personally, I haven't been interested in representing Asian/white couplings. The predominant relationships in my films have been between Asian and other Asian, black, or Native characters, and then only marginally, whites. In *Sally's Beauty Spot*, Sally's vacillation between white privilege and the prospect of a liaison with a black man (a pairing you'd be hard-pressed to find in Hollywood) reflects the tension of broaching an Asian presence in the stratified minefield of American race relations. On the soundtrack, different musical idioms and numerous abstracted voices interrogate this terrain. Clips from *The World of Suzie Wong*, photographs and voices of other Asian women, and images of Sally's body punctuate this narrative of discovery and subjecthood. The film maps this progression of psychic and theoretical attachments to the body, spectatorship, and voice with a simple story about an unwanted mole.

When I showed the film to Homi Bhabha, one of the critical inspirations for the film, he remarked how the mole or "beauty spot" on Sally's breast functioned as the *punctum* of the piece. Roland Barthes used the term to describe how a peripheral detail in a photograph may "prick" or unsettle the viewer in ways unexpected from the photograph's more conventionally coded meanings. The *punctum*'s effect is startling, like a "sting, speck, cut, little hole." Registering a visceral effect, "It also bruises me," Barthes writes, "is poignant to me."[8] Such a compelling detail may give a clue to how we come to "remember" an image or photograph, through the body. My sister, Sally (who by the way has no neurotic impulse towards her mole), had an immediate but different response to Bhabha's suggestion. To her, the *punctum* was not the mole but the stretch marks on her breasts. The film's final images are of a black man's lips dissolving into Sally's own, radiant smile.

She heard faintly the young girl uttering a sequence of words, and interspersed between them, equal duration of pauses. Her mouth is left open at the last word. She does not seem to realize that she had spoken.
—Theresa Hak Kyung Cha

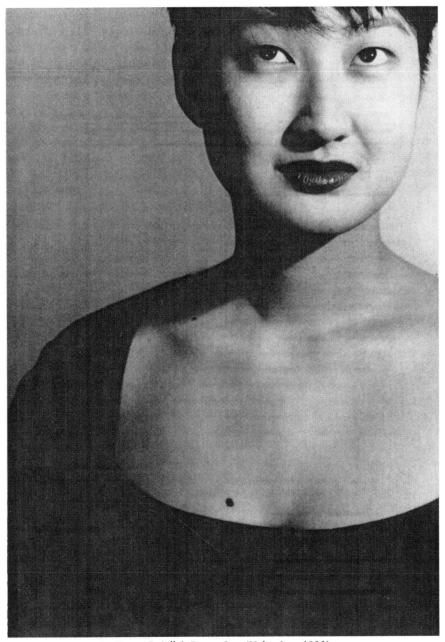

Figure 5. *Sally's Beauty Spot* (Helen Lee, 1990).

During the mid-1970s, Theresa Cha began producing work as a student at the University of California, Berkeley. The sheer formalism, elegance, and occasional opacity of her text constructions, in writing and media, reflect an excitement and curiosity about French poststructuralist ideas, which were then gaining importance on this side of the Atlantic. For the theoretically uninitiated, Cha's works can be daunting. Embracing a conceptual indeterminacy characteristic of avant-garde performance aesthetics, their meanings are often created provisionally in the encounter between the text and reader. The specificity of the reader as a social subject is always a precondition of performing the meaning. But different from her Euro-American intellectual peers, her thoughts were as much about Korea, which was marginal even to a Western understanding of "the Orient." Problems of language embody this sense of cultural displacement. The word, Cha implies, is not a universal or neutral signifier, not always in English or French. By a specific somebody, words are read, spoken, and breathed around, sometimes with considerable strain. In *mouth to mouth* (1975), the Korean language can offer the assurance and comfort of one's mother tongue, or is slippery as a cipher—depending on the viewer and her positioning. Cultural location, however, does not always guarantee a linguistic one. Language, once a repository and reliable signifier of culture, becomes contingent and fragile in the context of displacement.

  mouth to mouth opens with a continuous left to right panning movement over a series of written characters: simple vowel letters from *hangŭl*, the Korean phonetic alphabet. The movement fades into black, then fades up to a video snow effect, accompanied by static noise. This is followed by an image of a woman's mouth framed in close-up, superimposed over this snow/static. Her mouth widens ever slowly, but we don't hear her. Fade out. Fade in with another close-up of the same, her mouth forming a different, voiceless vowel. The video follows this pattern in a highly composed, almost ritualistic manner, with variations in sound treatments (static, water, bird sounds, sometimes silence) and the occasional camera movement. As in her other film and video work, the piece's formal austerity extends from the visual to the aural dimensions of the piece.

  Although *mouth to mouth* references the populist, physiognomic origin myths of *hangŭl*,[9] the functioning of language for the *kyop'o* speaker is not nearly so transparent. The supposedly neutral text of written language is gradually overturned by the arduous, subjective aspiration of speech. This tension between the text and speech mirrors the disintegrating relationship between sound and image in the videotape. While the disembodied voice may function as a radical, even liberatory tool for her feminist avant-garde contemporaries,[10] Cha's voiceless body suggests other problems of cultural legibility and knowledge. Here, the disconnection of voice and body alludes to the oscillatory nature of native/ non-native tongues where the transparency and certainty of language are suspended. The use of the vowel as a structuring absence of the word, as opposed to the positivity of consonants, underscores its supplementary but elemental nature. Significantly, two vowels are missing from the written text (compound vowels aren't even included here). The incomplete set suggests a child's or beginner's first apprehension of the language, or the imperfect recall of a native speaker whose mother tongue is lost. Cha's mute mouth, forming familiar/unfamiliar vowels, "performs" the Korean language with a desire for speech. The vowels' "absent" nature indicates the materiality of language, as building blocks. Where language itself is honed, however, is another question.

Cha's long-standing interest in negative space and silence is shared by the work of more recent video artists, most directly in Yunah Hong's work. Hong's first videotape, *Memory/all echo* (1990), is based on Cha's seminal poetic text, *DICTEE*.[11] The book itself is a complex document combining written text with graphic components, and covering topics ranging from modern Korean history, Catholic ritual, and cinema spectatorship, to topographies of the human body. Hong's video gathers together archival material from the Korean War and dramatic reenactments filmed in Korea and the United States, with visual montage elements such as computer-generated effects and photographic stills. Using *DICTEE* as a base text, the voice-over is comprised solely of selections from the book. But Hong's style is more allusive than illustrative of Cha's writing.[12] Rather than attempting an exhaustive, literal adaptation of the book, the video focuses mainly on themes related to Korean and American identity and issues of cultural and linguistic displacement, underscoring the interpretive possibilities and elliptical phrasings of the translation process itself.

Like the book, *Memory/all echo* attempts to engage the viewer in a self-reflexive, readerly relationship to the text. Hong tracks several discursive levels at once, extending the video's montage aesthetic to a multilayered presentation of voice. Three narrators with different accents (signifying varying levels of acculturation to the English language) adopt several forms of address. In one segment, Cha's eyewitness retelling of her brother's decision to join a 1962 student demonstration against their mother's will is narrated in third person. The video dramatizes this sequence, collapsing Cha's real-life experience with the story of a fictional character (played by the same actor). The use of the pronominal shifter (you/I; she/he) enables the subjective interplay between historical and autobiographical accounts locked by the accrual of time and memory. The sequence, although filmed in slow motion and extreme close-up, employs an arch, gestural performance style that drains the confrontation of any conventional dramatic intent or emotional identification. Linking her brother's anti-government position with a portrait of Yu Guan Soon (Yu Kwan-sun), the martyred nationalist heroine of 1919, the narrator/author/character traces the politics and history of modern Korean resistance to locate it within a personal, familial framework. The space between—tensions of nation and family, gaps between history and autobiography, the ellipses of story and memory—is transformed into a language of loss, displacement, and exile.

In Kim Su Theiler's *Great Girl* (1993), the haunting of cultural loss takes the form of a search for origins. The film's departure point is Theiler's own trip to Korea to find information about her birth mother. But this search doesn't function as a transparently autobiographical document or an effortless return of the subject to the mother/land. Laid out as a series of vignettes, the piece unfolds rather cryptically: a roomful of black hair, American dollar bills bandaged to a young girl's belly, an ambivalent childhood encounter with a U.S. serviceman (perhaps her father?), neutral adoption documents, uneasy travelogue footage of a hometown that existed before only in her mind. Like secret layers of a memory long repressed by familial and cultural silence, the discursive curiosity of this search unearths a place—Korea—sedimented by the absences and persistence of memory and silence in stark and unsettling ways.

Theiler's film begins with an extreme close-up shot of a black-and-white image, accompanied by music and a regulated scraping noise. The image is magnified to the point of illegibility. It is similarly difficult to locate the source of the sound, or its relationship to the image. This disjunctive relationship between the visual and aural is a primary stylistic trope of *Great Girl*, where sound is used contrapuntally or non-synchronously toward a redefinition of the subject, who is variously named in the film ("K," Sun-Mi, Cho Suk-hi, and implicitly, Kim Su Theiler). This non-realist use of sound, including voice-over, represents an interventionist strategy that feminist film theorists such as Kaja Silverman and Mary Ann Doane have deployed against classical realist cinema's reinforcement of male subjectivity and the illusion of a unified, coherent subject. The seamlessness of realist sound/image production masks "the potential trauma of dispersal, dismemberment, and difference,"[13] and the spectator's imagined plenitude or insufficiency of the image/subject. As the mirror opposite of realist filmmaking, identity-production seeks to expose its material workings. In *Great Girl*, Theiler's deconstructive task is to uncover the past trauma of dispersal (adoption and immigration), dismemberment (separation and loss of the mother), and difference (the *kyop'o*'s return to Korea).

In a key scene of the film, "K" is being interviewed about the trip and her experience meeting hometown folks who can give her information. The sequence is reenacted by an actress (Anita Chao) wearing a suit and coiffed hairstyle, and sitting obediently behind a desk. Strangely, her lips move out of sync with the monologue, followed by a slight echoing effect. As she moves into a story about how a scar on her body could definitively identify her, "K" detaches the microphone from her lapel and leaves the desk, as the camera follows her walking into another part of the room. She talks about meeting a woman who "could be my mother." The beating noise (the dislocated sound from the film's opening) is almost thunderous. But no one provides the right answers ("I looked nothing like the pictures"). Engaged in what Cha has called a "perpetual motion of search," the film's discursive explorations of self-identity and self-knowledge render an asymptotic relationship to "truth": the closer she comes, the more inaccessible and irrecoverable her past is. The carefully staged testimony of "K" 's faked performance undermines the documentary-like presentation of a unified, spontaneous, "authentic" subject. The film's visual and conceptual fragmentation, and the interpolated nature of the filmmaker's investigation—chance meetings, faulty memories, nasty rumors (the townspeople's suggestion of her mother as a prostitute with no prospects but American adoption of her biracial, illegitimate child), and implied wishes for a happy ending—reveal the impossibility of an innocent search for cultural and biological origins. Later in the film, the initial, illegible black-and-white close-up shot is widened to reveal the image's contents: curtains beating against the window of a fast-moving bus.

> *The effect of mass migrations has been the creation of radically new types of human being: people who root themselves in ideas rather than places, in memories as much as in material things; people who have been obliged to define themselves—because they are so defined by others—by their otherness; people in whose deepest selves strange fusions occur, unprecedented unions between what they were and where they find themselves.*
>
> *—Salman Rushdie*

The "in-betweenness" that characterizes films about immigrant experience, especially when faced with the physical or metaphoric possibility of return, is a persistent wound of the diasporic imagination. What is interesting is how these ideas take shape, depending on the form. The more free-wheeling language of experimental film and video can be immensely enabling in conveying a discursive complexity. It's possible to pack a film with dense ideas and a radical aesthetic, and be all the richer for it. The rules of narrative film, however, are far stricter. Still, the principle of diminishing audience (the more experimental your film is, the smaller your audience) plagued me as I contemplated a shift to narrative filmmaking. Why not try to communicate hitherto marginalized stories and characters through a more accessible form? At the same time, other models of contemporary innovative and subjective filmmaking that identified marginalized characters and the interplay of difference—cultural, psychic, sexual—showed it was possible to locate these ideas in a narrative context.[14]

My second film, *My Niagara* (1992), features a Japanese American/Canadian[15] protagonist, a twenty-year-old woman named Julie Kumagai. In continuing my exploration of displacement and assimilation, and racial/sexual representation in film, I wished to collaborate with another Asian writer on a film about an Asian/Asian relationship. This didn't come about innocently. One of my guiding lights, videomaker

Richard Fung, had an interesting reaction to *Sally's Beauty Spot* and the Asian/black dialectic it sought to set up. "So, you think that's radical, Helen?" he challenged (very gently, of course). "The Asian and black thing is provocative but you know what's really radical? Yellow on yellow."

My Niagara is a story of maternal loss and intercultural discovery. Written with novelist Kerri Sakamoto, the film explores the inner world of Julie Kumagai who, on the cusp of adulthood, faces choices to move her life forward. At the film's outset, she is breaking off with a boyfriend and contemplating a trip to Europe with her best friend, Enza. Julie lives at home with her incommunicative father, and her life is shadowed by the death of her Japanese-born mother (who, on a return trip there when Julie was a small girl, died in a drowning accident off the coast). At Julie's workplace, a stately water filtration plant by the lake, she meets a young man, Tetsuro, who, recently emigrated from Japan but of Korean origin, is obsessed with all things American. They make a connection, but Julie ultimately cannot escape her listless state; life goes on. While this is the plot proper and *My Niagara* is a drama, the film is essentially minimalist and counter-dramatic in design.

The central relationship that Kerri and I wanted to portray was Julie and Tetsuro's, and their evolving realizations of cultural difference. To us, the picture of an assimilated Asian in America was a sansei (third-generation) Japanese Canadian/American. But Julie's background also resembled my own upbringing in a predominantly white suburban envi-

Figure 6. *My Niagara* (Helen Lee, 1992).

ronment. What were the differences between being a settled Asian person in North America, and a recent immigrant; what were the similarities? What kinds of dynamics and perceptions existed among Asians of differing nationalities living here? Also, how does the fantasy of Japan in Julie's idealized memories (as a place of origin and the site of her mother's birth and death) change when confronted with Tetsuro's experiences of discrimination as a Korean in Japan? Although these were our didactic considerations in creating the story and our characters, we were also dead-set against making an earnest "race relations" drama. Once established, cultural identity would be a given, not constantly "rehearsed" for an assumedly "white" audience; our audience would already be knowledgeable and informed. As well, there would be no obvious or Orientalist signifiers: for instance, although we assume Julie's father, as a nisei (second-generation) Japanese, had an internment camp experience, this never comes up in the film, not as much because the story isn't his but that this would be the most obvious filmic representation of a nisei character. He was just an emotionally bottled-up dad, for personal as well as cultural reasons. Enza and Dominic (not coincidentally, both ethnic whites) have their own quirks, and Tetsuro his Memphis stylings.

Julie (Melanie Tanaka), Tetsuro (William Shin), and Mr. Kumagai (George Anzai) are played by non-professional actors, not because of the dearth of Asian actors, but because of a particular "non-performative" performance style which I had hoped to experiment with. Different from documentary-like naturalism, the style I was searching for was a convergence of real-life personas and scripted characters toward non-psychological portrayals. Reduced and flattened, they could suggest an inaccessible state of interiority. I thought their alienation wouldn't be properly served by gutsy, positivist performances. Muted or held-in, their canted expressions of emotional discord and cultural displacement alluded to theoretically based notions of absence and negativity. Suspicious of models of identification that relied on audience absorption, I hoped for some critical distance (was it possible to be both emotionally engaged and critically aware at the same time?). Similarly, the progression of the story is obliquely presented and ultimately subverted. Julie's own passivity is mirrored in the film's languid expository style. In the ending, Julie's momentary communion with her father (she finds a charged but constipated gift of a wooden box he's crafted himself—touching, but also oddly paralyzing) also denies specific narrative closure. But it is less a refusal than a deferral. The film's final notes, the daughter's dutiful gesture of filling her father's rice bowl and an image of her mother's watery grave, suggest another chapter of a continuing story.

Also dealing with families and parent/child dynamics, other narrative films by Korean American women filmmakers avoid a deconstructionist approach in favor of a realist, reconstructionist tone and spirit. These works feature critical dilemmas faced by Korean American families with female protagonists, interestingly all daughters, at their center. While issues of national culture and the family still coalesce around language, critical discursivity is transformed into dialogue and dramatic conflict.

Problems of language and cultural difference encountered by second-generation Korean Americans, compounded by biracial identity, are the subject of Kyung-ja Lee's *Halmani* (1988). Kathy is born of a Korean mother and U.S. serviceman father. Her home life is an example of middle-class assimilation, idyllic and erased of any signs of ethnicity. Living outside an urban center (and therefore outside a community of Korean Americans), Kathy's white-as-norm American comfort is uprooted by the arrival of her very Korean grandmother, Halmani. Oriental signifiers start to proliferate: gifts of a ceramic vase and traditional *hanbok* dresses, yucky foods, odd customs, and an unrecognizable language. Her mother's assurance that "Korea is a long way away" is threatened by Halmani's new-found presence, and a reminder of not the foreignness "over there" but of the difference within.

Kathy speaks only English, and Halmani only Korean, so grandmother and granddaughter literally cannot speak to one another. Halmani's Korean is left untranslated, reinforcing Kathy's sense of estrangement (and curiously, the viewer's; I craved for Halmani to be on equal footing but Lee decides not to subtitle Halmani's dialogue). Instead, their method of communicating transfers to the body, and oscillates between the physical connection/repulsion of Kathy's own biological and cultural ambivalence. Still, their bodies can correspond. The film's framing often places Kathy and Halmani within the same two-shot, emphasizing their shared physical stature. "Halmani noticed that you're left-handed, too," her mother says. It's when Halmani does something strange and visceral, like squatting on the earth, chanting while polishing the vase, or praying as she burns paper that Kathy's alienated American-ness seeks to excise any display of alterity.

When asked to draw a self-portrait in class, Kathy models her fingers around her face and is stymied; the drawing's a mess, and she runs away. After her father brings her home, Kathy proclaims, "She's disgusting. I hate her," and smashes the precious vase to the ground. Halmani's reaction is swift and perfect: fury and true disgust. This is a moment when Halmani's identity, throughout the film positioned as "authentic" and unknowable, won't be denied. The film's resolution, Halmani's forgiveness and Kathy's penance, plays out the banality of cultural compromise: Kathy eats her words after Halmani takes the blame for the broken vase, and she dons the *hanbok* for her family. Through the verbal and nonverbal communion of the film's final scene, a long shot of Kathy and Halmani together against a desert sunset, Kathy willingly accepts not just the signs of cultural difference, but the language itself. "*Kamsa-hamnida*, Halmani," she thanks her grandmother, her tongue humbled by the native.

The desire for assimilation takes a decidedly adventurous, sardonic turn in Christine Chang's *Be Good, My Children* (1992). At the film's outset, Chang boldly asks of her characters, "Why did you come to America?" A musical-comedy-drama, the film satirizes the saga of a struggling Korean immigrant family in New York City: Mom is a "Jesus freak" who works at a Harlem clothing store, Judy aspires to be an actress but tends bar on the sly, and Jimmy is failing out of school (the father is notably absent). Mom still hopes for mainstream professional success for her children, who opt for white boyfriends and wished-for car dealerships in L.A. Their entanglements and conflicts form the basis of the film's plot, but it is the extra-diegetic levels, in the form of two "narrators," which subvert our expectations of the conventional family drama.

The film opens with an Asian woman wearing impeccable makeup and a huge blonde wig languishing on top of a bed, clutching a teddy bear. This is Snow White (played by Chang herself). She addresses the camera directly, introducing the family via a photo album and acerbically decrying this "mean world." Snow White functions as an omniscient narrator, like a guardian angel to the family, but more devilish than angelic. In an early episode with Jimmy, she dribbles chocolate candies to lure him, fairytale-like, into a lesson of simple economics, NYC-style ("These are pennies; we throw them away. These are nickels; we give them to beggars"), before releasing her authority as the film's driving force ("Say it! I have absolute power"). Another figure, Mae East, who is first introduced as daughter Judy's alter ego but soon enters the story as a character in her own right, provides the impetus for the main musical numbers. It's high camp, with Mae East's torch songs and the sexually charged persona of Snow White, part sex kitten/part dominatrix, releasing the drama from the realist confines of the typical immigrant narrative.

Toying with the conventions of a morality tale, Chang discards the myth of hard-working, model minority citizens in an explicit critique of the American dream and white norms. Offset by the sheer jazziness of the musical interludes, the family's parables offer a deeply ironic perspective of Korean immigrant life (for me, marred only by some of the actors' inauthentic Korean accents). One of Mae's musical numbers is even set in a California drive-in theater in the middle of an earthquake. In another sequence, where Judy recounts a dream to a psychologist, several Asian women with names like Cherry Blossom, Miss Butterfly, and Lady Dragon first display themselves as stereotypical submissives but end up beating up on the white males, yelling, "That's not my name!" Later, the same women, including Judy, rally together in a self-affirming musical extravaganza led by Mae East's rebel femininity. By presenting an unequivocally sexual image of the Asian woman in a campy musical or melodramatic context, the film avoids essentializing the Asian American experience or "fixing" the stereotype as false/true. The film's radicality lies in this refusal to reinforce dramatic realist presentations of what Korean women are "really like." Its parody of Hollywood happy endings similarly denies escapist tendencies of the immigrant narrative. When Jimmy and Judy steal the weekly offerings from their mother's church to hail a cab to "somewhere over the rainbow," and Mom launches into the show tune of the same name, you know that Snow White (and Chang herself) is smirking. "Oh my, just the lullaby I needed," she says. "But forget it. This ain't no time to dream."

The dysfunctional family and personal compromises made to sustain the illusion of perfect nuclearity also propel the narrative of Hyun Mi Oh's *La Senorita Lee* (1995). The film follows the choices made by Jeanie Lee, a vivacious young woman ending an affair with Tomas, a Mexican worker who has left her pregnant. She feels pressured to marry Harry Kim, a childhood friend and young doctor, in order to bail out her mother and grandmother. The backstory is the financial ruin of the family's business during the L.A. riots, and the father's subsequent abandonment of his wife, mother, and daughter (even in a household containing only women, patriarchal pressures still assert themselves). Oh presents Jeanie's personal crisis as an example of the complex positioning of this generation of Korean American women in Los Angeles, poised on the edge of a continent bordered by desiring bodies, clashing cultural realities, and a "prodigality of tongues."[16]

The film's structure is circular, beginning and ending with Jeanie (also played by the filmmaker) lying on a highrise rooftop, moments after fleeing her traditional Korean wedding. The strains of a Korean folk song and the vivid colors of her *hanbok* and *chokturi* set against the smoggy backdrop of downtown L.A. and the sound of helicopters in the distance portray the conflict almost iconically. We enter the story through Jeanie's vision, a close-up shot catching her semiconscious state as she passes through dream, sleep, and memory. The film's flashback structure effectively internalizes the site of Jeanie's dramatic conflict into her body, so that the drama unfolds as part of Jeanie's consciousness and her subjectively drawn world. Struck by pregnancy cramps in the bathroom of a hotel room she's sharing with Harry on a whim, Jeanie's thoughts move to an idyllic scene on the same rooftop where she and Tomas speak Spanish to one another, and share a night of lovemaking. Later, in the operating room of an abortion clinic, the threat of terminating her pregnancy conjures up an image of a small girl—Jeanie herself as a child. This jolts her into a moment of self-apprehension, and she runs. Jeanie's "wildness" and its repression are also reflected in the film's structure, a continuous sublimation of her sexual identity into the filial role of dutiful Korean American daughter and, now, mother.

When Jeanie's feminist will and new world freedoms are overtaken by considerations of the family's future (ruled by the interdependency of different immigrant generations and, ironically, a continuation of patriarchal structures supported by women), her marriage to Harry is a sign of defeat. But Jeanie's radical decision to keep Tomas's baby shows the exact price of compromise. "I don't believe anymore," she tells a small Mexican boy on the rooftop in one of the film's last scenes. The "cosmopolitanizing of humanity" in a place like Los Angeles (which Tomas calls "the loneliest city in the world") can also signal what Rey Chow has named a "vanishing of human diversity."[17] Difference is subsumed by forces of urbanization, assimilation, and homogenization. At the film's closing, various spoken lines from the film create a voice montage over a single shot of Jeanie's quiet face, ending on a freeze-frame of her eyes opening, wide awake. Of the different languages that haunt her —Korean, Spanish, English—which will her child eventually claim as her own?

Hyun Mi Oh's script was a kind of revelation when I first read it several years ago. Encountering its cultural sophistication and astute writing recalled a time years earlier, when I first saw Pam Tom's seminal film, *Two Lies* (1989), a beautifully made black-and-white film about two Chinese American sisters and the psychological aftermath of their mother's eyelid operation. With strongly enacted characters and a compelling story, it struck a perfect balance of cultural identity exploration and expertly crafted narrative. The film spoke to me, and it spoke well. The film also made me laugh, the better to spit out, not swallow, the bitter pill of racial assimilation. For a fourth-generation Chinese American filmmaker like Tom, the question of language isn't such an issue (all the dialogue is in English). But for 1.5 generation filmmakers such as Oh and myself, language functions as a kind of primal site of conflict, a site that signifies torment, misunderstanding, or loss. Perhaps it is because I am now struggling with Korean language lessons, or crave certain foods to which I do not know the names, or cannot discuss intellectual topics in real depth with my parents, that I make the films I make, to recover this sense of loss.

The confluence of language and crisis surfaces in my third film, *Prey* (1995), a drama about a young Korean Canadian woman who falls for a shoplifter in her father's convenience store the morning after an overnight robbery. Taking place over the course of one day (but a day that will determine the next), Il Bae's everyday family routine is upset by this handsome Native stranger, Noel, who insinuates himself into her life and apartment. Is he to be trusted? A surprise visit by Halmoni, her grandmother who doesn't speak English, forces her to choose alliances, but Il Bae's defense is poorly negotiated by the fact of Noel's ethnicity and his disheveled, possibly dangerous appearance, as much as by Il Bae's unsure command of the Korean language. These problems of miscommunication and cultural perception are heightened by circumstance when Halmoni meets him not only post-coitally shirtless but also in possession of a gun (echoing a specter of violence familiar to Korean American store owners' lives). In the film's conclusion, a late-night confrontation set in their convenience store, Noel proffers this gun to Il Bae's father as a safeguard against future robberies. But to the father, Noel couldn't be anything but a robber, and he mistakes the gesture as a hold-up. Il Bae's final introduction ("Dad, this is Noel. Noel, this is my dad.") is in some ways just the beginning.

The meeting of Il Bae (Sandra Oh), a young Korean Canadian woman and Noel (Adam Beach), a Native man, creates an unexpected alliance. While they each come from totally different social spaces, there are also aspects which are shared—the same high school, a sense of cultural displacement, and lives shadowed by personal loss (the death of Noel's sister, Lucy; Il Bae's absent mother). I think of their relationship as a completely contemporary one, a phenomenon of the late twentieth century that allows such encounters between Asian immigrants and indigenous people to be possible. Since Koreans emigrated in significant numbers only in the past two decades, it's historically unlikely that Il Bae and Noel would have met until now. Native people, who suffer the same invisibility as Asians and other racial minorities in mainstream media, are practically unknown to the Korean American/Canadian community. It was important to me to explore how a Native character could impact on a Korean family who may have never before acknowledged the Native presence in their adopted land. Halmoni refers to Noel as a "foreigner," not suspecting the irony of her words. While Il Bae and Noel are similarly cast as star-crossed lovers, this "new world" narrative also creates an emotional space where ideas around ethnicity and belonging can be as meaningful and dramatic as cinematically coded elements like trust, desire, and gunplay.

In conceiving the film, I wanted to avoid reinforcing certain

Figure 7. *Prey* (Helen Lee, 1995).

A Personal Genealogy of Korean American Women's Cinema

dualisms that I thought typified some Asian American filmmaking. The binaristic opposition of tradition (old, backward "Orient") and modernity (progressive Western ideas and attitudes) particularly unnerved me. Although traditional perspectives play a large role in our lives, I don't believe that Korean identity played in simple conflict with living in North America. It wasn't an either/or choice; we live an incredibly hybrid existence. In the film, both English and Korean coexist, however fragilely, a balancing act of language and identity for 1.5 or second-generation immigrants of any nationality. Hyphenated existence (Korean-Canadian, Korean-American) from an adult perspective as opposed to the assimilating impulse of childhood affords the distance and desire, and sometimes necessity, for both tongues to exist in simultaneity. A typical convenience store was the perfect stage to enact this drama, a place where so many Korean Americans have spent their lives (my own movie-watching hours are just recently outpacing my days behind a retail counter). Il Bae's father, circumscribed by this setting, is a barometer of this tongue-twisting dance of language and race. Even he, as imperfectly "bilingual" as his daughter, misunderstands—his daughter, Noel's intentions, the unending drone of labor at the expense of love. By the film's end, Il Bae does not make an either/or choice, but mediates her father's position into a place of forced compromise and personal release.

The script for *Prey* was originally written for Sandra Oh and my mother's sister, In Sook Kim, to play the roles of Il Bae and Halmoni. I knew this would be an interesting process of not only pairing a highly trained actor like Oh with my aunt, who'd never performed before, but also because Oh, like the character, didn't speak Korean and my aunt doesn't speak much English. Since I cannot really speak Korean either, a process of translation was integral to the project. At every stage, from rehearsal to shooting to editing, the interpreter, Jane Huh, stuck close and ready. I wasn't prepared for the cultural wrangling over specific attitudes and sayings that I thought were authentic or convincing, but Jane insisted were off-mark. True to form, my aunt, herself a prolific essayist and poet, refused to play the role of the grandmother (who was initially written as very accepting of Noel and Il Bae's liaison) and demanded changes. My aunt wanted Noel out of Il Bae's apartment and out of their lives. While I never thought I'd take identity for granted, especially in a film about cross-generational differences, here I was making my own cultural assumptions. Ultimately, developing Halmoni's character was a collaboration between my aunt and myself, a creation of the Korean and *kyop'o* imagination. I doubt the film would exist without her.

> No one today is purely one thing.
>
> –Edward Said

From our "simultaneously split and doubled existence"[18] as Korean American women, we have learned to become adept, sophisticated readers of images. From this minoritized position, we have learned to focus on subversive readings and peripheral details, seeing how the *punctum* satisfies. Now, we take up the whole frame; as writers and filmmakers, we have created new images, enlarged those details. Can the production of an image of identity lead to the "transformation of the subject in assuming that image"?[19] The representation of Korean women is complex, figured by and interpolated through a variety of discourses, but each frame of these moving images elucidates us, bringing the image of the colonial subject one step closer toward self-identification. The ideas of home, memory, language, and desire obsess us; we try hard to translate these collective thoughts in ways never imagined for us. These narratives of the tongue, voice, and body, they all speak with newfound specificity. The velvet grain of Mae East's voice, Sally's crooked smile, the flaring of Jeanie Lee's *hanbok*, Cha's silent lips—all engaged in a "perpetual motion of search," these explorations signal a kind of *kyop'o* arrival. While the question of identity is never guaranteed, this new clamoring of images suggests other, curiously beautiful ways of traveling in a strange land.

A Personal Genealogy of Korean American Women's Cinema

SELECTED FILMOGRAPHY

This listing includes films and videos made by and about Korean American women, available through the following distributors or filmmakers:

Be Good, My Children, Christine Chang, 1992, 47 min. 16mm. Women Make Movies, 462 Broadway, #500, New York, NY 10012, 212-925-0606.

Camp Arirang, Diana Lee and Grace Yoon Kyung Lee, 1995, 28 min. video. Third World Newsreel, 335 West 38th Street, New York, NY 10018, 212-947-9277.

Comfort Me, Soo Jin Kim, 1993, 8 min. video. 201 Wayland Street, Los Angeles, CA 90042, 213-550-1772.

Daughterline, Grace Lee-Park, 1995, 11 min. 16mm. Grace-Lee Park, 6104 N.E. Sacramento, Portland, OR 97213, 503-223-2243.

Distance, Soo Jin Kim, 1991, 13 min. video. Soo Jim Kim (see *Comfort Me*).

Do Roo (Circling Back), Soon Mi Yoo, 1993, 14 min. 16mm. Yellow Earth Productions, 3900 Cathedral Avenue N.W., #501A, Washington, DC 20016, 202-338-9577.

A Forgotten People, Dai-Sil Kim Gibson, 1995, 59 min. 16mm. Crosscurrents Media, NAATA, 346 9th Street, 2nd Floor, San Francisco, CA 94103, 415-552-9550.

Golden Dreams, Alice Ra, 1995, 9 min. 16mm. Crosscurrents Media.

Great Girl, Kim Su Theiler, 1993, 14 min. 16mm. Women Make Movies.

Halmani, Kyung-ja Lee, 1988, 30 min. 16mm. Pyramid Film & Video, 2801 Colorado Avenue, Santa Monica, CA 90404, 310-828-7577.

Here Now, Yunah Hong, 1995, 32 min. 16mm. Yunah Hong, 223 East 4th Street, #12, New York, NY 10009, 212-677-8980.

An Initiation Kut for a Korean Shaman, Diana Lee and Laurel Kendall, 1991, 37 min. video. University of Hawaii Press, 2840 Kolowalu Street, Honolulu, HI 96822, 808-956-8697.

In Memoriam to an Identity, R. Vaughn, 1993, 5 min. video. Katharine Burdette, 15308 Alan Drive, Laurel, MD 20707, 301-725-0472.

Korea: Homes Apart, Christine Choy and J. T. Takagi, 1991, 60 min. 16mm. Third World Newsreel.

La Senorita Lee, Hyun Mi Oh, 1995, 26 min. 16mm. Cinema Guild, 1697 Broadway, #506, New York, NY 10019, 212–246-5522.

living in half tones, Me-K. Ahn, 1994, 9 min. video. Third World Newsreel.

Memory/all echo, Yunah Hong, 1990, 27 min. video. Women Make Movies.

Mija, Hei Sook Park, 1989, 30 min. 16mm. Visual Communications, 263 South Los Angeles Street, Suite 307, Los Angeles, CA 90012, 213-680-4462.

mouth to mouth, Theresa Hak Kyung Cha, 8 min. video. University Art Museum and Pacific Film Archive, University of California at Berkeley, 2625 Durant Avenue, Berkeley, CA 94720, 510-643-8584.

My Niagara, Helen Lee, 1992, 40 min. 16mm. Women Make Movies.

Permutations, Theresa Hak Kyung Cha, 10 min. 16mm. University Art Museum and Pacific Film Archive.

Prey, Helen Lee, 1995, 26 min. 16mm. Women Make Movies.

Red Lolita, Gloria Toyun Park, 1989, 6 min. video. Gloria Toyun Park, 3064 Cardillo Avenue, Hacienda Heights, CA, 91745, 818-336-6141.

re/dis/appearing, Theresa Hak Kyung Cha, 1977, 3 min. video. University Art Museum and Pacific Film Archive.

Sa-i-Gu, Christine Choy, Elaine Kim, Dai-Sil Kim Gibson, 1993, 36 min. video. Crosscurrents Media.

Sally's Beauty Spot, Helen Lee, 1990, 12 min. 16mm. Women Make Movies.

Through the Milky Way, Yunah Hong, 1992, 19 min. video. Women Make Movies.

Translating Grace, Anita Lee, 1996, 20 min. 16mm. Nagual Productions, P.O. Box 364, Station P, 704 Spadina Avenue, Toronto, ON M5S 2S9, 416-588-6976.

Undertow, Me-K. Ahn, 1995, 19 min. video. Asian American Renaissance, 1564 Lafond Avenue, St. Paul, MN 55104, 612-641-4040.

Videoeme, Theresa Hak Kyung Cha, 1976, 3 min. video. University Art Museum and Pacific Film Archive.

What Do You Know About Korea? R. Vaughn, 1996, 7 min. video. Katharine Burdette (see *In Memoriam to an Identity*).

The Women Outside, Hye-Jung Park and J. T. Takagi/Third World Newsreel, 1995, 60 min. 16mm. Third World Newsreel.

NOTES

I wish to thank Elaine Kim and the editors for their encouragement, all the filmmakers who supplied tapes, photographs, and comments, Abraham Ferrer for additions to the filmography, and also to Esther Yu, Richard Fung, and Cameron Bailey for their usual fabulousness.

1. Although I refer to "filmmakers," videomakers are also included here. Also, I use the term "Korean American" although it is properly "Korean North American," which includes Canada as well as the United States. To talk about the differences (and similarities) of Korean American versus Korean Canadian identities and histories would comprise another essay, so excuse my predominant use of the former.

2. "New" is relative, and everything is context. While the "history of cinema" recently celebrated its centenary, the respective histories of Asian American and feminist cinemas date back only some twenty-odd years. In this particular context, anything called "Korean American" would have been begging company, or collapsed into other definitions. Only in the past few years has this work reached a critical mass to be so named. In this sense, film and video work by Korean American women is still a cinematic project in its infancy, and this survey is provisional at best. For reasons of space and focus, this discussion centers around a selection of experimental and narrative works, not documentaries. Refer to the filmography for a more complete list of works by Korean American women filmmakers.

3. W. E. B. DuBois's concept of "double consciousness" is useful in cultivating possibilities for considering cultural difference in non-dualistic ways. Allowing the coexistence of objectification and subjecthood, he writes about "this sense of always looking at one's self through the eyes of others." This turn-of-the-century model of decolonization for postemancipation blacks uncannily resembles the tricky balance between identification and alienation marking the postcolonial, migratory experiences of the late twentieth century. See DuBois, *The Souls of Black Folk* (New York: First Vintage, 1990).

4. Trinh T. Minh-ha, *Woman, Native, Other: Writing Postcoloniality and Feminism* (Bloomington: Indiana University Press, 1989), 6.

5. One striking note is the dearth of filmmaking by Asian American lesbians, including Korean Americans. I can't speculate why, but the absence is astonishing considering the strength of lesbian work in feminist cinema, especially in recent years.

6. "Third cinema" (versus Third World cinema) was first coined by Argentinean filmmakers Fernando Solanas and Octavio Getino during the late 1960s as a rallying cry for anticolonial, revolutionary cinema. During the late 1980s, a renewed concept of third cinema was debated, especially among black British theorists and practitioners, to signify the work of diasporic, politically and theoretically minded filmmakers who were starting to see themselves increasingly in terms of a community. See *Questions of Third Cinema*, ed. Jim Pines and Paul Willemen (London: British Film Institute, 1989).

7. Homi K. Bhabha, "The Other Question: Stereotype, Discrimination and the Discourse of Colonialism," in *The Location of Culture* (London: Routledge, 1994), 66–84.

8. Roland Barthes, *Camera Lucida* (New York: Hill and Wang, 1981), 27.

9. *Hangŭl*, developed under the reign of King Sejong (1418–50), was designed to replace Chinese characters and achieve widespread literacy. The consonants are said to be based on the shape of the human tongue, mouth, and throat when forming these letters.

10. See "Disembodying the Female Voice: Irigaray, Experimental Feminist Cinema, and Femininity" by Kaja Silverman, in *The Acoustic Mirror: The Female Voice in Psychoanalysis and Cinema* (Bloomington: Indiana University Press, 1988), 141–86. Silverman examines the work of Yvonne Rainer, Sally Potter, Patricia Gruben, and Bette Gordon in relation to the asynchronous use of the female voice and female subjectivity.

11. Theresa Hak Kyung Cha, *DICTEE* (New York: Tanam, 1982), 168.

12. See also Walter Lew, *Excerpts from: Dikte, For DICTEE* (1982) (Seoul, Korea: Yeul, 1992). His book offers another example of a critical collage based on Cha's *DICTEE*.

13. Mary Ann Doane, "Ideology and the Practice of Sound Editing and Mixing," in *The Cinematic Apparatus*, ed. Teresa de Lauretis and Stephen Heath (New York: St. Martin's, 1980), 47.

14. Although I watched Korean movies whenever possible, they weren't a prime source of inspiration because, with the exception of a few works, the exported films I saw during the 1980s and 1990s were typically staid melodramas or slight comedies. Because I was interested in a subjective cinema, middle-aged male perspectives (from which the directors invariably worked) about Korean women and their representation in Korean cinema struck me as idealized or, again, marginalized or tokenistic.

15. Japanese American or Japanese Canadian, the interchangeability was intentional because the co-writer, Kerri Sakamoto, and I believed the social and political histories were so similar, why not the personal ones? This story was meant to transcend an arbitrary national border and acknowledge the similarities between the experiences of people of Japanese descent in North America.

16. Ella Shohat and Robert Stam, "The Cinema After Babel: Language, Difference, Power," *Screen* 26 (May–August 1985): 35–58.

17. Rey Chow, "Where Have All the Natives Gone?" in *Displacements: Cultural Identities in Question*, ed. Angelika Bammer (Bloomington: Indiana University Press, 1994), 137.

18. Frederic Jameson, "Modernism and Imperialism," in *Nationalism, Colonialism, and Literature*, ed. Terry Eagleton, Frederic Jameson, and Edward Said (Minneapolis: University of Minnesota Press, 1990), 51.

19. Homi K. Bhabha, "Interrogating Identity: Frantz Fanon and the Postcolonial Prerogative," in *The Location of Culture* (London: Routledge, 1994), 66–84.

Asian American Film
and Video in Context

Historical Consciousness and the Viewer: *Who Killed Vincent Chin?*

> The memory of past time depends on the present proj-
> ect of the subject: the intentionalization of the past
> changes with the intentionalization of the future.
> –Anthony Wilden, System and Structure

Who Killed Vincent Chin? (Renee Tajima and Chris Choy, 1988) examines the murder of Vincent Chin by Ronald Ebens and his stepson in 1982. Ebens was an out-of-work autoworker in Detroit who was reported to have mistaken Chin for Japanese. Ebens blamed Chin for his own lack of work and, in a street fight, killed him. The film uses a wide variety of source materials not only to raise questions about the structural conditions that might give rise to Ronald Ebens's specific form of social consciousness, but also to propose novel alternatives to the prevailing forms of historical representation found in nonfiction cinema.

Taking less than ten minutes of screen time, the opening succession of shots presents topless dancers from the Fancy Pants bar describing their jobs; a policeman recounting how Ronald Ebens and his stepson, Michael Nitz, beat Vincent Chin to death with a baseball bat in a McDonald's parking lot near this bar; Mrs. Chin on the Phil Donahue show, choking back tears at the loss of her son; neighbors of Ebens saying he and his family are "good people" and it (the murder) was "just one of those things [that] could happen to anyone"; Ronald Ebens, on a Detroit TV show denying that he has ever been a racist; men streaming out of an auto factory with an African American quartet singing "Get a Job" on the sound track; shoppers at a mall listening to groups sing ditties about "their city," Detroit; a friend of Ebens describing his and Ebens's ethic, "You work hard and you play hard"; Mrs. Chin, against a background of traditional Chinese music, recounting the shocks, hardship, and racism she discovered in America, such as being driven from a Detroit baseball stadium by (white) fans who refused to tolerate the presence of Asians; Ebens telling of his own courtship and marriage and the couple's move to Detroit as the same African American quartet croons "How sweet it is to be loved by you . . ."; and a group of auto workers who go from work to a bar where they talk about how the Japanese undercut American car prices by paying workers less for their labor.

If the future, like the past, is made and remade in terms of our changing present situation, it cannot be known in advance and made subject to dicta, dogma, or any other teleological imperative. And yet the future cannot be abandoned as merely unknowable or our decisions and actions would become meaningless. Intentionality, as Wilden's epigraph indicates, is that (phenomenological) process by which consciousness constitutes and addresses a world, by which consciousness is always *consciousness of* something.[1] That something, here, is the future, that time in which we act upon what we learn now. It is the ceaseless dialectic of past, present, and future that sustains historical consciousness for the historical actor as well as the historical spectator. It is the construction of such actors within a viewing context that provides the present focus of this essay. Political art needs to "convey the sense of a hermeneutic relationship to the past which is able to grasp its own present as history only on condition it manages to keep the idea of the future, and of radical and Utopian transformation, alive."[2]

For the film spectator, this "present" is the present moment of viewing. At issue, then, is the relation between this moment and previous moments (our past, including earlier moments within the film itself) as they coalesce into an intentionalization of the future (a consciousness of a necessary correspondence between now and what has yet to come). My claim is that *Who Killed Vincent Chin?* is the most important political documentary of the 1980s. It is so because it establishes a present moment of viewing in relation to what has already taken place in the film, such that we regard our own present as past, or, more conventionally, as prologue to a future outside the film which, through the very process of viewing, we may bring into being. I use the conditional mood and the phrase "*may* bring into being" because it remains a question of the content of the form as we apprehend it. Form guarantees nothing. Its content, the meaning we make of it, is a dialectical process taking place between us and the screen and among present, past, and future. The viewing process provides an analogy for a larger historical process. Our present, aligned to the film's re-presentation of past events, may construct a dialectical "will to transform" as our specific intentionalization toward the future. This is not to say that the engendering of a historical consciousness is determined by our apprehension of certain film forms; only that such a consciousness may follow from such apprehension, and that the content of *Who Killed Vincent Chin?*'s collage form seems especially conducive to this result.[3]

This claim—that *Who Killed Vincent Chin?* constructs a dialectical will to transform as an intentionalization toward the future—borrows from what Freud called *Nachträglichkeit* and White called "willing backwards" to describe a viewing experience that suspends us in time, between past and present, present and future. As prompted by *Who Killed Vincent Chin?* and certain other films, this experience stands distinctly apart from the form of historical consciousness arising from classic realist representation with its sense of linear causality and teleological determination. Here, by contrast, the future remains unknowable but simultaneously up for grabs. *Nachträglichkeit* joins more squarely with the question of modernism, as posed by White, and of postmodernism, as posed by Jameson.[4] As we view a film retrospectively, in the mode of "willing backward," we model a future on the basis of our present situation as it is mediated by how we now understand our past situation. The collage structure of *Who Killed Vincent Chin?* invites such a reading and as we retro-spect, re-read, re-construct, we assemble a story (*histoire*) from our present perspective that is mediated by what we now understand of past events in the plot, in "the story so far. . . ."

The sense of working a boundary that impinges on realism has fundamental importance to documentary film representation and historical consciousness (the fragments that comprise the film are themselves usually realist in construction whereas the assembly of the fragments resembles collage more than classic narrative realism). Within this border zone, the assembly of fragments, such as those presented during the first ten minutes of *Who Killed Vincent Chin?*, allows for the evocation of what is not manifestly present, what cannot be named or represented literally without shifting to a different, metacommunicative level (such as the one here). Collage, although comprised of realist fragments, has a distinct "content" from that of the classic realist narrative. The paradoxical status of realism as a mode of representation that attests to knowledge and to aesthetic pleasure remains acute: the fragments appear "merely" to replicate what already exists; the collage announces itself as a distinctive form of representation. To resolve this paradox in either direction so that a text is made transparent to the world, as unmediated knowledge, or rendered opaque, as a realm of aesthetic signification, is to dull the very edge that gives realism its power and continuing use-value. Collage, such as we find in *Who Killed Vincent Chin?*, retains the paradox while simultaneously aiming it in the direction of a will to transform.

Realism alone clearly will not suffice. *Who Killed Vincent Chin?* derails narrative without destroying it; it reconstitutes realism without abandoning it. Retardations, delays, slippages, diversions, incomplete reasonings, unfinished arguments, partial proposals, competing claims, jarring or strange juxtapositions, fissures, jumps, gaps, or other *perepetias* mark this distinct inflection of realist narrative. The film's form ties the present moment of viewing intimately to what has already been viewed as we actively try to make connections left unstated by the film. Various modes of documentary representation, distinct fragments, or units interlace with one another in configurations we might call sedimented, laminated, or marbled.[5] Disparate elements must be reread and reworked. Strange juxtapositions and unexpected fissures require us to fit fragments into place within a shifting field of reference. As Robert Burgoyne puts it regarding historical narrative (but the same would hold true for collage), "In short, historical narrative is seen as a performative discourse, a product of the same kinds of actions that produce historical events; the investing of the world with symbolic meaning."[6]

The contemporary search for alternative forms of representation parallels a waning of historical consciousness itself. A crisis of representation ensues from the failure of classic realist narrative models to convince us of their commensurability with the reality we experience beyond them. Different models arise and contend. The modern event (massively demonstrated in disasters, catastrophes, and social holocausts) eludes traditional historical understanding. Things happen but without identifiable agency, without a clear causal chain, without explanatory linkage. Questions arise that cannot be answered by traditional storytelling techniques. Too much of that excess magnitude we explain by saying that "history" remains unaccounted for; too much noise or dissonance, too many loose ends and dangling uncertainties remain. The (narrative) center will not hold. As Hayden White puts it,

> But not only are *modern*, post-industrial "accidents" more incomprehensible than anything earlier generations could possibly have imagined (think of Chernobyl), the photo and video documentation of such accidents is so full that it is difficult to work the documentation of any one of them up as elements of a single "objective" story. Moreover, in many instances, the documentation of such events is so manipulable as to discourage the effort to derive explanations of the occurrences of which the documentation is supposed to be a recorded image.[7]

Thus, *Who Killed Vincent Chin?* provides a surface upon which to inscribe both the sense and the senselessness of Chin's murder. The film presents surface traces of an absent subject. It is one of many films to do so: *Hotel Terminus: The Life and Times of Klaus Barbie* (Marcel Ophuls, 1988), *Roger and Me* (Michael Moore, 1989), *Far From Poland* (Jill Godmilow, 1984), and *Sari Red* (Pratibha Parmar, 1988) are a few others. This tactical choice reinforces the sense that these traces lack the "grit," the points of attachment, that would hold them within a given frame of reference or explanatory matrix. To re-present the event is clearly not to explain it. Multiple interpretations and meanings seem to explode outward. The event—up for grabs, decontextualized, or de-realized—produces a crisis for historical representation. The fractured, fragmented surface mirrors back assigned meanings ironically: it refracts them and denies them the closure or objective truth value that might otherwise be claimed for them.

Who Killed Vincent Chin?, with its superficial resemblance to an MTV visual style, poses the risk of sliding toward a discourse not of sobriety, but delirium.[8] The film presents us with a fraying away of the historical event from an explanatory frame; the logical impossibility of explaining the whole by means of any part; the reluctance to name the framework in which apparent disorder can assume pattern and meaning (intensified by an aversion to "master narratives"); the analytic impossibility of determining causality, intentionality, or motivation from the visual record; the heightened intensity brought to bear on the isolated event itself as though it *ought* to yield up its secrets, its meaning. All of these factors burden the interpretation of the event with an excess that threatens to become pure delirium.

Signs of this potential delirium appear in the film's complex array of source materials as well as in its remarkably diverse set of moods (subjunctive, conditional, performative), tenses (past, present, future), and voices (active, passive, middle). The film joins together home movies, interviews shot by the filmmakers, interviews conducted by others but reused by the filmmakers, photographs, "behind the scenes" observational footage of network news journalism, the reproduction of broadcast news and talk shows, cartoons, advertisements, and press conferences.

The film includes a diversity of moods, each of which contributes to its fragmented construction. These will each be described in turn. The first mood is the subjunctive, which *Webster's Third New International Dictionary* defines as "a set of verb forms that represents an attitude toward or concern with a denoted act or state not as fact but as something entertained in thought as contingent or possible or viewed emotionally (as with doubt, desire, will)." Such a definition is entirely in keeping with the dominant stress of performative documentary and historical fictions like *Who Killed Vincent Chin?*, where the effect of the absent subject and collage form prompts both interviewees and the viewer, respectively, to construct thoughts of what might have happened that fateful night, what should have happened in the courts, what may yet happen to the persistence of racism in our land.

The conditional mood, devoted to matters of supposition, and the ablative absolute case, specifying "time, cause, or an attendant circumstance of an action," also propose themselves as linguistic models for the types of text/event/viewer relations (hermeneutic relations) discussed here. For example, *if* the testimony of Starlene, one of the dancers at the Fancy Pants club, had been admitted in court, it *may have contributed* to a very different outcome. Similarly, *if* the courts were not so overburdened, there *might have been* time to insist that such testimony be considered. These sentences, in the conditional mood, loosely correspond to the retrospective construction we place on some of the fragments dealing with Ronald Ebens's trial and the subsequent appeals. (These conditional claims are implied, are not stated as such.) The move away from conventional declarative structures appears to correspond to a move away from "rationality," or linear causality, and toward something closer to chaos theory (the discovery of pattern within apparently entropic processes by reframing or recontextualizing them). This is distinct from classic notions of "deep structure" or "structuring absence," where what is not seen or given materially can still be specified within a routine linguistic protocol: it can be named or specified even if it cannot be represented.

The performative mood involves those aspects of the film that deflect our attention away from the referential claims of the text to the more expressive, poetic, or rhetorical dimensions of the text per se. This deflection does not target the organizational properties of the text or the viewer's apprehension of them in the way formal or political reflexivity does; performativity is, instead, an insistence on the expressive gesture itself. There is a strongly performative quality to the opening minutes of *Who Killed Vincent Chin?*, for example, where various types of source material kaleidoscopically invoke the social milieu of Detroit in 1982 without feigning any transparency to this milieu. The performative mood is more than stylistic flourish. It counters the ideological effect of a text: instead of surreptitiously substituting a sign system (realism, for instance) for the historical referent this system appears to capture or present, the performative mood heightens our awareness of how referential meanings are themselves produced without entirely dispensing with the meanings so produced.

Of particular interest in *Who Killed Vincent Chin?* is the use of the middle voice in addition to the more conventional active and passive voices. Middle voice originates in Greek grammar and refers to those verb forms that indicate an effect on the subject occasioned by the action described by the verb. "I take," for example, may become "I choose" in middle voice, carrying with it both a sense of self-agency and of heightened moral consciousness. In terms of this film, the interviews with Ronald Ebens that are conducted by Renee Tajima move from "I interview" to "I offer testimony of what another said." Similarly, the viewer's involvement shifts from "I see" to "I witness or understand." Such changes lack the linguistic markers that the middle voice would have in writing and thus they remain more speculative; I nonetheless believe this concept to be an apt one for the type of effect *Who Killed Vincent Chin?* produces.[9]

Through a collage of this rich array of moods, tenses, voices, and sources, *Who Killed Vincent Chin?* achieves a distinct linkage between the general and the particular. It evokes those conceptual categories by which we generalize from particular instances (racism, sexism, class conflict) but does not name them. As Robert Burgoyne comments regarding Bertolucci's *The Conformist,* "Moments of struggle are recoded in such a way that local, historical events acquire a secondary referent. The double coding can be understood as a kind of shift in perspective, manifested through the temporal and point of view structure of the film."[10] Filmmakers Choy and Tajima adopt a similar strategy, involving much more radical shifts than Bertolucci's, to bring into being an intentionality marked by the will to transform.

Their approach also differs sharply from that of Oliver Stone, a cinematic historian working in a more recognizably fictional mode. If Stone's film *JFK* seeks to find a frame that, in retrospect, will prove a fascist conspiracy behind Kennedy's assassination and risks sliding into paranoia along the way, *Who Killed Vincent Chin?* invokes a retrospective framing of Chin's murder precisely in terms of those complex social mediations that paranoia denies or represses.

Like *JFK, Who Killed Vincent Chin?* begins with an embedded, implicit explanation of what caused a specific murder built from a welter of fragments, a panoply of images and voices drawn from a wide range of sources. What the opening segment of *Who Killed Vincent Chin?* described above does is imply linkages that remain unstated. There is no voice-over commentary to orient us; scenes exhibit that "peculiar dispersal of documentary across a heterogeneous series of objects" without the guiding hand of a narrator.[11] The heterogeneity of images and sounds grows in intensity, signaling a double refusal: the film will neither play a surrealist game with the historically real (through an insistence on the strangeness of its juxtapositions) nor uphold realist epistemology (through the organizing unity of verbal commentary or continuity editing). *Who Killed Vincent Chin?* searches for a historical frame greater than a strict sequence of events with their presumably inexorable causality. The latter would have conveyed a very different, and outmoded, sense of history or culture. The film seeks out instead a frame that cannot be named, at least not without the risk of making the apparently paranoid leap that dooms Jim Garrison in *JFK.* To name that global form of agency that "determines" local events is to reify and naturalize. These names—"global economy," "social conditions," "capitalism," "the ruling class"—all invoke an imaginary agent rather than a symbolic process. Through its form, *Who Killed Vincent Chin?* challenges us to intuit, sense, or inferentially grasp, and thereby understand, the frame or perspective that gives this act of "random" violence its fullest meaning.

In the act of viewing the film, *Who Killed Vincent Chin?* pivots dialectically between past and present, present and future, and among issues of race, class, masculinity, sex, work, pleasure, and death. This pivoting upholds a tension between the particular and the general, the local and the historical, the need for abstract or conceptual knowledge, and the desire to impart a knowledge rooted in the concrete. *Vincent Chin's* investigative action supports an epistemological genealogy that holds embodied (local, concrete, experiential) and disembodied (general, abstract, conceptual) knowledge together without blending them into a unity or diminishing them through hierarchy. If Vincent Chin's murder is to be understood in relation to the more abstract categories of class, race, and gender (already embedded but not named in the opening sequence), it must be understood in all its specificity and existential horror. And if this horror, or terror, is to be understood dialectically, it must be understood in relation to an embodied intentionality that activates the abstract principle of a will to transform.

The full embodiment of knowledge hinges on the interpretive understanding of the spectator, not on any stated meanings in the realist fragments that come before us. Even the actual murder of Vincent Chin is never spelled out at any one place in the film. Any realist description of the murder that is presented becomes only one part of the story that we retrospectively construct from what the plot places before us. I resort to the description that follows since my goal is not to replicate the form and structure of the film but to understand it; the effect of the following account, therefore, is quite distinct from the effect produced by the film. The fatal event, as retroactively constructed by the viewer, is as follows:

> Ron Ebens shouts encouragement to a black stripper, Starlene, at the "Hot Pants" club, but Vincent Chin makes a derogatory comment. They start to argue with each other at the bar.
> Ebens, "It's because of you little motherfuckers that I'm out of work."
> Chin, "Don't call me a fucker."
> Ebens, "I'm not sure if you're a big fucker or a little fucker."
> A fight ensues. Chin knocks Ebens down and leaves. Ebens tracks Chin down and beats him to death with a baseball bat while his step-son holds on to Chin.

The "cause" of the murder is also destabilized and found dispersed through the film, particularly in different fragments of Ronald Ebens's comments:

> "If you want to construe that [his "motherfucker" remark] as a racial slur, I don't know how you could do that, but I didn't say that.
> "It was like this was pre-ordained to be, I guess; it just happened.
> "It's not something you plan on happening, but it happens.
> "I've never been a racist. And God is my witness, that's the truth.
> "I felt like a real jerk, being in jail, knowing the next day was Father's Day.

"[Protest by the American Citizens for Justice] is selfish, a way for Asian-Americans to get ahead, overcome their alleged plight, alleged because I know very few Asians, very few."

Ebens's statements represent a knowledge all too fully embodied, all too totally tied to immediate, personal experience and local context. Instead of a dialectical will to transform, there is a strong desire for permanence. Like Sartre's anti-Semite, Ebens wishes

> to be massive and impenetrable . . . not to change. Where, indeed, would change take [anti-Semites]? We have here a basic fear of oneself and of truth. What frightens them is not the content of truth, of which they have no conception, but the form itself of truth, that thing of indefinite approximation. . . . They do not want any acquired opinions; they want them to be innate.[12]

"The bigot's reduction" (the segregation of Us from Them across the social imaginary) represses the passionate urge to question and know. If anything, we glimpse the failure to make an imaginative leap toward uncertainty and speculation at all. Such a leap would catapult the viewer/historian toward the conceptual but unnamed perspective that the film itself requires of its viewers. Unlike the social paranoid who also leaps beyond facts, details, and other minutiae, but toward irreversible certainty, Ronald Ebens cannot embrace the explanatory frames of racism or jingoism openly.[13] The film itself, however, chooses to leave unnamed what Ebens represses. It retains the form of indefinite approximation, leaving it for us to fill in and complete what the text's gaps and fissures address but do not identify.

Ebens's refusal of the metaphorical dimension of language, his need to cling to the metonymic contiguities of literalism, fit more precisely with the profile of classic schizophrenia than paranoia (and contrast radically with the metaphorical work of collage evident in the film as a whole). He who has admitted killing another man uses as his means of defense *a refusal to see* (to frame, to bracket, to contextualize)—a ploy that *Who Killed Vincent Chin?* makes almost impossible for its viewers. For Ronald Ebens, retrospection, willing backwards, serves only to reinforce his profound sense of non-agency. Events take place in which those who exercised agency no longer recognize themselves as agents. "It was like this was ordained to be, I guess; it just happened."[14]

This may be Ebens's perspective, but it is clearly not the film's. Choy and Tajima take a position not of nostalgic passivity, but of passionate revision. Ronald Ebens clings to the literal model of the chronicle, unwilling to make the leap beyond an ahistoricized sense of destiny. The film, however, invites bold conjecture with every cut, every new juxtaposition, every shift and change of frame. Choy and Tajima reject the monad-centered, judicially required demand for *a guilty individual*. They take no interest (not even skeptical interest) in projects to inculcate the acceptance of personal responsibility for crimes by those who commit them.[15] Although they do not let Ebens off the hook, they avoid the sense of global conspiracy a paranoid view of racism might entail and do not create the debilitating sense of victimization that an Althusserian structuralism would produce as an "ideological effect."

The oblique subject brought into being by the viewer, by means of the collage principle at work in the film, clearly entails race, class, and gender—three words *not* spoken in the film itself but omnipresent in what the collage *shows* (in the interaction between shots and scenes). Willing backward, *Nachträglichkeit*, means aiming toward a future state in which these terms achieve the full expressivity of embodied knowledge, when the meaning and effect of such terms are liberated from the chains of abstraction and brought to realization in the hearts of people.

The *experience* of the text, then, is integral to grasping the content of its form. *Who Killed Vincent Chin?* proposes an alternative form of knowledge that may have recourse to abstractions such as "race" or "class" but that depends on a return to the concrete. This involves not only an evocation of the horror of an isolated killing, but, even more, the felt and active experience of *making sense* of what we see and hear.

Leslie Devereaux, writing in relation to debates within anthropology, critiques dominant representational strategies; her remarks have application here:

> The conventions of scientific writing work against the portrayal of experience in favor of elicited systems of thought, and observed regularities of public behavior, usually reported *as* behavior, that is, with the emphasis on action rather than interaction, and prescription rather than contingency, which amounts to grave distortion of human actuality. In this rhetorical form it becomes hard not to render people homogenous and rule following [or breaking], no matter the disavowals we utter about this. Our scientized standards of evidence privilege speech over feeling and bodily sensation, which is assimilated to the personal. The personal, the putatively private, is an indistinct category of suspicious character.[16]

Who Killed Vincent Chin? opts to eschew the conventions and standards of scientific writing and of juridical procedure, moral judgment, and traditional, or realist-based Marxist analysis. Feeling and bodily sensation occupy a central place in this alternative strategy of collage and *Nachträglichkeit*. What concepts and abstractions arise do so by dint of passage through a more experiential domain, and the knowledge that ensues may well be of a different order.

The film's dynamic editing, the technique responsible for the collage effect, functions to emphasize the "portrayal of experience," less Ronald Ebens's experience than our own as we take up the process of making sense of what we see and hear. The editing, through what it juxtaposes and what it omits, fosters a will to transform that revolves around a cry for justice that the judicial system has yet to hear. More obliquely, it presents as its subject a white racism that cannot speak its own name. White racism recognizes no name for itself insofar as it can be subsumed within the domain of what "was ordained to be."

Approximating Marx's challenge to rise from the abstract to the concrete, and charged with the intensity Jameson associates with existential historicism where the past retains a "vital urgency," *Who Killed Vincent Chin?* compels us to approximate the truth Ronald Ebens represses.[17] Ebens's petty bourgeois aspirations; masculinist sense of pride and chauvinism; his history of alcoholism; the implicit sexism in his choice to "let off steam" by visiting a striptease bar with his step-son; his ignorance of Asian cultures and people; the reinforcement of family, friends, work, a distinct subculture in which Ebens lived (in which, for example, people take turns bashing a Japanese car with a sledge hammer in a televised spectacle of frustration and anger), and official policies (which portray the Japanese as workaholics, incapable of pleasure, and indifferent to others) clearly contribute to the overdetermination of what actually happened (each factor could provide an answer to the question posed by the film's title).[18]

Choy and Tajima juxtapose these elements in ways we, if not Ebens, cannot fail to apprehend. Vincent Chin's murder required all these factors, acting in concert, through the "medium" of Ebens. Where, then, does agency reside? Everywhere and nowhere. It is in how we make sense of the juxtaposition or conjunction of these factors, just as a will to transform resides in the way we make sense of the gaps and fissures of the film's collage form. This is what makes the film's mixture of realist fragments and modernist collage so distinct and innovative within documentary film practice. To attribute responsibility or guilt to monadic agents (Ebens) or naturalized abstractions ("class conflict," "racism") would reify; to place it in "what's ordained to be" would mystify. Instead, *Who Killed Vincent Chin?* situates agency within the web of conflict surrounding overdetermined events itself.[19] This web consists of relationalities more than things. "Things happen," but less because of providence than because of the condensation of forces at strategic nodal points.

Who Killed Vincent Chin? poses its issues and questions of the historicality of an "event" with exceptional force. Its oblique (unnamed) subject (white racism) eludes both naming and address. And yet the film's result is very far from a lapse into quietism. We are called upon to complete elsewhere the story begun by the film. "Please, all you good and honest people," Mrs. Chin pleads near the film's conclusion, in response to the final judicial decision, which leaves Ronald Ebens a free man. Thanks to the meaning and effect of the film's form, we are left in a position where we, as both film viewers and historical actors, experience the potential to respond in our present, which is the film's future, to Mrs. Chin's plea. "It's up to you," says Jim Garrison at the end of *JFK*, looking toward this camera and hence toward us. But the challenge presented there, to identify and name those specific figures who did the dirty deed, to see that justice as already defined will yet be done, gives way, here, to a transformative intentionality of much greater magnitude. To paraphrase Jameson, *Who Killed Vincent Chin?* invites us to grasp our present as history in order to keep alive the idea of a radically transformed future. This is an achievement that earns the film singular distinction within the domain of historical representation.

NOTES

1. For additional discussion of intentionality in relation to film, see Vivian Sobchack, *The Address of the Eye: A Phenomenology of Film Experience* (Princeton, N.J.: Princeton University Press, 1992).

2. Fredric Jameson, "Marxism and Historicism," in *The Ideologies of Theory: Essays 1971–1986*, vol. 2, *The Syntax of History* (Minneapolis: University of Minnesota Press, 1988), 148–77.

3. This essay is strongly indebted to Hayden White's writing on history, particularly to his book *The Content of the Form: Narrative Discourse and Historical Representation* (Baltimore, Md.: Johns Hopkins University Press, 1987) and to White's Patricia Wise Lecture, "The Modernist Event," in *The Persistence of History: Cinema, Television, and the Modern Event*, ed. Vivian Sobchack (New York: Routledge, 1996). In his book, White takes on the central place of narrative in the construction of meaning about the world presumed to exist outside it. My concern here with the form of *Who Killed Vincent Chin?* as a collage text explores a type of narrative that White discusses in greater detail in "The Modernist Event." In either case, a prefatory comment by White helps clarify the centrality of the "content of the form" and its difference from such conventional notions as style: "[N]arrative, far from being merely a form of discourse that can be filled with different contents, real or imaginary as the case may be, already possesses a content prior to any given actualization of it in speech or in writing. It is this 'content of the form' of narrative discourse in historical thought that is examined in the essays of this volume" (*Content of the Form*, xi).

4. Hayden White, "The Modernist Event," and Fredric Jameson, *Postmodernism, or, The Cultural Logic of Late Capitalism* (Durham, N.C.: Duke University Press, 1991).

5. I discuss modes of documentary representation in *Representing Reality: Issues and Concepts in Documentary* (Bloomington: Indiana University Press, 1991). Jameson argues that new modes of narrative do not supersede previous ones but produce sedimentations in which previous modes continue to exist alongside more recent ones. See *The Political Unconscious: Narrative as a Socially Symbolic Act* (Ithaca, N.Y.: Cornell University Press, 1981), particularly 98–102. The corresponding notion that we are ourselves, as subjects, not unified entities, entirely available to consciousness, is the subject of my essay, "We, the People: Form, Rhetoric and Ideology," in *PostModern Discourses of Ideology*, ed. Mas'ud Zavarzadeh and Teresa Ebert (Gainesville: University Press of Florida, 1995).

6. Robert Burgoyne, *Bertolucci's 1900: A Narrative and Historical Analysis* (Detroit, Mich.: Wayne State University Press, 1991), 41.

7. Hayden White, "The Modernist Event," 23.

8. I adopt the term "discourse of sobriety" in *Representing Reality* (3–5) for expository discourse that regards its relation to the historical world as unproblematic and instrumental. Such discourse is unreceptive to fictive representations (hence the avoidance of fictional

experimentation in traditional historiography and the rhetorical construction of the news anchor as "father knows best"). Such discourse takes the tropes of realism literally. Discourses of sobriety make their operational or explanatory moves in relation to the historically real through metaphors (like all discourse), but here these metaphors are meant to be real, to "capture" with fidelity both characteristics of the world and what to do about them. This has the aura of a "serious" enterprise quite distinct from the "fun" implied by fictional representations despite the common use of metaphor and narrative.

9. For more on this point, see White, "The Content of the Form," in *The Content of the Form*, especially 190–93. See John Peradotto, *Man in the Middle Voice: Name and Narration in the Odyssey* (Princeton, N.J.: Princeton University Press, 1990), for more on the nature of middle voice. These thoughts on mood and voice are indebted to informal conversations with Hayden White and Karen Bassi.

10. Robert Burgoyne, *Bertolucci's 1900*, 11.

11. Raúl Ruiz, *Of Great Events and Ordinary People.* This comment is made on the sound track in voice-over. It is meant as a critique of the tradition whereby an array of images could be stitched together into a meaningful statement by means of voice-over commentary. Ruiz opts to insist on a heterogeneity that attests to the structural disjunctions in consciousness produced by pseudototalizations like the nation-state.

12. Jean-Paul Sartre, *Anti-Semite and Jew* (New York: Schocken, 1948), 19–20.

13. See Richard Hofstadter, "The Paranoid Style in American Politics," in *The Paranoid Style in American Politics* (New York: Knopf, 1966).

14. This line of reasoning, if we may call it that, also figured heavily in the defense lawyer's arguments in the case of the Rodney King beating. The Los Angeles Police Department officers argued that Mr. King "was in control" of the situation (and that they were not). They only "responded" to what Mr. King did. Willing backwards becomes an exercise in willing oneself into passivity, at best an agent of fate, or here, of police policy and procedures. I discuss the Rodney King case in greater detail in *Blurred Boundaries* (Bloomington: Indiana University Press, 1994).

15. This contrasts with the work of films like *El Chacal de Nahueltoro* (Miguel Littin, Chile, 1969) and *Death By Hanging* (Nagisa Oshima, France/Japan, 1976), which expose the enormous investment the judiciary and the state generally have in guaranteeing that the individual criminal accept responsibility for his or her crime. Without a sense of guilt, the premise of individual responsibility breaks down. When guilt is not evident, recourse is typically made to medicine and one or another concept of insanity as the explanation for a lack of guilt. Such recourse continues to remain localized at the level of the individual; it provides an alibi for sidestepping the more disruptive question of collective guilt or systemic responsibility, precisely the type of questions raised by *Who Killed Vincent Chin?*

16. Leslie Devereaux, "Experience, Re-presentation and Film" (unpublished ms.), 7.

17. Fredric Jameson, "Marxism and Historicism," 157.

18. Neither the film nor any subsequent commentary that I have seen stresses the fact that the most proximate cause of the initial quarrel between Chin and Ebens was not the effect of Japanese cars or workers on the American economy but the quality of a stripper's performance. Starlene, a relatively new, African American performer, claims that it was Chin's disparagement and Ebens's defense of her dancing that began the argument that led to Chin's death. (She was not called to testify at the original trial, but did testify at the second, federal trial, where Ebens was charged with violating Chin's civil rights; her testimony and that of another dancer in this venue apparently had an important effect on the jury.) Chin's failure to appreciate Starlene's dancing together with assumptions Ebens may have held about Japanese workers and their denial of pleasure (even though Chin was Chinese American and, of course, a patron of the Fancy Pants bar himself) complicates issues of racism with those of sexism and class as they pertain to nightclubs, striptease, audience involvement, banter, and the body.

19. The term "web of conflict" comes from Georg Simmel, "The Web of Group Affiliations," in *Conflict* (Glencoe, Ill.: The Free Press, 1955). Simmel's synchronic theory of con-

flict seems highly commensurate with contemporary notions of the divided and split subject, with relations of affinity, and with a politics of identity. These all render classic concepts of a binary class struggle chimerical. His theory complements the diachronic theory
of sedimentation as one mode of production leaves vestiges of itself (such as patriarchal relations) within the mode that succeeds it. (Together, these theories also suggest parallel sedimentations and conflicts among forms of artistic production.) Such models call for the
complementary concept of a dominant—that specific concatenation of factors that transforms existing, conflictual relations decisively. In this case, the dominant would seem to be
the global economy as it implants itself in the tacit knowledge and schizophrenic worldview
of one Ronald Ebens. Simmel's model is often regarded as a conservative one since the competing forces within the conflictual web may cancel each other out, sustaining the status
quo; Choy and Tajima demonstrate how such a web can be represented to promote a transformative intentionality.

Marita Sturken

The Politics of Video Memory: Electronic Erasures and Inscriptions

> *I remember that month of January in Tokyo, or rather I remember the images that I filmed of the month of January in Tokyo. They have substituted themselves for my memory. They are my memory. I wonder how people remember things who don't film, don't photograph, don't tape. How has mankind managed to remember?*
> *—Chris Marker,* Sans Soleil

The camera image has long been understood as a central artifact in the production, preservation, and cultural meaning of memories. Whether as photography, film, or video/television, the camera image has figured centrally in the desire to remember, to recall the past, to make the absent present. The image has been primarily understood as a receptacle for memories, an artifact in which they reside, or as the raw material of personal histories and historical narratives. Throughout the twentieth century, events were remembered because they were photographed and moments forgotten because no images of them were preserved, and these image artifacts worked in tension with unphotographed memories. History has come to be represented by a black-and-white photographic or cinematic image, a faded color film image, or a low-resolution television image.

Yet, memories do not simply reside in image artifacts so much as they are produced by them, and in offering itself as a material fragment of the past, the camera image also produces a kind of forgetting. As such, camera images can be seen as "screen memories." According to Freud, a "screen memory" functions to hide painful memories that are too difficult for a subject to confront; the screen memory offers itself as a substitute, while "screening out" the "real" memory. Thus, the camera image can often screen out other unphotographed memories and offer itself as the "real" memory, "becoming," as Chris Marker states, our memory.

Freud demonstrated that memory is essential to the notion of a self and described the complex ways that we repress, or disremember, those memories that are too damaging or painful. Similarly, the construction of memory and history is essential to a specific culture or nation; we often "forget" as a nation. The term "cultural memory" can be understood as the realm of shared memory that exists in relation to both personal memory and history. Cultural memory designates those aspects of memory that are collective, yet not official, and which are often in tension with historical discourse. It is not necessarily a site of resistance, but often where political differences operate in tension over what should be remembered, how, and in what form. Memories and cultural artifacts can move from personal memory to cultural memory to history, or from history to personal memory. So, for instance, a survivor's personal memory may become part of a historical narrative about a particular event, and the images of history can become incorporated into our personal memories. The image is central to this entanglement of memory and history.

Independent video constitutes a field of cultural memory, one that often contests and intervenes into official history. This is not to say that all memories produced with a video camera involve political intervention—in the 1980s and 1990s, with the proliferation of home video and cable television, the wielding of a video camera is no longer encoded as an act of cultural resistance. However, many independent videotapes are deliberate interventions in the making of history and conscious constructions of cultural memory.

The Television Image-Making History

The photograph, the documentary film image, and the docudrama are central elements in the construction of history. Yet electronic images have a constantly shifting relationship to history. The television image is an image of immediacy, transmission, and continuity. "Flow," as defined by Raymond Williams—the incorporation of interruption until it becomes naturalized in the stream of images—is a central aspect of television. Television is the image without an original, for which the status of the copy is ultimately irrelevant. Stanley Cavell has noted that the primary "fact" of television is its serial format; we do not distinguish the particular television episode so much as the ongoing series or event; hence, the series is what is memorable in television.[1]

In contrast, most videotapes that fall under the rubric of video art or independent video are meant to be seen not as interruptions in the flow but as unique events. Certain works are designed for the context of satellite transmission and other videotapes are identified as "art for television." However, most independent videotapes aspire to be seen in contexts that separate them from the ongoing information flow of television.

Yet the video image is implicated in the relentless electronic flow of the television image. Television is coded, like all electronic technology, as live and immediate; it evokes the instant present, in which information is more valuable the faster and more immediate it is. Television technology has thus never been conceived in terms of preservation, and videotapes deteriorate rapidly. Videotapes that were made as recently as the 1970s look like distant antecedents to contemporary television, with their blurred and worn images and muffled sound. Many videotapes and early television shows are in fact already irretrievable.

Despite this problematic relationship to preservation, television-video has inevitably become a medium in which memory and history are recorded. Since the early 1980s, an increasing number of "historical" incidents have been recorded on television (until the late 1970s, most television news footage was still shot on film). The *Challenger* space shuttle exploding, the lone Chinese student halting a tank in Tiananmen Square, people clambering on top of the Berlin Wall, and the "targets" taken from cameras on bombs in the Persian Gulf War: these are distinctly television images of history. Slightly blurred, often shot with the immediate feeling of a handheld camera, these images seem to evoke not a fixed history but rather history as it unfolds—the making of history. While the feverish immediacy of these images connotes an instantaneity, their status as historical images is somewhat muddied. They will, in a sense, always be coded as live, immediate images—their blurriness or lack of image resolution is often read as evoking the speed of information rather than their electronic materiality. The electronic image thus presents a paradox for memory and history, connoting the immediate instead of the past. This has led certain cultural critics to declare television as the site of memory's demise. For instance, Fredric Jameson has written: "But memory seems to play no role in television, commercial or otherwise (or, I am tempted to say, in postmodernism generally): nothing haunts the mind or leaves its afterimages in the manner of the great moments of film (which do not necessarily happen, of course, in the 'great' films)."[2]

Yet, despite Jameson's pessimism (and cultural elitism), it is too easy to declare memory dead in a postmodern context. Jameson nostalgically mourns the passing of history in the postmodern "weakening of history, both in our relationship to public History and in the new forms of our private temporality."[3] But what is the history mourned here, a pretelevision history? I would argue that the stakes in memory and history are ever present in electronic media (and postmodernism)—that despite its paradoxical relationship to the preservation of memory, television-video is a primary site of history and cultural memory, where memories, both individual and collective, are produced and claimed. It is a matter of understanding that memory is unstable, intangible, and often misread as forgetting. Video may indeed be the quintessential medium of postmodern memory.

Video Memories

In independent video, the preservation of images and recording of history has been an underlying desire in the accumulation of videotapes. Video collectives in the 1970s, such as the Videofreex and Raindance, were interested in compiling databanks of alternative images and in accruing an alternative visual history to the nationalist history produced by broadcast television. Yet, concerns with preservation were deemed irrelevant; consequently, most of the early videotapes by the collectives have not survived, and television stations routinely destroy master tapes of old programs. The maintenance of collective memory is a problem, it seems, in the case of bulky one-inch tapes or old heat-sensitive reel-to-reel videotapes. While the notion of a video databank utopically envisioned by these collectives conjured up alternative histories stored neatly in electronic space and accessible to everyone, in reality tapes are material objects that stick, erode, and warp.

Yet in this dual role of image retention and loss, video has increasingly become a medium in which issues of collective and individual memory are being examined. The politics of memory and identity, the elusiveness of personal memory, and the relationship of camera images to national and cultural memory have become topics explored by artists working in video. I would like to examine several of these artists' works in order to explore how the phenomenology of video—its electronic presence, screen image, and instantaneity—intersects with a contemporary politics of memory, and how video has been used to create counterimages to nationalistic histories: Woody Vasulka's *Art of Memory* (1987), Rea Tajiri's *History and Memory* (1991), Janice Tanaka's *Memories from the Department of Amnesia* (1990) and *Who's Going to Pay for These Donuts, Anyway?* (1992), and Jeanne Finley's *Nomads at the 25 Door* (1991). These tapes are concerned with the memory of political and historical events, how those memories are preserved and embodied, how they permeate the present, and the intersections of personal memory, cultural memory, and history. In all these works, the role of video as a technology of memory is ever present: remembering, forgetting, and containing, preserving, and producing memories.

Among these tapes, Woody Vasulka's *Art of Memory* is concerned most directly with the different phenomenological relationships of film and television-video to memory and history, and the fluctuating cultural meanings of images that are coded "history." *Art of Memory* takes as its material the black-and-white photographic and filmic images of the "historic events" of the twentieth century: the Spanish Civil War, the Russian Revolution, World War II, the atomic bomb. Vasulka mixes codes and images to make the signification of historicity his central topic. Cinematic tropes for the passage of time, such as images reeling past or flipping by, are contained within stylized, electronically created shapes that deny these cinematic codes their narrative potential. Vasulka's project is to use video to examine and ultimately consume cinema. Whereas the cinema preserved history, he seems to say, video will reshape it.

In *Art of Memory*, newsreel and documentary footage and still photographs are transformed into image objects that appear to sit on a southwestern desert landscape. These image objects are evocative, strange, and unpredictable. Sometimes they resemble large movie screens in the desert, at other times their shapes are awkward and bulky. They function to decontextualize the film images: one cannot read them as windows onto the world, but only as generic images of history. Some assert themselves to suggest narratives—Oppenheimer's famous postbomb speech, in which he quotes the Bhagavad Gita, for instance—but then are submerged again in the stream of images contained within the object forms that deconstruct narrative in the tape.

Yet within this dense layering of images, Vasulka does hint at a narrative of history and the image. In one of the few purely video images, a mythical figure with wings sits on a cliff. Seeing it from a distance, a man tries to capture its attention. He tosses a pebble at it, and then, when it turns toward him, he photographs it, causing it to rise up in apparent anger and swoop down upon him. The creature is ultimately unexplained in this tape, but it evokes many possible meanings—an unattainable, mythic man/beast that the nervous and distracted middle-aged man, haunted by images of history, tries to capture with his camera. It is as if he is trying to photograph the well-known "angel of history" described by Walter Benjamin:

> His face is turned toward the past. Where we perceive a chain of events, he sees one single catastrophe which keeps piling wreckage upon wreckage and hurls it in front of his feet. The angel would like to stay, awaken the dead, and make whole what has been smashed. But a storm is blowing from Paradise; it has got caught in his wings with such violence that the angel can no longer close them. This storm irresistibly propels him into the future to which his back is turned, while the pile of debris before him grows skyward.[4]

This sense of a propelling forward of history permeates *Art of Memory*. Vasulka's alter ego tries to create an image of the figure to hold it in place, to prevent it from hurtling toward the future, away from the photographic into the electronic grids created by Vasulka's machinery. The images of history lose their individual meaning and become a tangle of memories swallowed by the electronically rendered desert landscape. Voices echo and haunt these images; we cannot understand them, but we know, with their scratchy sound and intonation, that these are the voices of history. Still photographs, some of famous historical figures such as the anarchist Durruti and the revolutionary Rosa Luxemburg, scroll across the screen, processed until they become almost translucent and shredded by the passage of time. These images of history are set in the desert, a landscape coded as both timeless and postapocalyptic.

In its form and its contrast of the cinematic and the electronic, *Art of Memory* is an attempt to chart the death of cinema. Here, the cinematic is the past, the fading black-and-white images of history, swallowed up by the electronic. In the structure of the tape, Vasulka is attempting to configure an electronic language that defies the legacy of cinematic codes. He uses complex wipes and fades to avoid the "cut," which he considers to be a cinematic device that is not inherently a part of the language of electronic imaging. In creating image "objects" on the screen, he is attempting to defy the fetishizing aspect of cinema, to render the cinematic images into a relentless flow in which any pretense of realism gives way to the simple code of cinema as history. *Art of Memory* is a meditation on the ways in which cinema defines and creates history, and on redefining its legacy in the realm of the electronic.

While the status of the cinematic image as history propels *Art of Memory*, the work does not attempt to trace the meaning of its historical images or their consequences. In *Art of Memory*, the images of war meld together into a totalizing image of history, one that does not question the status of the image as history. In contrast, Rea Tajiri's *History and Memory* presents video as memory (as opposed to cinema as history) as a means to construct countermemories to history. For Tajiri, the critical issue is the construction of history and how the historical image screens out the images of personal memory. This is a dense work of found and reconstructed images, a cathartic reworking of history through the image.

History and Memory attempts to understand the intersections of personal memory and historical events, specifically the history and memories of the imprisonment of Japanese Americans in the United States during World War II. Tajiri is compelled by the gaps in her mother's memory and her own sense of incompleteness to counter the historical images of the internment of her mother and her father's family in California, specifically in U.S. propaganda films. The story of her family forms a microcosm of the consequences of racist American policy: her father served in the army while the government interned his family, all of them Americans, in concentration camps and took their possessions. Their house was not only confiscated by the government but literally moved away; they never found out where. Tajiri's task is a kind of retroactive witnessing; cameras were not allowed in the camps, so her raw materials are the images she has carried in her mind of this nonimaged past. From her mother's stories of the camps, recounted to her as a child, she creates an image of her mother filling a canteen at a faucet in the desert, an image for which she wants to find the story. When cameras are not there to witness, when memories fade and people forget, the sole witnesses are the spirits of the dead:

> There are things which have happened in the world while there were cameras watching, things we have images for. There are other things, which have happened while there were no cameras watching, which we restage in front of cameras to have images of.

> There are things which have happened for which the only images that
> exist are in the minds of observers, present at the time, while there are
> things which have happened for which there have been no observers, ex-
> cept the spirits of the dead.

Tajiri imagines the spirit of her grandfather witnessing an argument between
her parents about the "unexplained nightmares that their daughter has been
having on the twentieth anniversary of the bombing of Pearl Harbor." Where
are the memories of those events for which there were no witnesses? Where
are those memories when the witnesses are gone? Where are the unphotographed images? The prohibition of cameras in the camps asserts itself
often in the narrative weavings of this work. An unearthed home movie
image of the camps, made with a smuggled camera, contrasts sharply with
the evenly lit, steady, and clean images of government propaganda films in
its jerky camera movement and, unexpectedly, its everydayness.

When we do not have access to images to construct memories and
histories, Tajiri makes it clear, we make others. Her sister follows a young
man with her camera, too shy to talk to him except to ask him to pose for
her. His photo ends up in her box of movie stars that only years later Tajiri
realizes is filled only with images of white people. Her own task is to create images to fill the void of those absent images of the camps, to make
the absent Japanese American—absent from the box of movie stars and
from history—present. The war in the Pacific produced a kind of hyper-
visibility of the Japanese Americans. Tajiri notes, "Whereas before we
were mostly ignored and slightly out of focus, the war brought us clearly
into view and made us sharply defined." The historical camera focused
and saw not citizens but enemies of the state.

These are not just the memories of survivors, now fading, but the
memories of their children as well. Tajiri has lived this memory:

> I began searching for a history, my own history, because I had known all
> along that the stories I had heard were not true and parts had been left out.
> I remember having this feeling growing up that I was haunted by something,
> that I was living within a family full of ghosts. There was this place that
> they knew about. I had never been there, yet I had a memory for it. I could
> remember a time of great sadness before I was born. We had been moved,
> uprooted. We had lived with a lot of pain. I had no idea where these memo-
> ries came from yet I knew the place.

Her tape is in many ways an attempt to coexist with the ghosts of the past
by creating images in which to place them.

History is constructed not only through documentary images and
propaganda films, it is also constructed via popular culture. American cultural notions of World War II, for instance, are for the most part constructed through Hollywood films. These are screen memories that both
substitute themselves for the personal memories of survivors and supersede documentary images in signifying history. These are, in Tajiri's

words, the events that we restage in front of cameras. This era in American history is signified for Tajiri by the jingoistic film *Yankee Doodle Dandy* (1942) and the absent presence evoked by *Bad Day at Black Rock* (1955), in which Spencer Tracy investigates the death of a Japanese American man in the United States after the invasion of Pearl Harbor. Komoko, the murdered man, is never seen in the film; Tajiri notes that his murder was one the townspeople wanted to forget, just as the people who live near Poston, Arizona, where the internment camps were constructed on a Native American reservation, attempt to forget until an Asian face reminds them. The narrative film thus functions as a retelling, in Tajiri's terms, of the absent presence of the Japanese Americans. Like other historical narrative films, it works to fill in and supplant gaps in cultural memory, offering images when there were none. Tajiri's nephew, in reviewing the Hollywood film *Come See the Paradise* (1990), a sentimental depiction of the camps seen through the eyes of an internee's white husband, actively resists the capacity of these film images to replace memories, although, he says, his grandparents didn't tell him any stories.

Tajiri's desire to fill in the memory gaps with new images and reworked images of the past allows her to re-remember for her mother. When her mother cannot remember how she got to the camp, Tajiri goes back to videotape the drive for her. Imagining her mother filling the canteen, she reenacts it, saying, "For years, I have been living with this picture without the story. . . . Now I could forgive my mother for her loss of memory and could make this image for her." The camera image thus participates in a process of healing, allowing through recreating, reimaging, a kind of memory closure. Yet, Tajiri makes it clear that this is a partial memory and a partial healing, one remembered and constructed in opposition, one peopled with multiple subjectivities, racist images, counterimages, fragments of the past, absent presences.

Public commemoration, as a memorial or a videotape, is a form of bearing witness. Tajiri, in questioning historical narratives and creating countermemories, attempts to create memory out of forgetting. For Janice Tanaka the video form also becomes a means of bearing witness and reclaiming memories. Tanaka states that in her childhood home, "silence was the keeper of memories," and her videotapes are a means of speaking through that silence. *Memories from the Department of Amnesia* reflects on the death of her mother, and *Who's Going to Pay for These Donuts, Anyway?* chronicles her search for a father she hadn't seen since she was three, a father she continues to search for in the frail man with a confused memory whom she comes to know.

In both these tapes, Tanaka juxtaposes "official" historical accounts with personal memories and anecdotes. On paper, both her parents clearly suffered because of their internment as Japanese Americans during World War II, yet it is the different ways in which they responded to American racism that Tanaka investigates. In *Memories from the Depart-*

ment of Amnesia, she opposes a chronology of her mother's life events with the seemingly "unimportant" quirks and anecdotes remembered by herself and her daughter. Tanaka uses cryptic and dreamlike images to suggest the elusive nature of memory: a figure rides a bicycle through a restaurant; a surgeon walks through deep snow; a white figure stands in a white space, perhaps a hospital waiting room; the bicyclist and surgeon pass each other in the snow—images of passage, remembering, and death.

The photograph as a marker of the past, as a totem of death, infuses this work. A hand lays photographs on the screen, creating negative and positive layers of images, each shifting with movement, focusing and refocusing. The photograph is both stationary and moving, freezing the past yet moving within the present. As the hand lays these still images on the screen, they appear to briefly come alive and then resume their two-dimensional form, as if floating in and out of consciousness.

Tanaka and her daughter tell stories about her mother as the statistical events of her life are written on the screen: Born December 15, 1919, Los Angeles, California . . . Abandoned by mother, 1925 . . . Molested by father . . . Married, February 1940 . . . First child born, September 1940 . . . Government freezes bank account, 1941 . . . Interned Manzanar, 1942 . . . Spouse declared insane, 1942 . . . Nervous breakdown, 1963 . . . Finds mother, acknowledgment denied . . . This visual litany of trauma, abuse, and hardship displaces the amused rememberings of Tanaka and her daughter. We see the layered existence of a woman whose life is unalterably changed by the actions of the government, the memory behind the history, the memories that are stored in the "department" of amnesia. The history of Tanaka's mother is told through a roll call of the traumatic events of her life, the institutionalization of her life's events. Yet her memory is evoked through video images, hands touching photographs, voices remembering her humor and her humanness.

In *Who's Going to Pay for These Donuts, Anyway?* this tension between history and memory lies in the absence of memory of Tanaka's father. When she discovers him after several years in a halfway house for the chronically mentally ill in Los Angeles, it is unclear whether he ever recognizes her to be his daughter, although he knows he has a daughter named Janice. Similarly, it remains unclear whether or not his mental instability was sadly coincidental with or actually the direct result of the Japanese American internment. Tanaka remembers that her mother told her in anger not to make a hero of her absent father and, to prove his insanity to her daughter, stated that he had written letters of protest to the president about the Japanese internment, that he had been questioned by the FBI, that he was diagnosed as a schizophrenic with paranoid tendencies, and that he had outbursts of anger—all of them, on the face of it, potentially sane responses to being interned in one's native country. Tanaka says, "You hated being a Jap and you hated your wife and children for being Japs."

Tanaka juxtaposes this portrait of her father as a man destroyed by history with one of her uncle, whom she also rediscovers: a calm, reserved man who speaks of the events of the war and their effects with a sad irony. Just as her uncle has devised a personal philosophy to reconcile his memories of interrogation and internment, so clearly her father has lost his memory not only through shock treatment and drug therapy but also perhaps by a strategic forgetting of things too painful to remember. In this light, those things that he does remember seem remarkable—his understanding of redress, for instance, and why he was given money by the government to compensate for his internment.

Like Tajiri, Tanaka uses the video camera as a tool to mediate between herself and the past that is also part of her memory; she states, "Observing the effect of the past could only be dealt with from behind the distancing lens of the camera." Focusing the camera on her father, however lost, makes him finally tangible. Her videotaping is thus an attempt to counter the anti-memory of her family, the lack of souvenirs and memorabilia, the lack of family cohesion. Memory, according to Tanaka, allows us to live more in the present: "When you have a past, it is easy to believe the present has a reason."

Tanaka's tape serves as a countermemory to history, providing, like Tajiri's work, memories that tangle with history and disrupt its narratives. American national identity is constructed through the remembrance of certain historical events, as well as through the forgetting and rescripting of certain events. The historical event of the internment of Japanese American citizens during the war is not easily rescripted from its historical narrative—as necessary although regrettable, as different somehow from what other countries did. It is survivors, in particular their physical presence, who prevent history from being written smoothly and without disruption. In these three tapes it is the children of survivors who are refusing to leave history alone and whose image interventions place the bodies of their parents in the cracks of history.

The displacement so powerfully evoked in Tajiri's story of the house moved from its foundations and in Tanaka's image of her father as a man destroyed by history is echoed in Jeanne Finley's *Nomads at the 25 Door*, in which the ruthlessness of history-making and issues of home are presented within a context of bearing witness and memorializing fleeting moments in history's rapid accrual. The tape examines two separate worlds that are infused by displacement: Yugoslavia in 1990 and a women's prison in Carson City, Nevada. Finley toys with notions of history by drawing analogies between the two situations: the upheaval of Yugoslavia and the burden of its rapidly changing history, and the ways in which the displaced women in the prison create a sense of home and bear witness for each other.

That history is a process of displacement has been played out for over a decade in the upheaval of Eastern Europe. Finley captures this painful process of history via videotape and the television screens on which it unfolded. Ironically, the historical upheaval she documents seems trivial when compared with the brutal destruction of Yugoslavia that has taken place since that time. While in Yugoslavia she watches the televised images of the Romanian revolution that are broadcast twenty-four hours a day for a week. Yet the television revolution is confusing and chaotic. We see scenes of people speaking, lined up before the camera, trying desperately to get into its view. Finley remarks that the coverage was "incredibly confusing," and even the Romanians she knew could not decipher the scenes. A British newscaster tells us that "residents have placed their televisions in the windows of their homes so those who are engaged in street fighting can watch their own revolution as it is taking place." History is presented in the relentless flow of television, although finally it elucidates nothing except that power has changed hands. Yet the political stakes in what gets designated history and imaged as history are high. A friend of Finley's writes her notes every morning about tricky phrases in the Serbo-Croatian language, a hybrid language created by historical whim, which are minicommentaries on history and home:

> —You might think you are in a vacation *paradise*, but you are not. You're in a complicated part of the world, used by a cruel and ongoing history.
> —The possibility of a home for me has always been based on the whims of history. And history never seems too indulgent. It is always displacing people.

The search for a history represents a search for stability, community, a home. In the tape we see Finley write on someone's hands, "If only I could find history simply by pressing the palms of your hands against my chest." Yet history is elusive, intangible, ever changing: it stands outside these bodies.

It is through the unusual juxtaposition of the two disparate worlds of Eastern Europe and the women's prison that Finley pushes at notions of personal history, national history, and the desires within for both community and home. Her interviews with the women in the Carson City prison are moving and compelling and ultimately overshadow the images of Yugoslavia because of their direct emotional intensity. These women speak of lives of abuse and fear and, strangely for those of us on the outside, the ways in which they finally found acceptance, love, families, and a sense of home in prison. The tape centers on Mickey Yates, a young woman who very slowly tells her story of receiving two life sentences for her complicity in the brutal killing of her mother. For Yates, the notion of a home is profoundly troubling; she went home to find her mother dead. At first, she is reluctant to tell her story, her history, but then its telling becomes cathartic and essential. She actively constructs her history. Ironically, she reveals the paradox of history in a simple idiomatic expression: when the judge asked her about the sexual abuse she was subjected to, she started to cry—"I was history after that."

In its elliptical style, Finley's tape is about inserting personal memories into the mass of history. She begins and ends the tape with an image taken by her own mother of herself and her brother waving while going off to school. These were images her mother took for family calendars showing the children dressed in different outfits for each month, standing and waving—a project that crudely evokes the passage of time. They were instructed, says Finley, to stand and wave, walk, wave again, and then walk away without looking back. Yet clearly her tape is asking, How can we not look back? Isn't it cruel to ask a child not to look back? History and memory in this work are intimately allied, each pushing the boundary of the other, each permeating our lives.

The relationship of history and home is clearly evoked in Finley's tape. The women in the prison find their voices after establishing a sense of home. "I never realized that I would have to come to prison to find acceptance," one says. The displacement of the Japanese Americans during the war was equally a negation of home, of the right to call any place home. It is from the place of home that a historical voice can speak, and it is home where memories reside.

All these tapes are infused with the desire to create countermemories to official historical narratives. While Vasulka wants to reorchestrate the images of history and to show the empty frame of the totalizing historical image, these other videomakers want to bear witness: the prisoners in Finley's tape bear witness for each other; the Romanians bear witness before the television cameras, watching themselves "make history"; Tanaka bears witness for her mother and father; and Tajiri bears witness for her family. Video thus acts as a form of cultural memory, providing a form through which personal memories are shared, historical narratives are questioned, and memory is contested and claimed. Television will continue to play a central role in how Americans and other nations construct their national identities. Yet video's memories are tangling with its narratives, appropriating its images, and telling different stories.

In these tapes, memory is not seen as a depository of images to be excavated, but rather as an amorphous, ever-changing field of images. This memory is not about retrieval as much as it is about retelling and reconstruction. It is about acknowledging the impossibility of knowing what really happened, and a search for a means of telling. This is memory within a postmodern context, not absent but often disguised as something else, not stable or tangible but elusive and fragile, entangled with fantasy, longing, and desire.

NOTES

1. Stanley Cavell, "The Fact of Television," in *Video Culture: A Critical Investigation,* ed. John Hanhardt (Rochester, N.Y.: Visual Studies Workshop, 1986), 192–218.

2. Fredric Jameson, *Postmodernism; or, The Cultural Logic of Late Capitalism* (Durham, N.C.: Duke University Press, 1991), 70–71.

3. Ibid., 6.

4. Walter Benjamin, "Theses on the Philosophy of History," in *Illuminations,* ed. Hannah Arendt, trans. Harry Zohn (New York: Schocken, 1969), 257–58.

Peter X Feng

Being Chinese American, Becoming Asian American: *Chan Is Missing*

It was almost ten years ago. A small group of us perched on the rickety chairs at the old Collective for Living Cinema loft in Manhattan got a first glimpse at a low-budget, black-and-white feature by then experimental film-maker, Wayne Wang. The appeal of Chan Is Missing *(1981) went beyond its social relevance or the familiarity of the characters and themes. There was something original about the film, and something very Asian American.*
—Renee Tajima

Where's our jazz? Where's our blues? Where's our ain't-taking-no-shit-from-nobody street-strutting language?
—Wittman Ah Sing (Maxine Hong Kingston)

In the early 1980s, sometime between the inauguration of Ronald Reagan and the murder of Vincent Chin, a new voice began to intrude upon the cultural consciousness of the United States. That voice belonged, depending upon who named it, to Wayne Wang, a Hong Kong-born Chinese American filmmaker; to Asian American filmmakers as a group; or to Asian Americans as a filmgoing community. The film *Chan Is Missing* (1981) announced that Asian Americans could be artists, could be commercial filmmakers, and could support Asian American filmmaking (as well as successfully market Asian American films to wider audiences).

Asian American ethnicity is determined by a tension among many cultures; as such, Asian Americans are an especially hyphenate community. Manning Marable defines African American ethnicity in hyphenated cultural terms: "our ethnicity is derived from the cultural synthesis of our African heritage and our experiences in American society."[1] Thus the eth-

From *Cinema Journal* 35:4, pp. 88–118. Copyright © 1996 by the University of Texas Press. All rights reserved.

nic subject is a divided subject. Asian Americans are further divided, for the term "Asian" encompasses several distinct cultures—Chinese, Japanese, Korean, Filipino, Vietnamese, Indian, and Laotian, to name a few. Even Chinese culture can be broken down further: mainland Chinese versus Taiwanese, Cantonese versus Mandarin. Given this diversity of cultural experience, how can there be a voice that is distinctively Asian American?

This essay seeks to answer that question by examining the discourses of race and ethnicity within and surrounding the film *Chan Is Missing*.[2] Following a brief discussion of the meanings of the term "Asian American," I examine the usefulness and the limitations of theories of hyphenated identity (derived from and associated with debates about postmodernism) for the interpretation of Wayne Wang's film. I then show how *Chan Is Missing* works to destabilize notions of Chinese American identity, even while the film is marketed as an Asian American text: ultimately, I argue that the destabilization of Chinese American identity not only allows for, but actually contributes to, the construction of Asian American subjectivity. This can only be accomplished by focusing on process rather than end result, on the act of "becoming" rather than the state of "being"; otherwise we risk arguing "merely" that *Chan Is Missing* elaborates the fragmentation of Chinese American identity without suggesting what it offers in its place.

Chan Is Missing is a useful text for examining the contingency of identity, for the film lends itself to multiple reading formations, generic and otherwise. Surely the appeal of *Chan Is Missing* to those of us who teach film is due in no small part to the different cinematic traditions the film evokes. *Chan Is Missing*'s narrative structure allows us to discuss it as an arthouse film; the film plays with the conventions of detective fiction and thus contributes to a discussion of investigative narrative structures and epistemology; its claustrophobic visual style, combined with grainy black-and-white cinematography, suggests film noir; the film's low-budget aesthetic intersects with an auteur-based approach (insofar as it can be compared with other first features like Spike Lee's *She's Gotta Have It* [1986]); scenes that draw on direct cinema conventions locate the film in a tradition of international "new wave" films (such as John Cassavetes's *Faces* [1968]); and so on. Just as the identities of its characters are destabilized by the film, so is the identity of *Chan Is Missing* destabilized by a multiplicity of interpretations drawing on different aspects of cinematic history. But how many subject positions can one film occupy?

The Hyphen and the Interval: Being and Becoming

> "I remember one time a man bring a performing monkey to my village," Polly said. "The man divide the audience in two and give each side one end of a rope to hold. Then the monkey walk carefully back and forth

Being Chinese American, Becoming Asian American: Chan is Missing

> *between the two sides. At each end, he stop a little bit,*
> *but he cannot stay, and so he walk again until he so*
> *tired, he fall."*
>
> —*Ruthanne Lum McCunn,*
> Thousand Pieces of Gold

The term "Asian American" is a highly problematic label: insofar as "America" is popularly understood to refer to the United States (and not to other North and South American nations), "Asian American" yokes together a continent and a nation. Furthermore, in the United States the term "Asian" is usually taken to mean East (and sometimes Southeast) Asian: primarily Chinese, Japanese, Korean, and Filipino, and more recently Vietnamese; by contrast, in Britain the term "Asian" generally refers to South Asians, primarily Indians and Pakistanis.[3] Some Arabs have wondered if they are Asians, yet the term is almost never applied to "whites" from Asian nations such as Russia.

The term "Asian American" is thus highly contested, and as such it is better understood as a political rather than a cultural designation.[4] The term in fact has its genesis in the transformation of racial politics in the late 1960s, when Asians in the United States first began to articulate the diversity of their cultural and national traditions along with their shared histories of oppression.[5] The term thus not only replaces the derogatory "oriental" but also calls attention to the provisionality and contradictions that it contains (or fails to contain). Thus, while the term lumps Asians together, it does so in the service of a racial rather than a racist logic, unlike the term "oriental."[6] For example, Filipino Americans rejected the label "yellow" (inspired by the Black Power movement), arguing that they were not yellow but brown and drawing attention to both their ethnic specificity and their Spanish (some would say "Hispanic") cultural heritage: Yen Le Espiritu points out that Filipinos thus insisted upon inclusion under the Asian rubric while asserting their distinctiveness.[7] Thus in my view, to identify myself as Chinese American is to invoke a cultural label, while to call myself Asian American is to invoke a political label—and in different contexts I will use one term or the other, or both.

In the introduction to his study of literatures of subjective fragmentation and alienation, Phillip Brian Harper notes that while "postmodernist fiction foregrounds subjective fragmentation, a similar decenteredness can be identified in U.S. novels written prior to the postmodern era, in which it derives specifically from the socially marginalized and politically disenfranchised status of the populations treated in the works."[8] Harper notes that postmodernism might thus be understood as an attempt by the "center" to assert its own fragmentation, a process of decentering that somehow ignores the existence of already marginalized subject positions. Harper goes on to argue that "the experiences of socially marginalized groups implicitly inform the 'general' postmodern condition without being accounted for in theorizations of it."[9] His project is not to apply the theoretical concepts of postmodernism to the literature of socially marginalized peoples but rather to recover the discourses of race, gender, sexual orientation, and class for postmodernism, to bring these structurally absent discourses to the fore. But to talk about ethnicity (in Marable's sense) using the terminology of postmodernism is in some way to accept the appropriation of divided subjectivity (DuBois's double consciousness) by postmodernism, a discourse that has often been intent on erasing certain markers of difference (race, class, gender, and sometimes sexual orientation) in its effort to decenter that which previously had been (and I would argue still is) central: white male subjectivity.

Harper argues that a crucial component of the politics of postmodernist thought is "the notion of subjective decenteredness . . . even when it does not constitute a dominant term in the discussion."[10]

> Whatever their differences, Habermas, Lyotard, and Jameson all recognize fragmented or decentered experience as a constituent of the postmodern condition. Habermas's idea that postmodernity consists in the ramified nature of human activity such that it can no longer be comprised in an overarching metanarrative is an acknowledgment of its decentered quality. . . . Lyotard, in theorizing the postmodern as approximating the experience of the Kantian sublime . . . specifies subjective disjunction and fragmentation as key factors in the postmodern condition. And Jameson's sense that the contemporary period is characterized by the absence of a referential standard in relation to which the individual human subject might orient itself implies a sort of dispersal of that subject among the various "superficial" signifiers that now alone constitute objective reality. . . . However differently they might interpret the political meaning of subjective fragmentation, though, [these three] theorists conceive of that meaning in terms of macro-level social and economic structures, *leaving aside considerations of more contingent political phenomena*, in particular those having to do with the social identities of the various subjects who manifest fragmentation in the postmodern context.[11]

Harper argues that literature(s) of social marginality (he examines the writings of Nathaniel West, Anaïs Nin, Djuna Barnes, Gwendolyn Brooks, and Ralph Ellison at length) indicate "the degree to which subjective fragmentation of social marginality diverges from that of postmodernism";[12] he thus insists on discussing the "contingent political phenomena" that are effaced by postmodern theory. Harper's argument that postmodern theory effaces the markers of social marginality is assisted by his emphasis on literature that predates postmodern theory. Can such an argument be reasonably made for *Chan Is Missing*, which arrives in the midst of Habermas's, Lyotard's, and Jameson's writings on postmodernity?[13] In other words, does Wang's film belong to Harper's project or to the postmodernists'? Does *Chan Is Missing* critique the appropriation of social marginality by the postmodern subject, or does it equate Chinese American fragmentation with postmodern fragmentation? Is it possible that the film neither contributes to nor critiques postmodern subjectivity, and might this be an explanation for the film's popularity among multiple audiences?[14]

This essay argues that *Chan Is Missing* foregrounds the heterogeneity of Chinese American subjectivities, thereby arguing for the fluidity of Chinese American identity. If the film did no more than that, then it would simply exemplify postmodern fragmentation and its discourse would be recuperable by postmodern discourses that efface markers of social marginality. However, I would argue that *Chan Is Missing* also suggests the *contingency* of Chinese American subjectivities (in the passage excerpted above, Harper suggests that postmodern theorists ignore political contingency) and in so doing paves the way for Asian American subjectivities that might learn from Chinese American heterogeneity. *Chan Is Missing* thus can be reclaimed as a critique of postmodernist theory, but only if we as readers intervene. If we do not mobilize the insights into Chinese American subjectivity occasioned by the film into an effective strategy for understanding Asian American subjectivity, if we do not illuminate the emphasis on "process" and "becoming" Asian American, then we cede *Chan Is Missing* to the postmodernist project.

It would be a mistake to think that postmodernism is unaware of its own critical project, however. While there is much disagreement on the nature of postmodernism, it is surely not going too far to assert that postmodernism is closely associated with the critique of forms; indeed, the "post" of postmodernism refers not so much to temporal sequence as to this activity of critique. Postmodernism is not a stage that succeeds modernism but rather a critique that exists alongside modernism. Jean-François Lyotard argues that the postmodern "is undoubtedly part of the modern. All that has been received, if only yesterday . . . must be suspected. . . . In an amazing acceleration, the generations precipitate themselves. A work can become modern only if it is first postmodern. Postmodernism thus understood is not modernism at its end but in the nascent state, and this state is constant."[15] Harper notes: "While this conception of postmodernism salvages it as a politically progressive practice, it also obviously privileges it as a specifically *cultural* activity."[16] At least for this discussion, I am willing to restrict the postmodern to the realm of cultural activity, but I would argue that just because postmodernism coexists with and critiques modernism and therefore critiques its own project as well (as it passes into the modern, in Lyotard's terms), it does not follow that postmodernism calls attention to the process by which markers of difference were erased in its project to decenter (white male) subjectivity. If I remain skeptical about postmodernism's liberatory potential, I do find value in the claim that postmodernism calls attention to *process;*

however, it is premature to celebrate the identification of process, for such celebration itself halts that process. When investigating a process, one usually must stop it; when children disassemble clocks to see how they work, the clock is not often restored to function, and there is only so much that can be learned from a stopped clock.

What then is the nature of the postmodern critique? David E. Wellbery notes that "postmodern aesthetic experimentation should be viewed as having an irreducible political dimension. It is inextricably bound up with a critique of domination."[17] Wellbery's claim is qualified by Linda Hutcheon: "it must be admitted from the start that it is a strange kind of critique, one bound up, too, with its own *complicity* with power and domination, one that acknowledges that it cannot escape implication in that which it nevertheless still wants to analyze and maybe even undermine. The ambiguities of this kind of position are translated into both the content and the form of postmodern art, which thus at once purveys and challenges ideology—but always self-consciously."[18] Postmodernist critique attempts to make a virtue of its complicity by acknowledging and foregrounding it: Linda Hutcheon envisions postmodern discourses as aware of their position qua discourse, aware that their existence as discourses affirms the legitimacy of what they critique.

The affirmation of a hyphenate identity is a similarly complicitous action: for a Chinese American like Wayne Wang or myself to identify himself or herself as an Asian American is to accept "an externally imposed label that is meant to define us by distinguishing us from other Americans primarily on the basis of race rather than culture."[19] To identify one's self as an Asian American is a political move: "the racial classification of Asian Americans does in fact have its advantages for us. Our racial unity has been contributing to our strength, to our efforts to build community, and to the maintenance and development of a vital Asian American culture."[20] Thus to identify one's self as Asian American is to both accept and critique the externally imposed label that denies the specificity of one's cultural heritage and defines one's otherness in racial terms. As such, adopting a hyphenate identity is a means both of "purvey[ing] and challeng[ing] ideology."[21]

To claim a hyphenate identity is to assert a subject position while simultaneously asserting the impossibility of stable positioning. Fittingly, this is done in the label of the hyphenate term itself and thus critiques the discourse of identity and labeling. The hyphen, while yoking two terms together on the page, emphasizes the inadequacy of either term; furthermore, as the hyphen strains to hold the terms together and apart, it denies the creation of a stable third term in the space between the two. The strength of the hyphenate term then is the way in which it foregrounds the inadequacy of its discursive construction. Trinh T. Minh-ha notes, in a different context, that "meaning can neither be imposed nor denied. Although every film is in itself a form of ordering and closing, each closure can defy its own closure, opening onto other closures, thereby emphasizing the interval between apertures and creating a space in which meaning remains fascinated by what escapes and exceeds it."[22] The hyphen emphasizes the interval between apertures; it creates and maintains the space where meaning is exceeded.

That space between, perhaps better called an interval, is the space for which this essay fights. Fights for not in the sense of fights to claim, for that implies that there is already a territory that has been staked out, that can be claimed in the name of hyphenate identity, but fights for in the sense of fighting in the name of (if indeed one can fight for something without name). It is in the interval that much poststructuralist/modernist/feminist/colonialist theory has "centered" its attention, and such theory attempts to both bridge and expand the gap. This is the importance of the hyphen, which has been understood to be a bridge, a link, between two terms. But this essay, by rejecting the possibility of successfully bridging the gap, rejects the hyphen as well. The hyphen preserves the notion of a duality, of a binary opposition, a pattern of thinking that limits the answers to those posed by the question. If I continue to refer to the hyphen and to use the term "hyphenate identity," it is to recognize the binaristic mode of thought that posits a bridgeable space between terms; if I refuse to inscribe the hyphen myself, it is to emphasize the unbridgeability of the interval.

The gap between theorizing a hyphen and trying to live a hyphen is another way of describing the critique that is also complicitous, which purveys as it challenges. The presence/absence of the hyphen underscores the need to stabilize momentarily a position from which to speak and to destabilize that position immediately. Taking a text (such as *Chan Is Missing*) and discussing the ways it mobilizes notions of hyphenate identity is to venture "into that distance that has not been abolished but expanded to infinity by postmodern criticism: the gap between the politics of production, and of regimes of consumption."[23] To seize upon a text is yet another attempt to hold together and keep apart the terms on either side of a hyphen; that is the distance or gap to which Morris alludes. We who would discuss hyphenate identity seize upon Wang's film to do so, but our interpretations of the text must not lock down the range of meanings found in the gap between text and reader. In other words, we must approach *Chan Is Missing* in the same way that I have proposed we approach the term "Asian American": we will agree to refer to it as a label, but in doing so we must constantly foreground the inadequacy of the label; rather than accepting it as a term that obscures our differences and assigns an inflexible racial identity to us, we instead assert that the term will unite us politically but not culturally. Thus, we take advantage of the gap between the production of the term and the uses to which we put it. The question then becomes how exactly to mobilize such a label.

In *Chan Is Missing*, many courses of action are identified as being Chinese and others as being American, but a Chinese American course of action is difficult to identify. The realm of Chinese American—the gap between production and consumption—cannot be named, because it is constantly being negotiated by the characters in the film. Being Chinese American is not a matter of resolving a duality, for proposing to draw from two cultures inevitably results in not belonging to either culture. George, director of the Newcomers' Language Center, points to an apple pie baked by the Sun Wah Kuu bakery as an example of Chinese American negotiation. "It is a definite American form, you know, pie, okay. And it looks just like any other apple pie, but it doesn't *taste* like any other apple pie, you eat it. And that's because many Chinese baking technique has gone into it, and when we deal with our everyday lives, that's what we have to do."[24] But ultimately, such a negotiation proves untenable because it does not create anything new, it merely borrows forms.[25] Jo rejects the apple pie analogy, referring to it as George's "spiel," in his quest for a notion of identity that does not see the duality but creates a space in the gap between the two terms. "There is indeed little hope of speaking this simultaneously outside-inside actuality into existence in simple, polarizing black-and-white terms. The challenge of the hyphenated reality lies in the hyphen itself: the *becoming* Asian American."[26] The apple pie cannot be Asian American because it does not manifest the process of "becoming"—it is an expression of the uneasy encounter of two cultures, not revealing the process of accommodation so much as revising Asian techniques to produce American goods. To be Chinese American is to be constantly in the process of becoming, to negotiate the relationship between cultures; to be a Chinese American artist (whether baker or filmmaker), one must do more than introduce Asian themes into American forms— the artist must reveal the process that produces new cultural expressions and thereby preserve a sense of contingency. When an artist asserts that there is one way successfully to balance Chinese and American influences, that artist implicitly asserts that Chinese Americans exist in a fixed space, fulfill a fixed role. Rote actions are only successful when events operate predictably, and with rote responses one will not discover anything new, will not evolve, will not accept the challenge of "becoming" Asian American.

How then is the challenge of "becoming" Asian American explored by a film that draws on film noir conventions? Is a detective film with Chinese American characters simply an apple pie made in a Chinese bakery? Don't genre films, with their predictable events, call for the very rote actions (on the part of characters, and indeed on the part of filmmakers as well) which fix their characters in a state of "being" rather than a process of "becoming"? When Jo and Steve argue about their course of action, Steve asserts: "Hey, I understand the situation, man. . . . Here's how I see it. If you're sick, you go see a doctor, right? If you're going nuts, you go see a shrink. If you need some money, man, you go to a bank or a loan company. You know, somebody rips off your money, if you don't have no friends who can take care of it, you go to the cops and let *them* take care of it" (64). Steve thus advocates a rote response: if someone does this, then you do that. Steve is frustrated by the lack of results and so advocates conventional methods of resolving his problem. Jo, on the other hand, does not believe that conventional methods will work; "it's none of their [the police's] damn business" (64), he says, for he knows that Chan's disappearance is not conventional and therefore the police (who are bound by rote responses) will not be successful. When Jo says, "I'm no Charlie Chan," he is also saying, "This only appears to be a Charlie Chan case, a genre film; but we don't know what will happen next, we're just making this up as we go along." In other words, Jo is willing to wait and see what happens next, what kind of a film this is "becoming."

The challenge that Trinh describes "in the hyphen itself" is the challenge of trying to make a third term out of a binary. Other theorists have rejected the notion of the hyphen, as, for example, Maxine Hong Kingston's character Wittman Ah Sing:

> "And 'Chinese-American' is inaccurate—as if we could have two countries. We need to take the hyphen out—'Chinese American.' 'American,' the noun, and 'Chinese,' the adjective. From now on: 'Chinese Americans.' However. Not okay yet. 'Chinese hyphen American' sounds exactly the same as 'Chinese no hyphen American.' No revolution takes place in the mouth or in the ear."[27]

Wittman rejects the hyphen because he would like to assert an identity of his own creation, one that has not been foisted upon him. But even Wittman recognizes the inadequacy of the provisional identity which he adopts, and that inadequacy rests on the ambiguity of the articulation of the absence of punctuation. You can read and write the hyphen, but you cannot hear or speak it. We might take this to describe metaphorically the gap between theorizing and living; if the former happens on paper, then the latter happens in the air—one is literate, the other oral. While the distinction may seem crucial in the context of this essay, is the distinction livable? The term, with or without a hyphen, is only meaningful when it calls attention to its own discursive construction and thus destabilizes itself. "Meaning can therefore be political only when it does not let itself be easily stabilized, and when it does not rely on any single source of authority but, rather, empties it, or decentralizes it."[28] The cycle of stabilizing and destabilizing meaning—of the insertion and removal of the hyphen—is thus an attempt to evade fixity; as such, the cycle describes the process of becoming.

One way of reading *Chan Is Missing*'s critique refuses to fixate on the questions it poses about the nature of hyphenate identity and instead emphasizes the process of becoming. The film affirms through its textuality the impossibility of being, the insistence on becoming—in its refusal of closure and by questioning identity, appropriation, narrative, and temporality.

(These terms overlap: for example, appropriation is narrativized, temporality is expressed narratively, identities are appropriated as means to narrative and other ends.) But while *Chan Is Missing* may critique fixed notions of identity, it must be emphasized that many of the discourses that surrounded the film, discourses that contextualized its position in the marketplace, placed it firmly within a discourse that operated as if hyphenate identities were indeed fixed. These discourses of the popular media place Wayne Wang's films between the constructed poles of "Asian American" and "mainstream American" film markets. However, a closer look at the production, marketing, and reception of Wang's films reveals that he has moved freely between those poles, often bridging independent and Hollywood production, arthouse and mainstream theaters, Asian and white audiences.

You can take the filmmaker out of Chinatown . . .

> *So if a Hollywood producer came up and said, "I want you to make this Hollywood film," you would take it?*
> *Wang: I'd do it in a second. I love* Back to the Future; *I love the money that it's made. But I know I'll always come back to whatever I can charge up on my credit card to make a movie that I really want to make, even if it's in 16mm again.*
> *—Wayne Wang, interviewed in* American Film

The success of *The Joy Luck Club* (1993) followed by the "non-Asian" *Smoke* (1995) sparked comment as to whether Wang had "crossed over" and/or "sold out." Such comments imply that Wang's pre–*Joy Luck Club* oeuvre is in contrast to his more recent films, a contrast charted through such categories as casting (regional theater actors versus "established" film actors), budget (a term sometimes used interchangeably with "production values"), distribution (in terms of both the production company itself and the movie houses that screened the films), and subject matter (obviously in terms of "ethnicity" but also in terms of mainstream familiarity—after all, *The Joy Luck Club* was an "ethnic" film, but it was also based on a best-selling novel; in contrast, *Eat a Bowl of Tea* [1989] is a little-known book, rarely read outside Asian American literature courses and not even in print when the movie was released). *The Joy Luck Club* is undeniably a watershed film for Asian Americans, and yet it can also be argued that the film was not a watershed in Wang's career. For example, while *The Joy Luck Club* did play multiplexes in midwestern cities where none of Wang's earlier films had ever opened, it was also "rolled out" very slowly to allow "word of mouth" to build, in a strategy commonly employed by films much smaller (and without Oliver Stone's name above the title). Furthermore, arguing that Wang's recent films "cross over" ignores the fact that *Chan Is Missing* itself appealed to arthouse audiences as well as Chinese American and Asian American audiences. (*Chan Is Missing* was small, but it attracted the attention of nationally known film critics like Gene Siskel and Roger Ebert, both of whom reviewed the film for their own papers as well as on their show, "Sneak Previews." Granted, on PBS Siskel and Ebert were still a few years away from the "Two Thumbs Up!" days, but they did have national exposure.)

Indeed, *Chan Is Missing* did far better at crossing over or bridging audiences than *Life Is Cheap . . .* (1989), a film shot in Hong Kong with something of the feel of late-1960s Godard; and Wang's *Slamdance* (1987), released by Island Pictures and featuring "nonethnic" actors like Tom Hulce, Virginia Madsen, Harry Dean Stanton, and Adam Ant, had a tough time finding any audience. While the polish of *Dim Sum* (1985) puts it in a different category from *Chan Is Missing,* the film's arthouse style (Wang's homage to Ozu Yasuhiro) and appearance on PBS's "American Playhouse" suggest that it aimed for the same audience. Wang's career to date is not a gradual rise to bigger budgets and more "mainstream" subject matter, nor is it a series of small films followed by a sudden breakthrough. Rather, Wang's career from 1980 to 1995 reveals a series of idiosyncratic films that interconnect in surprising ways. Shrewd marketing seems to have been behind most of Wang's critical and financial successes, marketing that positioned the film vis-à-vis Asian American and arthouse cinema audiences.

Wayne Wang was born in Hong Kong in 1949 ("Really I was born when Hong Kong was born"); his father named him after John Wayne.[29] Wang came to the United States to attend college in the late 1960s, earning a bachelor's degree in painting at the California College of Arts and Crafts, where he also studied film history and production. Returning to Hong Kong in the early 1970s, Wang quickly found work as a director for a Hong Kong television comedy, but he was not satisfied working within the Hong Kong industry. Wang returned to the San Francisco Bay Area and became an administrator and English teacher for a Chinatown community organization (experiences he would draw on for *Chan Is Missing*); during this period Wang also learned "how to write grants and turn them in on time." Wang also developed a program for KRON-TV and occasionally worked on Loni Ding's "Bean Sprouts," a series of half-hour programs for Chinese American children.[30]

Wayne Wang's first film since returning from Hong Kong was supposed to be a thirty-minute video documentary on cab drivers. After securing $10,000 from the American Film Institute, Wang decided to make a feature instead. Wang and his crew shot the film over ten successive weekends and then settled down for the arduous process of editing and postproduction, going steadily deeper into debt; during this period, Wang supported himself by writing bilingual science curricula for San Francisco State University.[31] Eventually securing a grant from the National Endowment for the

Arts, Wang completed the film on a budget of $22,500. After good response at a few festivals (key among them the New Directors/New Films festival in New York), the movie was picked up by New Yorker Films.[32] The result was an extremely rough, immensely likable film that earned critical raves and more than recovered its investment.

According to Sterritt, "Though its initial audience has not been an ethnic one, Chinese viewers are being wooed through newspaper ads, and Wang would like to see a trial run in a Chinatown theater."[33] This statement, while anecdotal, indicates the underdevelopment (or outright absence) of venues for Asian American feature films in 1982. *Chan Is Missing* succeeded because it appealed to arthouse audiences and also brought Asian Americans into the theaters. In Asian American newspapers, articles about *Chan Is Missing* and its director often cited its mainstream success and quoted reviewers in mainstream publications,[34] as if to announce to the Asian American audience that the film is not an amateur production and that this is the film that is teaching whites about Chinese Americans. Reviews in the Asian American press often simply advertise the screenings; but the lengthier reviews usually refer to how white reviewers see Chinese Americans and how Asian American texts are received by non-Asian audiences.[35] One Chinese American critic points out that many texts produced *by* Asian Americans are not produced *for* Asian Americans: "*Chan Is Missing* . . . does not have the same tone of voice as some of the other artistic works which have come out of [the Chinese American] community—the grossest examples being the tour guides and cookbooks— where one again has the feeling that the readership which the author has chosen to write to is really the larger society, there being so much explaining, so many footnotes, sometimes so much apology for not being white."[36] Lem takes care to point out that the tourist mentality can be found within texts, not just in their reception; he thus positions *Chan Is Missing* as *from* and *for* the Chinese American community.

By contrast, the majority of mainstream reviewers take one of two critical approaches and often include both approaches despite their seeming incompatibility.[37] The first approach is to locate the film within a tradition of filmmaking represented by "canonical" U.S. films and foreign films that had arthouse success in the United States: several reviewers compare the film to *Citizen Kane* (Ansen, Seitz) and mention *The Third Man* (Denby, Ebert); the *Variety* review cites *L'Avventura*, while Hatch reviews *Bob le Flambeur* in the same column, emphasizing *Chan*'s appropriation of gangster iconography. The film is often positioned vis-à-vis arthouse cinema through references to its low budget, often favorably (Ansen, Canby, Denby, Ebert, Hatch, Kauffmann, Sterritt, *Variety*) but not necessarily so (O'Toole, Seitz), and/or through reference to the film's release strategy. One reviewer (Siskel) even alludes to the manner in which other reviewers have hyped the film's budget. The second approach is to describe the authenticity of Wang's film and praise it for presenting a "true portrait" of Chinatown (Ebert, Hatch, Siskel), often citing a specific stereotype that the film challenges; in other words, by addressing certain stereotypes head on the film is perceived by mainstream reviewers as representing an authentic Chinese American perspective.[38] The first approach locates *Chan Is Missing* in a tradition of arthouse cinema, while the second asserts the essential uniqueness of the film. While seemingly contradictory, these two approaches are of course entirely compatible.[39]

Following *Chan Is Missing,* Wang's career has alternated a few medium-budget films with forays into low-budget, guerrilla filmmaking. Like many Asian American filmmakers, Wang has stated a desire not to be limited to making films about his ethnicity ("'I Didn't Want To Do Another Chinese Movie' " states the headline of one article).[40] With *Smoke* and *Blue in the Face* (1995) he seems to have succeeded; it remains to be seen whether Wang will return to Chinese and Chinese American subjects. But *Smoke* was not Wang's first non-Chinese film, only the most successful, and a survey of Wang's career does not reveal a gradual growth of budgets counterposed with a gradual abandonment of Chinese American subjects.[41] Rather, all of Wang's films seem designed to appeal to multiple specialized film markets. Furthermore, Wang is perceived in some circles as a director of "women's films," on the basis of *Dim Sum* and *The Joy Luck Club,*[42] despite the fact that *Chan Is Missing, Eat a Bowl of Tea,* and *Smoke* depict men interacting in social spaces where women are allowed but not welcomed.[43] Wang's career has been characterized by the canny ability to position his films vis-à-vis competing, contradictory discourses, as a quick survey of his career will show.

After *Chan,* Wang came close to signing on a remake of *In a Lonely Place* (Ray, 1950). In an interview, Wang stated (rather unclearly), "There's a part of me that liked the script a lot. And a part that wasn't sure about it. It was all American characters, except for one Asian."[44] Opting out of that project, Wang made *Dim Sum,* an intimate film focusing on the relationship of a Chinese American woman and her immigrant mother, which aired on PBS's "American Playhouse." (The outtakes from an early "draft" of *Dim Sum* later appeared as a short film, now called *Dim Sum Takeouts* [1988].) Less abstract than *Chan Is Missing, Dim Sum* evinces a greater degree of production polish and develops its characters more thoroughly; however, *Dim Sum* still nods toward the arthouse audience through its allusions to Ozu Yasuhiro's late color films, and, like *Chan,* it does not resolve the issues it raises.

Wang's next film was *Slamdance,* a neonoir story about an underground cartoonist (played by Tom Hulce) whose prostitute girlfriend gets killed to protect the reputation of some elected officials. *Slamdance* featured white characters almost exclusively (Rosalind Chao had a very small part as an elementary schoolteacher), but it bombed at the box office. More important than the absence of Asian faces in the cast is the absence of unknown actors: heretofore, Wang's films had mixed professional and amateur actors, and his next few films would mix U.S. and Hong Kong professionals (along with a sprinkling of amateurs).

Following *Slamdance, Eat a Bowl of Tea* marked a return to "American Playhouse" and to Asian American subject matter. First published in 1961, Louis Chu's pioneering novel, set in the "bachelor society" of New York's Chinatown, described the pressures on two newlyweds who represent the next generation of Chinese Americans; the novel had previously been adapted for the stage by the Pan Asian Repertory Theater in New York City.[45] Wang brought a light, neoscrewball touch to the story, lightening the serious subject matter but also diffusing some of its historically specific edge.[46] Wang's cast mixed American (Victor Wong and Russell Wong) and Hong Kong (Cora Miao and comedian Eric Tsang Chi Wai) actors.

Citing a desire to return to guerrilla filmmaking, Wang collaborated with screenwriter-actor Spencer Nakasako on *Life Is Cheap . . . But Toilet Paper Is Expensive* (the cast again featured Victor Wong and Cora Miao). The nominal story line of *Life Is Cheap . . .* concerns a mixed-race Asian American courier charged with delivering a briefcase to Hong Kong gangsters. While well received by critics (*Variety, Rolling Stone*), *Life Is Cheap . . .* received only limited release in the United States. At present, the film is virtually unavailable, due perhaps to mistrust between the filmmakers and the film's U.S. distributor.[47] This is unfortunate, for *Life Is Cheap . . .* is a fascinating film, straddling European-influenced art cinema and guerrilla filmmaking, produced at the leading edge of the world's discovery of the vibrancy of Hong Kong cinema.

The Joy Luck Club was developed on speculation by Wang and screenwriters Amy Tan and Ronald Bass, eventually finding a champion in producer Janet Yang, then vice president of production for Oliver Stone's Ixtlan production company; the project ended up at Walt Disney's Hollywood Pictures.[48] Disney's producer, Patrick Markey, kept a tight rein on the film's "cut-rate" budget of $10.6 million. A shrewd marketing campaign and a cautious but deliberate distribution strategy helped the film gross approximately $30 million in the first three months following release.[49]

Wang's next project, *Smoke,* was developed in collaboration with novelist-critic Paul Auster, whose short story "Auggie Wren's Christmas Story" served as the initial inspiration.[50] Following *The Joy Luck Club, Smoke* represents a step toward both independent filmmaking and mainstream popularity. If examined in terms of budget and returns (smaller than *The Joy Luck Club*), exhibition venues (smaller, arthouse theaters), and production company (Miramax), *Smoke* is a much smaller production.[51] But if viewed in terms of ethnicity (non-Asian cast) and bankable stars (Stockard Channing, William Hurt, Harvey Keitel, Forrest Whitaker), *Smoke* represents a "step up" for Wang. True to form, Wang followed the tightly scripted and highly polished production with the largely improvised *Blue in the Face* (shot on the sets and with much of the cast of *Smoke*). While of an entirely different order than *Chan Is Missing* or *Life Is Cheap* . . . , *Blue in the Face* shares many of the Wang low-budget trademarks: a fascination with life on the street; improvised performances based on preconceived scenarios; an abbreviated production schedule (six days of shooting, two sessions of three days each, three months apart); and a mixed cast ranging from the mainstream (Michael J. Fox) to the independent cinema and avant-garde art worlds (Jim Jarmusch, Lou Reed), with a healthy dose of actors whose work itself straddles those worlds (Lily Tomlin, Giancarlo Esposito, Madonna, and RuPaul).[52]

Has Wayne Wang crossed over? In the summer of 1995, *Newsweek* ran a cover story on the "Overclass," a supposedly new class of upper-middle-class progressive Americans,[53] and Wayne Wang was included as an example of this new class because of his success with both *The Joy Luck Club* and *Smoke.* This paradoxical label—nouveau bourgeois but progressive, ethnically aware but not militant—seems to capture perfectly the ambiguous position that Wayne Wang finds himself in, an in-between position that Wang helped to create. As such, Wang's position vis-à-vis Hollywood is not unlike that of Asian Americans vis-à-vis mainstream society: American popular culture has begun to embrace hip Asian faces like Margaret Cho and Henry Cho, but still regards radical and lower-class Asian Americans with suspicion.

Charlie Chan Is Dead—Long Live Charlie Chan!

Perfect crime like perfect doughnut—always has hole!
—Charlie Chan in Paris, 1935

When *Chan Is Missing* begins, two San Francisco cab drivers, Jo and Steve, are searching for their friend Chan Hung, who has apparently absconded with $4,000. When the film ends, the money has been recovered, but Chan Hung has not been found, and Jo no longer knows who Chan Hung is. Each clue they find only raises more questions; indeed, the clues aren't even real clues: they include a gun that may or may not have been fired, a newspaper with the important article torn out, a spot on the wall where a picture used to hang, a series of former addresses no longer occupied by Chan Hung, and a Polaroid in which Chan Hung's face is obscured by shadows. Given the inconclusiveness of these clues, Jo is forced to rely on the testimonies he gathers from various people who knew Chan Hung, but the incompatibility of these stories evacuates them of any explanatory force.

Chan Is Missing can be interpreted as a revisionist Charlie Chan film; indeed, the marketing of the videocassette release of the film refers to Jo and Steve as "two 'subgumshoes' " who are "walking self-mockingly in the footsteps of Charlie Chan and his Number One Son." At one point, Steve introduces himself by pointing to Jo and saying, "That's Charlie

Chan, and I'm his Number One Son—The Fly!" (52). The videocassette's "self-mocking" label seems appropriate; the characters themselves seem aware that they are trapped in a pop-culture stereotype—trapped not in the sense that they have been placed there by the dominant, but in Linda Hutcheon's sense of a strange kind of critique, purveying and challenging their position. Later, while puttering around in his kitchen, Jo invokes Charlie Chan in voice-over: "I guess I'm no gourmet Chinese cook, and I'm no Charlie Chan either, although I did start watching some of his reruns for cheap laughs. Charlie says, 'When superior man have no clue, be patient. Maybe he become lucky!' The next night, I was cleaning out the cab Chan Hung was driving the day he disappeared. I found a letter in Chinese and a gun under the front seat" (57–58). In this scene, it is not only Jo who mocks his adopted role of Charlie Chan, but the narrative itself, which is bound up in the complicitous critique. Jo asks for a clue and he gets one: the film's sound track underscores this moment of deus ex machina by hammering out melodramatic music when the gun is discovered. The overdetermined emphasis on this narrative moment mocks the unfolding of the narrative and thus mocks the generic expectations of a Charlie Chan film.[54]

The title of the film presumably refers to Chan Hung and not Charlie Chan, but in this regard Earl Derr Biggers's famous detective still has something to say. In 1935, Charlie's doughnut reference alludes to the inevitable slip that will allow the detectives to capture the criminal, but I prefer to think of the doughnut in another way: as a metaphor for a mystery with a missing center. Whereas the typical classical Hollywood detective drama is characterized by a relentless narrative acquisition of clues that eventually climaxes in the solution of the mystery,[55] in *Chan Is Missing* each clue seems to take the narrative farther from a possible solution. Rather than closing down the narrative possibilities, each clue opens up the range of possible answers to the question, "Where is Chan Hung?" Jenny, Chan Hung's daughter, further deflates the narrative tension by returning the money to Jo and Steve, thereby removing the impetus to find Chan. If Jo's investigation continues, it is because the real problem posed by the narrative is not "Where is Chan Hung" but "Who is Chan Hung?" As Jo states at the end of the film, "I've already given up on finding out what happened to Chan Hung, but what bothers me is that I no longer know who Chan Hung is" (73–74). If no one knows who Chan Hung is, then who can know if he has been found?

> Mr. Lee says Chan Hung and immigrants like him need to be taught everything as if they were children. Mr. Fong thinks anyone who can invent a word processing system in Chinese must be a genius. Steve thinks that Chan Hung is slow-witted, but sly when it comes to money. Jenny thinks that her father is honest and trustworthy. Mrs. Chan thinks her husband is a failure because he isn't rich. Amy thinks he's a hot-headed

political activist. The old man thinks Chan Hung's just a paranoid person. Henry thinks Chan Hung is patriotic, and has gone back to the mainland to serve the people. Frankie thinks Chan Hung worries a lot about money and his inheritance. He thinks Chan Hung's back in Taiwan fighting with his brother over the partition of some property. George thinks Chan Hung's too Chinese, and unwilling to change. Presco thinks he's an eccentric who likes mariachi music. (74)

Jo's investigation, rather than closing in upon Chan, only serves to widen the hole in the doughnut.

Chan Is Missing's lack of closure is a manifestation of the process of becoming that the narrative describes. Any definitive answer to the questions, "Who or where is Chan Hung?" would serve to close off the process of becoming and solidify the film into a "became." That the narrative of the film is closely tied to the notion of hyphenate identity is underlined by the two questions that are actually the same question: "Who is Chan?" and "Where is Chan?" Both seek to locate an identity, to place it in relation to the grand narrative of subject positioning. Textually, the tie between narrative and identity is manifested in the destabilization of the identities of the various characters who seek to hypostatize Chan Hung. As the narrative "progresses," for example, Steve's identity begins to evaporate, as if the increasing indeterminacy of Chan's identity undermines everyone else's identity. The reasons for this are underlined in the suggestion Presco offers to Jo and Steve in their search for Chan. Presco says, "Look in the puddle" (34)—look to your reflection to answer your question.

Early in their investigation, Steve asks Jo if his feelings about Chan Hung are being influenced by his feelings for his ex-wife; both were FOB (fresh off the boat). By doing so, Steve reveals an assumption that all FOBs are alike—or, more specifically, that Jo would react to all FOBs in the same way. Steve tells a story about Chan Hung that reveals how the older man's inability to acculturate himself embarrasses the supposedly well-adapted Steve: after seeing Chan Hung take off his jacket and give it to a friend who had admired it, Steve told Chan that he liked his pants—was he going to take them off, too? Jo tells us in voice-over, "Steve doesn't realize that the joke about the pants is really on him. Chan Hung told me he sometimes play up being an FOB just to make Steve mad" (28).

The encounter between Steve and Chan Hung is a drama that resonates throughout the Chinese American community and has been dramatized before in playwright David Henry Hwang's *FOB*. In the prologue to *FOB*, an assimilated Chinese American "lectures like a university professor" at a blackboard.

F-O-B. Fresh Off the Boat. FOB. What words can you think of that characterize the FOB? Clumsy, ugly, greasy FOB. Loud, stupid, four-eyed FOB. Big feet. Horny. Like Lenny in *Of Mice and Men*. Very good. A literary reference. High-water pants. Floods, to be exact. Someone you wouldn't want your sister to marry. If you are a sister, someone you wouldn't want to marry. That assumes we're talking about boy FOBs, of course. But girl FOBs aren't really as . . . FOBish. Boy FOBs are the worst, the . . . pits. They are the sworn enemies of all ABC—oh, that's "American Born Chinese"—of all ABC girls. Before an ABC girl will be seen on Friday night with a boy FOB in Westwood, she would rather burn off her face. . . . How can you spot an FOB? Look out! If you can't answer that, you might be one.[56]

In the course of Hwang's play, the ABC is forced to revise his estimation of FOBs; meanwhile, the audience comes to understand that the image of the FOB is entirely a creation of the ABC, and a creation that the ABC depends upon to stabilize his own sense of identity. Similarly, Steve's identity is threatened by the destabilization of Chan Hung—Chan's process of becoming forces Steve to confront the fact that his identity is not fixed, that he too is in the process of becoming (rather than being). As the investigation continues and Jo begins to speculate about Chan Hung's identity crisis, Steve becomes more and more adamant: "That's a bunch of bullshit, man. That identity shit, man—that's old news, man, that happened ten years ago" (62). Jo asserts that the identity crisis is never over (that hyphenate people like Steve as well as Chan are always becoming), to which Steve replies that everybody has their roles in "the game." Steve tells a story about an old friend of his and then invokes his experience in Vietnam, "getting shot at by my own peo—; 'ey! The Chinese are all over this city. Why are you tripping so heavy on this one dude, man?" (63). Steve almost refers to the Vietnamese as his own people, but he stops himself; is it because he realizes that he is Chinese, not Vietnamese? Or is it because Marc Hayashi, the actor who plays Steve, realizes that he is Japanese?

The instability of Steve's identity—and that of the ABC in Hwang's play—is clearly tied to his insecure masculinity. Steve's references to combat in Vietnam, not to mention his repeated use of the interjection, "man," hint at the threat to his masculine identity posed by Chan Hung. Chan Hung's inability to assimilate threatens Steve's perception of himself as American and as a man. Similarly, the ABC in Hwang's play reveals his biases when he allows that "girl FOBs aren't really as . . . FOBish." Juxtaposed with his claim that "Boy FOBs . . . are the sworn enemies . . . of all ABC girls," the boy ABC reveals that he thinks it is okay for ABCs to date FOB girls but that FOB boys should stay away from ABC girls. The FOB stereotype, as articulated by Hwang's character, is rooted in the exchange of women in a sexual economy: women assimilate more easily than men, because women are sexual possessions and can be more easily absorbed into U.S. society.[57] *Chan Is Missing* reveals a similar logic: for example, Chan Hung's wife rejects her husband because he was unable to assimilate ("He doesn't even want to apply for American citizen. He's too Chinese" [46]), and Chan's daughter Jenny mocks Steve when he uses American idioms awkwardly (see below).[58] As is often the case, the more

Steve's masculinity is threatened, the more recourse he has to masculine posturing, as evidenced by his assertion that he understands "the game" better than Jo or Chan Hung.

Steve's metaphor of "the game" suggests that everyone's actions are prescribed by certain rules, that interpersonal dynamics are reducible to a repertoire of gambits. "The game" is Steve's description of his own reliance on situationally determined rote responses: "If you're sick, you go see a doctor." For Steve, succeeding in the game is not a matter of always reacting the same way but of recognizing and adjusting to the situation at hand: indeed, whenever Steve encounters someone new, he immediately riffs off the situation. When Jo and Steve visit Chan's hotel room, they are given some information by one of Chan's neighbors, who calls out to them from behind a closed door. The unseen speaker queries, "You Chinese, Jo?" Steve turns the question around: "Are you Chinese?" Then the voice asks, "Hey Jo, you police?" When the voice refuses to answer their questions, Steve squats down, makes a gun with his hand, and says, "Let's go in the other way—got your magnum?" (41–43). Steve adopts the posture of a cop, assuming the identity that the voice suggested for him.

The fluidity with which Steve shifts should not be mistaken for the process of negotiation that we have described as the process of becoming; instead, Steve reserves the right to shift from one fixed subject position to another. The fixity of the subject positions that Steve serially inhabits is emphasized by their mediated quality: each subjectivity is made available to Steve from pop culture. When we say that Steve adopts the posture of a cop, the word "posture" should remind us that such role playing involves the performance of visible actions metonymically associated with the roles in question. What then does it mean to say that Steve is a self-mocking Charlie Chan?

To celebrate Steve as a deconstructed Charlie Chan is to privilege the notion of postmodern critique. Such a reading assumes that Steve's situationally driven role playing displays his virtuosity. But Steve does not maintain any of his roles long enough to explore their uniqueness: instead, Steve isolates each subjectivity from its unique sociocultural context, so that it is evacuated of any political force. Instead of restoring markers of difference and hence historical specificity to the center, Steve confirms the emptiness of the postmodern subjectivity—the hole in the doughnut. This is evident in the reactions Steve elicits. The key scene in which Steve identifies himself as Chan's "Number One Son—The Fly!" begins with Steve misidentifying himself: "I'm Steve Chan—Choy—Chan—Choy" (52). Even the spectator who does not already know that *Chan Is Missing* evolved from an improvised script is likely to read this line as a "blooper," a moment of rupture, an actor's slip. In the spirit of improvisation, the other actors modify the trajectory of the scene to account for the dialogue: the scene continues with Jenny's friend mocking, "This dude doesn't even know his name!" While shaking her hand, Steve adopts the posture of a streetwise ghetto kid, clasping her wrist and rapping, "What's happening!" He then goes on a riff about Mrs. Chong's mah-jongg club, to which the girls reply, "Who do you think you are, anyway, you think you're Richard Pryor, something like that?" Steve reverts to his "normal" voice until they say goodbye, when he suddenly shifts into Chinese Uncle mode. "I got some spare change, go get yourself an icecream cone, man." The offer is rejected: "Who do you think we are, kids?" (51–54). The girls refuse to play along with Steve, to accept the roles that he is suggesting for them, leaving him trying on various identities, hoping he will find one that will work. Steve's self-conscious awareness of his position as a mock Charlie Chan does not occasion a critique of that role but instead reveals that Steve accepts the terms that the text lays out for him. Steve is trapped in a generically defined role.

"I'm Steve Chan—Choy—Chan—Choy": Steve's Chinese American identity is not in a process of becoming (of evolving from position to position) but of shifting from subjectivity to subjectivity, just as he oscillates between "Choy" and "Chan." Steve's character emblematizes the process by which Chinese American identity is interrogated by the film. Steve's various subject positions are deployed in response to interpellation ("Are you police?"), situation ("what's happening!" to begin a conversation, "go get yourself some icecream" to end one), and, most important, in contradistinction to Chan Hung, Steve's FOB/Other. This last dynamic is reversed by Presco's suggestion to "Look in the puddle": he advises that Chan Hung is best found by examining one's self. And indeed, everyone who offers an opinion of Chan Hung first looks in the puddle—defines her or his own identity—and then depicts Chan as he best complements that identity. Steve sees Chan as an FOB; Chan's wife sees him as an unsuccessful, unassimilated Taiwanese; Mr. Lee sees him as a small child who needs to be led by the hand. Each person sees Chan as the thing that she or he is not, or does not want to be. As such, each person sees Chan Hung as something to get beyond, or rather as something to avoid. "To get beyond" suggests that subjectivities exist on a continuum of becoming, emphasizing process and movement. However, each of the characters in *Chan Is Missing*, with the possible exception of Jo, attempts to fix Chan Hung's identity and in so doing fix her or his own identity. It is crucial that the differing opinions about Chan Hung are all expressed in his absence—Chan Hung becomes the Other that can be made to stand in for all insecurities, and through him the Chinese Americans can momentarily become one with the dominant.

It is telling that the suggestion to "look in the puddle" does not come from within the Chinese American community but from Presco, who runs the Manilatown Senior Center.[59] At the Senior Center, where Chan Hung went to enjoy mariachi music, the Filipinos know Chan Hung as "Hi Ho" for the crackers he carries in his pockets. Thus, it would be wrong to suggest that the Filipino American community is more aware of the processes of becoming, for they too have assigned Chan Hung a stable identity (as Hi Ho). By suggesting that Jo and Steve "look in the puddle," Presco does not abandon his own understanding of Chan Hung, nor does he ask Jo and Steve to accept his own interpretation. However, by taking the advice from Manilatown to Chinatown, Jo is provided with an opportunity to seek Chan Hung in the interval between Chan Hung's Filipino and Chinese identities, and it is in this interval that Chan Hung has been lost and that Asian American subjectivity can be found.

Characterization and Performance: The Question of Cross-Ethnic Casting

> *How To Tell Your Friends from the Japs: . . . Japanese are likely to be stockier and broader-hipped than short Chinese. . . . Chinese, not as hairy as Japa-nese, seldom grow an impressive mustache. . . . Although both have the typical epicanthic fold of the upper eyelid (which makes them look almond-eyed), Japanese eyes are usually set closer together. . . . the Chinese expression is likely to be more placid, kindly, open; the Japanese more positive, dogmatic, arrogant. . . . Japanese are hesitant, nervous in conversation, laugh loudly at the wrong time. . . . Japanese walk stiffly erect, hard heeled. Chinese, more re-laxed, have an easy gait, sometimes shuffle.*
> —Time, 22 December 1941

Just before *The Joy Luck Club* opened in New York, a Sunday *New York Times* article, "How to Tell the Players in 'The Joy Luck Club,' " came perilously close to declaring "all Orientals look alike": "it is in fact difficult to assemble a large cast in which one character is not mistaken for another. The conventional solution is to pepper a cast with blonds, redheads and brunettes and different ethnic types. But the 'Joy Luck Club' does not have that liberty."[60] Faced with casting over fifty female roles (in two languages, English and Mandarin), a task made more difficult by the fact that in some cases three actors of different ages would portray the same character at different stages in her life, Wayne Wang devised two rules when casting the film.

First, no Caucasians would play roles written for Asians. "During the 'Miss Saigon' controversy," he said, "there were a lot of people who said, 'Talent is talent, and anybody can play any character with makeup.' But it never happens that an Asian actress can go out for a major Caucasian role and get it. Until that day comes, there is no equity, so it was important to me that these roles all go to Asians."

Rule two was that actresses of various Asian backgrounds would be considered for specifically Chinese roles. "Because there are so few good roles for Asians, I didn't want to eliminate Japanese or Vietnamese or Koreans," Mr. Wang explained. "The important thing was that they felt right for the role and would fit into the ensemble."[61]

Wang's argument, as presented by the *Times,* is based purely on equity. He never says that a non-Asian actor cannot play an Asian role, only that such casting denies opportunities to Asian actors. However, by formulating the argument this way, Wang sidesteps the implications of casting non-Chinese in *The Joy Luck Club;* for example, when non-Asian filmmakers cast Rosalind Chao as a Korean in "M*A*S*H" or as a Japanese in "Star Trek: Deep Space Nine,"[62] many Asian Americans were less than pleased. Wang goes on to argue that there are other aspects of performance which might affect ethnic realism; for example, he admits that an actress was not cast because her speech rhythms were more Japanese than Chinese, conceding that realism is the ultimate deciding factor but leaving open the question of who defines realism. After all, did Wang foresee the complaints of some Mandarin speakers that all the Chinese characters in *The Joy Luck Club* spoke with Beijing accents?[63]

Realism and equity for Asian actors are thus the two key determinants in casting Asian roles. But how does ethnic specificity fit into the argument? Is it unrealistic or inequitable to cast a Japanese American in a Korean role, for example? And how does the politics of authorship affect casting: why is it bad form for a white filmmaker to cast Japanese American Tamlyn Tomita in the film *Vietnam, Texas* (Ginty, 1990) but okay for Wang to cast her in *The Joy Luck Club?*

It is not necessarily hypocritical to assert that a Chinese American filmmaker can cast across Asian ethnic lines while a white filmmaker should not: a similar logic allows us to call ourselves Asian Americans while we resist being lumped together as "Orientals." However, the purpose of this essay is not to justify Wayne Wang's casting decisions but rather to analyze the results of such a blurring of ethnic boundaries on the part of an Asian American filmmaker. Whether successfully verisimilitudinous or not, whether politically effective or not, cross-ethnic casting functions simultaneously to represent and deconstruct Asian American subjectivity. In *Chan Is Missing,* these issues coalesce once again around the figure of Steve or, more specifically, around the actor who plays him, Marc Hayashi. Perhaps the ease with which Steve performs a variety of identities—professional (ranging from Vietnam veteran to TV cop), Chinese American (ranging from deferential nephew to patronizing uncle), and racial (he adopts the voices of a Chicano *cholo* and a Filipino delinquent when reenacting a newspaper story)—can be traced back to the Japanese American actor cast in a Chinese American role.[64]

In a 1983 interview, Wang gave three arguments to justify casting Hayashi in a Chinese role:

> Ninety percent of the time I can tell if somebody's Japanese or Chinese. There's ten percent in the ambiguous zone. Marc was one of them. If you just show a picture of him to somebody, they'll say they're not sure whether he's Chinese or Japanese. Second, Marc grew up in Chinatown. He has a lot of Chinese friends and he can speak a little Chinese. Three, I think Asian Americans have more in common [than Asians, presumably]. I'm not putting them down, but they lack their own culture enough that you can lump them together. . . . all those factors, and also the fact that Marc is an extremely talented actor.[65]

The first argument, that Hayashi looks Chinese, is problematic but consistent with the paradigm of realism suggested by the second argument, that Hayashi knows Chinatown. But it is the third reason that intrigues me most: Wang suggests that later generations of Asian Americans have more in common with each other than with the specifics of their cultural ancestry. While this statement is not radical in and of itself, I would like to suggest that in the process of destabilizing Chinese American identity, Wang creates a space for Asian American subjectivity. That space is performative, contingent, and highly unstable, and in that it is consistent with *Chan Is Missing*'s central claim that identity cannot be fixed, Chan Hung cannot be located, the center of the doughnut cannot be described.

Voicing the Interval

> *I began to write stories using all the Englishes I grew up with: the English I spoke to my mother, which for lack of a better term might be described as "simple"; the English she used with me, which for lack of a better term might be described as "broken"; my translation of her Chinese, which could certainly be described as "watered down"; and what I imagined to be her translation of her Chinese if she could speak in perfect English, her internal language, and for that I sought to preserve the essence, but neither an English nor a Chinese structure. I wanted to capture what language ability tests can never reveal: her intent, her passion, her imagery, the rhythms of her speech and the nature of her thoughts.*
> *—Amy Tan[66]*

If the figure of Steve emblematizes the paradoxes that attend to the performance of multiple identities, Steve also emphasizes the link between identity and the acquisition of a voice.[67] Given the multiplicity of voices in the film, what is the distinctively Asian American voice that Renee Tajima heard when she first saw *Chan Is Missing* in 1981? If there is such a thing as an Asian American voice, what does it have to say?

The characters in *Chan Is Missing* repeat themselves over and over again; it seems that everybody whom Jo encounters has a favorite rap. George uses the anecdote of the apple pie and has a rehearsed spiel about Chinatown politics. Henry talks about solidarity with the people in China (except when cooking, when he sings, "Fry me to the moon," over and over). Mr. Lee gives advice over the phone on how to make business arrangements with Chinese people. Frankie says, "You don't know the Oriental people—when they say they haven't got it, they got something" (31–32). The faceless voice of Chan's neighbor recycles clichés from television shows like "Dragnet" and "The Rockford Files." Everyone who is asked to speak to the specificity of Chan Hung's position instead takes refuge in prefabricated speeches.

The need to find a voice is expressed in the tension between the two epigrams that began this essay. Wittman Ah Sing, the protagonist of Maxine Hong Kingston's *Tripmaster Monkey*, refers to African American culture and bemoans the lack of a similar hyphenate cultural expression for Chinese Americans. Wittman can only conceive of an Asian American voice in terms of already existing voices of subcultural expression, which would seem to ally him with Steve and his various appropriated identities. But both *Chan Is Missing* and *Tripmaster Monkey* demonstrate the ultimate untenability of appropriating voices; it is as if the characters seize upon the first thing at hand in an effort to plug the doughnut hole without really understanding what that doughnut is. By romanticizing African American cultural forms as resistant ("ain't-taking-no-shit-from-nobody street-strutting language"), Wittman and Steve fail to interrogate the extent to which American culture has absorbed African American cultural forms, as well as the specific processes of negotiation and contestation that produced African American culture(s).

The conflict between different modes of expression, between different voices, is described in *Chan Is Missing* by a lawyer (Judi Nihei) researching a paper on "the legal implications of cross-cultural misunderstandings" (17). When a police officer asked Chan, "You didn't stop at the stop sign, did you?" Chan answered, "No." In Chinese grammar, the answer must agree with the logic of the question ("No, I did not *not stop*"), whereas most native speakers of American English understand answers to agree with the logic of the statement ("No, I *did not* stop"). The lawyer, interested in the misunderstandings that result from this encounter, explicates the cross-cultural confusion in an attempt (presumably) to foster cross-cultural understanding. On the one hand, her voice is put in service of the two voices that preceded hers; on the other, her voice intervenes in their conversation, taking advantage of the confusion occasioned by the meeting of two voices to convey her own message.[68]

Following from this example of the interaction of hierarchized voices, it is important to maintain a distinction between the voice of *Chan Is Missing* and the voices of its characters, for the one contains the others and makes sense of them through mediation. In other words, *Chan Is Missing* (the film itself) is the third party that mediates between the various voices it contains. Furthermore, any encounter with the text of *Chan Is Missing* can itself be analyzed from a third position, as a critic does when analyzing different interpretations of a text. This should come as a surprise to no one: I am merely restating the terms of hermeneutic mobilization, suggesting that we make meaning out of terms that collide with each other. At the moment, this is the only way I can make sense of Renee Tajima's claim that there is something very Asian American about *Chan Is Missing,* for the interpretation proposed by this essay suggests that the film is about the multiplicity of assumed voices and the resulting confusion of identity. If we understand hyphenate identity in the terms that Trinh T. Minh-ha proposes, as a process of becoming, then there can be no hypostatized Asian American voice, just encounters between difficult-to-place voices that can be interpreted by third parties to be Asian American. The irony is that I myself am Asian American, but I can only understand my voice by standing apart from it, for if I try to arrest the process of becoming that my voice is undergoing, I remove myself from the realm of hyphenate identity and assert that I have a position somewhere. Perhaps then the importance of *Chan Is Missing* for the Asian American community is that it forces Asian Americans to reevaluate our own positions vis-à-vis our own identities.

I have argued that Asian American subjectivity cannot be founded upon any notions of stability, for such notions arrest the process of becoming and are not true to the fluidity of hyphenate identity. This is especially true given the diversity of Asian Americans, who represent a wide range of Asian ethnicities and cultures, different histories in the United States, and different generational removes from Asia. In this, I am echoing Lisa Lowe, who suggests that "it is possible to utilize specific signifiers of ethnic identity, such as Asian American, for the purpose of contesting and disrupting the discourses that exclude Asian Americans, while simultaneously revealing the internal contradictions and slippages of [the term] Asian American. . . . I am not suggesting that we can or should do away with the notion of Asian American identity . . . [but that we] explore the hybridities concealed beneath the desire of identity."[69] Wayne Wang's films explore the contradictions of Chinese American identity and in so doing propose a space for Asian American subjectivity. *Chan Is Missing* takes the interrogation of identity as its central project, presenting a variety of perspectives on Chan Hung from a variety of puddles.

While detective films are typically described as if they were jigsaw puzzles, I have proposed the metaphor of the doughnut.[70] Each character in *Chan Is Missing* holds a doughnut that contains the possibilities for Chinese American identity in its center; each character glances in the puddle and takes one bite from the doughnut in an attempt to find her or his access to the center. The big doughnut made up of all the little doughnuts—a doughnut akin to the construction of Chinese American identity that the spectator viewing *Chan Is Missing* is left with—is almost meaningless, almost wholly "hole." Whereas each character fixes Chan Hung in an attempt to fix her or his own identity, the spectator is not allowed to occupy any one of these fixed perspectives but must instead negotiate all of them. Thus each character's bite out of the doughnut—each character's attempt to limit the range of identities for Chan Hung—opens up the interval in the spectator's doughnut, widening the space for spectatorial subjectivity and, by extension, Asian American subjectivity. *Chan Is Missing*, by showing us why it is impossible to know precisely who we are as Chinese Americans, shows us how we might discover how we can become Asian Americans.

NOTES

The first draft of this essay was written under the guidance of Timothy Corrigan for a seminar on film theory and postmodernism held at the University of Iowa in 1992; my colleague Taylor Harrison also provided feedback on early drafts and shared research with me. Excerpts were presented at the Association for Asian American Studies Conference in Ann Arbor, Michigan, on 7 April 1994, under the title "Chinese American Subjectivity and Asian American Identity: The Films of Wayne Wang." Sandra Liu commented on the manuscript at this time, and I am grateful to all who read or heard the paper and shared their comments with me. I would especially acknowledge the generosity of Judi Nihei, who shared her insights and memories of the making of *Chan Is Missing*; my conceptions of the history of Asian American theater and cinema also owe much to our conversations. Thanks are also due to Spencer Nakasako for lending me a tape of *Life Is Cheap . . . But Toilet Paper Is Expensive*. Last but not least, David Desser and two anonymous readers offered invaluable advice in preparing this piece for publication.

1. Manning Marable, "The Rhetoric of Racial Harmony: What's Wrong with Integration?" *Sojourners* (August–September 1990): 14–18.

2. The term "ethnicity" is used in at least two distinct ways in this discussion. I usually use the term to identify cultural, national, and phenotypical distinctions within races (i.e., Vietnamese and Korean are ethnicities while Asian is a race; Italian and Polish are ethnicities while white is a race); this usage is consistent with Espiritu, and with Omi and Winant. Sometimes the term "ethnicity" is deployed to signify hyphenated or diasporic identities, as in Marable's use of the term to distinguish African Americans from the race of Africans and/or blacks, or in Werner Sollors's discussion of ethnicity as a product of descent and consent.

One other point needs to be made here. I at times speak of Asian Americans as hyphenated (the second use of the term "ethnicity") but I do not hyphenate the term "Asian American" even when using it as an adjective. Many Asian Americans, myself included, feel that the hyphen puts undue emphasis on our position between Asia and the United States, whereas our liminality might better be described as between a supposedly dominant culture and ethnic or racial subcultures. Of course, Asian Americans are not unanimous on this issue, and there are even Asian Americans who would argue that we have more important things to be worried about than punctuation. (Marable hyphenates "African-American," but other African Americans do not; I have omitted the hyphen to maintain consistency.) I discuss this issue more thoroughly in a sidebar, "The Politics of the Hyphen," that accompanies my article "In Search of Asian American Cinema," *Cineaste* 21, nos. 1–2 (1995): 32–36.

Yen Le Espiritu, *Asian American Panethnicity: Bridging Institutions and Identities* (Philadelphia, Pa.: Temple University Press, 1992). See also Michael Omi and Howard Winant, *Racial Formation in the United States: From the 1960s to the 1990s*, 2nd ed. (New York: Routledge, 1994); Werner Sollors, *Beyond Ethnicity: Consent and Descent in American Culture* (New York: Oxford University Press, 1986).

3. In June 1994, Mujibur and Sirajul toured the United States under the auspices of the

"Late Show with David Letterman": the news media referred to these two men interchangeably as "Bangladesh natives," "Asians," or "Asian Americans." This highlights another problem: some would restrict the term "Asian American" to U.S. citizens, while others would use the term to describe all diasporic Asians living in the West.

4. This contestation is also apparent in the existence of competing terms, sometimes used interchangeably and sometimes deployed in contradistinction to "Asian American": "Asian-Pacific American" and "Asian/Pacific Islander" (API).

5. Yen Le Espiritu's *Asian American Panethnicity* is an excellent discussion of the complexities of the Asian American label. Espiritu argues that the designation is uniquely American, depending as it does on a shared language of English, and serves both to unite diverse Asian ethnicities as well as emphasize our distinctiveness.

6. I am following the distinction suggested by Omi and Winant, *Racial Formation*. In their view race is both "an element of social structure rather than an irregularity within" and "a dimension of human representation rather than an illusion" (55). Racism is defined as "a fundamental characteristic of social projects which create or reproduce structures of domination based on essentialist categories of race" (162). There are thus racial projects, projects which rely on a sociohistorical analysis of the "structural and cultural dimensions of race in the U.S." (71), which can be distinguished from racist projects.

7. Espiritu, *Asian American Panethnicity*, 32–33. Espiritu makes a similar argument in a chapter entitled "Census Classification: The Politics of Ethnic Enumeration," which details the campaign by "Asian American individuals, advocacy groups, and legislators" to rewrite the 1990 census question on race: Asian Americans fought for expansion of ethnic enumeration (Asian Indian and Samoan were among the added designations) as well as for an umbrella category "Asian or Pacific Islander," which included a category of "Other API" distinct from the "Other race" category. Espiritu convincingly argues that the 1990 census campaign(s) should be seen as a "demand for separate counts of Asian American subgroups waged by a pan-Asian coalition" (112), a "protest [that] was mostly against the *absence* of the subgroup categories, not against the *presence* of the umbrella category" (132).

I have elected to use the term "Filipino" despite the lack of consensus; some use the term "Pilipino," to highlight the imperialist overtones of the term "Filipino" (since the *f* sound supposedly does not occur in Tagalog and is therefore perceived to be a Western import). However, some Filipinos have argued that some dialects do indeed have the *f* sound, suggesting that Tagalog should not be privileged as the authentic dialect of the Philippines. Other Filipinos continue to use the traditional spelling either out of habit or with the opinion that the debate is silly. As a Chinese American, I do not feel it is my place to take a side on this question, but I wish to emphasize that I am *not* using the traditional spelling of "Filipino" because it is more familiar (to non-Asians). Rather, in the lack of consensus, I have deferred to the traditional spelling (while hopefully problematizing it).

8. Phillip Brian Harper, *Framing the Margins: The Social Logic of Postmodern Culture* (New York: Oxford University Press, 1994).

9. Ibid., 4.

10. Ibid.

11. Ibid., 8–9, emphasis added.

12. Ibid., 19.

13. At the conclusion of his study, Harper examines three postmodern (nonmarginal) writers: Donald Barthelme, Robert Coover, and Thomas Pynchon. He then looks at a contemporary socially marginalized writer (Maxine Hong Kingston), who Harper argues evinces postmodern sensibility, albeit one that derives from the writer's "narrative treatment of social difference and marginality" (ibid., 28). In Harper's view, Kingston's writing represents a fuller theorization of postmodernism because it "engage[s] the sociopolitical issues that are unavoidably implicated in the concept" (186), whereas other writings evade the same issues.

Harper does examine contemporary texts produced on the margins, and so he directly engages the question I have raised: what is the role of "margin" texts vis-à-vis the postmodern in the contemporary period? However, while Harper argues that Kingston's writing is more fully postmodern than nonmarginal contemporary texts, I do not wish to claim similar status for *Chan Is Missing*. My own position is elaborated in the main text.

14. I am grateful to one of the anonymous reviewers of this essay for suggesting that Wayne Wang's "'cross-over' appeal" might be explained through an ambivalent relationship to theories of postmodern subjectivity.

15. Jean-François Lyotard, *The Postmodern Condition: A Report on Knowledge,* trans. Geoff Bennington and Brian Massumi (Minneapolis: University of Minnesota Press, 1984), 79.

16. Harper, *Framing the Margins,* 7.

17. David E. Wellbery, "Postmodernism in Europe: On Recent German Writing," in *The Postmodern Moment: A Handbook of Contemporary Innovation in the Arts,* ed. Stanley Trachtenberg (Westport, Conn.: Greenwood, 1985), 235, quoted in Linda Hutcheon, *The Politics of Postmodernism* (London: Routledge, 1989), 4.

18. Ibid.

19. Elaine H. Kim, *Asian American Literature: An Introduction to the Writings and Their Social Context* (Philadelphia, Pa.: Temple University Press, 1982), xii.

20. Ibid., xiii.

21. For example, for a second-generation, middle-class Chinese American like myself, adopting the label "Asian American" means that I have agreed to take a measure of political responsibility for a Laotian immigrant who wishes to attend MIT but is not assessed as a minority candidate because of the disproportionate representation of Chinese Americans in MIT's student body. Adopting the label "Asian American" means I make it my responsibility to show what the term excludes as well as what it includes.

22. Trinh T. Minh-ha, *When the Moon Waxes Red: Representation, Gender and Cultural Politics* (New York: Routledge, 1991), 49.

23. Meaghan Morris, *The Pirate's Fiancée: Feminism, Reading, Postmodernism* (London: Verso, 1988), 268.

24. Wayne Wang, *Chan Is Missing,* ed. Diane Mei Lin Mark (Honolulu: Bamboo Ridge, 1984), 50. Subsequent quotations of *Chan Is Missing*'s dialogue will be indicated parenthetically in the text and refer to the continuity script; however, when the script as published conflicts with what I hear on the sound track of the video release, I have opted to notate what I hear. My notations differ primarily in the way I have punctuated: I have attempted to indicate the rhythms of speech rather than grammatical logic.

While the continuity script has been an invaluable reference, it is no more than that, as is the script of any highly improvised movie. The principal actors (Wood Moy and Marc Hayashi) as well as some of the supporting players (in particular, Peter Wang and Judi Nihei) deserve credit for "rewriting" the initial script written by Wayne Wang, Isaac Cronin, and Terrel Seltzer.

25. The apple pie example does not combine American form with Chinese content (that might arguably result in something Chinese American) but rather combines American form with Chinese technique. Technique is not content but another manifestation of form. "To excel only in the mechanics of a language, be it verbal, visual, or musical is to excel only in imitation—the part that can be formulated, hence enclosed in formulas. Form as formulas can only express form; it cannot free itself from the form-content divide" (Trinh, *When the Moon Waxes Red,* 162). (Chinese content would perhaps be Chinese ingredients but not baking techniques.)

26. Ibid., 157.

27. Maxine Hong Kingston, *Tripmaster Monkey: His Fake Book* (New York: Vintage, 1990), 327.

28. Trinh, *When the Moon Waxes Red,* 41.

29. Wang's name rhymes with "hang." Whereas some Chinese Americans with Wang's surname pronounce their name "Wong," which is closer to the correct Cantonese pronunciation, other Chinese Americans accept the Americanized pronunciation; in this Wang is not unlike the descendants of European immigrants who have Anglicized or shortened their surnames. David Thomson, "Chinese Takeout: Wayne Wang Interviewed," *Film Comment* 21, no. 5 (September–October 1985): 24; Wang, *Chan Is Missing,* 101–2.

30. Thomson, "Chinese Takeout."

31. Tony Chiu, "Wayne Wang—He Made the Year's Unlikeliest Hit," *New York Times,* 30 May 1982, 17.

32. Richard Patterson, "Chan Is Missing, or How to Make a Successful Feature for $22,315.92," *American Cinematographer* (February 1983): 32–39.

33. David Sterritt, "Lively, Enriching Tale of the Chinese American Experience," review of *Chan Is Missing, Christian Science Monitor,* 1 July 1982, 18.

34. Michael Lam, "Program Notes: *Chan Is Missing:* Hard-edged, Gutsy," review of *Chan Is Missing, East/West,* 2 December 1981, 11; "Acclaimed Film to Be Shown at Art Academy," review of *Chan Is Missing, Honolulu Star-Bulletin,* 17 June 1982, D1. Of course, the *Star-Bulletin* is a local newspaper, not specifically an Asian American newspaper. However, it is not a "national" paper like the *New York Times* or the *Wall Street Journal,* and it does serve a city where Asians and Pacific Islanders comprise a significant proportion of the population.

35. Wayne Wang's published script for *Chan Is* Missing includes a detailed bibliography of reviews, of which I was only able to track down a small fraction, as Asian American newspapers have limited regional circulation. My thanks to the staff of Seattle's *International Examiner* for locating back issues for me and to the University of Iowa's Interlibrary Loan staff. Lam, "Program Notes," 11; Alan Chong Lau, "State of the Art," review of *Chan Is Missing, International Examiner,* 21 July 1982, 4.

36. Wing Tek Lum, "*Chan Is Missing* Marks New Age of Asian American Film," *East/West,* 28 July 1982, 9.

37. Reviews cited in this paragraph include David Ansen, "Chinese Puzzle," review of *Chan Is Missing, Newsweek,* 21 June 1982, 65–66; Vincent Canby, "'Chan Is Missing' in Chinatown," review of *Chan Is Missing, New York Times,* 24 April 1982, 13; "Caught at Filmex in L.A.," review of *Chan Is Missing, Variety,* 31 March 1982, 26; David Denby, "Movies," review of *Chan Is Missing, New York,* 7 June 1982, 72; Roger Ebert, "'Chan Is Missing' Warm, Funny Look at Chinese in U.S.," review of *Chan Is Missing, Chicago Sun-Times,* 20 April 1982, *Weekender* supplement, 55; "'Chan Is Missing' Journeys through Real Chinatown," review of *Chan Is Missing, Chicago Sun-Times,* 10 September 1982, 47; Robert Hatch, "Films," review of *Chan Is Missing, The Nation,* 3 July 1982, 26–27; Stanley Kauffmann, "Mysteries, Comic and Otherwise," review of *Chan Is Missing, The New Republic,* 16 June 1982, 24–25; Lawrence O'Toole, "Chinese Translations," review of *Chan Is Missing, MacLean's,* 6 September 1982, 54; Michael H. Seitz, "The Unhyped," review of *Chan Is Missing, The Progressive* (July 1982): 50–51; Sterritt, "Lively, Enriching Tale"; Gene Siskel, "'Chan' Reflects Life, Not Stereotypes," *Chicago Tribune,* 10 September 1982, sec. 3, 1, 4.

38. In analyzing the mainstream appeal of Amy Tan's novels, Sau-ling Cynthia Wong argues that counterorientalist rhetoric (e.g., when characters directly refute stereotypes) exists alongside hints of Chinatown exoticism, and together the two discourses constitute a "complex, unstable interplay of possibilities [that] makes for a larger readership" (191). I would go farther: the voicing of a counterorientalist position legitimates the novels' "authenticity" and reframes their own tendencies to exoticize Chinese culture. Such a rhetorical approach appeals strongly to progressive whites because it condemns overt racism while celebrating (unassimilable) ethnic difference.

Sau-ling Cynthia Wong, "'Sugar Sisterhood': Situating the Amy Tan Phenomenon," in *The Ethnic Canon: Histories, Institutions, and Interventions,* ed. David Palumbo-Liu (Minneapolis: University of Minnesota Press, 1995), 174–210.

39. Ibid.

40. Bernard Weinraub, "'I Didn't Want to Do Another Chinese Movie,' " *New York Times,* 5 September 1993, sec. 2, 7, 15.

41. At least one reviewer (Wilmington) went out of his way to mention that a minor character in *Smoke* was of mixed Asian ancestry, as if to assure readers that they were not mistaken, that Wayne Wang usually did Asian movies. Interestingly, Auster's screenplay specifies that the character (who has a larger role in the screenplay) is a Eurasian (a somewhat outdated term for a person of mixed Asian and white ancestry; Asian Americans generally employ the term *hapa,*

derived from the Hawaiian *hapa haole,* meaning literally "half white"). However, the press kit for *Smoke* does not single out this character or comment on Wang's Asian American identity.

42. Some anecdotal evidence for this is that Hollywood seems to have decided that the success of *The Joy Luck Club* is attributable to the fact that it is a film about women, not Chinese women specifically. The fall of 1995 saw the release of several films with non-Asian female ensemble casts—*Moonlight and Valentino, Now and Then, How to Make an American Quilt*—referred to by critics and marketing as "Caucasian versions of *The Joy Luck Club.*" *Waiting to Exhale* has more in common with *The Joy Luck Club* than the three films just mentioned, insofar as it also has a screenplay written by Ronald Bass in collaboration with the novelist (Terry McMillan) and it too was directed by a man (not a woman) of color; however, I have yet to see *Waiting to Exhale* referred to as "the African American *Joy Luck Club.*"

43. Examples include the bars and garages of *Chan Is Missing,* not to mention the key scene in the Manilatown Senior Center, which takes place in a back room (away from the dance hall); the barber shop, restaurant kitchen, and tong offices of *Eat a Bowl of Tea;* and the tobacco store in *Smoke.* (When women enter the store, like Ruby [Stockard Channing], the store literally and figuratively closes down; when the so-called "OTB men" hang out in the store, they talk about sports, politics, and women.)

44. Thomson, "Chinese Takeout," 25.

45. Louis Chu, *Eat a Bowl of Tea* (New York: Carol, 1993). Chu's novel made barely a ripple the year it was published; Renee Tajima points out that Rodgers and Hammerstein's *Flower Drum Song* was on stage that year, and it "offered up more palatable Chinese Americans in the age of model minorities" ("War Booty," review of *Eat a Bowl of Tea, The Village Voice,* 1 August 1989, 67). The book was rediscovered nearly a decade later, during the dawn of the Asian American Movement, and an excerpt was printed in the groundbreaking anthology *Aiiieeeee!* (1974), which was dedicated to Chu and Japanese American author John Okada (Frank Chin, Jeffery Paul Chan, Lawson Fusao Inada, and Shawn Wong, *Aiiieeeee! An Anthology of Asian American Writers* [New York: Mentor-NAL, 1991]).

46. Screwball comedy is referenced both by mainstream critics and by Renee Tajima (writing in *The Village Voice*).

47. I wish to emphasize that neither the filmmakers nor the distributor expressed any ill will toward each other; however, none of my sources would admit to knowing of the existence of any print aside from Wang's own. (Spencer Nakasako graciously lent me a VHS dub of the film.)

48. *The Joy Luck Club* press book, 9.

49. Actual figures: as of 21 November, the eleventh week of release, the film earned $28 million according to *Entertainment Weekly,* 3 December 1993. By Christmas, the film had earned $30.8 million according to *Variety,* 3 January 1994.

50. In an unusual move, *Smoke* broke with Hollywood tradition by crediting its screenwriter above the title ("A Film by Wayne Wang and Paul Auster").

51. Of course, Miramax is now owned by Disney, although that deal went through after *Smoke* and *Blue in the Face* went into postproduction. Presumably, Disney will leave the marketing of Miramax films to Bob and Harvey Weinstein, so as to retain Miramax's air of prestige (relative to Buena Vista/Hollywood Pictures): the very notion of "prestige" itself illustrates the cross-over paradox—better films seen by smaller (but more affluent) audiences.

52. According to the pressbook for *The Joy Luck Club,* the team of Tan, Bass, and Wang is developing a screenplay for Tan's second novel, *The Kitchen God's Wife,* but Tan told me (while in Iowa City in November 1995, promoting *The Hundred Secret Senses*) that they have not written a treatment and she is not convinced that her second novel can be effectively adapted for the screen. Wang has apparently optioned a novel set in contemporary Japan (according to a Pocket Books "Advance Reading Copy"): *Audrey Hepburn's Neck* (forthcoming in 1996) by Alan Brown. How the Hong Kong-born American director will go about adapting this book set in Japan will surely illuminate and perhaps challenge the arguments advanced in this essay.

53. Jerry Adler, "The Rise of the Overclass," *Newsweek,* 31 July 1995, 32–46. This is

not the place for a definition of "the overclass," but it may assist readers to envision these types if I point out that *Newsweek's* cover featured characters from the Doonesbury comic strip drawn by G. B. Trudeau.

54. It is ironic to cite the music as underlining and mocking a moment of intertextual reference in the film, for the score itself has been lifted from Michel Legrand's score for *The Go-Between* (1971). The musical quotation would suggest that the film's narrative approach belongs more in the realm of pastiche than of parody, to use Frederic Jameson's terminology. (The excerpt is not noted in the credits.)

55. I do not mean to imply that there is any such thing as a typical detective movie; rather, I have chosen this locution in the absence of satisfactory generic terminology. I am uncertain whether the detective film is best described as a genre, a mode, or a tendency; and the conflation of the terms "film noir" and "hardboiled detective drama" only adds to the confusion. Insofar as this essay is concerned with destabilizing terminology and the process of becoming, it rejects the notion that a rigorous definition of the detective film would assist us. Thus, I have used the word "typical" to call attention to the fluidity of the detective film.

56. David Henry Hwang, *FOB and Other Plays* (New York: Plume, 1990), 6–7.

57. The implication that women assimilate more easily than men is of course tied up with the U.S. attitude that it is more acceptable for white males to associate with women of color than it is for white women to associate with men of color. For a discussion of how these attitudes play out in U.S. films about romances between Asians and whites, refer to Gina Marchetti, *Romance and the "Yellow Peril": Race, Sex, and Discursive Strategies in Hollywood Fiction* (Berkeley: University of California Press, 1993). Marchetti discusses the roots of this attitude in (for example) rape narratives and captivity stories, two genres that revolved around attitudes toward non-Asian people of color, and how those genres were inflected when Asians were inserted.

58. Do Hwang's play and Wang's film buy into this logic or critique it? Due to space limitations, that question cannot be answered here. For a female perspective on this complex issue, readers may consult Velina Hasu Houston's play *Tea,* collected in Roberta Uno, *Unbroken Thread: An Anthology of Plays by Asian American Women* (Amherst: University of Massachusetts Press, 1993).

59. Presco is played by Bay Area writer Presco Tabios. For an audience familiar with Tabios's poetry, the figure of Presco marks a space where actor and character are not distinct and separable. More than an in-joke, the casting of Tabios as Presco underlines the self-reflexive advice that Presco dispenses.

60. Mimi Avins, "How to Tell the Players in 'The Joy Luck Club,' " *New York Times,* national edition, 5 September 1993, sec. 2, 14. According to the article, both Amy Tan and producer Janet Yang were approached by members of a preview audience and praised for their performances in the film. This was not an isolated case; filmmaker Jessica Yu reports that she was repeatedly mistaken for Ming-Na Wen at the 1993 Telluride Film Festival (Jessica Yu, "Only Yu," *Los Angeles Times Magazine,* 24 October 1993).

61. Avins, "How to Tell the Players."

62. Chao's character, Keiko O'Brien, first appeared during the fourth season (1990–91) of *Star Trek: The Next Generation* before moving to *Star Trek: Deep Space Nine,* which premiered in early 1993.

63. This discussion took place on the Internet newsgroup "alt.asian-movies" during the fall of 1993. I am grateful to Michael Raine for this information.

While Wang apparently insisted on casting only Mandarin speakers in the roles of Chinese women, Russell Wong (in the role of a Chinese man) is clearly dubbed.

64. *Chan Is Missing* is not Marc Hayashi's only feature film role to cast him as a decentered Asian American. In Peter Wang's *Laserman* Hayashi plays a Chinese American scientist with a Jewish mother, dating a white woman who knows more about Chinese culture than he does.

65. Erick Dittus, "Chan Is Missing: An Interview with Wayne Wang," *Cineaste* 12, no. 3 (1983): 19.

66. Amy Tan, "Mother Tongue," in *The Best American Essays: 1991*, ed. Joyce Carol Oates (New York: Ticknor & Fields, 1991), 196–202.

67. William Galperin ("'Bad for the Glass': Representation and Filmic Deconstruction in *Chinatown* and *Chan Is Missing*," *MLN* 102, no. 5 [December 1987]: 1151–70) refers to Steve as "the most attractive and accessible of the film's characters . . . [because] Steve attracts our fallen nature, makes us realize who we are and more important what we must resign to become like Jo or to imitate the still greater example of Chan Hung" (1167). While I agree with Galperin that Steve's character exhibits the contradictions of hyphenate identity most visibly, I resist the implication that Jo represents a more successful negotiation of Chinese and American cultures. To speak of how Steve has "fallen" and what Jo has "resigned" suggests not only a cultural hierarchy but also that the process of becoming forecloses even a partial "return."

Norman K. Denzin ("*Chan Is Missing*: The Asian Eye Examines Cultural Studies," *Symbolic Interaction* 17, no. 1 [1994]: 63–89), on the other hand, is interested less in the voice than the gaze. Denzin's reading focuses on Jo and pays Steve only lip-service, which is perhaps inevitable given Denzin's argument: he discusses *Chan Is Missing* as an interrogation of the Charlie Chan movies, in which he (reasonably) privileges Chan over his various sons. Denzin argues that Charlie is "rational, virtuous, mature, normal" when contrasted with "irrational, depraved, childish, violent, immature Westerners" (67), and he further notes, "Of course in the Chan series Number One Son played the part of the immature, irrational, childish Asian; yet even this conduct was neutralized, by having Charlie act as the traditional-white-paternal father figure" (86, note 17). I would take Denzin's argument one step farther: not only is Charlie the "Asian male [who] knew who he was, knew his place in society" (74), by disciplining his awkwardly acculturated sons Chan does not merely "act as" a white *patriarch* but rather serves to enforce white *patriarchy*. Unlike the Number One Son, however, Steve is not contained by Jo, as revealed by Jo's attempts to explain Steve to Steve ("two-faced, schizophrenic Chinaman" [48]).

Just as we should resist the temptation to read Chan Hung as a symbol of the diversity of Asian America, so should we as critics avoid reducing Jo and/or Steve to points of identification for the audience. Furthermore, we should not assume that our critical activity positions us as representatives of a unitary audience (a move that Galperin risks) nor as completely divorced from it (which Denzin risks when he argues that in *Chan Is Missing* "this self has become so thoroughly Westernized, no otherness is any longer possible" [79]).

68. Of course, the alternately bored, confused, and bemused expressions on Jo's and Steve's faces suggest that the graduate student is not communicating as effectively as she might hope, either.

69. Lisa Lowe, "Heterogeneity, Hybridity, Multiplicity: Marking Asian American Differences," *Diaspora* 1, no. 1 (spring 1991): 39.

In personal conversation, Lowe revealed her desire to rewrite her essay, which relies heavily on Chinese American and Japanese American texts to interrogate Asian American subjectivity. However, I have argued that the deconstruction of the cultural term "Chinese American" opens up the interval in which we might locate the political term "Asian American." I would therefore contend that neither Lowe's nor my project reduces Asian America to its Chinese American components but rather attempts to destabilize Chinese American texts in favor of Asian American subjectivity. (By contrast, Denzin's analysis conflates Asian American and Chinese American terms, e.g., "the Asian American [sic] must take a stand on the American experience that is either Pro-Tiawan [sic] and assimilationist, or anti-American and pro-People's Republic of China" [76]. The flip side is that Denzin conflates *Blowup*, *The Conversation*, *Sex, Lies, and Videotape*, and *JFK* as "Hollywood" films [83].)

70. See note 55.

Emigrants Twice Displaced: Race, Color, and Identity in Mira Nair's *Mississippi Masala*

The relationship between non-white minority groups in the United States today is an issue that requires our immediate attention. To recognize the gravity of the situation, one has only to look at such disputes in Brooklyn as the 1990 black boycott of two Korean grocery stores, and the clashes between the Hasidic and African American communities in the Crown Heights neighborhood. The much publicized April 1992 riot in South Central Los Angeles following the Rodney King verdict was not simply a black versus white incident, but one that involved members of African American, Korean American, and Latino communities. Peter Kwong explains the complex nature of the violence in "The First Multicultural Riots": "The fixation on black versus white is outdated and misleading—the Rodney King verdict was merely the match that lit the fuse of the first multiracial class riot in American history." Many Korean American stores located in Koreatown, north of South Central Los Angeles, were looted and burned down by Latino, mostly Central American, immigrants who lived in the area. The Korean American community was mobilized by the riots and "came to see themselves—for the first time—as victims of white racism" when neither local nor state police came to their aid.[1]

With the influx of immigrants from Latin America, Asia, and the Caribbean to the United States, American society has become more complex. The black/white dichotomy no longer provides an analytical model for the problematics of race, color, and identity. Many historians and cultural critics recognize the need for new coalitions, especially among marginalized communities and peoples of color. Manning Marable speaks of a new stage of black freedom in the United States that no longer involves only blacks but includes all people of color: "We must find new room for

From *Between the Lines: South Asians and Postcoloniality* edited by Deepika Bahri and Mary Vasudeva. Reprinted by permission of Temple University Press. © 1996 by Temple University. All Rights Reserved.

our identity as people of color to include other oppressed national minorities—Chicanos, Puerto Ricans, Asian/Pacific Americans, Native Americans, and other people of African descent."[2] Taking a broader perspective, philosopher and theologian Cornel West expresses the need for unity between different groups of people regardless of race, class, gender, or sexuality—while maintaining individual identity. The new cultural politics of difference "affirms the perennial quest for the precious ideals of individuality and democracy by digging deep in the depths of human particularities and social specificities in order to construct new kinds of connections, affinities and communities across empire, nation, region, race, gender, age and sexual orientation."[3] Like Marable and West, Edward Said suggests that binary oppositions rooted in imperialism have disappeared and that "new alignments made across borders, types, nations, and essences" have challenged the notion of identity: "Just as human beings make their own history, they also make their cultures and ethnic identities."[4] Contemporary debates on race and color in the United States must necessarily include relations between non-white minorities.

In her 1991 film *Mississippi Masala*,[5] Mira Nair depicts the complex relations between two non-white minorities in the United States, the Indian and the African American, prompting a reflection on issues of race, color, and identity.[6] The Indian family depicted in *Mississippi Masala* has migrated via England from Uganda, East Africa, to Greenwood, Mississippi. Expelled from Uganda by General Idi Amin in 1972, they are twice displaced: Indians by culture and tradition, Ugandan by birth, they move to the United States to live in a motel owned by relatives, themselves immigrants from India. The narrative includes many vignettes about the family's social and cultural adjustments in a small southern town, but the main thrust of the film is the violent opposition of the parents, father Jay (Roshan Seth) and mother Kinnu (Sharmila Tagore), to the relationship of their daughter Mina (Sarita Choudhury) with Demetrius (Denzel Washington), an African American who owns a rug-cleaning business. Mina and Demetrius's relationship brings to the surface the prejudices of the extended Indian family toward African Americans, rendered particularly poignant by the fact that they are both minority communities in Greenwood, as well as by their peculiar status with respect to the white community.

Preceding a detailed analysis of the film, some background information about Ugandan Indians is in order.[7] Mercantile and commercial ties between the East African coast and India date back a thousand years, when Indian merchants lived in Zanzibar and traders from Karachi and Bombay did business regularly with Madagascar. Soon the Indians moved inland, and by 1900 they "controlled wholesale trade along a two-thousand-mile stretch of coastline."[8] The British, who colonized Uganda, employed Indians first as soldiers, then as labor to help build the Ugandan railway. The railway opened up remote areas of the country, paving the way for more Indian immigrants, who arrived in large numbers, opened shops, and soon controlled most of the retail trade in Uganda. Although the British encouraged the prosperity of the Indians, real power in Uganda remained in British hands. As the Indians prospered, however, the black African population was relegated to the bottom rung of society: "Indians created a second-class [stratum] for themselves, while the Africans were automatically relegated to the third, and lowest," according to G. S. K. Ibingira. As the business class in Uganda, Indians controlled most of the wealth, excluding Africans from the economic structure. Soon Indians were involved in every aspect of the country's economy, from laborers to the professional classes; they hired Africans as servants, making them work long hours and paying them low wages. Africans resented the Indians not only for their wealth but also because they "lived an isolated communal life, they never mixed with Africans, and their interracial dealing never went beyond business matters."[9] In addition, Indians were not concerned with social change, preoccupied as they were with making a living, educating their children, and planning suitable marriages for them. The relationship between Indians and Africans deteriorated further with the growth of African nationalism and worsened after Ugandan independence. These social and economic conflicts were among the reasons invoked by General Idi Amin when he decided to expel all Ugandan Asians during a ninety-day period in 1972.

The Indian community in Uganda comprised a mixed group of Hindus, Muslims, Christians, and Sikhs. Most came from the states of Gujarat, Kathiawar, and Kutch on the northwest coast of India, while some were from the Punjab. In their social structure the Hindus were divided into caste and subcastes (*jati*), and the Muslims into two principal sects, the Sunnis and the Shias (which were further divided into subsects). Although Indian immigrants wanted to prosper in Ugandan society and were prepared to become Ugandan citizens, they were unwilling to give up caste and cultural differences. They were not able to transfer to Uganda the traditional hierarchy of the caste system as it existed in India, but "caste exclusiveness still remained."[10] For example, marriage within one's caste or subcaste was rigidly followed, and needless to say, marriage between black Africans and Indians was completely out of the question. (Members of the Muslim Ismaili sect, however, were encouraged by the Aga Khan, their religious leader, to become Ugandan citizens and to assimilate into Ugandan society.) Indians from Uganda and other African countries retained caste and kinship ties, maintaining customs such as endogamy, in the countries they migrated to after expulsion—England, Canada, and the United States.[11] In a study of East African Gujaratis in Britain, Maureen Michaelson observes: "Despite the double migration of Gujaratis from India to East Africa, and thence to Britain, Hindu Gujarati castes have retained remarkable resiliency and in many important aspects continue to operate according to traditional restraints."[12]

The historical and social context of the Ugandan Indian family is set up in the first frame of *Mississippi Masala* and continues by means of flashbacks throughout the film. Beginning and ending in Uganda, the film opens with an attempt to enunciate the rationale for Idi Amin's expulsion of Indians. The grim pre-credit sequence in Kampala, set in November 1972, shows Jay and his childhood friend Okelo (Konga Mbandu) in a car stopped at a roadblock, where a policemen shines a flashlight in their faces. After a tense moment, the policeman allows them to leave. We later learn that Jay, a lawyer, had been jailed for denouncing Idi Amin as an evil man during a BBC interview, and that Okelo had bribed the police in order to obtain Jay's release. Reluctant to leave the land of their birth, yet realizing that they have no choice, Jay, Kinnu, and Mina pack up whatever belongings they can carry, abandoning their home to their African servants. During the bus ride to the airport, Kinnu is forced out of the bus by Ugandan policemen, who jeer at her and throw a photograph depicting her husband in lawyer's robes into the mud. In a final humiliating act, one policeman tears a gold chain from around her neck with a rifle. Mira Nair based this scene on one of the many reports of harassment and mistreatment by Ugandan officials related by Ugandan Indians who had left during the expulsion period.[13]

We meet Mina's family again eighteen years later, in 1990, in Greenwood, Mississippi. Moving from the lush landscape of the Kampala hills overlooking Lake Victoria, the camera scans the North American concrete jungle of motels, highways, supermarkets, and automobiles. From the drumbeats of Africa to the rhythm of Mississippi blues, the sound track reflects the change of scene.[14] The now adult Mina is in a supermarket filling her shopping cart with gallons of milk. The camera follows Mina outside and slowly pans from an Indian woman counting dollar bills to a black teenager loading groceries into the trunk. Suggested here are the class differences between a typical middle-class Indian immigrant who has attained material success in the United States and a black teenager who is relegated to menial labor. Mina's own nuclear family, however, does not fit neatly into the stereotype of the successful immigrant. In a major change from their comfortable upper-middle-class existence in Uganda, in the United States they are forced to live in a motel, the Monte Cristo, owned by relatives. Mina's father spends his days filing lawsuits against the new Ugandan regime for the restoration of his property and possessions. Her mother runs a liquor store, purchased with money borrowed from relatives and located in a black neighborhood, much to the horror of other Indian women in Greenwood. Mina works as a maid in the motel, cleaning bathrooms and helping out at the front desk.

The motel motif is significant in *Mississippi Masala*. Motels are quintessentially American: convenient, inexpensive, and linked to working-class life both as rest stops for traveling families and as sites of illicit sexual encounters. Driving through South Carolina and Mississippi during research for the film, Mira Nair found a number of Indian-owned motels.

Many of the owners were sponsored and financed by relatives and, like Korean grocers, employed family members who needed only a limited knowledge of English to carry on their daily business.[15] In this "no man's land" of "truck drivers or prostitutes or lovers having a tryst," says Nair, the Indians continue to preserve their way of life, their religion and food habits.[16] Moreover, because motel chains are standardized nationwide, many have no character, no style; by and large they look the same everywhere. It is precisely this lack of identity, this standardization, this neutrality, which acts as a symbolic backdrop of a paradoxical nature for the Indian family seeking to maintain its identity. The motel creates a natural community for immigrants like Jay and his family. Nuclear families have their own living quarters and share other areas during social events such as weddings. Because the motel is self-contained, it is an ideal setting where the Indian family can practice social and religious customs without fear of interference from the outside world and maintain their exclusiveness, their separateness from other ethnic groups. History and tradition are preserved; family ties are strengthened. Yet at the same time the motel serves as a site of transition. For Jay, Kinnu, and Mina the chintzy environment of the Monte Cristo stands in stark contrast to their life of elegant comfort in Uganda.[17] The scenes of leave-taking from Uganda, as well as scenes of the extended family in the motel in Mississippi, symbolize the temporary and the transitional, emphasizing the binary structure of rootedness/rootlessness that operates throughout the film.

The "ghettoization" of immigrants suggested by the motel is not particular to Indian immigrants but typical of immigrant communities in general, for whom the ghetto becomes not only a space for maintaining their culture but also a space of empowerment in hostile surroundings. The motel in *Mississippi Masala* has allowed the Indians to maintain their cultural exclusiveness, but Mina's relationship with Demetrius forces them to leave that security and to confront not only questions of their own identity as Ugandan Indian immigrants in the United States but also their feelings toward other communities in Greenwood, especially the black community.

Although Nair's treatment of representation, identity, and displacement is complex and nuanced and has the potential for suggesting productive coalitions between Indians and African Americans, bell hooks and Anuradha Dingwaney are severe in their critique of the film, denouncing it as a stereotypical portrayal of blacks, Indians, and whites and lacking in political commitment.[18] Calling Nair's work "another shallow comment on interracial, inter-ethnic, transnational 'lust,' " hooks writes, "Nair's film compelled commentary because spectators in the United States have never had the opportunity to see a Hollywood narrative about Africa, India, and African-American cultures" (41). Dingwaney reports that fellow Indians found it "the only film that dared to represent working class Indian culture in the United States. They praised the film for conveying so much realism." Both hooks and Dingwaney, however, question the portrayal of a "real" that is already a selection by the director: "Often stereotypes are used to embody the concept of the 'real,' or the everyday" (41). These critics admit that *Mississippi Masala* shows familiar images but assert that the familiar "need not embody the stereotypical," which only confirms "hegemonic Western notions of Indian traditionalism or the parochialism of both the black and white in the deep South" (41). They also claim that although black and Indian viewers were uncritical in their enjoyment of the film—because they felt that it did indeed explore Indo-black relationships—nevertheless, the film's exploration of that relationship was "shallow, dishonest, and ultimately mocking" (41).

Their critique, less valid in some cases than in others, nevertheless facilitates the introduction of critical questions for the film in particular and for interminority relations in the United States in general. The issue of filmic "truth" and "realism" in ethnic or racial representations is a highly contested one. It is obvious that Nair makes a choice in her depiction of the Indian family and offers her version of the "truth," based on interviews with Ugandan Indians who had settled in the United States and were mostly in the business of operating motels in South Carolina and Mississippi. To that extent it is real. Although representations can have a real effect on the world, Ella Shohat and Robert Stam observe that they can also lead "to an impasse in which diverse spectators or critics passionately defend their version of the 'real.'"[19] hooks and Dingwaney's complaint that the film "offers only stereotypical portraits of southern whites and blacks" (43) is, however, valid to a certain extent. It is true that the film has its share of black, brown, and white stereotypes. Demetrius's brother Dexter (Tico Wells) is depicted as a wastrel spending his time on the streets with his friends and listening to rap music. In keeping with images of the sexual prowess of black males, much is made of the unbridled sexuality of Demetrius's partner Tyrone (Charles S. Dutton). The white motel owners depicted in the film hate the Indians yet hate the blacks even more. Some Indians, such as motel owners Anil (Ranjit Chowdhry) and Kanti (Mohan Agashe), are portrayed as greedy vultures. Yet it must be acknowledged that the film has its share of nonstereotypical, multifaceted characters: Mina, Kinnu, and Jay among the Indians; Demetrius and his Aunt Rose (Yvette Hawkins), with her heightened sense of self, among the blacks.[20] hooks and Dingwaney do not allow sufficiently for the multiplicity and plurality of Indian immigrant experiences, or for the complexities and diversities of the African American experience presented in the film. In contrast, while Shohat and Stam understand the importance of "the study of stereotyping in popular culture," they are aware of its downfalls: "First, the exclusive preoccupation with images, whether positive or negative, can lead to a kind of *essentialism*. . . . This essentialism generates in its wake a certain *ahistoricism*; the analysis tends to be static, not allowing for mutations, metamorphoses, changes of valence, altered function."[21]

Nair is careful to present a family situated in a very particular historical context; the film portrays the experiences of one Indian family that emigrated from Uganda. The temptation to read this family as representative of all Indian immigrants in the United States may be understandable in light of the paucity of Indian images in the American media; it may be more useful, however, to attempt to understand the complexities in their lives and the important issues that surface with regard to race relations in representing that family.

When hooks and Dingwaney remark that "there is little interaction between the two cultures when the focus is the United States" (41), they point to a lack that is all too exemplary of the huge gap that exists between minorities in this country. Mina and Demetrius's attempt to bridge this gap emphasizes both the gap and the difficulties that attend their effort. Mina does, however, share a meal with Demetrius's family at the celebration of his father Williben's (Joe Seneca) birthday, and Demetrius meets Mina's father on one occasion. Whereas Demetrius's family receives Mina very warmly, and they, especially his brother Dexter, are intrigued by her African-Indian roots, Demetrius's meeting with Jay is confrontational. This encounter must be understood in light of Jay's experiences in Uganda as well as his observations about race relations in the United States; no less important to the confrontation are Demetrius's own experiences with racism in America and the long history of African American struggles for recognition and acceptance.

Jay's reaction to Demetrius, complicated by his love/hate feelings for Uganda, brings multiple and conflicting histories to the fore. In a conversation early in the film, Jay agonizes over being forced to leave the country of his birth: "I've always been Ugandan first and Indian second," he exclaims to Okelo. "I've been called a bootlicker and traitor by my fellow Indians." He asks, "Why should I go, Okelo? Uganda is my home." Okelo sadly replies, "Not anymore, Jay. Africa is for Africans—black Africans." hooks and Dingwaney claim that Jay "never reflects on the power relations between Indians and blacks in Uganda, that the film so skillfully erases and denies" (43). On the contrary, Jay is fully aware of the exploitative relationship that existed between Indians and blacks in Uganda, and this understanding is depicted in one of the flashbacks: on their last night in Uganda, Jay is in a bar drinking with some Indian friends and reminiscing about their lives. When one of them raises the toast "Uganda, you have been so good to us until this madman [Idi Amin] came," Jay responds that it was the Indians who had created the "madman." Noting the failure of the Indian community to make itself a meaningful part of Uganda, he says, "Most people are born with five senses. We are left with only one, sense of property." Unlike the prejudices of other members of his extended family, there is a good amount of self-reflection on Jay's part as to the unequal relationship between Indians and Africans in Uganda.

Jay's character in the film is much more nuanced than it appears at first glance. Although he can easily be dismissed as prejudiced against blacks because of his rejection of Demetrius, he had, unlike other Indians in Uganda, established professional and social ties with blacks there, as his close ties with his childhood friend Okelo reveal.[22] There develops a definite strain in their relationship when he is forced to leave Uganda, perhaps because he unconsciously blames Okelo for Idi Amin's decision. Although his feelings toward blacks are clearly embittered after his expulsion and the loss of the social and economic status he had enjoyed, Jay still has mixed feelings about Ugandan blacks. When a fellow Indian in the United States comments that Jay was "a champion defender of blacks" in Uganda and that the "same blacks kicked him out," Jay insightfully remarks, "Cruelty has no color." Nevertheless, despite his liberal ideas (he also tells Demetrius that Mina is free to love whomever she wants), he warns Mina that, ultimately, "people stick to their own kind. You are forced to accept that when you grow older. I'm only trying to spare you the pain." It is precisely because the power relations between the races cannot be denied that Jay is sensitive both to exploitative relations between Indians and blacks in Uganda and to the struggle in store for those who abandon "their own kind."

Influenced by his own experience in Uganda ("After thirty-four years that's what it came down to, the color of my skin"), Jay expresses his misgivings about Demetrius's relationship with Mina, saying that he does not want his daughter to struggle as he had. Demetrius, in turn, is obliged to invoke the history of black men in the South. On hearing the word "struggle," he explodes: "Struggle, struggle, look, I'm a black man, born and raised in Mississippi, not a damn thing you can tell me about struggle." He continues, "You and your folks can come down here from God knows where and be about as black as the ace of spades, and as soon as you get here you start acting white and treating us like we're your doormats. I know that you and your daughter ain't but a few shades from this right here [points to his skin], that I know."

Demetrius's scathing critique reflects the Indian community's tendency to affiliate with the dominant rather than minority cultures in the United States. Discussing Indian attitudes toward race and racism, Mira Nair says that when asked if he had experienced racism, an Indian motel owner is reported to have said, "'I'm just a white person who stayed in the sun too long,'" thus identifying with the whites and implying that he considered himself light enough to be accepted by white society.[23] Attitudes toward skin color in the film likewise show that the Indians identify with the whites rather than the blacks; the preference for light skin color is frequently stressed. Mina makes light of her dark skin in conversations with her mother, who wants her to date the lighter-skinned Harry Patel, an eligible young Indian. Color also becomes the subject of gossip between two Indian women, who discuss the probable effect of Mina's skin color on her marriage prospects with Harry Patel. One of them sardonically remarks, "You can be dark and have money, or fair and have no money. But you can't be dark, have no money, and expect to get Harry Patel." The concern with gradations of skin color is something Indian culture shares with African American culture, but it serves to drive them apart rather than bring them closer.[24] Near the film's conclusion, as Mina and Demetrius try to reestablish their relationship after the scandal (which ensues when they are found in a motel room together), he asks Mina why she had not warned him that her family had "trouble with black folks." "You didn't ask," responds Mina, implying that her family was perhaps transferring its social segregation from blacks in Uganda to their American situation. But Shohat and Stam suggest that just as Spike Lee's film *Do the Right Thing* (1989), which deals with the tensions and affinities between Italian American and African American communities, "calls attention to how some members of recent immigrant communities have used Blacks as a kind of 'welcome mat,' as a way of affirming, through anti-Black hostility, their own insecure sense of American identity," so also racist behavior toward blacks may have been learned by the Indian family in *Mississippi Masala* after arrival in the United States, or reinforced if already present.[25]

The Indians' relationship with the whites in Greenwood is also conflicted. They may wish to maintain physical and social distance from the blacks and to identify with the whites, but white attitudes toward Indians are founded on racism and ignorance. Neighboring working-class white motel owners confuse the Indian family with American Indians. When one of them remarks, "Send them back to the reservations where they belong," the other responds, "How many times have I told you they are not that kind of Indian!" The very same white motel owners—who resent the Indians encroaching on their territory and complain to the police about the family making too much noise during wedding festivities—express a sense of solidarity with the Indians after learning of the Mina–Demetrius scandal; they call up Anil's father Jammubhai (Anjan Srivastava) and ask in a conspiratorial chuckle, "Are ya'll having nigger problems?" The whites in this incident are blatantly racist, and the "conspiracy" involves their assuming that the "brown" Indians share their virulent racist feelings against blacks. Another scene reinforces the stereotype of Indians as cow worshipers. As Mina is buying gallons of milk and buttermilk for Anil's wedding, the supermarket clerk jokes, "Holy cow! Are you opening a dairy?" Seeing that Mina is not amused, he apologizes for his flippant remark. White racist attitudes toward the black family are more overt, especially when the white bank manager threatens to repossess Demetrius's van. The discrimination suffered, albeit to varying degrees, by both Indians and blacks fails to create alliances between them and paradoxically widens the gulf that separates them.

That the community at large is unable to imagine the possibility of alliance with the African American community is underscored in a mock-coalitional scene—long before the confrontation between Demetrius and Jay—when members of the extended family fake a move to ally themselves with the blacks for selfish reasons. Mina first meets Demetrius when she accidentally runs into his van while driving a car that belongs to Anil, the relative who owns the motel her family lives in. Afraid of a lawsuit, Anil seeks the help of fellow motel owner Kanti, whose motel carpets are also cleaned by Demetrius and his partner Tyrone. In an attempt to find out if Demetrius is going to sue Anil, Kanti expresses solidarity with African Americans as members of non-white minorities: "Black, brown, yellow, Mexican, Puerto Rican, all the same. As long as you are not white, means you are colored." He concludes with "United we stand, divided we fall." Kanti's pat rhetoric is transparent in its slickness; we are not surprised to learn later that he was merely paying lip service to ethnic solidarity, using his color and minority status only to curry favor with Demetrius.

In fact, the gulf between the groups is only reinforced by Kanti's mouthing of a "line" that rings well but means nothing. Showing the Indians feigning friendship with the blacks, hooks and Dingwaney argue, only downplays "the significance of political bonding between people of color" and does not promote the coalition building among minorities "that subverts the status quo" (42).[26] On the one hand, they point out that the film does not emphasize enough that Indians in Uganda mediated between the oppressed blacks and the oppressing imperialist class; on the other hand, they criticize Nair's representation of Indians as conniving hustlers. But not all the Indians in the film are portrayed as conniving hustlers, any more than all the black or the white characters are. By placing minorities on the high ground, the critics can be faulted for reverse stereotyping. Should the Indians be judged by different standards because of their minority status? This critique in fact diverts attention from the possibility that Kanti's failure to internalize the values he so glibly musters might be read as a powerful comment on the larger failure of minorities to find common cause with one another. Later, when Anil and his friends discover Mina and Demetrius in a Biloxi motel room together, both African American and Indian communities defend their mutual isolation. Tyrone, when he bails Demetrius out of jail after that fiasco, observes bitterly, "Leave them fuckin' foreigners alone. They ain't nothing but trouble." He repeats with irony, "United we stand, divided we fall. Ain't that a bitch! Yeah, but fall in bed with one of their daughters, your ass gonna swing," referring to both the cultural value of female chastity in the Indian community and the false promise of unity that is destined to be belied.

If Jay is haunted by the ghosts of racial difference that constitute his betrayal by Uganda, and the Indian community is obsessed with maintaining its distance from blacks, Mina herself identifies more with the blacks than with the whites in Greenwood. In one incident, when Mina has a date with Harry Patel, they go to a club where she is perfectly at ease socializing with the predominantly black crowd, dancing with some black friends and later with Demetrius. Harry, however, becomes so uncomfortable that he angrily leaves the club without her. As an Indian who has never been to India, Mina also shares a common history with African Americans who, as Dexter explains, are Africans who have never been to Africa. Moreover, Mina also has fond memories of her childhood in Uganda and of her father's friend Okelo. She chastises Jay for his refusal to bid Okelo goodbye. "Okelo risked his life to save yours," she reminds him. "I don't know what more proof you need of his love. I remember his face when he came to say goodbye. You would not even look at him."

It may be true, as hooks and Dingwaney suggest, that Mina "is no civil rights activist in the making" (43), but she is acutely sensitive to the racism around her. She recounts to Demetrius the racism faced by Indian motel owners: "You know how many people come to the motel. They look at us and say, 'Not another goddam Indian.' Makes me so mad."[27] Moreover, although Mina is not given to making political speeches on racism and equality, her leaving Greenwood with a black man in a society where blackness has come to be feared and loathed is nothing less than radical. Breaking the social taboos of both her own community and the larger society around her, she is engaged in a revolutionary act for an Indian woman under any circumstances.

Although Mina's relationship with Demetrius is an attempt to transcend a devastating racial divide, after their actual sexual union the chasm between the two cultures gapes wider. Yet hooks and Dingwaney assert that the film's message is one of romantic love that breaks down racial barriers, a message that "deflects from the very real politics of domination that underlies our inability as individuals to bond and form sustained community while simultaneously embracing our difference" (41). They object to the use of romantic love as a means of bonding between the two groups. Mina and Demetrius are not blinded by the love that brings them together, however; they have a realistic idea of the problems they are likely to face. When Demetrius ironically asks Mina whether they will live on fresh air if they leave Greenwood, Mina responds, perhaps not so unrealistically, "I could be your partner. I know how to clean rooms." Demetrius is also fully aware of his financial responsibilities. The couple's departure demonstrates that they can be together despite their differences, thus rendering their bonding more challenging and circumspect.

Still more egregious to hooks and Dingwaney is the fact that whereas the film portrays the sexual frustrations of a newly married Indian couple, it shows Mina and Demetrius's sexual encounter as so "intense and so fulfilling that it empowers them to abandon familial ties" (42). These critics exaggerate the impact of the one sexual encounter shown in the film; the narrative structure does not allow for more sexual trysts, or even for the development of the relationship, especially since

Mina's relatives prevent her from meeting Demetrius after they are discovered together. Only when she finally slips away from her family's watchful eye to find him do they have a brief moment to connect emotionally and discuss their true feelings for each other. Admittedly, Nair may have forfeited the opportunity to represent a more complex and layered relationship between Mina and Demetrius; however, the sexual aspect of it is liberating for Mina, given her restrictive background and the repression of female sexuality within Indian society. The sexual difficulties experienced by the newlyweds may be perceived as an indictment of a certain Indian middle class, which treats sex as taboo and does not educate men and women, especially women, in sexual matters. Often Indian women (and on occasion, Indian men) are thrust into arranged marriages with little or no knowledge of sex, or of their future spouses.

Disapproval of Mina and Demetrius's sexual exuberance must be framed by another claim that appears in hooks and Dingwaney's review, that Nair mocks Indian traditions such as prayer and traditional weddings. They point to Jammubhai's speech during his son's wedding reception: "Even though we are ten thousand miles away from India, we should not forget our roots, our culture, our traditions, our gods." "By making these moments comedic," the critics remark, "Nair seems to stand with white Americans who insist that ethnic jokes and poking fun at non-white cultures is harmless and not meant to undermine respect for difference" (42). Yet they never question what aspects of Indian culture are being portrayed in the film. The social customs depicted are a potpourri of Hindu religious ritual and Indian pop culture: family members gather for daily prayers, celebrate a traditional Hindu arranged marriage, listen to Indian music, watch commercial Hindi films on video, and wear Indian clothes. When hooks and Dingwaney speak about the film's lack of respect for "Indian" culture, they refer to Nair's depiction of a Hindu culture, thus conflating "Indian" and "Hindu" identity. They do not consider the religious, regional, caste, and class differences within Indian culture.

Indeed, Nair appears to ridicule not the customs themselves but the manner in which they are conducted, underscoring the pompous tone of Jammubhai's declaration, followed by his leading a Hindu *bhajun* or hymn in which many of the younger Indians participate only halfheartedly. The practice of rituals may help the older generation maintain a sense of identity, but the rites are perhaps meaningless to the younger generation. In fact, given that many of the Indians in the film either left India many years earlier or have never been there at all, the customs themselves may be anachronistic in the contemporary Indian context. For Mina, who has never lived in India and who left Uganda as a child, these so-called traditions are merely symbols devoid of significance.

In their eagerness to present culture and tradition as sacrosanct institutions, hooks and Dingwaney do not acknowledge that Indian customs such as arranged marriages can be oppressive to Indian women. Anxious to see twenty-four-year-old Mina married, Kinnu encourages her to go out with Harry Patel. She admonishes Jay, who is less concerned about Mina's marriage prospects: "You want your daughter to be a thirty-year-old spinster, running a liquor store?" The sexual politics of propriety and shame are evident in Kinnu's remark. Both parents, although "Westernized" enough to encourage Mina to go out with eligible young Indian men, are shocked when she and Demetrius are discovered in bed together. Kinnu and Jay feel that she has brought dishonor to her family, although it is unclear whether they are upset because she has slept with a man before marriage, because Demetrius is American, or because he is black. The film's allowing Mina a measure of sexual liberation constitutes less a glorification of sex at the expense of family than an arraignment of a sexual economy that uses the female body as currency for cultural survival.

Moreover, far from celebrating Mina and Demetrius's "self-chosen homelessness," as hooks and Dingwaney contend (43), the film shows that the decision is wrenching for the couple as well as their families. Both Mina and Demetrius call their parents to wish them goodbye before they leave Greenwood; Demetrius receives his father's blessing, and Kinnu tearfully accepts Mina's decision, but Jay receives the news in stoic silence, refusing to speak to his daughter once he learns that she is with Demetrius.[28] Mina and Demetrius do not want to leave their families. It is the families and the community that force their departure by refusing to accept their relationship. Moreover, they decide to leave Mississippi for a more practical reason: Ostracized by Greenwood society, Demetrius is unable to find work; moving to another state offers him more employment opportunities. It is important to emphasize here that it is not they who fail the family, but the family and community that fail them.

Nevertheless, hooks and Dingwaney see in *Mississippi Masala* the suggestion that "personal fulfillment cannot be found within the context of nation or family where one is able to reconcile the longing for personal autonomy with the desire to function within community" (43). Their comment echoes that of Demetrius's ex-girlfriend Alicia (Natalie Oliver); observing that there is no shortage of black women in Greenwood, she accuses him of letting down his family, his community, and his entire race. Dismissing the couple's decision as a manifestation of "bourgeois white western . . . individuality" (41), hooks and Dingwaney do not allow for the complexity of the role of immigration, whose very nature complicates notions of "identity," "family," "community," and "nation," which are nuanced and not monolithic concepts. Mina was born in Africa of Indian parents, and raised in the southern United States. She cannot deny her "Americanness" any more than she can deny her "Africanness" or her "Indianness"—if it were possible to identify an essential Indian, African, or American. Therefore Mina does not reject her identity but accepts her multiple identities. Because of her unique experience she is forced to create her own space, which does not necessarily imply rejection of tradition and family. Mina describes herself as a *masala* or mixture, a "bunch of hot spices." For Mina, *masala* is a social construction, a means of explaining her Indian/Ugandan/American identities, an amalgamation of her ethnic roots, as well as her immigrant past.

The term *masala*, literally a blend of spices, has various connotations in the film. At times it refers to the hybrid nature of the family, which is Indian, Ugandan, and now North American. Nair herself defines *masala* in a more postcolonial sense as a "polyglot culture of the Indians who were colonized in their own nation by the British and then forced by poverty to seek survival elsewhere."[29] Shohat and Stam comment that culinary terms like *masala* have a metaphorical meaning for filmmakers: "'creating something new out of old ingredients'— as a key to their recipe for making films."[30] For several male characters in the film, however, *masala* is reduced to a description of Mina's sensuality and earthy good looks, a means of objectifying her as sexual object. Demetrius describes her as "hot and spicy." To Tyrone, Demetrius's oversexed business partner, Mina is "just ripe for plucking." He even mistakes her for a Mexican at first, reinforcing the Hollywood image of Latin American women as sex objects. When she corrects him and identifies herself as an Indian, he assumes she means a Native American (the only "Indian" he is familiar with) and refuses to believe her. Even the *New York Times* film critic Vincent Canby emphasizes Mina's sensual appeal as if it were the only thing that determines her relationship with Demetrius: "Her voluptuous presence defines the urgency of the love affair."[31]

hooks and Dingwaney's observations with regard to family and nation raise a number of important questions: Is the Ugandan Indian (Hindu) family in the film typical of all Indian immigrant families in the United States? What constitutes Mina's Indian identity, given the fact that she has never been to India? In their concluding paragraph, the critics write, "Exile is not homelessness, rather a deep engagement with 'home'" (43). The very question of "home" is central to the film, but what is "home" to the Indian family in the film—Uganda? India? the United States? What does Mina consider home?

There are no simple answers to these questions of identity and home. Cultural historians have discussed these very issues as they pertain to emigrant groups. Stuart Hall speaks about the notion of *migranthood* and the attitudes of migrants who know deep down that they are not going home, because "migration is a one way trip. There is no 'home' to go back to. There never was."[32] Ashis Nandy observes that South Asians in the diaspora "cling to the memories of [a] South Asia which no longer exists and to a myth of return to the homeland which is no longer shared by their children or grandchildren." Even Jay comes to realize that his home is now in North America, and that neither the India nor the Uganda of his memories exists anymore. "Home is where the heart is, and my heart is with you," he writes to Kinnu from Uganda, using a well-worn cliché to attain perhaps a reasonable compromise in his own mind to his personal dilemma. Jay's resolve signals an important moment of commitment, to his wife and, by extension, to the "home" he must build with her in their new domicile, thereby recalling Nandy's suggestion that "the diaspora must work towards dismantling links with the mother-country and entering the political realm of their new country."[33] In this context one might say that whether or not Mina and Demetrius's departure is a celebration of individualism, more urgently it is a call for minority communities to recognize and begin to resolve their differences in their immediate surroundings. That the film ends not with the couple's departure but with Jay in a Kampala marketplace holding an African child in his arms and swaying to the beat of African drums suggests that despite the admittedly mawkish display, it points to a more hopeful future—or at least a longing for a better world in which such hopes need no longer be quixotic.

The film demonstrates how essential migration and displacement are to an understanding of the behavior of the twice-displaced Indians as Mina's family transfers its attitudes and behavior toward black Africans to black Americans. It ends on a note of uneasy reconciliation: all conflicts appear to have been resolved, at least temporarily. Mina and Demetrius have left Mississippi for an uncertain future but with the "possibility" that the love relationship will work out. Both families have accepted the couple's decision, albeit with difficulty, and it becomes clear that the Ugandan Indian family must forge a new identity: a combination linking their Indian and Ugandan past with their present life in America.

Although *Mississippi Masala* does not have a radical political agenda, the film nonetheless makes a political statement by raising the necessary question of interminority politics, so rarely addressed in mass media. Given that minorities often seem preoccupied with making political statements of representation in opposition to the majority culture, the film creates a space where we can refine black/white issues in order to study the more subtle shades of relationships between minority groups in the United States. Indeed, the film urges that connections be made between different non-white minorities, old taboos broken, and new identities created. In a broader context, *Mississippi Masala* shows that binary oppositions such as black versus white, victim versus victimizer, are not necessarily the most significant oppositions in American society. The film declares that people of color must overcome mutual prejudice if they are to unite in a collective space of their own.

NOTES

Acknowledgments: I thank Deepika Bahri, George McClintock, Pia Mukherji, and Francesca Sautman for their helpful suggestions and patient reading of earlier drafts of this essay.

1. Peter Kwong, "The First Multicultural Riots," *The Village Voice*, 9 June 1992, 29, 32. Edward T. Chang similarly titles his article tracing the historical roots of the riots "Amer-

ica's First Multiethnic 'Riots,' " in *The State of Asian America: Activism and Resistance in The 1990's*, ed. Karin Aguilar-San Juan (Boston, Mass.: South End, 1994), 101–17.

2. Manning Marable, "Race, Identity and Political Culture," in *Black Popular Culture*, a project by Michele Wallace, ed. Gina Dent, Dia Center for the Arts, Discussions in Contemporary Culture 8 (Seattle, Wash.: Bay Press, 1992), 302.

3. Cornel West, *Keeping Faith: Philosophy and Race in America* (New York: Routledge, 1993), 29.

4. Edward Said, *Culture and Imperialism* (New York: Knopf, 1993), xxiv–xxv, 336.

5. *Mississippi Masala*, dir. Mira Nair, with Denzel Washington, Sarita Choudhury, Roshan Seth, and Sharmila Tagore, Michael Nozik, and Mira Nair, Samuel Goldwyn Company, 1991.

6. I use "African American" and "black" almost interchangeably, but I specifically use "black" when I want to stress the issue of color.

7. This historical background of the Ugandan Indians derives from four principal sources: Grace Stuart K. Ibingira, *The Forging of an African Nation: The Political and Constitutional Evolution of Uganda from Colonial Rule to Independence, 1894–1962* (New York: Viking, 1973); Jane Kramer, "Profiles: The Ugandan Asians," *New Yorker*, 8 April 1974, 47–93; J. S. Mangat, *A History of The Asians in East Africa, 1886–1945* (Oxford: Clarendon, 1969); and H. S. Morris, *The Indians In Uganda* (Chicago: University of Chicago Press, 1968).

8. Kramer, "Profiles," 48.

9. Ibingira, *Forging*, 69, 107–8. It is important to note that Ibingira's stance is an official one. He played a major role in the independence movement of Uganda, was a founding member of the Uganda People's Congress (UPC), and served as both minister of justice and minister of state in an independent Uganda.

10. Morris, *Indians in Uganda*, 27.

11. Within the United States, Suvarna Thaker's "The Quality of Life of Asian Indian Women in the Motel Industry" confirms that most of the Asian Indian women she interviewed (who had come to the United States from England and Africa) said they hoped to marry off their children within their "small caste." Others said that although their children might not marry within their own caste, they "would certainly appreciate it if the other partner were at least Indian." *South Asia Bulletin* 2.1 (1982): 72.

12. Maureen Michaelson, "The Relevance of Caste among East African Gujaratis in Britain," *New Community* 7.3 (1979): 350.

13. Bert N. Adams and Mike Bristow have written about Ugandan Asians' expulsion and later resettlement in their adopted countries; see, e.g., "Ugandan Asian Expulsion Experiences: Rumour and Reality," *Journal of Asian and African Studies* 14.3–4 (1979): 191–203, for the experiences of refugees they interviewed in 1973.

14. The move from Africa to the United States, part of the narrative of *Mississippi Masala*, is reminiscent of Indian commercial films where, in the course of a song sequence, for example, the protagonists often change both costume and locale.

15. In her introduction to Suvarna Thaker's "Quality of Life," 68, Sucheta Mazumdar observes that a high percentage of Asian Indians in the United States invest in the motel industry. When asked why, some cite the security of investment in real estate; others, the fact that it provides jobs for newly arrived immigrants. For still others a motel provides a living area for the extended family, bringing in higher returns on investment than house ownership; in addition, the family also provides the labor needed to run the motel.

Michaelson, "Relevance," 350–51, mentions similar settlement patterns of East African Gujaratis in Britain. Those who purchased homes in certain areas affected later settlement patterns: first, their homes served subsequent migrants from East Africa; second, they were "nuclei around which later immigrants clustered in specific suburbs or centres of Britain."

16. Quoted in Samuel G. Freedman, "One People in Two Worlds," *New York Times*, 2 February 1992, H14.

17. James Clifford offers a contrasting interpretation of the potential for motels to preserve a sense of history of the Indians: in his "Traveling Cultures," in *Cultural Studies*, ed.

Lawrence Grossberg, Cary Nelson, and Paul A. Treichler (New York: Routledge, 1992), 106, he quotes from Meaghan Morris's essay "At Henry Parkes Motel" (*Cultural Studies* 2.1 [1988]: 1–47): "Motels, unlike hotels, demolish sense regimes of place, locale, and history."

18. bell hooks and Anuradha Dingwaney, *"Mississippi Masala"*; *Z Magazine*, July–August 1992, 41–43. Quotations from this review are cited by page number in the text.

19. Ella Shohat and Robert Stam, *Unthinking Eurocentrism: Multiculturalism and the Media* (London: Routledge, 1994), 178. For further discussion, see the introductory section (78–82) to the chapter entitled "Stereotype, Realism, and the Struggle over Representation."

20. Rose is quick to point out that her brother, Demetrius's father, owed nothing to his white employers, given that they had only recommended Demetrius to the bank for a loan: "All you and the rest of them want is that he [Demetrius] know his place and stay in it. But the days of slavery, they're over, Williben."

21. Shohat and Stam, *Unthinking Eurocentrism*, 198, 199.

22. hooks and Dingwaney observe that Nair's portrayal of the relationship between Okelo and Jay is ambiguous. At no point, however, does the film explicitly indicate, as they suggest, that Okelo is Jay's servant. Although one might concede that Nair perhaps waits too long to reveal that he is a schoolteacher, there are several instances in the film where we see the two men drinking and conversing together as equals.

23. Quoted in Freedman, "One People," 14.

24. Although color is not really presented as an issue for the black family in *Mississippi Masala*, it has played an important role in films by black Americans, such as Spike Lee's *School Daze* (1988), whose plot revolves around the tensions between the lighter and darker-skinned African Americans, as well as his *Jungle Fever* (1991).

25. Shohat and Stam, *Unthinking Eurocentrism*, 237.

26. Mark A. Reid, "Rebirth of a Nation," *Southern Exposure*, Winter 1992, 27–28, disagrees. He says that three films, one of them being *Mississippi Masala* (the other two, *Daughters of the Dust* and *Fried Green Tomatoes*), "suggest that there is an alternative vision of Southern race relations gradually finding its way into mainstream media. . . . The community represented in each film represents the uneasiness of a society faced with emerging coalitions fighting the privileges of the status quo." These films "resist beliefs, socio-cultural customs, and detrimental ideas and practices which would inhibit the growth of their central characters." Mina and Demetrius, Reid argues, fight the forces that claim that love between people of different colors is unacceptable.

27. Sonia Shah, "Presenting the Blue Goddess: Toward a National Pan-Asian Feminist Agenda," in Aguilar-San Juan, *The State of Asian America*, 157, asserts that Mina is portrayed as "unconcerned with issues of race, history, culture and gender"—yet we have seen that Mina is aware of issues of race, history, and culture, although she may not be taking an obvious feminist position. I also disagree with Shah when she claims that Nair hurts the South Asian American cause by portraying Mina as one of those "little more than exotic, browner versions of white women, who by virtue of a little color can bridge the gap between black and white." Given the diversity of the South Asian Indian community, what "cause" could she be hurting? Again, what would be an appropriate representation of an Indian woman?

28. R. Radhakrishnan, "Is the Ethnic 'Authentic' in the Diaspora?" in Aguilar-San Juan, *The State of Asian America*, 225–26, sees in *Mississippi Masala* a "commodification of hybridity" as "the two young adults just walk out of their 'prehistories' into the innocence of physical, heterosexual love." He remarks that the term *masala* "trivializes histories" by allowing for "individualized escapes." "Just think of the racism awaiting the two lovers," cries Radhakrishnan. Yet the decision to leave their families is not an easy one for either Mina or Demetrius, and neither is blind to the problems ahead, racial or otherwise.

29. Quoted in Freedman, "One People," 13.

30. Shohat and Stam, *Unthinking Eurocentrism*, 314. There is a resemblance between *masala* and Gloria Anzaldua's definition of the "new mestiza" in her *Borderlands/La Frontera: The New Mestiza* (San Francisco, Calif.: Aunt Lute, 1987). Anzaldua describes her Mexican

American heritage as a hybrid mixture resulting from living on the "borderlands." Despite certain liabilities, the mestiza is seen as a positive, empowering force that strengthens rather than weakens: "This mixture of races, rather than resulting in an inferior being, provides hybrid progeny, a mutable, more malleable species with a rich gene pool" (77). The "new mestiza consciousness" is the creation of a new self, the amalgam of the different parts. It has political and feminist overtones, resulting in "a conscious rupture with all oppressive traditions of all cultures and traditions" (82). Implicit in *Mississippi Masala* is the notion of hybridity, but without the political and feminist agenda.

In Srinivas Krishna's film *Masala* (1991), the term has multiple meanings. It refers not only to the various story lines but, at another level, to the narrative structure, which borrows from video, television, and popular Hindi film. *Masala* is also used literally to mean the spices the grandmother grinds together to prepare a curry. Finally, it describes the hybrid quality of the Indian Canadian families portrayed in the film, who live their lives in a hodgepodge of Indian kitsch (Hindu gods and idols, Indian food, arranged marriages) and the reality of a racist Canada (the protagonist, Krishna, is stabbed to death by a white teenager at the end of the film).

31. Vincent Canby, "Indian Immigrants in a Black and White Milieu," *New York Times*, 5 February 1992, 19.

32. Stuart Hall, "Minimal Selves," *ICA Document* 6 (1987): 44.

33. Nandy quoted in Nikos Papastergiadis, "Ashis Nandy: Dialogue and Diaspora—A Conversation," *Third Text: Third World Perspectives in Contemporary Art and Culture* (special issue: "Beyond the Rushdie Affair") 11 (1990): 103, 105.

Linda Peckham

Surname Viet Given Name Nam: Spreading Rumors & Ex/Changing Histories

A society that imposes on its people a single way of thinking, a single way of perceiving life, cannot be a human society.
—Thu Van, thirty-five years old, health technical cadre, Vietnam, 1982

It has been noted that the war in Vietnam demonstrated the literal translation of ideology into violence, or rather the war in Vietnam illustrated to a divided public that ideology and violence are never separate. The war was fought in the media first, a war whose victory was measured in increments of meaning, in terms of the success with which events were matched to their interpretation. "If war is the continuation of politics by other means, then media images are the continuation of war by other means."[1] By implication then, wars are won or lost in history, in retrospect, and in the playing out of various resolutions in the cinema minigenre of films on Vietnam. Thus the war continues, paradoxically, in the urge to resolve it. The Time-Life war, the "Platoon" war (war-is-hell-for-young-American-men), is one where the Vietnamese people become the bystanders, the audience, no longer the witnesses.

　　Trinh Minh-ha's *Surname Viet Given Name Nam* does not directly address the war or the extrapolations that constitute its representation in this country. Perhaps it can be described as a film about the side effects of a monolithic point of view, about the aftermath of violent division and opposition, and especially about the margins of social upheaval, to which Vietnamese women have been confined like refugees of their own history. Between the cultural ideal of self-effacement and the social actuality of double exploitation and exclusion from power, women are suspended in silence.

From *Framework* 2:3. Reprinted with permission from Los Angeles Center for Photographic Studies.

Surname Viet Given Name Nam brings together Vietnamese women's voices in the form of interviews with women in the United States and reenactments of interviews conducted with women in Vietnam; other absent voices are in the form of letters and reminiscences, as well as the folk poetry that speaks of the condition of women in Vietnam. The film bears witness to "the misfits of history,"[2] as one woman says, but not merely to fill in the gaps, as if women represent only an omission from an already written text. Their silence is the strong presence of unwritten stories and unspoken testimonies, and the film itself forms a record of the process of bringing histories and meaning into being, specifically as it integrates and problematizes translation and the interview form.

His surname is Viet, his given name Nam. It is his identity she acquires with the status of marriage. It is her national and ethnic identity as perceived by the West. It is a dance she performs that has been step-printed to isolate each gesture in a freeze frame, and which is then reanimated in percussive synchrony to the beat of a drum; it is an identity with a strict form.

> *Cong Dung Ngon Hanh.* What are these four virtues persistently required of women? First, Cong: you'll have to be able, competent and skillful—in cooking, sewing, managing the household budget, caring for the husband, educating the children—all this to save the husband's face. Second, Dung: you'll have to maintain a gracious, compliant and cheerful appearance—first of all for the husband. Third, Ngon: you'll have to speak properly and softly and never raise your voice—particularly in front of the husband or his relatives. Then fourth, Hanh: you'll have to know where your place is; respect those older than you and yield to those younger or weaker than you—moreover, be faithful and sacrifice for the husband.

Who speaks when she speaks according to Ngon and Hanh? Absenting herself as a presence, presenting herself as an absence, the very act of speech is self-effacement. Between the Four Virtues and the Seven Deadly Sins of a Girl,[3] there is little room for self-government. A project to bring together the voices of Vietnamese women must therefore have hidden difficulties. And in socialist Vietnam, forms of speech for women may be modernized, but censorship takes different appearances. Anh, a doctor, relates how her female patients' bodies are still "an unnamed place, a non-existent and not-talked-of place. . . . Ignorance drives women to a world of silence." Cat Tien, also a doctor, recalls how she was required to produce and periodically update "a resume of my past life," obviously a political document of "right" speech and action, a socialist version of Ngon. (She observes dryly that she simply recopied it verbatim each time she was required to submit it, a subtle form of silence and resistance on her part.)

And yet, in apparent contradiction to this image of the Vietnamese woman as silent and decorative, there is a strong presence, in popular history and folklore, of rebellious, iconoclastic women. Both images are represented in the popular metaphor of woman as a lotus blossom, which, while being beautiful, grows in the mud and is of the earth. Most prominent is the nineteenth-century poetry of Ho Xuan Huong, whose work is frequently quoted in the film. The poems were "notorious for the scandal they caused, and they continue today to defy the principles of right speech and good manner of womanhood," by being flagrantly erotic and insolent. The voice-over also mentions two sisters (Hai Ba Trung) who led early resistance movements against the Chinese, and a peasant, Trieu Thi Trinh, "who led thirty battles against the Chinese. She was said to be 9 feet tall with frightful breasts 3 meters long flying over her shoulders as she rode on an elephant." Even the folk poetry (sung a capella by Ngoc Tu) which prescribes and represents women's conduct, takes on the tone of a lament in the context of the film ("Daughter, she obeys her father / Wife, she obeys her husband / Widow, she obeys her son").

All of these figures and works speak out against the stereotype, yet each has a story or is a story of a struggle to survive. Ho Xuan Huong's (female) authorship and very existence have been denied. The sisters Trung and Trieu Thi Trinh committed suicide in the face of defeat and captivity (rather than return to the confinement of their conventional roles). The national epic poem *The Tale of Kieu* survives as a text although its meaning has suffered reinterpretation and appropriation. The poem "recounts the misfortunes of women in the person of a beautiful talented woman, Kieu, whose love life has repeatedly served as a metaphor for Vietnam's destiny. The heroine, a perfect model of Confucian feminine loyalty and piety, was forced by circumstances to sacrifice her life to save her father and brother from disgrace and humiliation, and to sell herself to become a prostitute, a concubine, a servant and a nun, before she was able to come back to her first lover."

In the final minutes of the film, Trinh Minh-ha refers again to the poem as an allegory of the "tragic fate of Vietnam under colonial rule," and also as an allegory of the exploitation of the image of women. "Each government has its own interpretation of Kieu. Each has its peculiar way of using and appropriating women's images." There is a terrible irony, as Thu Van points out in an interview, in deifying women, both before the revolution and since: "Socialist Vietnam venerates the mothers and the wives. . . . The image of the woman is magnified like a saint! . . . The revolution has allowed the woman access to the working world. She works to deprive herself better, to eat less." The liberation of women is understood as "a double exploitation." To her and to others, "the very idea of heroism is monstrous!" Thu Van goes on to say that women need to demystify the image of themselves in order to understand and resist exploitation, "the illusion that we are full citizens." Citizenship versus the illusion "nationality," the name "Viet Nam." In the footage of the Miss Vietnam 1988 Pageant it is anonymity we see on display in her identity, as if she were simply an annual blossom. ("When he claps his hands, she has entertained / When she claps her hands, he has made a significant contribution—to his village, his town, his country. The fatherland, as they call it now.")

It is only by gathering together multiple images and voices of women that a dialogue can be established between them; only by including the silent interstices, the attendant contradictions in the way women see themselves and each other, the mediated portraits of their realities, can a history be traced. The film is like a marketplace, which is "women's city. It is the heart of daily life where information is exchanged, and where rumors are spread," unlike political meetings, where—as Ly, an employee, remarks—"adverse or different ideas are minimized." Trinh Minh-ha brings herself as a presence, a subject, to the film, not just in the commentary she provides, or by participating as a voice, but in the same way as the other women who play a role: she is herself a textuality, an inscription of history. "I—the writer do not *express* (a) reality more than (a) reality *im*presses itself on me. Expresses me," she has written elsewhere.[4]

Interviews are conducted and reconstructed according to this sense of articulation, being-as-writing, rather than being-as-photograph, reflecting and embodying "truth" value. The assumption that an individual is a passive receptor, a static reflection of experience, is the same as the assumption that documentary can restore to the present that experience as unmediated testimony. Thus the "antiquated" device of interview takes on new potential when its limitations—the hidden artifices of its construction—are used to augment the reality of a woman's story. There is no more powerful way of underscoring Cat Tien's narrative of her husband's internment in a reeducation camp than the implementation, through the "artifice" of style and form, of the content of her words. The routine of her life as a doctor was at once tedious and fraught with fear of political suspicion until finally her husband was arrested and she herself sustained a breakdown. The actress sits in a dimly lit interior, almost in profile as she speaks off screen, delivering the painful narrative that tedium and fear have reduced to a toneless, relentlessly inexpressive rhythm. It is like a debriefing session, where the reluctance of the speech reflects at the same time the will to remember. The whole interview is one sustained, ten- or twelve-minute take, where the passage of time is etched in space by the minutely slow zoom out, from a conventional tight framing of the subject through empty space until, in the corner of the frame in the extreme foreground, part of a formal flower arrangement is glimpsed, a disturbing demarcation of an abyss between the camera and the woman, between the viewer and the experience. It is when we recall that the speaker is an actress, a substitute, a "fake," that the interview style becomes in a way subversive—for the artificial subject points to the absence of the "real" speaker, an absence that suggests internment, censorship, and death, as well as the survival of a witness, a record—a history.

Another technique of (documentary) authenticity used to disguise mediation is the style of "direct address," where the interviewee speaks into the camera. In the first part of her interview in this style, Thu Van says immediately, "In our socialist society, we discard all disturbing subjects so that we don't have to deal with them. We prefer to cultivate fear and suspicion." Addressing first the politics of silence, she says shortly after, "Before, I would not dare speak up to say what I thought. But today, the situation is different. I have deeply rebelled." Thus Thu Van's look into the camera is as direct and critical as her gaze at her own political existence. Raised as a "child of the Party" and "fed . . . with revolutionary discourses since my childhood," her disillusionment with the language of politics is profound. Her interview, conducted in glaring brightness against a wall, with the minimal set of a table and chair, evokes the austerity of her environment, as well as interrogation, especially in her interaction with the camera and the way she divulges her personal/political opinions. The art direction and set also depict her sense of ideological division, for the table is split at the middle, and the color of light falling from opposite sides of the frame is orange and blue.

In the final part of her interview she paces back and forth as she speaks against the oppression of bureaucracy. The framing is tight, a medium close-up of her profile, rather like a "mug shot," and the camera follows her for a while, then is stationary, a long empty frame of white, a cell, a long stare at the texture of a whitewashed wall.

In these reenacted interviews in the first half of the film, documentary devices are "hybridized" stylistically into narrative devices—the obvious mise-en-scène combined with the interview format, the Hollywood cutting to the reverse angle that is conspicuously "unmotivated," and so on. In other words, devices like addressing the camera which, in documentary, attempt to effect a literal realism, are now reconceived as a metaphorical reference to reality. Similarly, the fictional spaces of the interviews represent externalizations of the content of the interviews.

By contrast, the interviews in the latter half of the film in which the women speak as "themselves" (speaking mostly in Vietnamese) and directly address their roles as "acting" are shot in the more conventionally naturalistic—even unconscious—style of documentary (handheld camera, available light, prosaic environments). It is an interesting reversal of the expectation that the film should make the critical progression from the less obviously fictional footage, the conventional interviews, to the more obviously crafted scenarios, thereby rendering visible the instrumentality of the devices that were previously "invisible." It seems to do the opposite (although within the segment of reenacted interviews there is a progression from the more conventional documentary technique to conspicuously stylized mise-en-scène). However, the shift from one strategy to the other is also the shift between Vietnam and the United States, between absent interviewees with their histories and the present interviewees for whom Thu Van, Cat Tien, Ly, and Anh represent, in a sense, the past. And it is through this frame of narrative and the past that we see the new lives of emigrants; it is through the eyes of the women's experiences that we watch scenes of normal—even banal—moments where the style of naturalism works again metaphorically, this time representing cultural assimilation, perhaps an opportunity to resume a continuity and a fabric of life undisturbed by rupture and trauma. It is an acknowledged formal decision to shoot in this style as well as the other, for both are complementary to each other, as Trinh Minh-ha says in the voice-over: "By choosing the most direct and spontaneous form of voicing and documenting, I find myself closer to fiction." And just as in the fictional mise-en-scène, "truth is selected, renewed, displaced, and speech is always tactical" in the naturalistic footage. These strategies together with the use of found footage raise the question, "What, then, is documentary?"—a question that conceals a distinction from fiction (what is real and what is artificial?).

Lurking in that question is another (anarchical) question, the question of identity and witnessing (to whom did it really happen?). Khien, the actress playing Thu Van, is seen in a sequence filmed in the "direct cinema" (verité) style: it is during a lunch break in the shooting and she is describing her own living conditions after reunification. She had to conceal her identity and her plans to escape from the local political officials, whose suspicion extended even to the surveillance of the food eaten in her house. But her greatest fear was of the discovery of her education, an event that would lead her to a camp of reeducation. Her manner of speech and her presence are similar enough in the staged and unstaged interviews to give an effect of eerie continuity, at this simple level, of both personalities; at the same time, the difference between the spontaneous outpouring of her own story and the more restrained delivery of Thu Van's inserts itself as a rupture, a gap in history; at the level of narrative there is continuity and discontinuity between two experiences, one a rebellion against a life of political orthodoxy, one in flight from it; one woman in Vietnam, one in exile in the United States. If an actress playing the character of a real person in the style of documentary then appears in a documentary as herself, the question "who is speaking?" becomes a much more radical question of identity itself, or at least a questioning of the demarcation of (a) subjectivity with respect to history. Looking for the authentic origin of a memory, for the single truth in witnessing is to subscribe to the fiction of separateness, what Todorov (1984) calls "the pseudosingularity of the I," and to deny the collective experience that inscribes us.[5] Or perhaps a more accurate metaphor than writing is translation. "Grafting several languages, cultures and realities onto a single body." Translation is a truer image of the interpenetration of textualities that occur in an individual.

There is a moment in the film where the framework that forms the sovereignty of the individual collapses—the frame of progression past, present, future, the frame of situation and place, the frame of address "I":

there is a voice-over whose identity is suspended or withheld until much later in the film; the voice is that of a young American woman, a somewhat incongruous choice for the texts she reads, which are folk poems (it is she who says, "Easy young man, you're spilling my rice! Yes I am with husband, his surname is Viet and his given name is Nam"). It is only later in the film, when she pronounces some untranslated words of Vietnamese, that we realize the American voice is also a Vietnamese voice, and that in her reading she spans not just the bilingual identity of Vietnamese American, but the multilingual identity of (Vietnamese) women. She appears, in later documentary footage, as her "contemporary" self, Lan, joking about her accent from Pennsylvania.

The film itself represents a body of "grafted" texts. As well as the interviews in English there is the variety of found footage of Vietnam, which, like the reenactments, is a reality seen with another's eyes at another time and place. It has been translated into/by a new context, as have the optically printed dances, in which the alteration and manipulation of images emphasize translation as a process of reading, or rather, rereading. Rereading as performed by the filmmaker ("spoken, transcribed and translated") and also rereading as a task or responsibility transferred to the viewer as a self-reflexive event, where, for example, subtitling no longer facilitates unconscious translation/consumption, but ruptures the reading process; sometimes it is absent and part of a conversation remains inaccessible; sometimes there are two voices speaking simultaneously, giving equal importance to both, when they are in English, or English and Vietnamese. When two voices are only in Vietnamese, the texts are fragmented by being selectively subtitled. Rereading and subtitling are taken to a literal extreme, however, in the interviews that are conducted in English, where text covers and invades the entire image. There is a rather absurd redundancy in subtitling English for an English-speaking audience, and especially in filling the whole frame with printed text, print that is too large and too bold. The text is a transcription of what is being said, but it interferes in several ways, drawing attention to the act of reading (and writing)—it either emphasizes the content of the words by appearing simultaneous with speech, or it reiterates and repeats the content by appearing after it is said, or it preempts (and renders redundant) the performance of the speech by appearing beforehand.

This strategy of translating English into English calls for a response to "the way the content is framed" as inseparable from meaning, and calls attention to the movement between "a language of inwardness and that of pure surface." But translation is necessarily foregrounded as a political issue, for translation is the primary struggle of the exile; at the most practical level, it is a problem of "mastering elevators and escalators" and "distinguishing dog's canned foods from human canned foods." More profoundly, it is the transcription of a new culture onto one's very being while still speaking the language of the original.

Surname Viet Given Name Nam can be read in the light of Thu Van's insight, that "a society that imposes on its people a single way of thinking, a single way of perceiving life," is a society organized around intolerance and around war. The divisions of Northern and Southern, capitalist and socialist, Vietnamese and American, are the constructions of identity that maintain mistrust and hostility between women. It is precisely in the fact that women share collectively the effects of division, regardless of regional differences and the diaspora, that the potential for unity lies. As Anh says, echoing Thu Van, "if woman could trust woman, then we could talk about a revolution." It is in this context of social division that the film documents the war, and from the critical perspective of the exploitation of "images of mothers holding their child in their arms to flee from war." For the film has a different concern than those films that represent conclusions about the war in Vietnam: it is a concern that history will not be rewritten, "the fear of a time when the [women] witnesses themselves die without [women] witnesses."

NOTES

1. From the script of *Surname Viet Given Name Nam*. This statement is credited in the script to Jean Baudrillard.

2. Quotations without notes are cited from the spoken text of the film.

3. "The seven deadly sins of a girl: one, sitting everywhere; two, leaning on pillars; three, eating sweet potatoes; four, eating treats; five, fleeing work; six, lying down too often; seven, wolfing her nephew's sweets."

4. Trinh T. Minh-ha, *Woman, Native, Other* (Bloomington: Indiana University Press, 1989).

5. T. Todorov. *Mikhail Bakhtin: The Dialogical Principle* (Minneapolis: University of Minnesota Press, 1984).

Thomas Waugh

Good Clean Fung[1]

A subjective handheld camera moves attentively through a gay male sauna past towel-wrapped clients in the corridor and the cubicles, to an upbeat disco-ish sound track. The subject, soon revealed as a slim young Chinese man in a jaunty baseball cap, considers several potential sexual partners and is declined by others, before finally coming to an unspoken agreement with a South Asian man of the same age. In the latter's mirrored cubicle, the two engage in kissing and caressing and then anal intercourse, the seated Chinese man penetrating his partner who is astride his lap. The men's bodies as well as their condom and lubricant are all carefully and graphically shown in close-up operation. Safe sex slogans scroll by in several languages and then the final credits.

This 1990 videotape, *Steam Clean,* has a symptomatic place in the videography of Richard Fung, positioned halfway through the nine-work career spanning from 1984 to 1996. But it is absent from Fung's own personal c.v., perhaps because it is a commission produced jointly by the Gay Men's Health Crisis of New York (GMHC) and the AIDS Committee of Toronto. I start with it, because neither my auteurist training nor my affinity toward social activist documentary allows me to discount commissions, especially those undertaken with community organizations, and also because the growing literature on Fung prefers to canonize the postcolonial queer hybridity of his more complex autobiographical works rather than something as bluntly instrumentalist as this and other community-based tapes. This literature also downplays the sexual discourse and performance, queer at that, that I think are at the center of Fung's production, and thus downplays the full constellation of intersecting identity and political practices that his work embodies. I would first like to reclaim *Steam*

From *Wide Angle* 20:2 (1998), 164–175. © Ohio Univ.: Athens Center for Film and Video. Reprinted by permission of Johns Hopkins University Press.

Clean as the key to his oeuvre and its full range of issues, and, second, to take Fung's *Dirty Laundry*, and hang it out to dry.

Let me make several points about *Steam Clean*, first by quoting Sara Diamond's Foucauldian reading of the tape:

> In *Steam Clean*, a safe sex tape addressed to Asian men by Richard Fung, a surveillance camera happens to discover two men having sex in a steam bath.[2]

An obvious error, stemming from the fact that not only does the author presumably prefer French theory to Greek active, but also because like most of us academics and theorists, she writes about the works *she* would like to see and make rather than what is on the screen—as if a political modernist overlay about the panopticon could possibly help Fung in achieving his goals of encouraging the discourse and practice of safer sex, of saving lives among the gay Asian community.[3] Here is a typical example, I am afraid, of the demotion of the sexual in academic discourse around queer culture. Sexual representation, in fact queer sexual performance, is an important but unacknowledged commonality that Fung shares with a disparate body of contemporary work in hybrid documentary that Nichols has lumped together as performative,[4] from Pratibha Parmar's *Khush* to Marlon Riggs's *Tongues Untied*, and one can certainly add artists from Sadie Benning to Gregg Bordowitz to his grouping. Laura Marks has called the sexual element in so many of these works the "engaging [of] desire," the "reclaiming [of] sexual pleasure on their own terms."[5] But the critical reception of all such artists often reveals a symptomatic softpedalling of the hanky-panky. As another example, one reviewer of *Dirty Laundry*

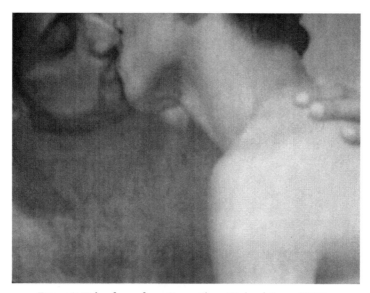

Figure 9. Video frame from *Steam Clean* (Richard Fung, 1990).

repeatedly intones the trimmed mantra "race and gender" when he clearly should be saying at the very least "race, gender, and sexuality" and perhaps even nationality—but we'll come back to that in a moment.[6]

Diamond was able to slip her error past University of Minnesota Press's vigilant readers no doubt because this whole network of so-called performative work is a slippery and chameleon-like commodity, susceptible not so much to state censorship as to discursive manipulation and appropriation in the academic marketplace, partly because of its cultivated open-endedness and obliqueness. Fung's own articles amusingly recount his own personal appropriability as artist persona, not only by GMHC and the Canadian cultural hierarchy (more of that later) but also by those dreaded institutions of the opportunist liberal academy, the "bomber crew" panel and the multicultural studies anthology. In these settings, he is drafted—indeed eagerly enlists—to wear the Asian hat today, and tomorrow the queer hat, the video hat, the leftist hat, occasionally the Canadian hat, and sometimes, within our pathological confederation up north, the Anglo hat. Fung is the ideal postcolonial panelist, more accessible and funnier than Trinh T. Minh-ha, queerer and arguably sexier, and certainly one-twentieth the cost.

Coming back to what is on the screen, as you have seen, or rather what the insider in me sees, first of all the camera's point of view wanders down the bathhouse corridor and who should pass with a characteristic cruise of the lens but hairy-chested wasp hunk Tim McCaskell, Fung's real-life partner of over twenty years. Then who should be in cubicle number 2 but pioneering Toronto video artist Colin Campbell reading, no doubt *Resolutions*, and who should be seen in cubicle number 4 by what is now revealed as the embodied look of our fetching protagonist, but Fung himself, together with second-generation video artist activist John Greyson, and McCaskell again, no doubt too busy plotting their next collaboration to engage in a hot foursome with the camera. No, we do not meet any other Toronto video art stalwarts in the next cubicle. But, as the protagonist passes an unwilling white presumed racist and a willing black leather man in their respective cubicles, to end up in the arms and anus of the tender and well-prepared stubble-chested South Asian man, it is clear that we are in a real place. We are in the middle of not only the incestuous universe of the Toronto art video community, not only a community education network staffed by activists from Toronto's queer Asian and anti-racist education organizations, but also a real Toronto sauna, the Spa on Maitland. The sense of networking and location for this fully dramatized piece of instructional porn is thus as strong as in any of Fung's realist, more conventional documentaries, all set in Toronto, dealing with political refugees, police racism, and consciousness raising by Asian gays and lesbians. So strong that the U.S. Asian sector of the intended audience must have felt a sense of bewildering dis-location, not only by the admonition in formal French to "enculer en sécurité," seemingly towering over the messages in Tagalog, Hindi, Chinese, and Vietnamese, but also by the specificity of this space. This is not a virtual panopticon or a porno set, but an earnest, brightly lit space that feels less like a sauna than a seminar room for a discourse of sobriety conducted by serious young community educators.

Nevertheless, let's think of the sauna as the setting for what we might call the "homoscape," borrowing Arjun Appadurai's figure of the "scape"—as in ethnoscape, mediascape, financescape, technoscape and ideoscape—scapes being "different streams or flows along which cultural material may be seen to be moving across national boundaries," which resonate through the perceived stabilities and localities of our everyday lives.[7] Shifting the notion's application from the ethnic diasporas to that of the queer diasporas, the Homintern, the queer global village, the homoscape is the transnational scene of sexual spaces, commodities, communications, and identity performance. The homoscape is shaped, as in Fung's tape, by flimsy partitions, corridors, half-opened doors and mirrors, and textured by the easily inflected (and disguised) accoutrements of baseball cap and towel, stubbled chest and leather harness, condom and lubricant. It is inhabited by the coded rituals of looking and cruising, the negotiations of consent, and ultimately of course the protocols of sexual exchange. In the space of the sauna, the scape is stable because it is so hermetic, scarcely disrupted by the performance of rejection, racist or otherwise, channeled down the corridor through the serial process of selection, and culminating in the mirrored space where not only sex is enacted, but where also, thanks to narrative conventions and expectations, the conjugal drive is resolved.

Figure 10. Video Frame from *Fighting Chance* (Richard Fung, 1990).

The romantic narrative of couple formation epitomized by this smiling, tender, safe coitus has in fact shaped all of Fung's queer Asian tapes. They may be so shaped obliquely, as in what I call the straight gay documentaries *Orientations* and *Fighting Chance*, in the sense that individualized talking heads are gradually transformed in the editing into talking couples. They may also be shaped by the absence and problematization of couple narratives, as in *Chinese Characters*, where the anxious and solitary cruisers, masturbators and life-narrators recount the stresses of couple formation but show its visual consummation only on its plane of impossibility, through the artifice of the video key. The last tape in my corpus, *Dirty Laundry*, is shaped directly by the narrativization of conjugality, with its romantic couple, not Pan-Asian this time, but Pan-Chinese. The consummation takes place, not across ethnic lines as in *Steam Clean*, but across class and cultural lines, namely, between the Chinese-speaking steward and the non-Chinese-speaking intellectual passenger on the Occidental Express. It thus provides a strong narrative impetus to that tape's documentary explorations of ethnic history undertaken in more experimental modes. With this couple, as in *Steam Clean*, Fung has literally accomplished his goal, announced repeatedly in his writings, of moving beyond "pulling apart" sexual discourses, to "constructing an alternative erotics . . . articulating counterhegemonic views of sexuality,"[8] constructing a utopian Pan-Asian sexual subject, sexuality, every bit as rhetorical and ideological as Marlon Riggs's *cri de coeur* and political manifesto, "Black men loving black men."

The non-Chinese-speaking protagonist is at once the most dramatized persona of Fung's oeuvre and the most documentary, an obvious stand-in for Fung the image maker and historical researcher, as he shifts through punning titles for a documentary on Chinese Canadian history. He is also engaged in family reconstruction as well, with the possibly queer ancestor, possibly complicit aunt, and fully complicit lesbian surrogate sister. This extended family is located by Fung elsewhere as the crux of difference:

> In the context of North American racism, families and communities can have particular significance for Asians in affirming identity. So while white gays and lesbians can avoid personalized homophobia by separating from their families or formative communities and still see themselves reflected in the society around them, their Asian counterparts do not always share this mobility and often find their sexual/emotional and racial/cultural identities in conflict.[9]

Despite the relatively conventional narrative construction, the hybrid scape of *Dirty Laundry* is a far cry from the unitary homoscape of the Spa on Maitland. Here in the spatial complexity of virtual train studio set and real nature landscape hurtling past, present space and historical space, documentary space of interview and dramatized space of reenactment, there is what Appadurai calls the "fundamental disjuncture" of scapes. The clash of homoscape with ethnoscape articulates more vividly than ever the identity disjuncture of queer and Asian that Fung has been so expressive in documenting since 1984. Such a disjuncture had

Figure 11. Video frame from *Chinese Characters* (Richard Fung, 1986).

Figure 12. Video frame from *Dirty Laundry* (Richard Fung, 1996).

been epitomized in the moments in *Chinese Characters,* where Asian gay men, anchored in the foreground ethnoscape, are videokeyed against the imaginary background of a white porno homoscape. In *Dirty Laundry,* in the corridors and discreet compartments of its expansive studio-constructed train, Chinese diasporas repeatedly come together with the queer nation. The lush canopy of the essentialized historical homeland that Fung had pastiched in *Chinese Characters,* before finally deconstructing it in his parental diptych, is here meticulously restored with great attention to historical and cultural authenticity. And now there is an intensified awareness of the secret corners and crevices of this homeland, where the homoscape bubbles through the surface, a probing of the ambiguities of its homosocial spaces. The video key is again deployed, setting fictive characters and documentary witnesses alike against rare archival still photos and newsreel shots from the Canadian Pacific Railway, which catch almost accidentally the Asian workers who built its tracks and tunnels. A decade after *Chinese Characters,* a more confident and diverse array of other devices is now engaged in creating this artistic confrontation of previously disjunctive scapes.

I would now like to approach the question of scapes and space in Fung's work from a slightly different angle, placing *Out of the Blue* alongside *Dirty Laundry* in our focus. Critical attention to postcolonial narrative and performative video alike has frequently underlined the uprootedness, the dislocatedness of space. For José Muñoz, a Hispanic American publishing in the British journal *Screen,* Fung's *Mother* and other tapes are situated in "contact zones," "locations of hybridity" such as the Asian community in Toronto, and are "uniquely concentrated on issues of place and displacement." That is, "Fung's place, in both Canada, Trinidad, gay male culture, documentary practice, ethnography, pornography, the Caribbean and Asian diasporas, is not quite fixed."[10] In similar vein, Appadurai can generalize, on behalf of a whole body of postcolonial theory, about "deterritorialization," "human motion," and the ethnoscape as the "landscape of persons who constitute the shifting world in which we live: tourists, immigrants, refugees, exiles, guest workers, and other moving groups and individuals." He argues in general that cultures are no longer nationally and spatially centered, but that locality is felt globally rather than spatially.[11]

These descriptions could of course not be more apt if we think of Fung's cast of migrants, both fictive and real, whose spatial coordinates are indeed "not quite fixed." Think of Fung's repeated return to a voyage or quest narrative structure as in *Steam Clean* or in his two autobiographical tapes where he literally travels to the homelands of his parents, mythical and historical; of his deft use of the video key for confronting two disparate spaces, for example, the closeted Chinese Canadian gay man keyed against the busy Toronto Chinatown street in *Chinese Characters;* of his reliance on abstract symbolic space shot in the studio, for example, the group of feet seen on a shower floor or the gestural play with petals in *Fighting Chance*, the masked and bannered choreography in *Orientations*, or in *Dirty Laundry* the devastating tableaus of the prison walls being scratched by the calligraphy of anonymous detainees.

But this reading of Fung's imagery cannot explain his work fully. For if we look at his oeuvre as a whole, and even within the works that we might call most migrant, the hybrid shifting space of the migrant is anchored in a strong sense of locality and rootedness. We find the situatedness of the social activist and the documentarist whose aesthetic integrates the postmodern and the non-referential performative in a strong realist and instrumentalist framework of localized agendas of city and nation. Fung recently casually mentioned to me the "pedagogical strategy" that had dictated the relatively conventional interview-based format for the tapes on refugee rights and police racism, *Safe Place* and *Out of the Blue*. These are his two most pragmatic works in terms of specific localized audiences and short-term community goals in the vivid urban environment in which he has worked for over twenty years (they are also his least "homocentric" works, but that may or may not be another story). Subtending the autobiographical searches for my father's village and my mother's place in his hybrid canonized work, then, is the assumption of "my place."

That may be why *Dirty Laundry*, parachuted into the pristine mountain landscape surrounding the Banff Centre for the Arts, where Sara Diamond produced the work during an artist's residency, has an exotic feel—not unlike Fung's father's China or his mother's Trinidad. *Laundry* seems unrelated to the Toronto urban rootedness of all of his other work. The western mountain setting coincided with his historical project investigating the presence of Chinese immigrants within Canadian history; the apparently generous budget and production facilities allowed full use of the scripting, dramatization, and archival compilation necessary for reconstituting the historical and geographical space of "the nation," an imagined community to be sure, but one attached firmly to the materiality of territory, economics, and a state apparatus. *Laundry* allowed further exploration of, in his words, "a country where the nation is always viewed as fragmentary and where Canadian nationalism has always been defensive and reactive."[12]

The image of transcontinental locomotion is a traditional Canadian cultural and historical motif, the Canadian Pacific Railway (CPR) construction of the 1880s allowing the British colonies to defensively and reactively cement their precarious confederation against American imperial designs. The railway set in motion a literary and cinematic procession over the next century of East-West rail passengers, claiming or reclaiming, discovering or rediscovering national trajectories, bonds, and fissures through moving over the land. Fung thus turns a nation-building myth inside-out into a subversive vehicle of alternative national history. Likewise the traditional trope of the immigrant staring in ambivalent horror and wonder at the sublime but treacherous natural space is now altered through the eyes of the Chinese laundress/prostitute/seamstress staring up at the Rockies, just as the image of the two men of color fishing in the northern lake in *Out of the Blue* matter-of-factly echoes and subverts a pastoral cliché of our national white settler mythology.

The *Screen* article on Fung's queer hybridity introduces the question of the national as an afterthought, after mistakenly identifying the artist as Chinese American and pointing the reader in footnotes to a couple of hook-ups between postcolonial theory and the Canadian entity. My intention is of course not to reclaim another internationally recognized artist for the Canadian pantheon à la William Shatner, but rather to point out how limiting it is to disregard crucial settings of Fung's practice, the urban locality and the national arena. These settings have seen Fung's canonization and co-optation in the name of multiculturalism, to be sure, but have also felt the benefits of his strong and influential interventions on cultural and social debates and policies.

In conclusion, Fung's brilliant marshalling of the ethnoscape and the homoscape, their overlaps and convergences, cannot properly be understood without reference to their rootedness in the metropolitan and the national, dynamic places not only of hybridity and dislocatedness, but also of rootedness, coalition, and intervention. We may want to make a postcolonial guru of Fung, and a panopticon of his work, but it also looks like old-fashioned activist documentary to me.

RICHARD FUNG: VIDEOGRAPHY

1984 *Orientations,* 56 min. Pioneering documentary on lesbian and gay Asians in Toronto.

1986 *Chinese Characters,* 22 min. Experimental documentary essay on Asian gays in the face of the North American white gay erotic mainstream.

1988 *The Way to My Father's Village,* 38 min. Autobiographical investigation of genealogy and "homeland."

1989 *Safe Place: A Videotape for Refugee Rights in Canada* (co-directed with Peter Steven), 32 min. Documentary of a spectrum of individual voices claiming the right to asylum.

1990 *My Mother's Place,* 50 min. Autobiographical exploration of Caribbean roots.

1990 *Steam Clean,* 3 min. A safe sex tape for Asian gay communities.

1990 *Fighting Chance,* 29 min. Documentary on people with HIV within North American gay Asian communities.

1991 *Out of the Blue,* 28 min. Documentary on resistance to racist abuse by police in Toronto.

1996 *Dirty Laundry,* 30 min. Experimental narrative documentary hybrid on the sexual undercurrents of Chinese Canadian history.

1998 *School Fag,* 17 min. Monologue by nineteen-year-old Shawn Fowler.

2000 *Sea in the Blood,* 26 min. Autobiographical exploration of illness (including thalassemia and HIV) and the artist's bonds with affected sister and lover.

NOTES

1. Author's note: I have maintained the somewhat informal, oral tone of this piece's first presentation in September 1997 at the Visible Evidence conference at Northwestern

University. I thank Richard Fung for his kind support of this project; Montreal's Oboro Gallery, whose invitation to curate their Fung retrospective in the fall of 1997 was its trigger; and Quebec's provincial Fonds pour la Formation des Chercheurs et l'Aide à la Recherche as well as Concordia University for their financial support of my research in sexual representation. The present chapter was first published in *A Festschrift in Honor of Erik Barnouw*, ed. Patricia Zimmermann and Ruth Bradley, *Wide Angle*, Vol. 20, No. 2 (April 1998): 164–75, and is reprinted here, with only minor updatings, with permission of Johns Hopkins University Press.

2. Sara Diamond, "Sex Lies with Videotape: Abbreviated Histories of Canadian Video Sex," in *Resolutions: Contemporary Video Practices*, ed. Michael Renov and Erika Suderburg (Minneapolis: University of Minnesota Press, 1996), 203.

3. In fact, Diamond, the distinguished Canadian video artist, *has* made this tape, or rather film, or rather participated in this film. *In Black and White* (Michael McGarry, 1979) is an undeservedly neglected short from the 1970s about gay toilet sex, captured by surveillance cameras, but that is another story.

4. Bill Nichols, "Performing Documentary," in *Blurred Boundaries: Questions of Meaning in Contemporary Culture* (Bloomington: Indiana University Press, 1994), 92–106.

5. Laura U. Marks, "Sexual Hybrids: From Oriental Exotic to Postcolonial Grotesque," *Parachute* 70 (1993): 23.

6. Peter Steven, "The Art of Calculated Risk: Richard Fung's *Dirty Laundry*," *POV* (Toronto), No. 29 (Spring 1996): 30–33.

7. Arjun Appadurai, *Modernity at Large: Cultural Dimensions of Globalization* (Minneapolis: University of Minnesota Press, 1996), 45–46.

8. Richard Fung, "Looking for my Penis: The Eroticized Asian in Gay Video Porn," in *How Do I Look: Queer Film and Video*, ed. Bad Object Choices (Seattle, Wash.: Bay Press, 1991), 165.

9. Richard Fung, "Center the Margins," in *Moving the Image: Independent Asian Pacific American Media Arts*, ed. Russell Leong (Los Angeles, Calif.: UCLA Asian American Studies Center, 1991), 64.

10. José Esteban Muñoz, "The Autoethnographic Performance: Reading Richard Fung's Queer Hybridity," *Screen*, Vol. 36, No. 2 (1995): 97–99. Reprinted in Muñoz, *Disidentifications: Queers of Color and the Performance of Politics* (Minneapolis: University of Minnesota Press, 1999), 77–92.

11. Appadurai, *Modernity at Large*, esp. 33, 182–99.

12. Fung, "Burdens of Representation, Burdens of Responsibility," in *Constructing Masculinity*, ed. Maurice Berger, Brian Wallis, and Simon Watson (New York and London: Routledge), 292.

"From the multitude of narratives . . . For another telling for another recitation": Constructing and Re-constructing *Dictee* and *Memory/all echo*

[Dictee] *draws from multiple codes of reference, which are carefully made to echo or correspond with each other.*

–Shu-Mei Shih

Film is put together as a multiplicity of movements. Each movement has its centre of gravity; and centers do move, they are not static.

–Trinh T. Minh-ha

In all of Theresa Hak Kyung Cha's creative and theoretical works, whether performed or written, she challenges the notion of a singular and fixed meaning that can be found in language, in words; she challenges the idea of a linear, unified narrative that can be read and interpreted in order to yield some essential "truth." Cha writes in her preface to *Apparatus,* her anthology of film theory, that one of her aims for the book as a whole is to lay open "the machinery that creates the impression of reality whose function, inherent in its very medium, is to conceal from its spectator the relationship of viewer/subject to the work being viewed" and in doing so, make the book exist as a "'plural text' making active the participating viewer/reader, making visible his or her position in the apparatus."[1] Accordingly, in making meaning from Cha's print text *Dictee* and from *Memory/all echo,* Yun-ah Hong's video work based on *Dictee,* I resist the urge to construct a singular narrative to "explain" these texts; instead, this project intends to build upon narrative, multiply the layers of narrative, being represented in the dialogue between Cha's printed text and Hong's cinematic text.

Theresa Hak Kyung Cha published her print text, *Dictee*, in 1982. Throughout the 1990s, this experimental prose/poetry/pictoral imagery text was extremely influential to writers and theorists;[2] it has been discussed in many critical essays by scholars of Asian American Studies and is generally recognized as part of the Asian American literary canon. Within its diverse sections, the text combines several themes: exploration into Korean as well as Korean American history, examination of Eastern and Western modes of discourse, and search for lost or displaced Korean memory(ies)/identity(ies) in newly formulated Korean American subjectivity(ies)/self(ves). In order to faithfully represent these disparate tensions and the interplay between them, Cha does not attempt to create one cohesive narrative of Korean history or of Korean American identity, but instead presents the pieces, the fragments, in their ruptured and discordant state: as Shu-Mei Shih notes, "We see in Cha's work . . . how borders both form and coalesce, contest and yield; hence there is no set 'in-between' or 'interstitial' location. As borders shift in time and space, so does the location of the subject. . . . Just as space is fragmented, so is time: occupying multiple places and shifting locations means being in different temporalities at the same time."[3]

In 1990, eight years after the publication of *Dictee*, Yunah Hong, a filmmaker born in Seoul, Korea, in 1962 and educated in both Korea and New York, adapted Cha's text into a video work entitled *Memory/all echo*, distributed by a New York-based company called Women Make Movies, Inc. Speaking of *Dictee*, Joan Retallack says that translation always involves cleaving, that "translation always proposes an original only to insist on a simultaneous departure from the original";[4] with *Memory/all echo*, Hong accomplishes a similar cleaving. In translating the text into video, she has attempted to make the viewing experience work "in both form and content in a way similar to the way *Dictee* was written."[5] Thus, Hong further fragments Cha's original fragmented narrative: she does not adhere to the order of presentation in Cha's text but instead excerpts and resequences sections; she translates some of the text into images while presenting some of the text as voice-over narration in the video; she adds sounds and the voices of several narrators; and she layers the work with intertextuality, alluding to omitted sections of *Dictee* and to other "texts" or "narratives" from Korean and American history and contemporary cultural discourse.

A good example of such intertextuality can be seen in examining the musical score that plays throughout the video. Hong chose to use the flute music of Korean-born Isang Yun as a sound narrative, connecting the sequences of the video with strains of music from his "Five Etudes for Flute." This selection of musical score contextualizes this American-produced video in a history of Korean diasporic art as well as a history of Korean political unrest; as noted in the CD jacket for Yun's "Cinq Etudes pour flute," "The circumstances of [Yun's] life have led him to compose in the name of humanity. . . . Having its origin in suffering, in tears, and in laughter, it is a protest against all forms of violence and cruelty."[6] Yun's protestations come directly out of his experiences fighting against many of Korea's oppressive political powers; because of his ongoing activity as a political dissident, he was imprisoned by the Japanese colonial forces as well as the South Korean Secret Service under the Park regime. In *Dictee*, Cha draws connections between the various uprisings against oppressive political systems; she unites student-led rebellions against the Park and Syngman Rhee regimes to the Tonghak uprisings against Japanese colonial rule. In *Memory/all echo*, then, Yun's music provides a similar connection between these types of resistance; his music, and the life experiences that prompted him to compose such music, audibly link the scenes of suffering and rebellion, of war, death, and eventual rebirth, which the video presents.

Yun's life and music also provide other interesting parallels with Cha and *Dictee*. On the one hand, his music is rooted in Korean culture and artistic traditions: "The use of flute is particularly significant. . . . The instrument plays an essential role in Korean music," and each etude "suggests an imaginary universe based on East Asian mythology."[7] In choosing to use this music throughout *Memory/all echo*, Hong places the actions of the video into a Korean epistemology, creating an Asian world-space within the film that serves as a setting in which Cha's theme of a return to a Korean sense of identity becomes enacted. Concomitantly, however, Yun's music embodies the interplay of Eastern and Western influences with which Cha also struggles in her work. As someone who studied music in Paris and East Berlin in the 1950s and who taught music composition at Berlin Arts College from 1970 to 1985, Yun continually attempts to negotiate tensions arising from "his background in Korean music and his mastery of the musical technique in the west."[8] Reminiscent of Cha's own negotiation in *Dictee* of her mastery of the Western languages of French and English interspersed with her desire to recoup her heritage and "mother tongue," Yun's music interspersed with scenes of Korea and sounds of the English language provides another lens through which to "read" the conflicting narratives of East and West at play in Hong's work.

Hong's video opens with the words "memory/all echo" imprinted onto a black screen. The title is taken from a line in a passage of *Dictee* from the Terpsichore/Choral Dance section, the narration of which will appear later in the film. The title foregrounds the issue of memory and the tensions between dismemberment (of Korea and Korean tradition/language/history) and re-membering that Cha also makes central in the original text.[9] The opening inscription of the words "memory/all echo" onto the black screen also perhaps has resonance with the frontispiece of *Dictee*, a black-and-white photograph of a wall inscribed with Korean script that translates as "Mother, I miss you, I want to go home to my native place."[10] This carving, found on a wall of a tunnel "leading to a castle being constructed during World War II to provide a safe haven for the Japanese Emperor" in Nagaro Prefecture, Matsushiro City, Japan, has been assumed to have been etched by one of the "hundreds of thousands of Korean peasants [who] were pressed into forced labor in Japanese mines and factories" in the 1930s and 1940s.[11] In its actual construction, this message disrupts the imposed linguistic homogeneity that Japan forced on Koreans by disallowing the use of the Korean language in any of its forms and mandating instead the use of the Japanese language; in its reproduction in Cha's text, this script (the only evidence of the Korean language found in the book) disrupts the tales of linguistic colonization that Cha relates. In the video, Hong reproduces the experience of linguistic homogenization in that no Korean script appears on the screen; however, we see many characters (the little girl speaks and calls, the mother pleads, the tutor scolds and demands, the brother asserts his right to die, the woman at the well talks with the little girl) speaking what is possibly the Korean language although these voices are muted, and instead of hearing the language, we hear a narrator's English voice-over, translating, interpreting, and speaking in place of the original language/speakers.

In *Dictee*, the theme of home and roots is prevalent and is significant to Cha's overall literary/cultural project. The "home" referred to in the frontispiece exceeds the signification of an actual house and family; it comes to signify a metaphorical type of home. As Eun Kyung Min notes, "(t)he Korean word translated as 'home' here designates not so much a family house as a native place of birth, a province, town, country, community of belonging."[12] Similarly, the word "mother" must also be read and interpreted metaphorically, not as a physical person or even a biological mother, but as a symbol of a type of origin or locus of cultural birth. The frontispiece introduces us to this idea, and it is a motif of doubling and tripling that extends throughout Cha's text; thus, whenever the text reads Mother, we must take it to mean mother on many levels: Cha's actual mother, her other Korean foremothers, Korea itself as a Motherland, Korean identity as a type of motherculture passed down through language, tradition, and memory, the parts of Cha herself that make up the Koreanness in her Korean American identity. In *Memory/all echo*, Hong builds on this theme by using the same narrator to tell the stories of Cha's personal history, her mother's history, Guan Soon's history, and so on; additionally, the characters of Cha as a young girl and her mother are played by the same actors (girl and woman) who will play the characters of the little girl and the woman at the well in the end of the video, playing with the idea of doublings and triplings, playing with the conflation of identity and signification.

After the title, the video begins with the first narrator speaking a series of lines taken from the middle of page 80 in the Melpomene/Tragedy section, the fourth section[13] of the nine in *Dictee*.

Text: taken from Melpomene/Tragedy p. 80	Cinematic Image:
The population standing before North standing before South for every bird that migrates North for Spring and South for Winter becomes a metaphor for the longing of return. Destination. Homeland.	birds flying map of Korea
No woman with child lifting sand bag barriers, all during the night for the battles to come.	Korean news footage of war: soldiers running, trenches, guns, and so on
There is no destination other than towards yet another refuge from yet another war. Many generations pass and many deceptions in the sequence in the chronology towards the destination.	refugees walking with belongings train carrying people/freight

The first narrator of the video, a narrator whose accent is suggestive of a native speaker of English,[14] speaks these words taken from a letter in *Dictee* addressed "Dear Mother" on 19 April from Seoul, Korea, written ostensibly by Cha to her mother in 1980 when Cha visited Korea. The spoken text instantly prepares the viewer to think about a journey, or the process of journeying, using the words "migration," "return," "destination," and "homeland." The words "migration" and "return," references to the concept of journeying as in moving, uprooting, and change as well as the concept of journeying as in a coming back, function to document several types of physical movement: the many Koreans including Cha's parents and grandparents who were forced to migrate from Korea to Manchuria in order to evade the hardship of Japanese colonization, the migration of Cha's family when she was twelve from Korea to the United States during the Korean political unrest of the 1960s, the movement of people and armies between North and South Korea, as well as Cha's journey back to Korea to visit her homeland and the land of her ancestry. The reference to journeying also serves as a metaphor for the symbolic journey Cha is making in her visit to Korea when writing the letter: the journey into her Korean roots and heritage, the journey into her past and into memory, the journey into herself that she makes not only in visiting Korea, but also in the creation of the text that will become *Dictee*. Thus, when we read "Destination. Homeland," this homeland is not just a physical space but also a metaphorical or mental place, a place inside the mind or the self where memory and heritage reside. The video pairs with this spoken text the image of migrating birds; significantly, this image of migration as a "natural" phenomenon performed by the birds contrasts the "unnatural" migrations, forced uprootings or movement because of political or economic necessity enacted by the people of Cha's text and Korean history, but also prompts the viewer to "read" the migration back into memory and heritage as natural and necessary.

As the text alludes to the migration of birds North and South, this initial passage also foregrounds the idea of a split in the self, a split between two worlds, identifiable in the two oppositional locations of "North" and "South." Literally representing the two counterposed homespaces of the migrating birds, the entities North and South (capitalized for their emphasis as proper nouns, distinct places rather than simply directional markers) also obviously allude to the divided Korea, North Korea versus South Korea, a sign of the war and strife separating Korea as well as highlighting the dismemberment, the non-unification, of Korea as a single "self." This analogy is furthered as the narrator goes on to speak of the battles to come (meaning the battles between North and South in what was labeled in the United States as "the Korean War") and as the screen projects battle footage. Moreover, as North and South Korea have been allying respectively with the Eastern communist systems and bodies of government as opposed to the Western "democratic" systems and bodies of government, North and South here can also stand for East and West, bringing us back to Cha herself as again interchangeable with Korea; as Cha exists as a divided self into her Eastern (Korean/Asian) roots in conjunction (or perhaps disjunction) with her Western (American/French) education, the theme of journey into self, or journeying back and forth between parts of self, is reemphasized.

In this short passage (textual passage combined with visual images passing across the screen), Hong introduces the viewer to the major themes Cha explores in *Dictee* and prepares us for a journey into memory, the past, the parts of the self, in search of a self that can wholly be called one's own, a self not imposed by others, outsiders: "Destination. Homeland." However, this notion of an attainable destination, of a unified self or safe homeland of one's own, is immediately destabilized. The narrator relates that the only destination is further migration, further attempts to seek refuge elsewhere from the war that seemingly does not end when or if physical fighting ends. Displacing a fixed destination will always be the search for this elusive destination; thus, many "deceptions" figure in place of a real place of refuge.

Text: from p. 81	Cinematic Images:
Our destination is fixed on the perpetual motion of search. Fixed in its perpetual exile. Here at my return in eighteen years, the war is not ended. We fight the same war. We are inside the same struggle seeking the same destination. We are	a handheld camera shows a road, people marching, demonstrating; sounds of people chanting; soldiers trying to suppress demonstration; tanks shooting

severed in Two by an abstract enemy an invisible
enemy under the title of liberators who have
conveniently named the severance, Civil
War. Cold War. Stalemate.

tear gas into crowds;
black/white chess/checkerboard

The second portion of this segment beginning "We are severed in two . . ." serves to indict the Western cultures, mainly the United States but also its allies, which have used and continue to use Korea as simply a pawn in their own political and military games/maneuvers, rather than allowing Korea to exist as an independent player. The abstract and invisible enemy is named as the cause for the divided and warring Korea, symbolized by the map flashed onto the screen directly before this section of narration begins, depicting the landmass of Korea as split into North Korea and South Korea with a De-Militarized Zone in the middle. Hong uses the image of the black-and-white, computer-generated chessboard as a static and sterile foil to the images of real-life people protesting war and dying; the language of war is thus abstracted into the symbolic language of the chessboard, into the unreal, non-personal conception of how the West views the Korean "conflict." The black-and-white checks also recall the Western philosophical discourse of binary opposition, where a Self is constructed as never separate from but always in opposition to some designated "Other,"[15] creating a conceptual stasis where subject positions are fixed, where no overlap can occur. Hong contrasts this type of discourse and epistemology with the fluid language of multiplicity and simultaneous narratives/positions that she and Cha seek to represent in their work.

Emblematic of Cha's printed text and Hong's cinematic text is a conflation of time between past and present, between the experiences of the daughter writing home in the "present" of the letter (1980) and the mother's past experiences told to the daughter sometime in the more distant past (and also between the experiences of the viewer learning all of this information in the present, which is the actual viewing time of the video). The narrator remarks that in the present, there are no women "lifting sand bag barriers" in defense against the siege of war as had happened some time in her mother's recollected past. This current retelling of the past, however, narrated and commented on in the present, compared to and contrasted with the narrator's present, and falling in between sections of her present discourse, serves to fuse past and present time into an inextricable intermingling. Furthermore, the sense of the unhinged nature of time is heightened with the next sequence of text.

Text: taken from p. 80

It is not 6. 25. Six twenty five. June 25th 1950.
Not today. Not this day. There are no bombs
as you had described them. They do not fall,
their shiny brown metallic backs like insects
one by one after another.

Cinematic Images:

Korean footage of war/trenches/
soldiers/tanks/bombs/ships firing
missiles

The narrator says that "(i)t is not . . . June 25th 1950" and that "(t)here are no bombs," yet the video disproves this statement as images of bombs and bombing are projected onto the screen, again conflating the experience of the "present" with the experience of the past. Although the official "Korean War" has ended, this sequence combining word and image suggests that a type of war is still waged in Korea or in the construction of a Korean/Korean-American identity; the past, then, does not remain contained in a sealed and distanced place, but instead creeps into and infects the present. In fact, the year 1980 (the present of the text's letter) when Cha visited Korea proved to be one of political unrest as the Kwanju Uprising occurred on 18 May.

One of the most interesting and illuminating sections of *Memory/all echo* is the "beach scene," a cinematic translation of an excerpt from the Calliope/Epic Poetry section of *Dictee*. In this sequence, Hong transforms the setting of seemingly a dream scene or hallucination experienced by Cha's mother in Manchuria, as related in the mother's diary. The passages from Cha's text reading "From the opposite direction, three women are approaching you. . . . You notice that they each carry a large dish of food. . . . The first one stands in front of you and asks you to eat from it"[16] as well as similar passages concerning the actions of the other two women[17] get transposed in the video onto a beach; through a combined zoom and unfocus, the view of the beach becomes obscured, and three women appear, as if coming out of the water, as the camera comes back into focus. These three women advance slowly up the length of the beach until they can be clearly seen by the viewer, and begin the offerings of their dishes. The camera centers on the first woman, an Asian woman, while the narrator speaks the corresponding text.

Text: taken from Epic Poetry p. 52	Cinematic Images:
Then was Jesus led up of the Spirit into the wilderness to be tempted of the devil.	first woman—Asian
2 And when he had fasted forty days and forty nights, he was afterward ahungered.	grapes on a white plate still frames of the Asian eyes
3 And when the tempter came to him, he said, If thou be the Son of God, command that these stones be made bread.	steeple clock reading 7:00 drawing of Jesus and devil with stones
4 But he answered and said it is written, Man shall not live by bread alone, but by every word that proceedeth out of the mouth of God.	painting of Jesus pointing to an angel and speaking close-up on Asian eyes

The video then stages the following line from Cha's text: "The second one offers you from her dish."[18] The camera focuses on the second woman, a black-skinned woman, who holds out a white plate with a miniature red plastic toy car on it.

Text: taken from pp. 52–53	Cinematic Images:
5 Then the devil taketh him up to the holy city, and setteth him on a pinnacle of the temple,	a modern city (American?)
6 And saith unto him, If thou be the Son of God, cast thyself down: for it is written, He shall give his angels charge concerning thee: and in their hand they shall bear thee up, lest at any time thou dash thy foot against a stone.	second woman offers her plate close-up on her eyes and nose a TV showing a red car driving in a ramp garage
7 Jesus said unto him It is written again, Thou shalt not tempt the Lord thy God.	rounding corners to Levels 2, 3, and up to the roof

The camera then moves to the third woman, a white-skinned woman who holds a book on her plate, apparently written in English, possibly intended to represent the Bible or some other book from Western literary or educational circles. Cha's text reads: "The third one says to you, 'then you must eat from mine' "; in the video we see and hear the third woman speak these words. The narrator then continues relating the following biblical passage taken from the pages of *Dictee*:

Text: taken from p. 53	Cinematic Images:
8 Again, the devil taketh him up into an exceeding high mountain, and showeth him all the kingdoms of the world, and the glory of them;	a collection of clips from American TV commercials for cruise lines, vacations;
9 And saith unto him, All these things will I give thee, if thou wilt fall down and worship me.	cruise ship; people walking on deck; servant carrying
10 Then saith Jesus unto him, Get thee hence, Satan: for it is written, Thou shalt worship the Lord thy God, and him only shalt thou serve.	plate; ship in harbor; couple walking on beach Gavin McLeod, captain
11 Then the devil leaveth him, and behold, angels came and ministered unto him.	on *Love Boat*, speaks to audience, selling the idea of cruising; waiter serving wine at table; ship; couple riding in horse-drawn carriage, waving; ship; woman being hugged, kissed; we see but do not hear the third woman speak her line again; close-up of the plate with book; book turns into grapes; grapes turn into little red car; steeple clock, showing same time: 7:00

Faithful to the printed text, the third woman speaks again, this time saying,"If you do not eat, you will become a cripple."[19]

With the images used in this section as accompaniments to the narrator's speech, Hong takes the most liberties with the text of *Dictee* but, in doing so, makes much of the social commentary on the West (and on the United States in particular) which Cha accounts for in other ways in her text. For example, later in the Epic Poetry section, Cha includes a textual selection that focuses on the Korean immigrant experience of naturalization as a U.S. citizen: "One day you raise the right hand and you are an American. . . . Somewhere someone has taken my identity and replaced it with their photograph. The other one. Their signature their seals. Their own image."[20] Cha also talks about her experience as a Korean American woman returning from her trip to Korea and having her identity as an American questioned, disbelieved; she doesn't "look like an American" and therefore the officials "have the right, no matter what rank, however low their function they have the authority"[21] to question and search her. Finally, Cha describes the process of Americanization, naturalization, assimilation as "smell[ing] filtered edited through progress and westernization,"[22] critiquing the imposed identity transmutations that necessarily accompany the process of becoming American. These textual sections do not appear at all as spoken text in *Memory/all echo*; instead, as enacted in the beach sequence, Hong provides us with the implications suggested by this discourse: she allows the viewer to see the traps and pitfalls of Westernization and the always "othering" experience of the East, of the Korean part of the self, which comes from accepting oneself as American.

As previously noted, the textual content of the scenes depicted are taken from the section in *Dictee* where Cha seems to be reading and talking about her mother's diary; exiled in Manchuria, teaching at a school where she knows no one and is forbidden to speak Korean or practice any Korean traditions, her mother contracts a fever and appears to have a dream in which she is "going somewhere" and yet there is an endless stillness as if she is really going nowhere.[23] In the video, Hong places this scene on a beach where waves crash endlessly but of course go nowhere except in and out. Instead, motion is produced from the fade-out and fade-in, revealing the appearance of the women. It is unclear whether this beach is meant to represent a beach in Korea or perhaps a beach in California, but it seems to double as both in that it is some land, either Eastern or Western, which is separated from the other by this ocean. The three women seem to walk out of the ocean, up the length of the beach, and face the camera/viewer; the viewer seems to now occupy the role of the mother being talked about or of one of the video's narrators whose experience this might be: as the women look and speak and offer their goods directly into the camera, the viewer occupies the position of recipient. Here, the experiences of the mother whose diaries this sequence comes from, the narrator who reads and relates this, and, now, the viewer who experiences it vicariously, become conflated.

The three women are dressed in pristine white nurses' uniforms, seeming to reference Red Cross missionaries; this is significant in that Korea has been the site of much proselytizing, of attempted "colonization" by Western religions as well as by Western political organizations, and the Red Cross embodies the intersection of these two entities. This section and its references to religious missionary activity also recall early sections of *Dictee* that talk about the forced learning of the language of the catechism that Cha encountered in Catholic school in California. Additionally as Lisa Lowe notes, the French Catholicism section of *Dictee* "also alludes to the long history of French Catholic missionary activity in Korea that dates from the early 19th century"[24] linking Hong's Red Cross missionaries/nurses to Cha's Californian Catholic nuns.[25] The analogy between Korean missionary experiences and American Catholic school experiences is appropriately applied to this section of the video as its narration deals directly with a textual source from the Bible, further complicating the conflation of "shores" between the Korean and American shores; potentially, the video suggests that this type of religious colonization and oppression is transoceanic.

Whether on the shores of Korea or California, this scene represents the many discursive and epistemological systems offered to, or forced upon, the Korean or Korean American subject by the institutions of the West. The experience of the women walking up the beach, and their subsequent roles played in this scene, illustrates the disparate constructions of subjectivity imposed by Western dominant culture upon white-skinned, black-skinned, and Asian persons, respectively. For example, when the women walk toward us, the black-skinned woman's face remains in shadow, and we cannot make out any of her features, only her blackness; also, in the part she plays in this scene, she acts the role of the beguiling seducer, offering her plate to us with a sly smile, effectively constructing her as a sexualized subject (object). Similarly, the Asian woman offers grapes on her plate, a food associated in Western literary tropes as that which would be offered to a master by a slave girl or to a woman by a man in an act of sexual seduction. This sexualizing of the Asian subject (object) is reinforced by the association of her with the word "tempter": when the narrator speaks this word, the camera focuses in on her Asian-shaped eyes, thus exoticizing her sexuality as well. Moreover, neither the Asian woman nor the black-skinned woman is granted voice; they exist only as bodies that we can see and as entities that offer us various pleasures. In contrast, the blond-haired, blue-eyed, white-skinned woman is granted voice and issues an ultimatum: "If you do not eat, you will become a cripple." Her voice carries the weight of some authority; even if it is not her own authority and is simply the authority of the discursive system that produces her (she holds out a book), she speaks assertively and with some power behind her words, effectively symbolizing her status as a white woman in relation to the other two women as positioned in Western culture.

As this section of the video depicts the deceptive lures yet also the coercive oppressiveness of the languages of colonization and Americanization, it seems especially significant in that it seems to represent the notions of forced feeding of language and ideology that Cha represents in *Dictee* through her dictation sections and her focus on the workings of language, the mouth, and diction. Hong coalesces these ideas into a symbolic and imagistic representation of the workings of language and the discursive ideology we consume as we enter into and participate in any language system; this compulsory participation in language is what the viewer experiences in participating in the act of viewing itself and ingesting these images offered to us.

In this section, Hong not only critiques the Western language of religion, but also other languages that espouse a Western ideology: languages of capitalism, consumerism, global tourism, orientalism, technology, advertising, and Western "Words," whether religious doctrine, Western philosophy, or simply the book learning that is the product of Western education. The temptation scene opens with the image of a steeple clock flashed onto the screen with the hands of the clock fixed on seven o'clock; later in the sequence, the clock is flashed onto the screen again, and the hands remain unmoved. This repeated image references a conception of time, of Time, that is fixed and immutable and that is contrasted to the conflations and bending of time that Hong plays with throughout the video; this strategy recalls the contrasting of the Western calendar/system of measuring the passage of time to the Eastern calendar/system that Cha plays with in her text. The arbitrariness of the notion of time is thus highlighted, called to our attention. The authority to designate time, and to unnaturally fix time, is thus debunked as simply another language/tool of power wielded by Western culture over the rest of the world.

Additionally, the video challenges the cultural currency of advertising as a language utilized by the dominant culture to indoctrinate viewers/consumers in its epistemological systems.[26] The advertising clips used by Hong reveal much of the underlying assumptions about what is considered to be desirable in American culture, what it means to be a "real" American. First, the clips expose the inherent materialism and consumerism that thrives in American culture and is promulgated by the media; the allure of acquiring things is shown, for example, in the ads for the shiny red new car that will take you to great heights, presumably heights in social status as the car will represent upward class mobility (although this assumption is also mocked in the video as the car goes up and up but never really leaves the parking garage). Ideal American identity is thus articulated in terms of class status, which in turn is evidenced by the acquisition of material things; the desired vacations on cruise ships that can allow one to explore the far regions of the world are also evidence of the ascendance into the middle- and upper-class strata; the servants, waiters, and drivers seen in the clips are not those who have earned the freedom/privilege/money to travel. Further, the clips expose the heteronormativity that accompanies ideal American identity while also playing with the media's obsession with the Hollywood notions of romance permeating our discourse concerning relationships between the sexes; the repetition of couples walking, couples driving, couples expressing their affection, mocks (in its oversaturation) this incessant language of heterosexuality and ideal romantic love rampant in the American media. This critique also echoes Cha's own explorations in *Dictee* into gender dynamics and the traditional role of women in heterosexual and marriage relations.[27]

Similarly, in this section, Hong lays bare the current global economic system and critiques the inherent orientalism employed by the West in economic transactions as well as overall worldview. The devil perches himself on top of the highest mountain in the world; this mountain viewpoint is shown to represent the U.S. viewpoint/worldview where it has placed itself in the highest position in the hierarchy of nations composing this world and from where it can look down at everyone else. The vast shores of the world that the devil shows us from this mountain are those that are symbolically (as well as sometimes literally) controlled by the West; these shores are shown by U.S. advertising (as illustrated on the television screen we view in this sequence as well as the clips from television advertisements) as playgrounds to be enjoyed and toured by U.S. vacationers.[28] The shores exist for this purpose only and for the pleasure of the Western tourists; these images recall the way in which "exotic" cultures are perceived not as equal or as even valid cultures in their own right, but are seen to exist merely in relation to the West, for the enjoyment of the West, as objects to admire or amuse oneself with. This montage of images also recalls the exploitation of the "exotic" peoples not only for the tourism industries, and not only by governmental systems, but also by multinational corporations that use Asian people as cheap labor but deny them basic human rights and the employee benefits mandated to workers in the West. The discourses of oppression, therefore, do not only issue from the mouths of people and are not only forced into the mouths of people, as explicated in Cha's text with her emphasis on dictation and language acquisition; Hong's images bare (also bear) the many other cultural languages (religion, art, the Word of the Bible or the Words of Western philosophy and education, the rhetoric of media and advertising, consumerism, capitalism, the language of economics and the global marketplace, orientalism, etc.) which also serve to create an oppressive and silencing cultural hierarchy.

Finally, this scene highlights the inherent conundrum faced by people who immigrate into a Western language and Western cultural system: how can you negotiate these cultural discourses working upon you while still maintaining your original cultural identity or even an autonomous cultural identity? The white-skinned woman parrots the voice of dominant culture in explaining that "if you do not eat, you will become a cripple"; if you do not accept the dominant discourse into your mouth/identity, you will not be able to function effectively as a member of Western society. The woman's words suggest that if you do not partake of cultural assimilation, you will be crippled by your "past" cultural identity, that you will lack or be deficient in the Western knowledges of language and differences in world-view, that the inability to blend in and acquire new traditions and cultural rituals will inhibit your maneuverability within the new social environment.

Hong chooses to end *Memory/all echo* with a representation of a story told in the final section of *Dictee*: Polymnia/Sacred Poetry. A Korean-accented[29] narrator, Hong's third of three narrators in the video, plays the role of the storyteller in these final segments.

Text: taken from Polymnia/Sacred poetry p. 167	Cinematic images:
She remembered that she had once drank from this well. A young woman was dipping into the well all alone and filling two jars that stood beside her. She remembered that she had walked very far. It had been a good distance to the village well. It was summer. The sun	image of well, from outside then inside, water within the walls of the well; woman sitting next to well, filling large black jars with water; girl running down a path through

Figure 13. *Memory/all echo* (Yunah Hong, 1990).

became brighter at an earlier hour, the
temperature soaring quickly, almost at once.

trees, spots of sunlight and
shadows of trees on ground

Flute music then plays as the girl walks slowly across a courtyard, stands next to the well, and watches the woman who continues to ladle water into the jars. The girl sits, obviously exhausted as her eyes drop momentarily; when they open, the woman looks at her directly for the first time. Walking to the woman, the girl drinks the water the woman offers. Both smile and sit together, as the narration resumes:

Text: taken from p. 169

Cinematic images:

The young woman asked her what she was doing
so far away from home. The child answered
simply that she was on her way home from
the neighboring village to take back remedies for
her mother who was very ill. She had been walking
from daybreak and although she did not want
to stop, she was very tired and thirsty, so she
had come to the well.

image of the woman and girl,
sitting and talking together;
girl running along dirt path
surrounded by trees, goes into a
house, close-up of stove with
something cooking; girl goes into
another courtyard area; again we
see her come to the well; girl and
woman talking together

After this, flute music again plays as the girl opens the package she has been carrying, and the woman helps her to rewrap it along with the cup she has drunk from at the well. In this story[30] used by Cha and Hong, a young girl travels to a neighboring village to obtain medicinal remedies for her ailing mother and stops at a well in order to revive herself as well, having become fatigued from her journey. Critics and readers of *Dictee* have identified this story with the Demeter and Persephone myth, seeing the girl's journey to heal her ill mother as the culmination of the theme of rebirth of all that had been destroyed, re-memberment of all that had been dismembered: after waiting for nine days, the return of Persephone from Hades to her mother "brings the promise of regeneration of the earth and restoration of spring."[31] However, Shu-Mei Shih notes that this tale also has roots in Korean mythology and sacred ritual:[32] "The Korean myth of princess Pali (*Pali Kongju*) . . . tells of the princess's search for remedies for her ill mother and her acquisition of nine pockets of medicines from the well keeper."[33] Thus, Hong reproduces Cha's fusion of classical Greek mythology with traditional Korean mythology, fusing the Western and Eastern facets of her identity, the mother and daughter symbolizing not just two specific people and not just a personal history but instead signifying the larger concepts involved in a return to one's roots and a healing of one's severed identity.

This well from the tale, then, becomes the well of memory in that it represents the destination for the journey of the little girl (at once Cha, at once a symbol of Korea and Korean identity) and in that its restorative powers return Cha's narrator's/character's history, tradition, and language of mythology to her. The well is also coded in the print text as symbolic of a receptacle for memory, for the language and experience of the Korean people, a place that contains the voices of the Korean people and the place where all their memories echo:

Text: from Terpischore/Choral Dance p. 162	Cinematic Images:
All rise. At once. One by one. Voices absorbed into the bowl of sound. Rise voices shifting upwards circ-ling the bowl's hollow. In deep metal voice spiraling upwards to pools no visible light lighter no audible higher quicken shiver the air in pool's waves to raise all else where all memory all echo	people walking in snow with bundles (refugees?); demonstrators running as tear gas is fired at them; black-and-white footage of man speaking to people, megaphone, man directing traffic; people crossing a street, trains, cars driving

In the video, this section directly precedes the section illustrating the well myth; additionally, the image of the inside of the well, its stone structure and its pool of water, is presented on the screen just prior to the speaking of this text, making the images of the well frame these images of travel-ing into Korean history/memory. Thus, Hong solidifies the connection between the well that the girl drinks from and a well of memory, of restoration of "mother" voices, and of echoes of past identity; visiting the well, drinking from the well, and gaining healing medicines from the well, the girl travels into her self and into her collective Korean identity/ history and attempts to heal the breaks and fissures.

Coming directly prior to the well scene, this segment is also instrumental in contrasting finally the discourse of the West that Cha/Hong hope to expose as a discourse that breeds the suppression of non-conformist, non-Westernized identity with the discourse of memory that Cha/Hong hope to pose as recuperative of past, cultural voice, cul-tural identity. Accordingly, Hong's narrator opens this section with the words "All rise" from Cha's text; in the video, the narrator's emphasis on these two words recalls their formal usage in Western discourse as one might hear in a courtroom, commanding people to rise in deference to the figure of authority whose words represent the law of the state as well as "justice"; one also might see these words written or hear them spoken in a church, again to show deference to an authority figure such as a priest in conjunction with raising voices in prayer to the higher authority of God. However, Hong plays with these notions and with the standard Western connotations of this phrase by pairing the speaking of these words with images of war, revolt, armed fighters, Korean resisters. Here, then, the "all rise" serves as an injunction for political dissenters to rise up in arms against their oppressors, partially the Western-instituted and -supported government systems. This serves to destabilize the power sometimes wielded by these words themselves but also to undercut the authority systems they speak for. In place of this dismantled discourse, the discourse of memory, symbolized in the well, can begin to reconstruct the girl's/Cha's/Korean and Korean American cultural identity and knowing/representation of oneself. Finally, with the repetition of the title here, the video circles around on itself and brings the viewer back to the beginning, back to the idea of a journey through memory toward some desired destination.

After drinking from the well and gaining the medicine for her mother, the girl returns to her village and to her mother's house:

Text: from Polymnia/Sacred Poetry p. 170	Cinematic Images:
Already the sun was in the west and she saw her village coming into view. As she came nearer to the house she became aware of the weight of the bundles and the warmth in her palms where she had held them. Through the paper screen door, dusk had entered and the shadow of a small candle was flickering.	girl running on path through trees, shadows on ground from trees and sunlight; girl stops, looks, continues running; goes into the entrance to the house grounds, through an opening in fence surrounded by trees and vegetation; she enters into sunlit area from shadowed wooded area

The girl thus returns to her homespace as seemingly revived, and also in order to revive her mother, her motherland cultural identification. The weight of her revived cultural awareness infuses her consciousness, and the negotiation of her disparate selves is not minimized, but neither is it represented as overbearing. The setting reveals a combination of the sun of the West and the dusk of her village, symbolizing the two facets of the girl's identity that come together in this final scene. Finally, the image of the small candle flickering leaves the viewer with a sense of hope of the continuation of life with renewed vigor.

In *Dictee*, the text moves on from this space/idea to show us the aftereffects of this cultural revisiting; Cha's narrator recrosses the ocean, returning to the United States (suggested as her final narrator addresses her mother in the American colloquial appellation of "mom"). The final scene of *Dictee* portrays this child asking her mother to lift her up to see out of the window of her house; ostensibly, she (a child who doubles for the girl who visited and drank from the well) has reentered the house of her cultural origins and asks to see out the window, to see her world from within her new memory/identification, to see her world from a new lens (her eyes/the window of her house). Hong chooses not to include this passage, instead ending *Memory/all echo* with the image of the girl entering the house; however, recalling the title, it seems like this change in worldview is implied. The journey into memory prompts a change in worldview in that memory no longer exists as something sealed in the past, untouchable, but now functions as an echo: the past is no longer wholly lost, but instead informs the present; the past comes back through memory and reverberates in the present as a constant echo.

NOTES

1. Theresa Hak Kyung Cha, ed., *Apparatus: cinematographic apparatus: selected writings* (New York: Tanam, 1980), preface.

2. Some renowned examples of work following *Dictee* include Elaine Kim and Norma Alarcon's collection of critical essays *Writing Self Writing Nation* and Walter Lew's *DIKTEE*, yet many other creative and critical works continue to be produced in Cha's legacy.

3. Shu-Mei Shih, "Nationalism and Korean American Women's Writing: Theresa Hak Kyung Cha's *Dictee*," in *Speaking the Other Self: American Women Writers*, ed. Reesman Jeanne Campbell (Athens: University of Georgia Press, 1997), 146.

4. Joan Retallack, "RE: THINKING: LITERARY: FEMINISM: (three essays onto shaky ground)," in *Feminist Measures: Soundings in Poetry and Theory*, ed. Lynne Keller and Cristanne Miller (Ann Arbor: University of Michigan Press, 1994), 54.

5. From a personal email interview with Hong; she notes further that she views *Dictee* as a "conceptual work" and that she approached the making of *Memory/all echo* as attempting to construct a "visual montage of *Dictee*."

6. Paul Mefano, *Isang Yun: Garak/5 etudes pour flute/Octour/Concerto pour flute et Orchestre* (Paris: Adda, 1990), text from CD jacket.

7. Ibid.

8. Ibid.

9. Shu-Mei Shih, for example, remarks on the nature of the bulk of the text with its references to war, death, and mutilation, describing it as a "text profuse with dismemberment" ("Nationalism and Korean American Women's Writing," 149) but later observes how, through the themes of memory and regeneration, the book "articulates a sense of salvation and transcendence of the darkness, dismemberment, and tragedy" (157). This theme is one that Hong capitalizes on and makes the central focus of her narrative as well as the source of the video's cohesiveness/continuity (despite the fragmentation of its parts).

10. This is how Elaine Kim (in her essay from *Writing Self Writing Nation*) translates the hangul script on the frontispiece (10), although other critics have translated the last line as "I want to go back to my home" or "my homespace." This carving has been assumed to have been etched by a Korean worker during the 1930s or 1940s, but Kim notes that it may in fact have been done by a resister at a later time; the implication of the message the carving sends, I think, is not diminished regardless.

11. Elaine Kim, "Poised on the In-between: A Korean American's Reflections on Theresa Hak Kyung Cha's *Dictee*." *Writing Self Writing Nation*, ed. Elaine Kim and Norma Alarcon (Berkeley, Calif.: Third Woman, 1994), 10.

12. Eun Kyung Min, "Regarding the Figure of Dictation in Theresa Hak Kyung Cha's *Dictee*," in *Other Sisterhoods: Literary Theory and U.S. Women of Color*, ed. Sandra Kumamoto Stanley (Chicago: University of Illinois Press, 1998), 314.

13. It may be interesting to note here that literary/cultural critic Michael Stephens cites the importance of the number 4 in Korean tradition as the number associated with death in that this section features the themes of the split of Korea during the Korean War as well as the killing of students and other political activists in various uprisings.

14. In a personal interview, Hong has reflected on her choice of narrators by saying, "I employed three female narrators in order to recreate the distinctive sensibilities found in

the experimental writings of DICTEE. As non-native speakers of English these three women maintain the contradictions explored in DICTEE and M/AE, that of melding a native identity with an adopted language."

15. The use of black and white as binary oppositions here also references the undertones of a racial hierarchy at play in the constructions of Self and Other in Western culture.

16. In *Dictee*, the "you" here is the mother: theoretically, the narrator (Cha) is reading her mother's diary and directing her speech (which relates her mother's experience or her reading of this experience) to the absent mother, the mother in her thoughts, as well as to the reader simultaneously.

17. Theresa Hak Kyung Cha, *Dictee* (New York: Tanam, 1982), 52, 53.

18. Ibid., 52.

19. Ibid., 53.

20. Ibid., 56.

21. Ibid., 57.

22. Ibid., 57.

23. Ibid., 50.

24. Lisa Lowe, *Immigrant Acts: On Asian American Cultural Politics* (Durham, N.C.: Duke University Press, 1996), 132.

25. This is also related to the picture we see earlier in the film of the Yihwa Girl's school; Shu-Mei Shih explains that this school, located in Seoul, where Guan Soon was educated, was "run by American missionaries" ("Nationalism and Korean American Women's Writing," 158).

26. Although this critique of the imposed and sometimes coercive language of advertising and media is not addressed specifically in *Dictee*, this motif is synchronous with Cha's work; as Susan Wolf explains in her article "Recalling Telling Retelling" in *Afterimage* (Summer 1986), "At the time of her death, [Cha] was working on . . . an aesthetically executed critique of advertising." Clearly, Hong is then not deviating from Cha's work, but instead carrying it to its logical conclusions.

27. This critique of gender norms and women's traditional roles can be seen in the Erato/Love Poetry section of Cha's text, a significant portion of which Hong adapts and deals with elsewhere in the film.

28. This theme also recalls a dominant American approach to cultural difference, a distinctly American notion of "multiculturalism" as internal tourism of "other" cultures.

29. It seems important to observe that the Korean myth is told by a narrator who has an Asian accent, but this narrator's struggle with articulating her story in the English language also seems extremely significant; the narrator speaks fluent English, but sometimes her diction is stilted or her words are hard to understand, marking her linguistically as a nonnative speaker, as "other" in terms of linguistic outsiderness. Her difficulties in translation and in mastering the English language in her narration connote the struggles with pronunciation and sometimes incorrect translations found in the dictation sections of Cha's text. Perhaps this is one of Hong's strategies for translating this section of the text into her video.

30. It should be noted here that much of Cha's original text does not get spoken by the narrator in this sequence but instead gets translated into image and actions performed by the characters on the screen; for example, the text telling about the girl walking to the well, sitting down, watching the woman, closing her eyes, and so forth, is not spoken in the video, but the viewer watches these actions being played out on the screen.

31. Shih, "Nationalism and Korean American Women's Writing," 156.

32. Michael Stephens, "Theresa Hak Kyung Cha," in *The Dramaturgy of Style: Voice in Short Fiction* (Carbondale: Southern Illinois Press, 1986), also notes that "Koreans are shamanistic first, and the number nine has mystical associations going back to an ancient text entitled *Nine Cloud Dream*" (199), and the woman at the well could almost be "a *moodong* (a shaman)" (210). This connection between this scene and shaman ritual would be also consistent with the flute music that dominates the sound space of this entire segment

as the flute music is said to be often found in Korean "religious ceremonies such as the sham-man" (Mefano, Isang Yun CD jacket). Further, Shu-Mei Shih observes that the myth of Princess Pali is "most often evoked in Korean shammanistic rituals for the dead" ("Nationalism and Korean American Women's Writing," 157).

33. Shih, "Nationalism and Korean American Women's Writing," 156.

Mark Chiang

Coming Out into the Global System: Postmodern Patriarchies and Transnational Sexualities in *The Wedding Banquet*

As a film that depicts diasporic Chinese communities in the United States, *The Wedding Banquet* offers one popular mapping of the trajectory of Asian and Asian American sexuality in the global system. Made on a $750,000 budget (minuscule for a major theatrical release), it became the highest-grossing film in Taiwan, with great success in the United States and other international markets. Surpassing *Jurassic Park* as the film with the highest profit ratio in 1993, it catapulted director Ang Lee to international fame. Lee, whose parents are part of the Chinese émigré population of 1949, is a native of Taiwan who went to college and film school in the United States. *The Wedding Banquet* was shot on location in the United States with an American production company, but funding, cast, and crew came from both sides of the Pacific.

Although the film gives a positive depiction of its gay protagonist, Gao Wai Tung—a Taiwanese businessman living in New York City with Simon, his white lover—its focus on reconciling the conflicts between the competing demands of sexuality and ethnic identity can hardly be regarded as much more than mildly progressive. Nevertheless, the intent of the reading here is not simply to cast judgment on the degree to which the film subverts or capitulates to the "dominant ideology." Rather, this essay seeks to raise the question of context, by asking how, or where, we locate such transnational cultural productions in the first place, a necessary precondition for any attempt at evaluation.

The film opens a space for gay people in homophobic Asian and American communities, but, from a slightly different perspective, it also seems to promote the co-optation of the gay male in the reconstruction of Asian patriarchy. This agenda is, in fact, announced quite openly by the filmmakers. James Schamus, who collaborated with Lee on all three of his films, remarks that "if the [three films] could be said to have a common theme, it is the question of the father, of the role of the patriarch in a world where the patriarchy is under justifiable fire. In one way, *The Wedding Banquet* is very much about making the institution of fatherhood safe for the contemporary world" (xi–xii). Thus *The Wedding Banquet* offers a useful test-case for investigating "how patriarchies are recast in diasporic conditions of postmodernity," in the words of Caren Kaplan and Inderpal Grewal, and my analysis seeks to respond to their call for a transnational feminist cultural studies: "What we need are critical practices that link our understanding of postmodernity, global economic structures, problematics of nationalism, issues of race and imperialism, critiques of global feminism, and emergent patriarchies" ("Transnational Feminist Cultural Studies," 439).[1]

My argument thus proceeds in two directions. First, I demonstrate that the complex entanglements of sexual and ethnic identity in *The Wedding Banquet* cannot be read solely from within the frameworks of national culture, either Chinese or American, but must be read across them in a transnational analysis that attends simultaneously to the local and global. Second, I register some of the problems that accompany the globalization of sexuality and identity. In particular, I critique certain queer studies formulations of a global gay identity politics, which generalize the challenge that homosexuality poses to national constructions of identity in the global system without fully accounting for the radically different valences of sexuality in relation to transnational capital and postmodernity. My reading centers on two key moments in the film: (1) the ill-fated wedding banquet itself, which epitomizes the crisis of the nation-state, whose cause and solution are both encapsulated in (2) the consolidation of the reconfigured family unit at the end of the film. This closure operates not at the level of national culture and identity, but at the level of the global system. In these terms, *The Wedding Banquet* tells us a great deal about the vicissitudes of national/ethnic identity in the era of postmodernity and about the function sexuality serves in mediating between modernity and postmodernity, the nation and transnational capital.

The film opens with Wai Tung's parents pestering him from Taiwan (via transpacific audiocassette) to get married and raise a family. Meanwhile, Wai Tung, who owns some property, is having trouble collecting rent from Wei Wei, a poor Chinese woman artist who is trying to evade the Immigration and Naturalization Service (INS). Simon suggests to Wai Tung that he marry Wei Wei in order to placate his parents, a marriage that will also net Wei Wei a green card and Wai Tung a tax break in the bargain. Complications predictably ensue, however, when Wai Tung's parents immediately fly to New York for the wedding of their only son.

Simon moves out so that Wei Wei can move in, and the reluctant couple try to feign intimacy for the parents. Ultimately, everything works out: Wai Tung succumbs to Wei Wei's charms on their wedding night and produces a son, satisfying his parents' desire for grandchildren, and he retains his relationship with Simon, who manages to come to an understanding, of sorts, with Wai Tung's father.

The international success of *The Wedding Banquet* as a traveling text offers some indication of its capacity to signify in multiple national contexts. The processes of translation and resignification activated by the text not only cross cultural and national boundaries, they also appeal to an emergent global/transnational culture that achieves concrete form in the growing cohesion of the global system. One hypothesis that I advance is that the success of independent (that is, non-Hollywood) films in the international arthouse and film festival circuit is most often tied to that text's proximity to the culture and values of the transnational capitalist class that comprises the main audience for these venues. I suggest, therefore, that *The Wedding Banquet* is a transnational allegory, insofar as it ultimately charts the Chinese diaspora's coalescence in the global system as the agents of transnational capital.

My analysis centers on Wai Tung's family, the Gaos, as members of one segment of what Leslie Sklair calls the transnational capitalist class, which is transnational insofar as its members "tend to have global rather than local perspectives" (71).[2] This global perspective finds its visual correlate in the film's aesthetic, its mise-en-scène, the most conspicuous quality of which is a kind of generic blankness. It is this generic and formulaic quality of the film that, apart from its main theme of homosexuality, renders the rest of the film nearly transparent. The primary instance of this evaporation of materiality in the film's cinematography is surely the extent to which Manhattan is resolutely stripped of all its iconic distinctiveness, converting it into the simulacrum of urban space in any number of metropolitan centers around the globe. Fredric Jameson describes this process as a "kind of representational laundering of ideologically marked contents," in which all signs of the socioeconomic system or of ideological struggle must be excised to avoid interference with the consumption of the film product (*Geopolitical Aesthetic*, 119).[3]

This characteristic of the mise-en-scène is indicative of the film's seemingly superficial nature, but it seems to me that it is precisely this very generic transparency that proves most indexical of its transnational origins. The transparency of *The Wedding Banquet* stems from its peculiarly deterritorialized signifiers. Therefore, the generic quality of its narrative is in some sense a consequence of the abstraction of the thematic content from its sociohistorical location in specific material contexts. The space that achieves material visibility in the film, in other words, corresponds to the generalized cosmopolitan space constructed by transnational capital and inhabited by the transnational capitalist class. In order to read a text like *The Wedding Banquet*, then, we must rematerialize or reterritorialize its signs, by restoring to them some of their concrete ideological and historical density, a project that this essay returns to in its conclusion.[4]

The plot of *The Wedding Banquet* is set in motion by the tension between Wai Tung's sexual desires and his father's nationalist desires. This antagonism is mediated through the trope of the closet and its attendant narratives of coming out. Much of the work in queer studies, however, has been oriented toward the critique of gay identity politics, the closet, and coming out, as being defined by bourgeois constructions of identity. This critique has been extended in the work of lesbian and gay scholars in Asian American Studies. If coming out is tangled in epistemological knots, as Diana Fuss has elaborated (1–10), these entanglements are multiplied by the geometrical complications of race and ethnicity. David Eng remarks that "coming out for Asian gays involves many irreconcilable choices between aligning oneself with a predominantly white gay community often tainted by overt racism or an ethnic community often marked by cultural homophobia" (9).[5] Eng concludes that "if nothing else, *The Wedding Banquet* illustrates in exacting detail the inevitable compromises that a tortuous, pathological, and unnatural system of compulsory heterosexuality demands from us all" (10).

While I certainly do not disagree with this assessment, the particular configurations of Wai Tung's negotiations of the closet and coming out encode a considerable amount of information about the material and institutional contexts surrounding these acts or performances. Eng's strategic reading of the film attempts to negotiate the mutual exclusions of racial and sexual communities and identities, yet it also operates within a context of U.S. identity politics, which cannot account for the complexities of sexual and ethnic identities in the global system. What is occluded in a national reading is the way in which the closet itself is reconstructed, in the course of the narrative, under the pressure of globalization. From an initial problematic of assimilation, in which it is a question of competing national identities, the choice gradually becomes recast as one between a national and a transnational/global identity.

Let us begin, then, by investigating some of the meanings attached to homosexuality in Asian and Asian American communities, in order to elucidate the cross-reference of race and sexuality in anxieties of assimilation. In the growing literature by lesbian and gay Asian Americans one can find numerous refutations of the persistent charges that homosexuality affects only white people and that being gay means wanting to be white. Eric Wat states that "for most Asian parents, being Asian and being gay are mutually exclusive. It is not only that homosexuality is a forbidden topic in most Asian communities. More significant, there is not a need to talk about 'it' because it is only a *problem* for white people: 'it' is a white *disease*. For example, in Hong Kong, a Westernized colony where

a gay community has become more visible in the last few years, the colloquial word for a gay man is simply *gay-loh* (gay fellow)" (155).[6] The
underlying narrative about homosexuality here is that it is an effect of
Westernization. The similarities of this conjunction across a number of
different national/ethnic contexts suggest that this association has less to
do with the homophobia or traditionalism of ethnic communities than
with discourses of nationalism and their particular mechanisms for defining and enforcing normative definitions of community and identity.
Nayan Shah explains that in some South Asian communities, "the conservative ideologies of heterosexist South Asians equate queer sexualities
with an already well-defined yet adaptable arsenal of 'Western evils'—
divorce, drinking alcohol, eating meat, or drug abuse. Any unfavorable
value is displaced onto a non-South Asian source" ("Sexuality, Identity,
and the Uses of History," 119). Shah further notes the irony implicit in the
rejection of homosexuality as Western, and therefore foreign to the native
culture, when such judgments are themselves structured by a Western
dichotomization of sexuality.

Sexuality is obviously one important semiotic field in which
social relations are negotiated, and the meanings assigned to homosexuality in the West and non-West are implicated in global relations of
inequality. Although homosexuality in American culture is primarily perceived as a form of deviance from prescribed *gender* identities—connoting a threat that arises from within national borders—Wat and Shah
suggest that for Asian communities in both Asia and the United States,
the phantasmic danger that homosexuality poses to national/ethnic identity may supersede other axes of alterity. The figure of the homosexual
becomes a sign for the Western domination that enters from without and
disrupts the community's ability to reproduce the structure of social relations. The homophobia that lesbians and gays of color face in their ethnic
communities finds its corollary in the racism that they confront in
gay communities that are predominantly white. Domestic racism is
inevitably tied to the epistemic structures of imperial domination in the
international sphere. And the imposition of Western categories of identity—whether in the name of oppression or liberation (it is not always
clear which is which)—may restrict alternative codifications and traditions of sexuality in the non-West within the homosexual/heterosexual
opposition. Instances of same-sex relations can, of course, be found in
almost all cultures, but they may not appear as "homosexuality" outside
Western regimes of sexuality/knowledge.[7]

Against a nationalist homophobia, then, one major function of
homosexuality in *The Wedding Banquet* is precisely to contest the
demands of national/ethnic identity, by performing the counternaturaliza-
tion of assimilation, on the impure and inauthentic ethnic subject. By uti-
lizing the sign of homosexuality, the film manages to appropriate whatever
legitimacy has been achieved by lesbian and gay constructions of homo-

sexual desire as essential, inherent, and therefore "natural." In the first half of *The Wedding Banquet*, sexuality and national/ethnic identity are elaborated together, so that every representation of sexuality is also simultaneously a negotiation of ethnicity. The narrative of coming out, the other major thematic that derives from the figure of homosexuality in the film (to which we will return later in the argument), is also evident here: following the conjunction of sexuality with ethnicity, the trope of the closet also signifies the deviation from ethnic identity that must be covered up. What becomes immediately apparent is that all of the younger generation of Chinese/Taiwanese in the United States are engaged in the masquerade of authenticity insofar as none of them are capable of enacting the forms of tradition that the older generation continually seeks to re-create.

The convergence of these two thematic strands is most obvious in the case of Sister Mao, Wai Tung's "perfect match" according to the Taiwanese dating service in which his parents enroll him. Far from being the good Chinese wife who will bring Wai Tung back into the fold of Chinese tradition, she is actually too much like him, since they are both highly educated, Westernized, upper-class Taiwanese. Both of them, after all, let their parents enroll them in the dating club because they have white lovers and don't want their parents to know. The closet is thus a function here of ethnicity as well as sexuality. Per Wai Tung's requirements, Sister Mao is an opera singer, but her training is in Western opera, and she performs for Wai Tung an aria from *Madama Butterfly*. Her name thus activates a certain irony in its subtle connotation of a more authentic Chinese identity, one that seems rather to belong to Wei Wei.

If Wei Wei seems closer to tradition, however—in her mainland origins and her familiarity with classical Chinese calligraphy, customs, and manners—she is completely incapable of the "traditional" housekeeping duty of the wife. In fact, we first encounter her in a sweat-drenched tank top, guzzling vodka from the bottle—somewhat excessive signifiers of Westernization, which are later reinforced (in case there was any doubt) by her sexual aggressiveness and her violent, abstract expressionist-style canvases. It is paradoxically the Western male, Simon, who is most capable of maintaining the domestic space and (re)producing traditional Chinese cuisine, an indication of the loosening of national/ethnic characteristics from any essential ties to race or blood as a consequence of their international commodification in the global economy.

If the signifiers of sexuality establish themata of assimilation, inauthenticity, and masquerade in the first half of the film, they do so against the nationalist assertions of cultural identity posed by the father. In one interview Lee himself explicates the film (which is based on the true story of one of Lee's friends) in terms of the history of Taiwan:

> *The Wedding Banquet* is a comedy about identity. Identity is an issue that for us Taiwanese is central but also rather muted by our short, contra-

dictory history. In the story, cultural, national, family and individual identities all work at cross-purposes with one another. A gay son, naturalized as an American citizen, can't "come out" to his father, a nationalist general who fled the mainland and whose entire family was wiped-out by the communists. If the wedding allows the son to continue to live "free" in America, he is still imprisoned by the weight of a history his father has shaped, a history that—because he won't be "continuing the family name"—will end with him. But, of course, the end of history is only the beginning of our story. The son's fake marriage to a girl from the mainland unites the "two Chinas," but in a new union that isn't quite what the elders were hoping for. (quoted in "Review," 44)

Note that in Lee's remarks, sexuality is conspicuously absent from the various categories of identity, an indication that homosexuality is a sign for the very confusions of identity that the film seeks to resolve. Rather than a form of identity, sexuality is the discourse in which questions of identity are negotiated. Furthermore, the fact that the son is gay seems almost inseparable from the fact that he is "naturalized as an American citizen." If this synopsis seems to pose the contradictions of Taiwanese identity within a typical nationalist problematic—that is, how to get crossed identities to align themselves, to work toward the same purpose, in order to guarantee the unity of the nation—we should note this passage's ambiguous relation to the nation and the subtlety with which nationalism is invoked only in order to be finally evaded.

The very effort to construct a "national allegory" (Jameson, "Third-World Literature," 65–88) is a performative attempt to script a unitary national narrative out of the contradictions and conflicts of Taiwanese society.[8] I suggest that the national allegory of Taiwan in *The Wedding Banquet* refers to the recent history of the transition from an authoritarian state to a liberal democratic one. The watershed moment was the 1986 lifting of martial law and the legalization of opposition parties that followed. The crisis of the patriarch signifies the crisis of the national state and the necessity of coming to terms with the demands of the global system. From the perspective of the nation, therefore, the fantasy evoked in the film may be the possibility of regaining some measure of control over the destabilizing operations of the global system.

As the organizing sign of the film, the wedding banquet is the hinge upon which the narrative pivots from one trajectory to another. It is, in other words, the transitional moment that must be converted from an end into a beginning; it marks a "generic discontinuity" (Jameson, *Political Unconscious,* 144) between comedy and melodrama that signals the film's status as a transnational allegory masquerading as a national one, just as the younger generation performs a masquerade of tradition.[9] Marriage is, of course, one of the central institutions of bourgeois society, and the family has long been conceived as analogous to the nation, so the failure of the wedding to effect closure indicates that the nationalist appeal to cultural authenticity is no longer sufficient to mediate the conflicts that are destabilizing the authority of the state in the global system.

If marriage constitutes the end point of traditional comedy in the West—Schamus cites Shakespeare as the locus classicus (ix–xiii)—the scenes of the wedding banquet mark the end of that generic strand in the text: the film suddenly shifts modes and turns into a melodrama, which does seem to be the generic form in which the narrative of "coming out" is usually cast in American culture. (One function of homosexuality in the plot, then, is to obstruct the closure offered by the wedding in favor of the closure presented at the end of the film.) This generic opposition also corresponds to the contrast between the arranged marriage, as one of convenience or expediency, and the marriage of love, which is supposed to typify the bourgeois version—love being the affective glue that binds together the conflictual elements of liberal society.[10] Because these two generic narratives (comedy and melodrama or sexuality and ethnic identity) are both insufficient, however, the film must seek a new mode of resolution, one that finds its material analogue in the creation of new familial relations.

The inability of the marriage plot to resolve the conflict between Wai Tung and his father over national/ethnic identity reflects the impossibility of appealing to an originary Chinese identity for Taiwan—given the erosion of Nationalist Party (KMT) hegemony. The quest for a new site of reconciliation requires the disarticulation of the nation from the state, that is, the reconstruction of a transnational patriarchal order. The reason for this—at least in the semiotic economy of the narrative—is made explicit in the last line that Wei Wei utters before the film cuts away from the bed where she lies atop Wai Tung. In response to his anxious question, "What are you doing?" Wei Wei replies, "I am liberating you." The Chinese word for "liberate" here is the same one used to denote 1949 as the year of Liberation, when the Communists forced the Nationalists into exile on Taiwan (significantly, although inexplicably, this is a line that is omitted from the English version of the screenplay). The anxiety expressed in the threat of a reluctant "liberation" is anxiety over the threat of mainland invasion, which is a very real possibility, as recent events remind us, but is also the justification used by the KMT government to legitimate martial law and authoritarian rule.[11]

The trope of liberation thus condenses both the fear of mainland invasion and the KMT state's imposition of a Chinese ethnic identity upon the heterogeneous population of Taiwan. This was a scripting of "fictive ethnicity" (Balibar, "The Nation Form," 86–106) that involved tracing genealogies back to their mainland origins, maintaining an entire legislative body composed of representatives of mainland provinces, and enforcing the use of Mandarin Chinese (the official dialect of the mainland empire) over the various local Taiwanese dialects.[12] The source of anxiety, therefore, is no longer simply the mainland and the Communists, but in some sense the nation itself, since the demand for national identification is now seen as emanating from both the mainland and KMT states. Liberation also connotes, of course, the Western narrative of individual emancipation, but during the course of the narrative, that emancipation is transposed from the national to the transnational, from the heterosexual to the homosexual. As a gay man, Wai Tung does not simply represent a Western threat to the Chinese nation; rather, he is eccentric to the nation as such.

The threat of mainland invasion thus serves to obstruct the nationalist resolution, but it does so by legitimating Wai Tung's homosexuality and, therefore, his rejection of his father's effort to impose upon him an essentialized national/ethnic identity in the form of a heterosexual union. In opposition to the authentic Chinese identity demanded by his father, Wai Tung's homosexuality stands in for the hybrid, inauthentic state of the Westernized ethnic subject. On a more basic level, though, the wedding fails to resolve the issues, because it rests on a fundamental conflict. The trope of liberation signals that competing liberations are at stake here; in other words, Wai Tung and Wei Wei cannot *both* be liberated simultaneously.[13] "Liberation" thus functions as a signifier encapsulating the antithetical relation between Wei Wei's escape from the global underclass of the undocumented, transnational migrant laborer and Wai Tung's evasion of his father's demand for heterosexual reproduction. Between these two forms of liberation, however, Wei Wei's desire is only understood by Wai Tung (and the film) as ventriloquizing the father's imperative, a conflation that effectively excludes any possibility of autonomy for Wei Wei or release from the dictates of the international sexual division of labor.

The film's resolution, however, depends most intently upon disciplining Wei Wei as the figure of resistance, so that it is only Wai Tung's impregnation of her, which turns out to be the mechanism of his control over her, that allows the ending to take place in a configuration that resolves the conflicts between the men. The consolidation of a transnational patriarchy of capital is fundamentally dependent upon the subordination of women and labor, and these are conflated in the film, so that woman becomes the very sign of labor. Therefore, if we reconstruct the film around Wei Wei as the main protagonist, we suddenly perceive an entirely new narrative, one that details the cooperation of national and transnational patriarchies in the exploitation of labor and the reconciliation of global capital across national borders. This leads us to the recognition of Wai Tung's occupation in the beginning of the film as essentially that of slumlord. Although we are given no other information about his business in the United States for the previous ten years, it certainly appears that he has been profiting from the exploitation of undocumented immigrants like Wei Wei. In this respect, we may begin to suspect that the crisis of legitimation allegorized in the decline of the father is the displacement of a crisis that afflicts the son. Or, rather, these are perhaps interrelated moments in the relation of capital to labor in the global system.

The transformation of Wai Tung into a patriarch, the declared project of the film, can now be seen as fundamentally dependent not so much upon the reconciliation with his father as upon the solicitation of ideological consent from Wei Wei and her submission to his hegemonic dominance. Returning to the first invocation of the trope of liberation in the film, recall that it occurs in the scene when Wai Tung goes to Wei Wei's loft to collect the three months' back rent she owes him. When Wai Tung announces on the intercom that the "evil landlord" has arrived, she refuses to let him in at first, declaring, "The sixth floor has been liberated!" (Lee, *Eat Drink*, 124). Although the anxiety provoked by this encounter is played for laughs, I take it to be perhaps the most fundamental sign of what propels the entire narrative. It is not only the national allegory and the drama of sexual identity, but also the situation of the transnational capitalist class in the diaspora, which finds itself in the tricky situation of having to negotiate between the demands of "its own" ethnic communities and those of global capital, without the institutional apparatuses of the state to enforce its position.

If the second half of the film consists of two moments of crisis—coming out and abortion—they are both registered through the mother. But it is important to note that they are, in fact, asymmetrical: Wai Tung's reconciliation with Simon depends on Wei Wei's decision to have the baby. This is structured into the very diegesis, since Wai Tung's father's recognition of Simon as "also" his son comes between Wei Wei's demand for a hamburger and her decision to keep the baby. The moment that Wei Wei comes closest to escaping the domination of the global system is stigmatized in the film through the act of abortion; once this possibility is closed off, her subordination is inevitable. Thus, the multicultural, non-heterosexual family formed by Wai Tung and Simon at the end of the film is in sharp contrast to the representation of women's liberation offered to Wei Wei. Although it is unclear what kind of arrangement she and Wai Tung will eventually come to, the decision to keep the baby drastically reduces her options, foreclosing the possibility of withdrawal from the global system. Her dependence upon global capital is vividly dramatized in the act of consuming that quintessential transnational food commodity and symbol of Americanization, the hamburger.

Cynthia Liu has discussed the antagonism between the anti-homophobic and feminist discourses in the film, comparing Wai Tung's acquisition of relative personal freedom with Wei Wei's destiny, which is eventually reduced to biology (1–60). Citing Biddy Martin's caution against "antifoundationalist celebrations of queerness [that] rely on their own projections of fixity, constraint, or subjection onto a fixed ground, often onto feminism or the female body, in relation to which queer sexualities become figural, performative, playful, and fun" (104), Liu argues that *The Wedding Banquet* "purchases queer-positivity and gay Asian male sexual and class mobility at the expense of a 'miring'-Asian female ground. Even the queer-positive elements are muted by the film's 'enabling' capitulation to patriarchal and procreative imperatives" (C. Liu, "'To Love, Honor, and Dismay,' " 43). Situating this analysis in terms of the global system and postmodernity, however, we can begin to locate this antagonism within the ideological antinomy between modernity and postmodernity or, to put it in more concrete terms, the nation-state and the global system. The tension between an apparently anti-homophobic or homophilic resolution and an anti-patriarchal or feminist one is the tension between sexuality and gender as two divergent challenges to the authority of the nation-state. This discontinuity cannot be parsed as one in which sexuality is inherently more or less efficacious a subversion than is gender; rather, we need to attend to who is being recuperated, the first-born son or the working-class woman.

Although the denouement can be read as offering the reconciliations of East and West, or tradition and modernity, or filial duty and individual freedom, the new structure of sexual and familial relations represented seems to exceed the simple resolution of binary oppositions. If the wedding as nationalist resolution is no longer capable of soliciting consent to bourgeois hegemony, we need to elucidate how the reconstituted family unit at the end of the film represents one attempt to imagine a new structure of social relations—one that would be capable of mediating the contradictions and antagonisms in the global systems. The film's ending seems to be striving toward an alteration in the ideological value and structure of the family to signify no longer the unity of the nation, but rather the unity of the global system as embodied in the concrete institution of the transnational corporation, with Wai Tung as the representative of the transnational capitalist class at the apex.[14] Thus in the publicity photo for the film, Wai Tung bends down to embrace Wei Wei on one side and Simon on the other. The baby that Wei Wei carries is the signifier for the vast Chinese labor force, and the money that is exchanged between Wai Tung's father and Simon is the symbol of their common interest as the owners of global capital.

The fact that this is an international confederation means a diminishment of national distinctions, which also entails leveling the opposition of heterosexuality and homosexuality. This opposition, if we are to agree with a number of accounts of gay history, is foundational to the construction of the modern nation.[15] In contrast, Donald Lowe characterizes sexuality in the era of postmodernity in these terms: "Separated from social reproduction, sexuality thus becomes a sign to energize, in effect to sexualize, late-capitalist consumption. The result is a sexual lifestyle, as distinct from the bourgeois assumption of an interiorized sexual identity. No longer respecting the outer/inner, the public/private oppositions, the new sexual lifestyle is subverting the opposition between heterosexual norm and its other, i.e., the so-called homosexual vice. We are verging toward polysexuality, i.e., sexual *differences without* stable sexual *identities"* (127). Sexual lifestyle rewrites the homosexual/heterosexual opposition, resulting not so much in the dissolution of the closet as in its reconfiguration in response to the material conditions of the global system. The parameters of the closet are redrawn in the noneuclidean geometries of cyberspace, making it increasingly difficult to speak of being in or out, since Wai Tung is simultaneously both inside and outside in some new and more complex relation of public and private. This remodeling of the closet and of the discourse of sexuality allows the film to pivot from a nationalist problematic of assimilation (competing national identities) to a transnational problematic of global identities. We can discern this shift in the now-naturalized oxymoron of "global citizenship"; of what global entity does one declare oneself a "citizen" here? This hybrid epithet is an acute index of the transitional moment in which, despite all pronouncements to the contrary, the global system has not yet completely formed and the nation has definitely not been superseded.

It is in this conjuncture that gay men and transvestites can become the emblematic embodiments of the transnational subject. Implicit in such figurations, however, is the unexamined universality of the nation-state as the referent of all subjectivity and the location of all forms of domination. To identify any opposition to the nation as inherently liberatory is to restrict questions of power and inequality within a zero-sum binary of domination and emancipation, such that any reduction in one automatically produces an increase in the other. The description of queer transnational subjectivity as a liberation from the limits of the nation reinscribes Enlightenment narratives of universal history and hierarchies of development. This occludes an inquiry into what material conditions enable or produce subject positions outside of or opposed to the nation—for example, global, diasporic, or transnational ones. In the twenty-fifth-anniversary celebrations of Stonewall, for instance, Martin Manalansan notes that the "official" march started not at the Stonewall Inn but at the United Nations. Documents, souvenirs, and artifacts associated with the anniversary demonstrate how "the textualization of Stonewall has changed—from localized descriptions of a police raid on a Greenwich Village bar to globalized descriptions of a revolutionary moment for gays and lesbians everywhere" (427). These proclamations of an "international" lesbian and gay movement risk subsuming heterogeneous forms of sexuality under a gay identity that is implicated in a specifically Western and bourgeois construction of subjectivity, with its topoi of voice, visibility, and coming out.

The progression from ethnicity to sexuality according to a teleological narrative of modernization constitutes such a foundational narrative of postmodern understandings of gay/queer identity that even as acute an observer of the crossings of race and sexuality as Dana Takagi can address the division separating ethnic communities from gay communities with this analogy: "Imagining your parents, clutching bento box lunches, thrust into the smoky haze of a South of Market leather bar in San Francisco is no less strange a vision than the idea of Lowie taking Ishi, the last of his tribe, for a cruise on Lucas' Star Tours at Disneyland" (6). The ethnographic analogy exemplifies the rhetorical construction of ethnic identity as primitive or premodern against sexuality as the very signifier of (post)modernity. Manalansan provides an important critique of the continuing structural force of such epistemological categories, when he refers to Barry Adam's distinction between anthropological, or historical, homosexuality and "modern" homosexuality as one in which "gay" becomes "synonymous with capitalist expansion." The consequence of this periodization, Manalansan argues, is that "all same-sex phenomena are placed within a developmental and teleological matrix that ends with Western 'gay' sexuality. Non-'gay' forms are seen as archeological artifacts to be reckoned with only when excavating the origins of pancultural/panglobal homosexuality" (427–28). The narrative of gay liberation thus reproduces narratives of universal history that gauge the evolution of civilization from tradition to modernity. But in *The Wedding Banquet*, this antinomy takes the form of a hierarchical opposition between sexuality and race, in which the latter constitutes the essential ground for the postmodern play of queerness.

In a discussion of representations of homosexuality in recent Asian film, Chris Berry provides a good example of the pitfalls of queer theory in the international arena. Referring to Lee Edelman's reading of *Fanny Hill*, Berry writes that "just as sodomy confounds male and female, before and behind, I will argue that the sight of homosexuality today in the simultaneously postcolonial and neo-Confucian construction known as East Asia can confound the logic of East and West and of past and present that underpins that construction and that it does so in a manner that constitutes this essay as a project of 'sexual disorientation' " (159). Putting aside the transposition of queer theory from *Fanny Hill* to East Asia, Berry contends that the visibility of homosexuality in Asian popular culture may be capable of destabilizing postcolonial Asian orientalist constructions of Asian identity—specifically the nominally postnational construction of an East Asian regional identity that would include the "Newly Industrializing Countries" (the so-called "Four Tigers" or "Four Dragons": Hong Kong, Singapore, Taiwan, and South Korea).

Although Berry's argument engages a number of the problems outlined here, let us focus on his conclusion that homosexuality may serve to disrupt the consolidation of an East Asian identity that relies on a colonial division of East and West. Listing a number of East Asian films and videos that deal with the topic of homosexuality, Berry writes, "The disparities between these films themselves confound any notion of a common Confucian East Asian identity, culture, or set of values. However, it is not the range of different representations that I am focusing on here; rather, it is what they all share, namely, the act of representing homosexuality that is of interest. . . . By making homosexuality visible at all, every one of these films and videos resists the conservative, government-centered ideologies of collective identity (whether national or regional) that attempt to other homosexuality" (167). One of the principal questions that I have attempted to pose in this essay is precisely the extent to which the visibility of homosexuality always and everywhere produces resistance or "sexual disorientation." Images of homosexuality may indeed disrupt homophobic nation-state discourses of identity, but the question that Berry fails to pursue is, To what end? What replaces the nationalist ideologies of collective identity that homosexuality subverts? Berry's statecentric, postcolonial framework restricts his argument within the opposition between homosexuality and the nation that is part of nationalism's own self-consolidation, occluding an investigation of sexuality as a component of various transnational practices.

In discussing the case of Singapore, Berry fails to take adequate account of how the crisis of state paternity—the discursive nexus through which the Singapore government constructed a Confucian identity, one that resonates with the phantasmic decline of the patriarch in Lee's films—may have contradictory effects within the decentered ideological field of the global system.[16] Homosexuality's function in the nationalist rhetoric of the Singapore government requires a more complex account than one that simply attends to binaries of East and West, gay and straight. Despite the vast differences between Singapore and Taiwan, we can discern in their resurgence of nationalist sentiment and anxieties of identity their common function in crisis management, in deflecting popular unrest occasioned by the destabilizations of global restructuring. The mobilization of homophobia as part of this tactic, then, cannot simply be countered with "deviationist" projects that disseminate the subversive sight of homosexuality. Homosexuality (especially in films made by producers/artists who, like Lee, are not gay) may be visible only as an ideological mirage of transnational capital and is therefore implicated in a process of globalization in which the nation-state is complicit and which the return to nationalism seeks to disavow.

The point here is simply that one main political imperative in the analysis of transnationalism or globalization is to define and specify the analytical frame within which we are evaluating any particular object or action. The reconciliation of the nationalist patriarch with the gay man may indeed be progressive in the context of the normative and regulatory forms of the nation-state, but this political effectivity cannot be guaranteed or taken for granted in other contexts. My reading of *The Wedding Banquet* suggests that one tendency in the reconstruction of nationalist patriarchies in postmodernity is the recuperation/incorporation of the "homosexual threat"; in fact, this may be one of the signal processes by which nationalist patriarchies become postmodern patriarchies. The politics of sexuality in the global system, then, cannot be directly extrapolated from within the nation. Rosemary Hennessy provides an incisive critique of queer theory's failure to address the commodification of objects and practices rather than their purely semiotic or discursive production. She argues that

> the appropriation of gay cultural codes in the cosmopolitan revamping of gender displays the arbitrariness of bourgeois patriarchy's gender system and helps to reconfigure it in a more postmodern mode where the links between gender and sexuality are looser, where homosexuals are welcome, even constituting the vanguard, and where the appropriation of their parody of authentic sex and gender identities is quite compatible with the aestheticization of everyday life into postmodern lifestyles. In itself, of course, this limited assimilation of gays into mainstream middleclass culture does not disrupt postmodern patriarchy and its intersection with capitalism; indeed it is in some ways quite integral to it. (Hennessy, "Queer Visibility in Commodity Culture," 170).

Similarly, Caren Kaplan and Inderpal Grewal ("Transnational Feminist Cultural Studies") suggest that within the context of the tensions that have developed in the global system between transnational capital and the nation-state, First World advocates of global identity politics risk becoming the unwitting agents of transnational capital in its struggle against the resistances posed by Third World states.

Hennessy argues that the visibility of queer spectacle often serves to detract attention from, or mask, labor and inequality, the process that Jameson refers to in *The Geopolitical Aesthetic* as "representational laundering." Signifying on Chinese American history, though, we might say that the laundry is one of the things that is laundered out; that is, the visibility of Asian American labor in *The Wedding Banquet* is precisely what is erased. We could characterize the aesthetic of the film, then, as a form of visual gentrification, the cinematographic mode that corresponds to Wai Tung's diegetic venture to convert his abandoned industrial building into condos. What must be excluded from the visual field is the actual community that is riven by differences of class, gender, ethnicity, nationality, and sexuality, and Asian American communities are locations of the Third World in the First World where the labor of production that fuels the operations of global capital can still be glimpsed from time to time. If Asian American communities are not visible in the film, however, they still surface through a kind of diegetic Freudian slip, condensed into the heat, humidity, and noise of Wei Wei's loft/work space—conditions that evoke Taipei and a Third World industrial past but also the Third World ethnic enclave in the First World, composed of sweatshops as well as small, paternalistic family businesses.

Therefore, we need to register what is elided in *The Wedding Banquet*'s representations of the Taiwanese diaspora in the United States. But the most striking example of the disappearance of the Asian American from the film is one that is literally invisible. The hotel (perhaps the paramount signifier of the film's transnational locations) where the scenes of the wedding banquet were shot sits almost in the center of Flushing, New York, a community that has become one of the largest concentrations of Chinese and other Asian immigrants in the past decade (much like Monterey Park in Los Angeles). Yet despite the fact that Lee drew on the resources of this community both for his first film, *Pushing Hands*, and for *The Wedding Banquet*, there is absolutely no hint in the film of anything that exists outside the hotel. What begins in the film as an apparent conflict between East and West is transformed in the course of the narrative into a conflict between the two halves of the global system, a new division that is apparent in the racialized class polarization of the contemporary United States.[17]

I have emphasized the dimensions of the film that have been expelled from the visual field or forced into the closet. Foremost among these are Asian American communities as the site of class inequalities and the extraction of surplus value, as well as the site of the underclass, which is excluded from production altogether. The restoration of the materiality of those contexts, as against the abstractions and commodification of capital, is one urgent project for an Asian American cultural studies. It can be conceptualized along the lines of Hennessy's definition of "critique" as a "political practice and a mode of reading that establishes the intimate links between the visible and the historical by taking as its starting point a systemic understanding of the social" (176). Cultural analysis in the global system must seek to return to political "consciousness" the Third World as the locus of offshore production no longer apparent in the First World, and it must trace the contradictory flows of sign, image, and commodity in the global system. This project cannot be undertaken unless our analysis is capable of restoring the interconnectedness of multiple vectors of inequality. An Asian American transnational cultural studies must attend to both poles of the local-global conjunction, in order to make the multiple erasures of globalization reappear in the field of action.

WORKS CITED

Ahmad, Aijaz. *In Theory: Classes, Nations, Literatures.* London: Verso, 1992.

Balibar, Etienne. "The Nation Form: History and Ideology." In *Race, Nation, Class: Ambiguous Identities.* Trans. Chris Turner. London: Verso, 1991. 86–106.

Berry, Chris. "Sexual DisOrientations: Homosexual Rights, East Asian Films, and Postmodern Postnationalism." In *In Pursuit of Contemporary East Asian Culture.* Ed. Xiaobing Tang and Stephen Snyder. Boulder, Colo.: Westview, 1996. 157–82.

Cazdyn, Eric. "Uses and Abuses of the Nation: Toward a Theory of the Transnational Cultural Exchange Industry." *Social Text* 44 (1995): 135–59.

Ching, Leo. "Imaginings in the Empires of the Sun: Japanese Mass Culture in Asia." In *Asia/Pacific as Space of Cultural Production*. Ed. Rob Wilson and Arif Dirlik. Durham, N.C.: Duke University Press, 1995. 262–83.

Chow, Rey. *Primitive Passions: Visuality, Sexuality, Ethnography, and Contemporary Chinese Cinema*. New York: Columbia University Press, 1995.

Cobham, Rhonda. "Misgendering the Nation: African Nationalist Fictions and Nuruddin Farah's *Maps*." In *Nationalisms and Sexualities*. Ed. Mary Russo, Andrew Parker, Doris Sommer, and Patricia Yaeger. New York: Routledge, 1992. 42–59.

Eng, David L. "*The Wedding Banquet*: You're Not Invited and Some Other Ancillary Thoughts." *Artspiral* 7 (1993): 8–10.

Foucault, Michel. *The History of Sexuality*, Vol. 1: *An Introduction*. Trans. Robert Hurley. New York: Vintage, 1980.

Fung, Richard. "Looking for My Penis: The Eroticized Asian in Gay Video Porn." In *How Do I Look?: Queer Film and Video*. Ed. Bad Object Choices. Seattle, Wash.: Bay Press, 1991. 145–68.

Fuss, Diana. "Introduction: Inside/Out." In *Inside/Out: Lesbian Theories, Gay Theories*. Ed. Diana Fuss. New York: Routledge, 1991. 1–10.

Gold, Thomas B. "Taiwan's Quest for Identity in the Shadow of China." In *In the Shadow of China: Political Developments in Taiwan Since 1949*. Ed. Steven Tsang. Honolulu: University of Hawaii Press, 1993. 169–92.

Gregory, Steven. "Race and Racism: A Symposium." *Social Text* 42 (1995): 16–21.

Halperin, David M. *One Hundred Years of Homosexuality*. New York: Routledge, 1989.

Heng, Geraldine, and Janadas Devan. "State Fatherhood: The Politics of Nationalism, Sexuality, and Race in Singapore." In *Nationalisms and Sexualities*. Ed. Mary Russo, Andrew Parker, Doris Sommer, and Patricia Yaeger. New York: Routledge, 1992. 343–64.

Hennessy, Rosemary. "Queer Visibility in Commodity Culture." In *Social Postmodernism: Beyond Identity Politics*. Ed. Linda Nicholson and Steven Seidman. Cambridge: Cambridge University Press, 1995. 142–83.

Hom, Alice Y. "Stories from the Homefront: Perspectives of Asian American Parents with Lesbian Daughters and Gay Sons." *Amerasia Journal* 20.1 (1994): 19–32.

Hoo, Maurice L. "Speech Impediments." *Asian Pacific American Journal* 2.1 (1993): 107–12.

Jameson, Fredric. *The Geopolitical Aesthetic*. Bloomington and London: Indiana University Press and British Film Institute, 1995.

———. *The Political Unconscious: Narrative as a Socially Symbolic Act*. Ithaca, N.Y.: Cornell University Press, 1981.

———. "Third-World Literature in the Era of Multinational Capitalism." *Social Text* 15 (1986): 65–88.

Kaplan, Caren. "'A World Without Boundaries': The Body Shop's Trans/National Geographics." *Social Text* 43 (1995): 45–66.

Kaplan, Caren, and Inderpal Grewal. "Introduction." In *Scattered Hegemonies: Postmodernity and Transnational Feminist Practices*. Ed. Caren Kaplan and Inderpal Grewal. Minneapolis: University of Minnesota Press, 1994. 1–33.

———. "Transnational Feminist Cultural Studies: Beyond the Marxism/ Poststructuralism/Feminism Divides." *positions: east asia cultures critique* 2.2 (1994): 430–45.

Katz, Jonathan Ned. *Gay/Lesbian Almanac: A New Documentary*. New York: Harper and Row, 1983.

Lee, Ang. *Eat Drink Man Woman/The Wedding Banquet: Two Films by Ang Lee*. Woodstock: Overlook, 1994.

Liu, Cynthia W. "'To Love, Honor, and Dismay': Subverting the Feminine in Ang Lee's Trilogy of Resuscitated Patriarchs." *Hitting Critical Mass* 3.1 (1995): 1–60.

Liu, Lydia. "The Female Body and Nationalist Discourse: *The Field of Life and Death* Revisited." In *Scattered Hegemonies: Postmodernity and Transnational Feminist Practices*. Ed. Caren Kaplan and Inderpal Grewal. Minneapolis: University of Minnesota Press, 1994. 37–62.

Lowe, Donald. *The Body in Late-Capitalist USA*. Durham, N.C.: Duke University Press, 1995.

Manalansan, Martin F., IV. "In the Shadows of Stonewall: Examining Gay Transnational Politics and the Diasporic Dilemma." *GLQ: A Journal of Lesbian and Gay Studies* 2.4 (1995): 425–38.

Martin, Biddy. "Sexualities Without Genders and Other Queer Utopias. " *diacritics* 24.2–3 (1994): 104–21.

"Review of *The Wedding Banquet*." *Migration World Magazine* 22.2–3 (1994): 44.

Schamus, James. "Introduction." In *Eat Drink Man Woman/The Wedding Banquet: Two Films by Ang Lee*. Woodstock: Overlook, 1994. ix–xiii.

Sedgwick, Eve. *Epistemology of the Closet*. Berkeley and Los Angeles: University of California Press, 1990.

Shah, Nayan. "Sexuality, Identity, and the Uses of History." In *A Lotus of Another Color: An Unfolding of the South Asian Gay and Lesbian Experience*. Ed. Rakesh Ratti. Boston, Mass.: Alyson, 1993. 113–32.

Shih, Shu-mei. "The Trope of 'Mainland China' in Taiwan's Media." *positions: east asia cultures critique* 3.1 (1995): 149–83.

Sklair, Leslie. *Sociology of the Global System*. 2nd ed. Baltimore, Md.: Johns Hopkins University Press, 1995.

Sommer, Doris. "Irresistible Romance: The Foundational Fictions of Latin America." In *Nation and Narration*. Ed. Homi K. Bhabha. London: Routledge, 1990. 71–98.

Takagi, Dana Y. "Maiden Voyage: Excursion into Sexuality and Identity Politics in Asian America." *Amerasia Journal* 20.1 (1994): 1–17.

Wat, Eric C. "Preserving the Paradox: Stories from a *Gay-loh*." *Amerasia Journal* 20.1 (1994): 149–60.

The Wedding Banquet. Ang Lee, director. Samuel Goldwyn, 1993.

NOTES

1. See also Kaplan and Grewal, "Introduction," 1–33.

2. The transnational capitalist class, according to Sklair, "consists of those people who see their own interests and/or the interests of their countries of citizenship, as best served by an identification with the interests of the capitalist global system, in particular the interests of the transnational corporations" (8).

3. Jameson suggests, however, that "it would be too simple and functional to impute this particular stylistic motivation . . . to marketing strategies alone and an attention to a potentially international public; or rather, it would be crucial to affirm such base, external motivation, such determination by the extra-aesthetic, as realities in the object-world that ultimately, at some wider level of analysis, always rejoin the subject (and the formal and aesthetic) in unexpected internal ways" (*Geopolitical Aesthetic*, 118).

4. In his discussion of the flow of Japanese media and culture into Taiwan, Leo Ching provides an apt analogy for the difficulties of contextualizing narratives and representations in *The Wedding Banquet* (despite its own attempts at invoking national allegories and identities, which are as much marketing devices as plot devices). Ching notes that despite the history of Japanese colonization of Taiwan, the influx of Japanese culture is generally not regarded as cultural imperialism by the Taiwanese in the same way that the influx of U.S. culture is. He accounts for this disparity by suggesting that because much of Japanese cultural production is, in fact, reengineered simulacra of First World, especially U.S. culture, it carries no national ideological or cultural markers. Commenting on Tsan Hung-Chih's analysis of the proliferation of Japanese cultural products in Taiwan, Ching remarks that "Tsan rightly observes that the cultural merchandise imported from Japan is gradually and increasingly discarding the shade of traditional Japanese culture and ethnic character. What is perceived as Japanese cultural products can easily be of American or British origins. Japan

simply reassembles and packages other cultural commodities and sells them to other countries" (277). The result is "a repackaged secondhand cultural commodity that has no specific 'national' origin or discernible ideology" (278) and cannot therefore be read as signifying Japanese national or cultural superiority. Shu-mei Shih furnishes corroborating evidence, citing Taiwanese critic Luo Zhicheng's remark that there are no longer any forms of hegemonic thought in Taiwan, because ideology itself has been commodified, a phenomenon somewhat facetiously confirmed by the appearance of an advertising agency named "Ideology" (Shih, "The Trope of 'Mainland China,' " 155).

5. For other discussions of the problematic of the closet for Asian American lesbians and gays, see Fung, "Looking for My Penis," 145–68, Hom, "Stories from the Homefront," 19–32, Manalansan, "In the Shadows of Stonewall," 425–28, and Wat, "Preserving the Paradox," 149–60.

6. See also Hoo, "Speech Impediments," 107–12.

7. Rhonda Cobham suggests, for example, that "the existence of the social category 'homosexuality' within Western discourse makes it virtually impossible for African writers who make use of the novel form to write about sexual intimacy in their societies without positioning their narratives in relation to the meanings associated with the 'foreign' term" (47–48).

8. For critiques of the concept of "national allegory," see Ahmad; Chow; and L. Liu, "The Female Body and Nationalist Discourse," 37–62.

9. Jameson proposes that the formal configurations of the text can be read as a "host of distinct generic messages—some of them objectified survivals from older modes of cultural production, some anticipatory, but all together projecting a formal conjuncture through which the 'conjuncture' of coexisting modes of production at a given historical moment can be detected and allegorically articulated" (*Political Unconscious*, 99). The juxtaposition of different generic modes in *The Wedding Banquet*—mainly comedy/farce and family melodrama—articulates the particular conjunction of nationalism and transnationalism that characterizes Taiwan's position in the global system.

10. For an example of the relation between romance and nationalism, see Sommer, "Irresistible Romance," 71–98.

11. The first direct presidential elections in Taiwan, held in March 1996, prompted military exercises by the mainland navy in the Taiwan Straits and renewed declarations by the communist government that Taiwan was a province of the mainland.

12. "Although the [KMT] regime acknowledged that Taiwan had regional particularities, like any other locality in China, the KMT assiduously promoted the idea that the island was the repository and guarantor of Chinese tradition as well as the mainland's rich diversity. The national political bodies, such as the Legislative Yuan and National Assembly, kept in place delegates representing mainland districts even though they were divorced from their constituents. Regional cuisines and operas flourished and native place associations were established. Popular culture stressed mainland roots, addressing history and life on the mainland, not the island. Politically and to some extent culturally, then, Taiwan became a microcosm of pre-1949 mainland China as interpreted by the KMT. Ironically, while telling its people that Taiwan was an integral part of China, the KMT forbad contacts with the mainland, establishing in effect a great wall across the Straits" (Gold, "Taiwan's Quest for Identity," 171–72).

13. In Switzerland *The Wedding Banquet* was shown in English, with the Chinese dialogue dubbed in French. Furthermore, Wei Wei's crucial bedroom line was translated as "Women's liberation!" which was greeted, at one showing, by a roar of laughter from the audience. I thank Nida Surber for this information.

14. The reconstructed family seems to partake of something like the fantasy that Caren Kaplan describes in her analysis of the Body Shop's "Trade Not Aid" program as the *"representation* of a corporate *replacement* of the nation-state. It appears to be The Body Shop that funds and manages development projects, just as it appears to be The Body Shop that addresses health care, financing, and environmental concerns in its global reach" ("World

Without Boundaries," 58–59). For a related discussion of the Japan Exchange and Teaching (JET) Program, see Cazdyn, "Uses and Abuses," 135–59.

15. See Foucault; Halperin; Katz; and Sedgwick.

16. See Heng and Devan, "State Fatherhood," 343–64 on the crisis of state paternity in Singapore. See Shih, "The Trope of 'Mainland China,' " 149–83 on "orientalizing" constructions of China in Taiwanese media.

17. Steven Gregory describes this race/class polarization as dividing the United States "into two nations, one 'black' and the other 'white,' but the meanings and the socio-spatial terrain of both terms are shifting, as they always have. Whereas the 'underclass,' a hyper-exploited race/gender/class fraction, is emerging as the nodal point in the articulation of postindustrial blackness, 'whiteness' has opened its arms to a gorgeous mosaic of differences, whose inscription in the global economy, rather than the federal census, increasingly defines belonging" (21).

Gayatri Gopinath

On *Fire*

In his critique of the globalization of lesbian and gay politics and identity, the anthropologist Martin F. Manalansan IV notes that within the rhetoric of certain international gay organizations, "*gay* gains meaning according to a developmental narrative that begins with an unliberated, 'prepolitical' homosexual practice and that culminates in a liberated, 'out,' politicized, 'modern,' 'gay' subjectivity."[1] The Indian Canadian director Deepa Mehta's 1996 film *Fire* both adheres to and challenges this developmental narrative of gay and lesbian identity, which underlies dominant Euro-American discourses on non-Western sexualities. The film opens with a scene of the adult protagonist Radha's memory/fantasy of herself as a young girl, sitting beside her parents in a wide open field of yellow flowers. Her mother urges the young Radha to "see the ocean" lying just beyond the landlocked field: "What you can't see you can see, you just have to see without looking." This scene, with its exhortation to 'see' without looking, to 'see' differently, recurs and resonates throughout the film, and suggests an analogy with the ways in which *Fire* interrogates the notion that the proper location of lesbianism is within a politics of visibility in the public sphere. However, the film's counterhegemonic representation of queer female desire is undercut and complicated by its own history of production, distribution, reception, and consumption. Funded largely with Canadian money, *Fire* has been shown mostly at international film festivals in India, Europe, and North America and had a lengthy arthouse release in major U.S. cities. Thus it was available to a limited audience in India but gained a significant South Asian diasporic viewership as well as a mainstream lesbian and gay audience in the United States and Canada. Given the trajectory of the film's reception, it is worth asking how the film has become available and legible to its diasporic and international audiences.

From *GLQ* 4:4 (1998), pp. 631–36. Copyright 1998 Duke University Press. All rights reserved. Reprinted with permission.

Fire takes place in the middle-class neighborhood of Lajpat Nagar, in New Delhi, and tells the story of the burgeoning love and desire that emerges between Radha (Shabana Azmi) and her new sister-in-law Sita (Nandita Das), in a joint family household. Mehta quickly establishes the familiar familial violences and compulsions that inhabit the household: the women do most of the labor for the family business while their husbands ignore or abuse them. Radha's husband Ashok is tender and attentive not to Radha but to his guru, with whom he spends all his free time and who preaches sexual abstinence, while Sita's husband, Jatin, is too preoccupied with his "Westernized" Chinese girlfriend to attend to Sita. The two women eventually turn to each other for sex and emotional sustenance.

Mehta rather conventionally frames the dilemma of her heroines as one in which the pull of "modernity," with its promise of individual freedom and self-expression, pulls inevitably against "tradition," which demands that the women adhere to the roles prescribed to them as good Hindu wives and remain chaste, demure, and self-sacrificing. Indeed their very names bespeak these roles. In Hindu mythology, Radha is the devoted consort of the god Krishna, who is famous for his womanizing; together Radha and Krishna symbolize an idealized, transcendent heterosexual union. Sita, the heroine of the Hindu epic *Ramayana*, proves her chastity to her husband, Ram, by immersing herself in fire, and thus represents the ideal of wifely devotion and virtue. The image of Sita emerging unscathed from her *agni pariksha*, or trial by fire, is the inescapable motif around which the women's lives revolve throughout the film: for instance, the background noise in their daily lives is the popular serialization of the *Ramayana*, which plays incessantly on the television. Das's Sita, however, refuses to inhabit the overdetermined role of her legendary namesake: with her penchant for donning her husband's jeans instead of her heavy silk saris, and her willingness to pursue her attraction to Radha, she becomes the emblem of a "new India" and its promise of feminist self-fulfillment. Conversely, the stultifying effects of "tradition" are embodied in the character of Biji, the mute, paralytic grandmother who keeps a disapproving eye on the activities of her daughters-in-law.

The dichotomies through which the film is structured—between Biji and Sita, saris and jeans, silence and speech, self-denial and self-fulfillment, abstinence and desire, tradition and modernity—implicate it in a familiar teleological narrative of progress toward the individual "freedom" offered by the West, against which "the non-West" can only be read as premodern. Indeed a number of U.S. critics have used the film as an occasion to replay colonial constructions of India as a site of regressive gender oppression, against which "the West" stands for enlightened egalitarianism.[2] Within the dominant discursive production of India as anterior to the West, lesbian or gay identity is explicitly articulated as the marker of full-fledged modernity. After Ashok spies the two women in bed together, Sita comments to Radha, "There is no word in our language to describe what we are to each other," to which Radha responds, "You're right; perhaps seeing is less complicated." U.S. film critics, most notably Roger Ebert, have taken this exchange (as well as Mehta's own pronouncement in the press notes that "Indians don't talk about sex") as proof of the West's cultural superiority and advanced politicization: "Lesbianism is so outside the experience of these Hindus that their language even lacks a work for it."[3] Indeed, almost all mainstream U.S. reviewers stress the failure of "these Hindus" to articulate lesbianism intelligibly, which in turn signifies the failure of the non-West to progress toward the organization of sexuality and gender prevalent in the West.[4] To these critics, ironically, lesbian or gay identity becomes intelligible and indeed desirable when and where it can be incorporated into this developmental narrative of modernity.

Because *Fire* gains legibility within such narratives for at least some North American, non-South Asian viewers (both straight and gay), it is helpful to resituate it within discourses of non-heteronormative sexuality that are available to Indian and South Asian diasporic audiences. Indian critics have noted that *Fire* is based on the 1942 short story "The Quilt," by the Urdu writer Ismat Chughtai.[5] Reading the film through the story provides an alternative to the tradition-modernity axis by foregrounding the complex model of queer female desire suggested by the film but foreclosed by its mainstream U.S. reception. Restoring "The Quilt" as an important intertext to *Fire* underscores the film's critique of colonial constructions in which non-Western sexualities are premodern and in need of Western political development, and challenges dominant Indian nationalist narratives that consolidate the nation in terms of sexual and gender normativity.

Chughtai's story depicts the lesbian relationship between a sequestered wife and her female servant/masseuse in an upper-middle-class Muslim household. The narrator tells of their curious activities as she remembers having seen them through the eyes of her childhood self. Every night, the young girl is alternately fascinated by the servant's relentless massaging of the wife's body, and alarmed by the energetic contortions of the two women under the quilt. Memory in the text does not evoke a narrative of nostalgia in which "home" is imagined as a site of subjective wholeness or originary, heterosexual identity; rather, the narrator remembers the domestic arena of her childhood self as the site of complicated, non-normative arrangements of pleasures and desires. The anti-nostalgic narrative radically destabilizes conceptions of the domestic as a site of compulsory heterosexuality, while the decidedly partial knowledge afforded by the child's gaze allows Chughtai to resist naming the women's homoerotic relationship within prescribed frameworks as "lesbian" or "homosexual." This resistance is not so much a failure to articulate queerness as an acknowledgment of the inadequacy of such articulation in expressing the range and complexity of non-heteronormative sexual practices and allegiances as they emerge within sites of extreme heteronormativity. Indeed, in the story female homo-eroticism is simply one form of desire within a web of multiple, competing desires. While the servant, the wife, and the girl circulate within a particular female homosocial-homoerotic economy, there are similarly uneven male homosocial-homoerotic economies in the text: the husband, for instance, has a penchant for entertaining young boys. Queer desire, then, is quilted into the very fabric of the heterosexual, hierarchical configurations of the domestic arena.

Chughtai's depiction of queer female desire at the interstices of rigidly heterosexual structures is echoed in *Fire*, as it details the ways in which desire is routed and rooted in the space of the home. In the film, the men in the family access pleasure and fantasy through "escape hatches" from the strictures of conjugal heterosexual domesticity. Ashok, for instance, immerses himself within the homosociality of religious discipleship, Jatin trades in porn videos and escapes into sex with his exotically "other" Chinese girlfriend, while the servant Mundu (who nurses an unrequited love for Radha) masturbates to pilfered porn videos in front of Biji. Male desire, blocked by the officially sanctioned gender and class arrangements of the home, nevertheless emerges and is gratified. Radha and Sita, however, are shut out of such economies of desire; they, like Biji, must mutely witness men's pleasure, fantasies, and desire while being denied their own.

For Radha and Sita, as for the women in Chughtai's story, queer desire becomes a means of extricating oneself from patriarchal heteronormativity by creating alternative circuits of pleasure and fantasy. While some critics suggest that *Fire*'s depiction of lesbian sexuality capitulates to the familiar notion of lesbianism as merely a reaction to failed heterosexual marriages,[6] I would argue that, at least in the middle-class urban Indian context that Mehta details, it is from within the very fissures of rigid heteronormativity that queer female desire emerges. The attraction between Radha and Sita is enabled by those spaces of female homosociality that are sanctioned by normative sexual and gender arrangements. Whether rubbing oil into each other's hair, or massaging each other's feet during a family picnic, the women exploit the permeable relation and slippages between female homosociality and female homoeroticism. Similarly, *karva chauth*, a North Indian ritual in which "dutiful" wives fast at home to ensure their husbands' well-being, is transformed from a female homosocial activity into an intensely homoerotic one, as the two women dress up in silk saris and gold jewelry for each other's pleasure.

By depicting the privatized, seemingly sanitized "domestic" space as a site of intense female homoerotic pleasure and practice, both "The Quilt" and *Fire* interrogate the teleological Euro-American narrative according to which lesbian sexuality must emerge from a private, domestic sphere into a public, visible, subjectivity. Both suggest that "lesbian" desire looks and functions differently in an Indian context than in Euro-

American social and historical formations. Thus one critic's assessment that *Fire*'s depiction of lesbian sexuality is "extremely tame by Western standards" must be read as symptomatic of the very narrative that the film reiterates and revises.[7] In *Fire*'s "modernized" version of "The Quilt," however, the two women eventually leave the confines of the household rather than continue to exist within it, as Chughtai's characters do. Thus *Fire*, coming fifty years after "The Quilt," is available for recuperation within (and bears the marks of) the narrative of sexual emancipation and public visibility circulated by contemporary international lesbian and gay politics even as it provides a critique of this narrative.

In its representation of the complicated and wild desiring relations between women in the seemingly "traditional" space of the home, "The Quilt" directly confronts notions of proper Indian womanhood upon which anti-colonial nationalist ideologies depend.[8] Similarly, *Fire*'s representation of female homoerotic desire within the home challenges contemporary Hindu nationalist ideologies that rely upon Hindu women's sexual purity and sanctity as a means of ensuring group solidarity and vilifying Muslim minorities. Indeed, the film's rejection of the image of Sita as the ideal Hindu woman takes on an added significance given the increasing power and virulence of right-wing Hindu nationalism in India today, as seen in the current electoral victories of political parties such as the Bharatiya Janata Party. Thus queer desire in the film functions (albeit obliquely) as a modality through which the women resist a complicity with the project of Hindu nationalism and its attendant gender and sexual hierarchies. Within the film's logic, escaping heterosexuality is synonymous with escaping the violence of Hindu nationalism: the few moments where the two women are seen together outside the home take place within explicitly non-Hindu spaces such as mosques and tombs. Indeed the film ends with a shot of the two women in an Islamic shrine, having finally left the confines of the household.

Fire, then, gains multiple and contradictory meanings as it circulates within India, within the South Asian diaspora, and within film festival circuits and theaters in Europe and North America. While it may, on the one hand, critique Hindu nationalism (and the financial support it receives from South Asian diasporic communities), the film both resists and plays into dominant developmental narratives of sexuality, visibility, and identity. Ultimately, *Fire*'s reception outside India raises the question of how queer-themed films made by diasporic or Third World filmmakers have to reproduce these narratives to gain international circulation.[9]

NOTES

1. Martin F. Manalansan IV, "In the Shadows of Stonewall: Examining Gay Transnational Politics and the Diasporic Dilemma," in *The Politics of Culture in the Shadow of Capital*, ed. Lisa Lowe and David Lloyd (Durham, N.C.: Duke University Press, 1997), 487. An earlier version of this essay appeared in *Gay and Lesbian Quarterly* 2 (1995): 425–38.

2. E.g., one critic writes that *"Fire* is a plea for women's self-determination that . . . will probably strike viewers in this country as a bit obvious" (Walter Addeago, "Fire Cool to State of Marriage in India," *San Francisco Examiner,* 26 September 1997, C7). Similarly, other critics describe the film as taking place within the "suffocatingly masculine" and "pre-feminist" culture of contemporary India (see, e.g., Owen Gleiberman, "Take My Wife: *Fire,* a Tale of Illicit Lesbian Love in India, Evokes the Early Days of American Feminism," *Entertainment Weekly,* 12 September 1997, 110).

3. Roger Ebert, *"Fire* Strikes at Indian Repression," *Chicago Sun Times,* 17 September 1997, 38.

4. See Margaret McGurk, "Tradition Broken in Indian Tale of Forbidden Love," *Cincinnati Enquirer,* 16 January 1998, W26; and Bill Morrison, "Women on the Verge of a Cinematic Breakthrough," *News and Observer* (Raleigh, N.C.), 21 November 1997, WUP10.

5. Shoma Chatterjee, "One Sita Steps Beyond the Lakshmanrekha," *Calcutta Telegraph,* 12 January 1997. See Ismat Chughtai, *The Quilt and Other Stories,* trans. Tahira Naqvi and Syeda Hamid (New Delhi: Kali for Women, 1990).

6. Ginu Kamani, "Interview with Deepa Mehta," in *Trikone Magazine,* v. 4, n. 4, October 1997: 11–13.

7. Brian D. Johnson, "Forbidden Flames," *Maclean's Magazine,* 29 September 1997, 86.

8. Various feminist critics have argued that anti-colonial nationalism in India constituted itself through the construction of the Indian woman as a "modern" national subject who nevertheless acted as "the guardian of national culture, indigenous religion and family traditions." See, for instance, Kumari Jayawardena, "Introduction," in *Feminism and Nationalism in the Third World* (London: Zed, 1986), 14.

9. This question becomes all the more urgent given the proliferation of queer-themed films made by Indian directors who self-consciously proclaim their own heterosexuality and rarely show their films in the very national sites in which they are set; clearly such films are made with an international film festival audience in mind. *The Square Circle* (dir. Amol Palekar, 1997) and *Darmiyaan* (dir. Kalpana Lajmi, 1997) are but two recent instances.

Contributors

MARK CHIANG is an assistant professor of English and Asian American Studies at the University of Pennsylvania. He is currently at work on a book entitled *Representing Asian America: National and Transnational Contexts of Asian American Culture*, as well as a project examining questions of institutionalization and the production of value in the controversy over the Association for Asian American Studies Fiction Award.

PETER X FENG is assistant professor of English and Women's Studies at the University of Delaware. He has published articles in the *Journal of Asian American Studies, Cineaste, Jump Cut, Amerasia Journal*, and *Cinema Journal*, and is currently completing work on a book-length study of Asian American cinema.

STEPHEN GONG is associate director of the University of California Berkeley Art Museum and Pacific Film Archive. Previously, he has served as a program officer in the Media Arts Program at the National Endowment for the Arts, and as the associate director of the National Center for Film and Video Preservation at the American Film Institute. He is a board member of the National Asian American Telecommunications Association, has taught for the Asian American Studies Department at UC Berkeley, and writes and lectures on film history, preservation, and independent media.

GAYATRI GOPINATH is an assistant professor of Women and Gender Studies at the University of California at Davis. Her work on sexuality, migration, and South Asian cultural production has appeared in the journals *GLQ, Positions*, and *Diaspora*, as well as in the anthologies *Asian American Sexualities* (ed. Russell Leong), *Burning Down the House:*

Recycling Domesticity (ed. Rosemary George), and *Queer Asian Cinema: Shadows in the Shade* (ed. Andrew Grossman). She is currently working on a book manuscript entitled *Contradictory Desires: Queer Diasporas and South Asian Public Cultures.*

JENNIFER GUARINO-TRIER, a doctoral candidate at the University of Delaware, is writing a dissertation on theories of representation and children's literature authored by women of color.

SABINE HAENNI is a Harper-Schmidt fellow and collegiate assistant professor at the University of Chicago. Her work has appeared in *Cinema Journal* and *American Literature.* This essay is part of a book-length project, currently entitled *The Immigrant Scene: The Commercialization of Ethnicity and the Formation of Public Cultures in New York, 1890–1920.*

LAURA HYUN YI KANG teaches Women's Studies and Comparative Literature at the University of California, Irvine. Her book, *Compositional Subjects: Enfiguring Asian/American Women* (forthcoming in 2002 from Duke University Press), examines the mutually vexing protocols of academic disciplinarity and social identity. She is currently at work on a second book project that tracks the local-global manufacture of Asian female embodiedness through emergent technologies and political economies of visual surveillance, exhibition, and circulation.

HELEN LEE is a Toronto-based filmmaker. She is a graduate of the University of Toronto, New York University, the Whitney Independent Study Program, and the Canadian Film Centre. Her short films, *Subrosa, Prey, My Niagara,* and *Sally's Beauty Spot,* have screened extensively at festivals and events worldwide. She is currently preparing her feature film debut, *The Art of Woo.*

BINITA MEHTA has most recently taught French at Brandeis University in Waltham, Massachusetts. She has completed a book-length manuscript, *Widows, Pariahs, and 'Bayadères': The Spectacle of India in French Theater,* which will be published by Bucknell University Press in 2002. She has published articles in *Medieval Folklore: An Encyclopedia of Myths, Legends, Tales, Beliefs, and Customs* (ABC-CLIO, 2000) and the *Dictionary of Literary Biography,* volume 192: *French Dramatists, 1789–1914* (Bruccoli Clark Layman, 1998). She is currently working on a book-length project that examines how India's material culture helped shape representations of India in French literature and painting.

BILL NICHOLS is director of the Graduate Program in Cinema Studies at San Francisco State University. His book, *Representing Reality,* is commonly cited as an authoritative source on the theory and structure of documentary film. His textbook, *Introduction to Documentary*, will appear in 2001. He has also completed an anthology on the work of Maya Deren.

LINDA PECKHAM is a documentary editor and writer whose articles on film have appeared in *Discourse, Cinematograph, Framework*, and other journals, and in anthologies: *Psychoanalysis and Cinema* (AFI Film Readers Series), and *Out There: Marginalization and Contemporary Culture* (The New Museum of Contemporary Art). Her current projects include a documentary on preventing hate crimes and healing racism in her Buddhist community.

MARITA STURKEN is associate professor at the Annenberg School for Communication at the University of Southern California. She is the author of *Tangled Memories: The Vietnam War, the AIDS Epidemic, and the Politics of Remembering* (University of California 1997), a British Film Institute monograph on *Thelma & Louise* (2000), and, with Lisa Cartwright, *Practices of Looking: An Introduction to Visual Culture* (Oxford University Press 2001).

ROLANDO B. TOLENTINO is an associate professor at the Department of Film and Audiovisual Communication, University of the Philippines. He has edited a collection on Philippine cinema, *Geopolitics of the Visible: Essays on Philippine Film Cultures*, and has written a book on Filipino movie icons. He chairs the Congress of Teachers and Educators for Nationalism and Democracy (CONTEND-UP).

THOMAS WAUGH (Concordia University, Montreal) has been teaching film studies, and more recently queer studies and interdisciplinary curriculum on AIDS, since 1976. His books are *Show Us Life: Towards a History and Aesthetics of the Committed Documentary* (Scarecrow, 1984), *Hard to Imagine: Gay Male Eroticism in Photography and Film from their Beginnings to Stonewall* (Columbia University Press, 1996), and *The Fruit Machine: Twenty Years of Writings on Queer Cinema* (Duke University Press, 2000). The essay in this volume is part of a larger ongoing book project, *The Romance of Transgression*, on queer film and video in Canada.

EUGENE F. WONG received his Ph.D. from the Graduate School of International Studies, the University of Denver. He currently teaches sociology at Voorhees College, Denmark, South Carolina. He has published a book entitled *On Visual Media Racism: Asians in the American Motion Pictures*, and articles on Asian American issues in the *Journal of Ethnic Studies*. His most recent publications include contributions to *The Encyclopedia of Popular Culture*, while research continues for his forthcoming book on the South Asian diaspora in film.

Index

AARW. *See* Asian American Resource Workshop
ACV. *See* Asian CineVision
affirmative action, 2
African Americans and Asian Americans, 13, 43, 52n72, 208
Ali Singh. *See* Fu Manchu: precursors and related characters
"American Playhouse," 197, 198
anthropology, 71–72
anti-Japanese sentiment, 63; Japanese government and, 55; Japanese nationalism and, 62
Arabian Nights compared with Chinatown, 48n26
Araki, Gregg, 120–121
Art of Memory (1987), 176–178
Asia on film, 2–4
Asian American (as term), 187, 190; and hyphen, 190–191
Asian American Arts and Media, 107
Asian American cinema, 6–7; black British cinema compared with, 116–117; canonization and, 7; diaspora and, 13; dispersion and, 7; documentary ethos of, 4; ethnic marginalization within, 112–113, 136; exhibition, 196; other cinematic traditions and, 11, 114, 116–117, 135
Asian American filmmakers and mainstream cinema, 3–4
Asian American Resource Workshop (AARW), 106
Asian American Studies and diaspora, 16
Asian American women conflated with Asian women, 95n3
Asian Americans: African Americans and, 13, 43, 52n72, 208; as audience, 11; body politic and, 1, 5; cinematic condescension toward, 3; diversity within, 10–11, 12, 109, 111, 112–113, 185–186; family structures, 14; foreign perception of, 1, 5; globalization and, 14–16; hyphenate identity and, 191; protests by, 67n23, 69n41, 97n19, 108; racial discourse and, 2

Asian Canadians, 11
Asian CineVision (ACV), 101; Asian American Resource Workshop compared with, 106; film festival, 6, 105; funding, 109; genesis, 104; publications and other programs, 105
Asian migration to U.S., 94
Asian Pacific Americans, 111. *See also* Asian American
Asian women: as protagonists, 91–92; conflated with Asian American women, 95n3; orientalism and, 74–76; white masculinity and, 74
avant-garde cinema, 114

Bad Day at Black Rock (1955), 180
Bass, Ronald, 198, 214
Be Good, My Children (1992), 147–148
Bean Sprouts (television program), 195
Bemis, Polly, 78, 80. *See also Thousand Pieces of Gold*
Bhabha, Homi, 9, 138
Bharatiya Janata Party. *See* Hindu nationalism
Biggers, Earl Derr, 59
black British cinema compared with Asian American cinema, 116–117
Blauvelt, Bill, 106
Blood, Sweat and Lace (1994), 122
Blue in the Face (1995), 197, 198–199
body, mutability of, 8, 21, 22–25, 37, 46n2, 51n71
body politic and Asian Americans, 1, 5
Bontoc Eulogy (1996), 120
Boxer Rebellion and Yellow Peril, 57, 66n18
Broken Blossoms (1919), 4–5, 49n41, 52n50
Bulosan, Carlos, 119–120

casting and ethnicity, 205–207, 215
Castro, John Manal, 118, 120
Cha, Theresa Hak Kyung (themes), 136, 138–140, 253, *See also Dictee*

CPSIA information can be obtained at www.ICGtesting.com
Printed in the USA
BVOW021851101012

302626BV00013B/7/P